The Authors

Ajit M. Banerjee, received his MA and Ph.D. in Public Policy and Management from Maxwell School, Syracuse, and New York as a Fellow in Social Sciences of Rockefeller Foundation, born in India, a US citizen, was a career UN diplomat almost throughout his professional life, being stationed in Bangkok as UN Regional Advisor for Asia and the Pacific, ESCAP, Kuala Lumpur as Deputy Director, UN Asian Centre for Development Management, New York as Special Advisor, United Nations Secretariat and worked extensively with over fifty developing countries, dealing with strategic issues of public policy and management, peacekeeping and peace building. He has served as a Senior Faculty Member with the National Institute of Public Administration, Consultant on administrative reforms to Government of India and State Governments. He retired as Senior Special Advisor to the United Nations and continues to be an ad hoc consultant. He has contributed numerous articles in professional journals, co-authored books, "Renewing Governance", (McGraw Hill, 1996), "Reinventing the United Nations" (Prentice-Hall, 2007).

Murari Raj Sharma received his Master's degrees in Public and International Affairs from the University of Pittsburgh (USA) and in Commerce and in Economics from Tribhuvan University (Nepal). He has closely worked with the United Nations since 1993, including as Member of the UN Advisory Committee on Administrative and Budgetary Questions, Chairman of the Fifth Committee, Vice President of the General Assembly and of the Economic and Social Council as well as Nepal's Ambassador to the United Nations in New York, Foreign Secretary, and chief of the United Nations Division in the Ministry of Foreign Affaires. He has served as Nepal's Ambassador to the United Kingdom as well. An expert in administrative reforms, he has advised the Government and various public enterprises of Nepal in that area. Mr. Sharma has published several articles in various professional journals, authored the book "Murari Adhikari's Short Stories" (2000), and co-authored the book "Reinventing the United Nations" (Prentice-Hall, 2007).

United Nations International Civil Service

Perceptions, Realities and Career Guidance

MURARI R. SHARMA • AJIT M. BANERJEE

ACADEMIC FOUNDATION
NEW DELHI

First published in 2009
by

ACADEMIC FOUNDATION
4772-73 / 23 Bharat Ram Road, (23 Ansari Road),
Darya Ganj, New Delhi - 110 002 (India).
Phones : 23245001 / 02 / 03 / 04.
Fax : +91-11-23245005.
E-mail : books@academicfoundation.com
www. academicfoundation.com

Cataloging in Publication Data--DK
Courtesy: D.K. Agencies (P) Ltd. <docinfo@dkagencies.com>

Sharma, Murari R. and Banerjee, Ajit M.
United Nations international civil service : perceptions realities and career guidance/Murari R. Sharma and Ajit M. Banerjee.
p. cm.
Includes bibliographical references (p.).
ISBN 13: 9788171887729
ISBN 10: 8171887724

1. United Nations—Basic Structures and Functions. 2. Major Features of International Civil Service. 3. Human Resource Management: Major UN Entities. 4 Human Resource Policy and Execution. 5. Making of International Civil Service. 6. Types of UN Personnel. 7. Position Classification, 8. Justice. 9 Conditions of Service. 10. Staff Development.

DDC 352.113 22

Typeset by Italics India, New Delhi.
Printed and bound in India.

In Memory of Our Fathers'

Jibon Mohan Banerjee

Dina Raj Adhikari

Contents

List of Tables, Figures and Annexures

Tables

Figures

Annexures

Preface

Even a cursory reading of its Charter tells us that the United Nations has not been able to rise to the expectations of the founders and our own generation. But that does not mean that we should give up on it, neither should we be complaisant about its poor performance and invite once again the kind of uncertainties, wars and agonies that marked the period before its establishment. What has become urgent and imperative for the organisation, however, is that it must identify its failures, redouble change efforts to reinvent and revitalise, and continuously strive to improve and move closer to its objectives.

We, as authors, are not some of those who are out to bash the United Nations as an ineffective organisation. Neither are we those who are pleased with the status quo. From our long, arduous association with the United Nations from within and without, from our study of the official documents and existing literature and from our interaction with staff members at different levels in course of preparation of this book and our previous book, *Reinventing the United Nations*, we have witnessed and learned that the organisation has many deficiencies, which need to be fixed to make the body more transparent, meritorious, inclusive, efficient and effective. We have not pulled punches when it comes to pointing out the weaknesses. But our purpose is not to diminish the entity, neither is it to criticise it for the sake of criticism; our objective is to prompt and prod reforms in the organisation, because we cannot change it for the better unless we identify its inherent lacunae and take measures to address them based on our experience and selected best practices.

Critiquing the United Nations, in essence, is engaging in our own self-examination as a global community. It is so, simply because the world body is a collective embodiment of the international community, whether the countries that have joined take it as a symbol of identity or as an instrument of their foreign policy. Its successes and failures collectively reflect on the community of nations as a whole, because it is responsible for managing the world body. Often, we as member states, have given the United Nations so many mandates, including a lot of them archaic, that it cannot deliver on them all with equal attention and tenacity; we have not been clear in what we wanted from the world body; we have not been able to agree on priorities and actions; and we have not provided enough resources to the organisation to do the job.

That does not, however, absolve the Secretariat and its staff of the failure on their part to inform and provide practical inputs to policy-making bodies and to implement the mandates once they are given; neither does that deprive them of the credit for success stories, particularly in some peacekeeping operations. We all know for a fact that there are woeful deficiencies in the Secretariat—in its structures, systems and processes; that the lack of proper management of resources at its disposal some times has contributed to the failure of the world body as a whole; and that better delivery is possible by discarding the outdated methods and practices and embracing what works to make the organisation more transparent, efficient and cost-effective. One of the areas where the deficiencies are especially pronounced is human resources management due to excessive use of patronage, insider connections, poor quality supervisors, and bureaucratic inertia.

Human resources constitute the organic part of an organisation. They are the brain, the heart, the limbs, and the voice that think for the organisation, nurture it; acquire, produce and deliver goods and services for it; and articulate its vision and inform the global community about its actions. Organisations succeed and fail mostly on account of the quality of their human resources, more than structures and procedures. Indeed, competent staff and efficient processes alone may not ensure success out of a bad policy but they can, if not make a modest success out of an impending egregious failure, certainly make the failure less painful. Sadly, human resources management in the United Nations is anemic at best, and it cannot be revived unless all stakeholders are candid to admit it and begin to take serious measures.

So the United Nations must accord the highest priority to reforming human resources management. While we welcome the initiatives being undertaken with respect to discontinuation of permanent appointments and harmonisation of staff rules for 100, 200 and 300 series, among others, our view is that they do not go far enough. Deeper efforts are required particularly in upgrading the recruitment and selection methods for posts at the P5 level and above and setting up of an independent entity dedicated to this vital function; improving the performance evaluation system; reorganising work; retrenching the excessive staff and downsizing the staff strength by at least 20 per cent through the use of established tools of management audit, managerial skills analysis, and work process flows. Excessive use of resources for employing consultants, contractors, and retired staff should stop forthwith. We find it difficult to accept the continuing use of over 80 per cent of the total UN budget on staff, especially in an environment of increasing scarcity of resources.

Measures have been taken to improve facets of human resources management in the Secretariat, but they have not been able to bring much needed change due to resistance from one quarter or another. Today, the United Nations is one of those few large organisations that is still trapped in too bureaucratic structures, outdated methods and hackneyed procedures, leading to the perception of "business as usual." Its recruitment tools—like Galaxy, rostering and others—are not effective; its recruitment practice is so designed that it does not attract the best and brightest to apply; its processing of application is so sluggish that those who apply give up after a while in utter frustration. There was a time when professionals waited patiently to join the organisation as long as it took, as they were drawn to it by the power of its ideals and attracted by the conditions of service it offered. Today, professionals often look at the United Nations as one of the various career options, and the opportunities and incentives it provides do not have the same old magnetic pull for them anymore.

This is a rather sad predicament for the staff and member states of the United Nations as well as for those who are imbued by its ideals and values and by its cardinal objectives of promoting peace and security, development, human rights and humanitarian services. We are deeply disappointed about this, and this has prompted us to write this book in an effort to identify the deficient areas in human resources management and to suggest a roadmap for change in the International Civil Service that could catapult the world body into a much better role model of transparency, purposefulness, innovative practices and individual motivation for achievement. We hope all stakeholders will redouble their efforts to modernise the United Nations' management practices with a sense of urgency and find the ideas contained in this book meaningful in that process.

We are pleased that Secretary-General Ban Ki-Moon is committed to bringing transformational change in human resources management. He has started the mobility of staff with his own executive office, and this should serve as an example for other departments and offices in the Secretariat. We are grateful to him for sharing his vision about this most important aspect of the world body for our book in a discussion with us.

Murari R. Sharma

Ajit M. Banerjee

Acknowledgments

Many illustrious and remarkable people have unreservedly supported us emotionally, logistically and with valuable information and insights in course of writing this book. We are grateful to them all.

In particular, we are deeply thankful to the following senior UN officials for kindly sharing their thoughts and insights with us: Chef de Cabinet and Under Secretary-General, Vijay Nambiar, Under Secretary-General of the Department of Public Information, Kiyo Akasaka, and Assistant Secretary-General of the Office of Human Resources Management, Catherine Pollard, and Victor Kisob, Chief, Staffing Service, Ms. Haiyan Qian, Director, Division for Public Administration and Development Management, Department of Economic and Social Affairs.

We are equally thankful to Ambassador of Chile to the United Kingdom, Rafael Moreno for sharing his views generously.

This book could not have been written without the active and willing support and information from Ambassador Andrzej T. Abraszewski, Member of the Advisory Committee on Administrative and Budgetary Questions. We express our deep gratitude to him.

We appreciate US Congressman John Mica's continued support to our endeavour and valuable information.

Our thanks go to Danise Jaen, Administrative Officer of the International Civil Service Commission, as well as the following individuals from the Dag Hammarskjold Library, for their assistance and support: Loraine Waitman, Chief of the Library Users Services, Martina Paniagua, Coordinator, UN Reference Team and Cyril Emery, UN Reference Team. We also thank the United Nations for documents.

We also express our deep thanks to all those writers and authors from whose books and writings we benefited in terms of acquiring knowledge and getting citations for our book. No less thankful we are to those websites from which we have learned and quoted.

We are profoundly grateful to Dwight Ink (USA), Prof. Surya Subedi and Sir Richard Jolly (UK), and Mr. Rajiv Sharma (India) for reading the manuscript and providing their extremely helpful comments.

Our appreciation goes to Mrs. Uma Banerjee and Amita, Ajoy and Arun Banerjee as well as Mrs. Nila Adhikari and Munish and Anish Adhikari for their support and encouragement.

Last but not least, we are profoundly grateful to the Academic Foundation for publishing this important book on time.

1

State of the World

Introduction

In the face of a global economic crisis unprecedented in several decades, governments and private organisations worldwide have been forced to change the way they do business. They have been tightening their belts, enhancing the efficiency and productivity of their staff, downsizing their workforces, reorganising their processes, eliminating redundant units and programmes, outsourcing functions and seeking more value for money. At such times and in the future, the United Nations cannot and must not expect business as usual. The world body ought to learn from its own experiences and from that of governments and the private sector, and seek to catapult to a higher plane its organisational capacity and staff competencies and productivity to be able to do more with less in the days ahead.

Due to the economic downturn, the paradigm of economic management is already shifting. Even if the downturn has been triggered by the sub-prime mortgage crisis in the West and related failures of seemingly unbeatable global banks, it has sent shattering shockwaves throughout the globe. This has compelled governments and peoples to view capitalism, the dominant economic model for so long, in a new light and global economic management, in a new context. At the same time, so many other developments have been happening: Growing population, rising food prices, quickly depleting finite resources, accelerating consumption of renewable resources—faster than they could be replenished, increasing pollution and climate change, to name a few. The recent respite in fuel prices after a prolonged spike, at best, is temporary, for the prices will go back up as soon as the economic slump bottoms out. Tensions are rising in many parts of the globe as states have to compete over decreasing pool of natural resources, and new conflicts and disruption of development activities could not be far off. The United Nations must be ready to come to grips with such emerging new realities.

No organisation other than the United Nations is equipped to deal with the challenges of the international community. Its mandates, functions and objectives are uniquly overarching, broad and inevitable, though somewhat ambitious. The world body can make laws and decisions, something no other entity can, many of which could be binding on the global community. It is charged with functions and objectives no other body can match in their scope and content. Those people who fear change and defend the status quo have been using this uniqueness to resist reform to the detriment of the organisation. They should not be allowed to do so if they want the world body to remain relevant and effective for all time to come.

If it fails to change, the United Nations will face existential crisis. It will continue to stagnate and atrophy and become increasingly irrelevant, as we have witnessed on many occasions in the past. And the international community will have to think of another organisation that can change with times and stand up to the existing and emerging crises before humanity.

To avoid such prospects, the world body must seize this moment to restructure itself and reshape its human resources management. In the past, the organisation has focused its reforms on treating the symptoms of its ailments, but that has not produced expected result, neither will it in the future. Therefore, the United Nations must think afresh for change and redouble its efforts anew, bringing to bear creative thinking, innovative practices and political will on an unprecedented scale to make itself much more transparent, democratic, efficient and effective.

Unfortunately, in many tumultuous and convoluted events, the United Nations has starkly failed to play a significant role. Take, for example, the ongoing economic slump. Member states are concerned as to where the Economic and Social Council has been hiding all this time. To be sure, in times of such major economic crises, world capitals and the IMF and the World Bank become more evident in their fire-fighting roles. However, what has struck most is the conspicuous absence of ECOSOC, the formost universal economic and social forum, as a player in seeking to arrest the economic meltdown and revive the global economy. The United Nations, particularly ECOSOC, spectaculourly failed to demonstrate leadership.

At long last, General Assembly President Miguel D'Escoto has set up a distinguished commission of experts under the Nobel Prize winner in Economics, Joe Stiglitz, on the economic crisis, and the commission started its work on June 24, 2009. The commission is reviewing a number of counter-cyclical measures of stimulus which are aimed to hasten recovery from the crisis, to hold back protectionist actions by states and to introduce greater regulation over financial markets. These measures are set in a frame of longer term initiatives to grapple with the climate change and other environmental threats. The membership of this group is heavily weighted towards developing countries.

While new problems are emerging, old challenges to humanity continue to persist. Conflicts have continued to destroy societies in many parts of the planet. Weapons of mass destruction continue to pose serious threat to the very existence of humanity. Rampant and unregulated use of small arms and light weapons has been taking countless innocent lives and destabilising countries shore to shore. Poverty has been holding billions of people back in misery and deprivation. Climate change has been threatening the very existence of human beings and animal species on earth, not to speak of island and costal countries that could submerge under the rising sea levels. The train of globalisation has left many peoples by the way side; and growing gaps between rich and poor have further been destabilising countries and communities.

Since its inception, the United Nations has played major role in trying to tackle some of these challenges, marginal part in some others and none in yet others. No one expects the world body to wield a magic wand that can vanish all the problems of our planet at once, but the international community quite reasonably hopes that this most universal of all multilateral organisations should be a critical instrument and central forum to fashion collective responses to common problems of humanity. Only a strong, competent and motivated United Nations—which is able to devise innovative and practical solutions to the existing and emergent problems and to implement them robustly and effectively—can rise to the occasion.

The United Nations ought to break itself from the catch-22 trap. Obviously, it cannot deliver unless it has necessary wherewithals, and resources would not be available unless it proves its ability to perform. The best way, perhaps the only way, to break out of this tricky trap would be for the Secretariat to demonstrate first that it can do more with less and to win the credibility and confidence from world leaders. Which essentially means the world body must accord high priority to sprucing up the Secretariat by restructuring it and changing its arcane management practices that have been stuck in the 1940s, when the organisation was established. The organisation must also strenghten its internal controls to prevent the likes of the Oil-for-food scandal and sexual abuse in its field missions and removing inefficiencies across the system.

It is but a pity that the United Nations today is so redolent of a bygone era. We need a 21st century body to tackle the challenges of today and tomorrow. Only committed, capable and competent staff can make an organisation strong and effective in fulfilling its mission. Therefore, dramatic improvements—call them a organisational shock and awe, if you will—are critical in the personnel system of the world body to ensure that it has the most efficient management and the best, brightest and most dedicated staff to attain its purposes and mandates. The new challenges in political, economic and social governance of the international community cry out for a sense of urgency and for a new vision and coherent practical philosophy to revitalise the United Nations.

Interstingly, challenges always come with opportunites. The economic meltdown, growing food prices, climate change, rising fuel prices, continued failure to revitalise the United Nations, etc., have given governments and peoples a new level of awakening that they must redouble their efforts to fashion collective responses to common problems and to create a peaceful, prosperous and just society where every individual, community and country enjoys freedom, respect and dignity.

Main Challenges

Global Economic Situation

The global economic meltdown has proved a daunting mountain for the community of nations to move. Triggered by the sub-prime loans in the United States, the slump has crashed the prices of stocks, houses and other assets; people have lost trillions of dollars; several banks and investment banks and insurance companies have failed; most notable among such failures have been Lehman Brothers; AIG, the insurance giant, and Citi Group are still standing thanks to huge bailout from the US government. The US economy, the largest, that had been the engine of growth for over a decade, is in deep recession. Many other wealthy countries are in the same boat. No one knows for sure how much of the bad credit every surviving bank is sitting on. So banks do not trust and lend each other; in turn, they do not extend credit to people and businesses, bringing the wheel of market economies to a grinding halt. The situation is so bad that even the bail-out and stimulus packages that have been put in place by several countries have failed to revive the sluggish economies.

No one that could make a difference to change policy thought that the housing bubble that was building over a period of time would burst until it did. Neither did anyone realise that business cycle was here to stay. Alan Greenspan, the Chairman of the US Federal Reserve Bank, had explicitly denied the existence of such a bubble, arguing in Congressional testimony and other public pronouncements that the run-up in housing prices was driven by fundamentals.[1] Yet while several economists contemplated a financial crisis, only a few could predict for sure that it was going to come along and hit the world community so badly. Among them was Nouriel Roubini, an economics professor at the New York University, who had emphatically predicted in September 2006 that the United States was likely to hit a crisis of this size.[2]

Evidently the adverse impacts of this situation have spread all over the world, putting a break on more than one and a half decade long spectacular expansion in world output. World output had begun to decelerate from the middle of the first decade of the 2000s. For instance, it slowed down from 5 per cent in 2006 to 3.7 per cent in 2008. In that period, the advanced countries expanded by 2.33 annually, whereas developing and emerging economies achieved 7.47 per cent growth rate, with China and India taking the lead. In 2009, growth is expected to decline to 3.9 per cent for the globe, 1.3 per cent for the advanced countries and 6.6 per cent for the developing and emerging economies.[3]

Thus a long stint of respectable economic expansion worldwide has come to an end. But before that happened, the economic buyoancy of more than a decade was able to lift millions of people out of poverty and improve enrolments in schools and availability of health facilities. So much so that a number of developing countries are well on course to meeting the Millennium Development Goals (MDGs) by 2015.

But in many other developing countries, the enormous problems of poverty and underdevelopment continue to persist for a large chunk of humanity. The number of people living on less than $1 a day is still more than 880 million, and most of whom live in rural areas.[4] The recent food crisis is likely to push an additional 100

---

1. Baker, Dean and David Rosnick, *Will a Bursting Bubble Trouble Bernanke*? Washington DC: Center for Economic and Policy Research, November, p.2.
2. Mihm, Stephen (2008). "Dr. Doom", in *The New York Times Magazine* of 15 August.
3. Mihm, Stephen (2008). "Dr. Doom", *The New York Times*, 15 August. *http://www.imf.org/external/pubs/ft/weo/2008/update/03/index.htm#table1*
4. United Nations (2008). *Report of the Secretary General on the work of the Organization*. p.4.

million people into extreme poverty.[5] Nearly 41 million primary school age children in sub-Saharan Africa and 31.5 million in South Asia remain out of school. About 1.2 billion of the world's poorest suffer from tropical diseases, malaria kills 1 million people every year, 33.2 million people live with HIV, one billion people do not have access to safe drinking water and 2.6 billion people lack adequate sanitation facilities.[6] Rural women constitute the overwhelming majority of those who suffer from poverty, illiteracy and ill health. The situation in sub-Saharan Africa happens to be worst.

Consequently, many unstable and poor nations will miss the MDG targets unless they are helped by their development partners to ensure political stability, good governance and capacity building. They need greater support from the North, in terms of increased development assistance and investment and improved access to markets and technology.[7] Although development assistance has been on the rise over the last several years, wealthy countries are still far from providing 0.7 per cent of their GNP as official development assistance to developing nations. The Doha round of trade negotiations, which aims at promoting investment and trade for developing countries, has faltered and missed several deadlines.

Globalisation has aggravated the wide gap between rich and poor. Those countries that had had the significant infrastructure for growth—such as roads, power, technical skills—prospered. Others lacking these critical elements for progress were left out high and dry. Even where globalisation succeeded, its benefits have disproportionately gone to the rich, be it in rich or poor countries. Food shortage over the last two years or so, too, has pushed millions into abject poverty. These factors have further increased the gulf between the rich and poor and aggravated the already inherent tensions and political instability across the world.

---

5. Ibid

6. Ibid.: 4-5.

7. See United Nations (2002). *Monterrey Consensus of the International Conference on Financing for Development*, (the final text), Monterrey, Mexico, 18-22 March, for details of the commitments made by developing countries and their development partners.

The economic meltdown facing the world today, supposed to be the serious most after the Great Depression of 1929, is likely to reverse many gains of the past. Many of those who had barely lifted themselves from the abyss of poverty will be pushed back down. Those who live on the margins of society, eking out a bare survival, will fall down the precipice of poverty, as jobs vanish, savings erode and governments cut down services to keep their fiscal balance going out of kilter. What is more, a prolonged economic gloom might titilate countries, both rich and poor, to pursue protectionist policies which are sure to jeopardise the achievements made under a freer trade regime, and this will work more to the detriment of poorer nations and peoples. The greatest challenge for the world community today is to prevent such reversal.

Experience in the economic arena has taught us many lessons. We now know that, while a rising economic tide does not lift all boats, when it does, it does not buoy them all equally. So we must conclude the Doha round of trade negotiations with a sense of renewed commitment and determination to lift all boats; developed countries need to meet the official development assistance target of 0.7 per cent of their GNI and provide greater access to their technologies to those poor countries that need it; and developing countries should strive their best to impove their governance and service delivery, optimise the use of domestic and external resources and work relentlessly to realise MDGs. The most shocking lesson we have learned has been three-fold: Greed might be good to a certain extent but too much of it might sink the economic boat built over time with sweat and blood, in a matter of few months; the Washington Consensus, which presumed that the private sector is the panacea to all ills in developing countries, was a complete failure; and prudent oversight of free market is critical to maintain sanity in national and global economic management.

Energy, Environment and Climate Change

Although the exorbitant rise in fossil fuel prices has eased up for now, the prices are unlikely to remain low for long. Energy prices rose from under $25 a barrel in 2003 to $147 in 2008. Now they have come down to just above the 2003 levels, but they are not sustainable and will go back as the global economy rebounds from the current crisis. Unfortunately, this decline in gas prices has dawned a sense of complacency among some people: Consumers have switched back to sports utility vehicles; governments' enthusiasm for alternative sources of energy—biofuels, solar, wind, wave, etc.—seems to have been sagging. The rise in food prices did not help the push for biofuels either, as the development of such energy began to undermine the prospects of feeding people. The imminent depletion of gasoline, an exhaustible source of energy, is a question of when, not whether; and gas prices are sure to go back up. It is truly disheartening that the international community has not yet put together a sustainable global energy policy; neither has the United Nations taken any concrete action in this vital and urgent respect.

Equally frustrating is a lack of sufficient attention paid to arresting climate change and reversing environmental degradation. To be sure, the world community has taken some measures to restore the deteriorating environmental health of our planet under Agenda 21, the Johannesburg Summit and the Kyoto Protocol on Climate Change. However, the implementation of the agreed provisions has remained woefully wanting, and the health of our environment is constantly declining. Meanwhile, imprudent expansion of human habitat and unsustainable use of energy and other resources have contributed to deforestation, soil erosion and pollution, excessive release of CFCs into atmosphere, etc.; many countries still do not have strict emission control rules, let alone appropriate institutions to implement them. Resultant climate change, loss of natural habitat, desertification and rise in sea levels have taken serious toll on birds, animals and plants, as well as threatened the ecosystem's balance and the very existence of many countries. Mostly the developing world has become the main victim of this phenomenon.

It is however heartening that those members of the global community that were reluctunt to hold the beast of environment degradation by its horns before are now more favourably disposed to tackling the issue. The United Nations must seize this opportunity and take and advance its initiatives in the area of green energy and green technologies.

Conflicts

Despite some successes to come to grips with them, conflicts continue to wreak havoc in societies across the world. Major wars have been few and far between, after World War II, and Cold War has petered out. But the fear of weapons of mass destruction continues and, in fact, is increasing with the proliferation of their technologies.

The United Nations was able to restore and keep the peace through its peacekeeping and political missions in Cambodia, Nepal, Mozambique, East Timor, Guatemala, Namibia, and some other countries. But several conflicts such as in the Middle East, Sri Lanka, Kosovo, Iraq, Afghanistan, Georgia, Sudan and the Democratic Republic of the Congo continue to rage unabated, defying solutions. Some of these conflicts have been over the control of finite resources—land and natural endowments—and others have been caused by cultural differences, mutual intolerance and injustice.

International terrorism and crimes have emerged as new but grave threats to peace and security. Hijacking planes, abducting people, murdering opponents, extorting money, running drugs, engaging in human trafficking are not necessarily new, but these crimes are now being perpetrated with increasing audacity and expanding reach to destabilise nations. Globalisation has considerably encouraged migration and reduced distance between states. It has expanded the scope of operation of outfits engaged in those crimes; and increased access to weapons has made criminal gangs more menacing and deadly. Greed, poverty and clash of civilisations are at the heart of such menaces.

Therefore, silencing guns for a while and calling on parties to find a negotiated settlement alone will not banish conflicts. To find durable resolution for them, governments, regional groups and global organisations must invest in addressing the root or contributing causes of conflicts—poverty, intolerance, xenophobia, injustice, discrimination, etc.—and building prosperous, tolerant and just societies for everyone. There is no shortcut to durable peace, security and harmonious global community.

As we have indicated above, there are many sources of disputes that give rise to conflicts and destabilise societies. Whenever you have an aggrieved population overlooked and refugees and internally displaced people neglected, you have a fertile ground for extremists to recruit terrorists. Such causes of conflicts should be nipped in the bud by deploying preventive diplomacy and mitigative measures. It is sad that efforts are seldom brought to bear on all levels—national, regional and global—in trying to prevent conflagration and resolve wars. What is more, many countries, as well as regional and international organisations are yet to sufficiently equip themselves to deal with the complex, existing and emergent peace and security challenges.

For example, take the United Nations. The foremost international organisation with a clear mandate to deal with global security issues is largely unprepared to grapple with many of its most serious challenges. Although we might be in the first decade of the 21st century, the world body continues to be trapped in outdate structures and processes established more than 60 years ago. Its security organ, the Security Council, reflects the geo-strategic realities and power configuration of 1945, rather than 2009. Efforts to strengthen and update the Council by expanding its structure and reforming its methods of work have faced a wall of resistance from those who do not want new claimants to share their privileges and those who do not want new countries to enjoy those undemocratic privileges. Although the foreign policy interests of its key members will always have a role to play in the decision-making process, the organisation will never rise to its challenges unless its members begin rising above their parochial interests and start acting in the larger interest of the world community.[8]

---

8. Carpenter, Ted (2007). "The Great Powers and the Security Council", in Ajit M. Banerjee and Murari R. Sharma (eds.), *Reinventing the United Nations*. Prentice-Hall of India. pp. 23-34.

Many other peace and security agendas have also become serious causes of concern for the global community. Eroding the disarmament regime is one of them. Some countries have made the mockery of the Nuclear Non-proliferation Treaty by developing or keeping nuclear weapons. Some others have done the same by scrapping the Intercontinental Ballistic Missile Treaty. Small arms have proliferated; defense expenditures have gone up and arms race has started anew in some global quarters; the Conference on Disarmament has become dormant, if not dead; UN peacekeeping capacities and resources remain precarious; and peace-building efforts remain either unfunded or under-funded. The United Nations ought to push further to make progress in these vital areas.

Inequity, Injustice and Lack of Democracy

Inequity, injustice and a lack of democracy also are at the root of instability and backwardness. Such situations exist not only within individual societies but also between countries. To start with, our societies are fragmented across class, caste, ethnic, linguistic, gender or religions lines. Often people from different groups do not see eye to eye; quite frequently, those from the dominant culture tend to exercise more state power, take disproportionate benefits from society, and even engage in reckless exploitation of the minoirites. When they find the situation right for them, the minorities fight back to get their grievances redressed. Conversely, the elite and privileged minorities have also exploited the disadvantaged majority, creating more explosive inter-group and intra-group relations.

Differences and irritants also exist among member states, and efforts are being made to remove them. For instance, developing countries feel that they have been largely shut out from decision-making bodies and processes by their wealthy partners. That is true of the Security Council, the World Bank, the International Monetary Fund and other international organisations. There is a widely held belief that the dominant North is bent on preserving its extant privileges as much as possible.

Communication and commerce work as a double-edged sword. Explosion in transportation, communication and commerce has tremendously increased interaction among peoples within and between nations and brought them closer. It has also given us the opportunity to see for ourselves how much better or worse other peoples and communities live and to emulate a better life. However, equity, justice and inclusion within and between countries that promote peace and harmony remain largely elusive, partly due to democracy deficit in much of the world and partly sectarian impulses running amock in developing societies and new, unstable democracies.

Humanitarian Crises

Disasters—natural and man-made—leave on their trail serious political and development consequences for societies affected by them, more so in developing countries. Many communities frequently suffer from such natural disasters as floods, landslides, volcano eruptions, hurricanes, tornado, etc. Others have been suffering from man-made disasters such as wars, conflicts and pollution and other forms of environmental degradation. These disasters take lives, destroy properties, displace people, produce refugees and internally displaced persons, and generate political instability and economic dislocation. Today there are close to 20 million refugees and many more internally displaced persons, both groups requiring humanitarian assistance for their survival and well-being.

Natural disasters spare no one, and man-made disasters strike the poor more. In developed countries, they would have the resources to provide immediate humanitarian relief, rescue and rehabilitation support to the victims of disaster as well as to carry out development activities to reduce the incidences of disasters and mitigate their impacts in the long run. As a result, these countries are often spared of serious economic and political fall outs of such disasters.

However, developing countries are not so lucky. They lack institutional capacities and financial resources to offer enough short-term help and provide sufficient long-term development support.

Settlements in inappropriate places and deficient building codes make physical structures susceptible to disasters and aggravate their consequences. Excessive exploitation of natural resources by people and animals for their survival also invites disasters and worsen their consequences in poor countries. So these countries suffer the pain of such disasters longer and harder and often end up having political turmoil or economic chaos in the aftermath.

Leadership and Accountability

Organisations that do not value leadership and do not pursue accountability are certain to fail. The United Nations is wanting on both counts. Although the UN Charter stresses merit as the principal basis and geographical representation as a key consideration for recruiting staff, both these fundamental requirements have received short shrift in the world body, unlike in most of its member states or its private sector bretheren. More often than not, political expediency and connection, rather than competence and quality of leadership, determine who is appointed as secretary-general. Appointment of other senior managers is fraught with similar problems, creating a senior management team that is unable to inspire and lead and unwilling to accept accountability and link it to incentives and disincentives.[9]

Change of culture is essential in the United Nations—in the Secretariat and in intergovernmental bodies—to make it a more effective organisation. People, not politics, should come first and foremost, and priorities must be so set that the world body can implement, within its limited resources, those resolutions and decisions that contribute most to improving human lives, as well as can monitor and follow up the execution undertaken by member states. The United Nations must make itself credible before it counsels member states to adopt democracy, leadership and accountability, somethings which this organisation has been doing to the rest of the world.

---

9. See Foreword by Boutros-Ghali, Former UN Secretary-General, to Banerjee, Ajit M. and Murari R. Sharma (2007). *Reinventing the United Nations*. Delhi: Prentice-Hall, for an illuminating discussion on leadership and accountability in the United Nations.

The world body must make a clear departure from the debilitating status quo if it wants to build its capacity to deliver. For instance, the Assembly and the Security Council should choose the Secretary-General on the basis of merit rather than backroom political deals; and he in turn should appoint senior managers based on their competence and geographical representation, as stipulated in the UN Charter, after a thorough and systematic vetting and approval prior to their appointment. The Charter provisions are not only applicable to junior officials, they should be equally applicable at senior levels as well.

Several other steps will also be necessary to strengthen leadership and accountability in the United Nations. For instance, intergovernmental bodies should not pass more resolutions than the Secretariat can handle and implement. The Secretary-General should be given clear authority to deploy staff and non-staff resources within his broad mandate and within the pool of approved resources. He should also have complete independence from member states in staffing decisions. On the other hand, the Secretary-General also must understand that member states will not give him such broad powers until and unless he convinces them that he is going to use them prudently and makes him and his senior staff accountable for their failure to use resources optimally and and to deliver on their duties and obligations.

Difficulties for UN Reforms

The United Nations remains woefully wanting in terms of transparancy, efficiency and effectiveness. Reform efforts of the past have made some marginal improvements to these elements in some pockets, but the overall situation remains far from satisfactory, to say the least. Two reasons stand out for this: One, it is not always easy to have consensus from 192 member states that come from different political, economic, social and geographical conditions and orientations. Two, by the former Secretary-General Kofi Annan's own admission, the United Nations has often tried to address symptoms rather than root problems most of the time.[10]

---

10. See Chapter 13 of this book for details.

Often financial difficulties or cataclysmic events have stirred the United Nations into reform. Secretary-General, Boutros-Ghali, presented *An Agenda for Peace*[11] and *An Agenda for Development*[12] when the world body was under tremendous financial strain. His successor, Kofi Annan, proposed a series of reforms during his tenure,[13] most of them under one circumstance or another of serious consequences for the organisation. In particular, events and controversies leading to the Iraq war raised existential questions for the organisation, and Kofi Annan constituted a High-level Panel on Threats, Challenges and Change[14] to help him formulate far-reaching reforms. He also set up an Independent Inquiry Committee to look into the allegations of corruption in the Oil-for-food programme that led to suggesting several measures to strengthen oversight functions.[15] In response to the allegations of sexual exploitation in peacekeeping mission and elsewhere, Mr. Annan asked Prince Zeid of Jordan to prepare a report—A comprehensive strategy to eliminate future sexual exploitation and abuse in United Nations peacekeeping operations—that contained measures to remedy the situation.[16] Based on those reports, the Secretary-General presented his reform proposals—*Investing in the United Nations*[17]—to the General Assembly to redeem the sullied image of and restore humanity's faith in the organisation. The summit level meeting of the General Assembly in 2005 approved some of those proposals and asked the Secretary-General to resubmit others with additional information.[18]

The Secretary-General presented his fully developed reforms requiring legislative action to the 61st session of the General Assembly in the fall of 2006. These reforms fell broadly into three categories: (i) Reforms in governance, (ii) improvements in oversight

11. United Nations (1992). *An Agenda for Peace*, A/47/277-S/24111, 17 June.
12. United Nations (1994). *An Agenda for Development*, A/48/935. 6 May.
13. See his reports, among others, *Investing in the United Nations* (2006); *In Larger Freedom* (2005); *An Agenda for Further Change* (2002); *A Programme for Reform* (1997).
14. See the Panel's Report (2004). *A more secure world: Our shared responsibility*, United Nations.
15. See United Nations (2005). *Report on the Manipulation of the Oil-for-food Programme*, 27 October.
16. See UN document A/59/710.
17. United Nations (2005). *Investing in the United Nations*, United Nations.
18. See United Nations (2005). *World Summit Outcome*, GA resolution 60/1 of 24 October.

mechanisms, and (iii) management reforms. In the realm of governance, the Secretary-General suggested, among others, that the General Assembly reorient itself towards topical issues, retire outdated mandates, reduce the length of the budget consideration process, and eliminate the Committee for Programme and Coordination. He proposed to create audit and oversight committees, provide more independence to internal oversight entities in terms of staffing and funding mechanisms, and introduce new accounting and information technology systems. Greater staffing and financial flexibility to SG, creating an ethics office, improving human resources and procurement management and induction of a staff buy-out programme constituted the key elements of his management reform.

Secretary-General, Ban Ki-Moon has continued the zeal for reform, even though he is far from portraying himself as a reform Secretary-General like his immediate predecessor. The first thing Mr. Ban did was to transfer all staff from his executive office, giving a boost to the notion of mobility that remains stagnant in the UN house. Breaking up of the Department of Peacekeeping Operations into the Department of Peace Operations and the Department of Field Service was another measure that came within months of Mr. Ban's taking the helm of the unversal entity.

Opportunities

As we have mentioned in the beginning of the preceding section of this chapter, challenges come with opportunities. And for the United Nations, that indeed happens to be the case. We shall look at some of the opportunities the world body has to revitalise itself and make it a credible, effective and efficient organisation.

Revolution in Science and Technology

Revolution in science and technology has opened up new frontiers for humanity to conquer and equip people with increased ability both to take human lives and to save them. Thanks to this phenomenon, man was able to land on the Moon in 1969 and has now been sending spacecraft to explore other planets. Ocean floors no more remain beyond the reach of humanity. We have a vastly more educated world now, as education has been spreading in every nook and cranny of the globe. Health services have expanded and improved, and life expectancy has increased significantly due to better transportation, availability of more effective drugs and better methods of diagnosis and treatment, and awareness about and capacity to afford nutrition and hygiene.

New technologies have revolutionised agricultural and industrial production and enabled the world to feed and dress the growing global population. Inputs have improved and methods of production have become more efficient, pushing up human productivity. You can travel across the world within 24 hours and send communications and transfer billions of dollars from one corner of the globe to another within the fraction of a second. We can harness these wonderful resources and capacities together for the collective benefits of humanity as a whole.

Interdependence

Growing recognition by societies across the world that they are interdependent and their interests are inextricably intertwined has opened up new opportunities for the global community and for the United Nations. Globalisation of communication, trade, investment, crimes, etc., has already driven that point home. The September 11 terrorist attacks on the United States, in a sad manner, underlined that point, as never before. So has the current financial crisis.

We now know more than ever that we cannot be safe and prosperous when everyone else is not. The current financial crisis started with subprime lending in the United States but has sunk with it economies around the world. The attacks on the World Trade Centre and the Pentagon in the United States by the terrorists—most of them Saudi nationals trained in Afghanistan—made it amply clear that festering conflict and insecurity elsewhere could come haunting people and states half way around the planet. Turmoil in the Middle East could turn off the tap of oil supply and benumb the entire world. Besides, conflict and insecurity in one part of the globe could cause obstructions to the free movement of people and goods, influx of refugees and migrants, disruption of social harmony and deterioration in environmental health. Conflicts, crimes, disputes, drugs and diseases defy national and regional borders.

In view of all this, world leaders are now more willing than ever before to join forces to address problems even in remote parts of the globe, though not sufficiently yet, as they recognise that their countries would not be immune from problems elsewhere. Freer movement of people and commerce across national and regional boundaries has enormously contributed to the creation of wealth and dissemination of information, which are vital tools to address the challenges of poverty, crimes, drugs and insecurity with which humanity is confronted. Collective measures by the international community to keep the peace, resolve disputes, eradicate poverty, promote sustainable development, arrest climate change and control crime and corruption are some of the examples of the new opportunities created by growing globalisation and intensifying interdependence.

Spread of Democracy

Spread of democracy has been one of the most remarkable phenomenons of our time. Today more people live under democratic freedom and liberty around the world than ever. While democracy has opened room for internal conflicts as the disadvantaged and wronged people have risen to have their grievances addressed, it has also given ordinary people more voice and power to determine their destiny and deter the ruling elite from engaging in reckless adventures at home and abroad.

Ordinary people want improved life for them and for their children more than war. They want to make a living, send their children to school, have treatment when they fall sick, and enjoy a decent life. So free societies where people have voice in government want to engage in promoting trade and creating wealth more than firing guns at each other. Checks and balances built into a democratic system force the ruling elite to respect public opinion and accept the loss of power without violence. The subsided, if not completely vanished, threat of annihilation of the entire humanity at the switch of a button during Cold War is a good example of this.

In other words, expanding democracy has created new opportunities for the international community to work together. Shared values tend to increase understanding between peoples and to bring them closer in friendship, fellowship and cooperation. Russia and the United States, the archrivals of the Cold War era and now both friendly democracies, have been working together to prevent North Korea and Iran from acquiring nuclear weapons and to tackle the global financial meltdown fomented by the credit crunch together rather than trying to weaken and hurt each other.

New Organisations

Over the last few decades, the world has witnessed the rise of many new global and regional organisations, some formal and some informal. These organisations have offered some competition, though limited in scope, to the United Nations and the Bretton Woods Institutions, and generated new and exciting opportunities for collaboration and complementarities for the world body. There are several such organisations.

The European Union is one of them. It has been growing bigger and perhaps stronger and increasingly coordinating its foreign and domestic policies; it has also embraced the Euro as a common currency. The Union works within the region as well as across the world. Strong regional groups that are seeking greater economic integration have also emerged elsewhere—South America, Africa, South East Asia, South Asia and North East Asia. Group of 8, an informal forum of the wealthy nations, has become a permanent feature of the global landscape with increasingly decisive impact on the global economy. Trading blocs have also emerged across the planet. There are organisations of emerging democracies, least developed countries, landlocked developing countries, small island developing states, and many others.

The United Nations, its regional commissions and its peacekeeping and political missions, as well as its specialised agencies, often work with those regional bodies to come to grips with the problems besetting their membership. Also the world body works with non-governmental organisations and multinational private organisations that have of late emerged as powerful players in the global arena. What is more, it can learn from their strengths and from their methods and systems; it can work with them to pursue shared objectives in areas of their common engagements; and it can avoid their weaknesses and mistakes.

Revamping United Nations

The United Nations is now at a favourable juncture where it can embrace singificant reforms, more easily than ever. There are new opportunites and prospects, as we have discussed above. In addition, member states have witnessed that their preconceived ideas and dogmas have not worked to improve the United Nations and that they need to try new methods and demonstrate more flexibility for reform. Leaders have also now realised more than ever that their countries could not be immune from the impacts of political and economic disasters half way around the world. They have realised more than ever that the United Nations still remains the only international forum that has not only universal membership but also widely accepted legitimany to work on behalf of common humanity. This indeed is the best opportuntity for the United Nations to start revitalising itself through restructuring the organisation and rearranging its work flows and to convince member states that it can add value as an independent and objective player to efforts for thrashing out global solutions to global problems. The world body should seize this opportunity.

This is not to suggest that revamping the United Nations is going to be easy now. Member states might not always agree on everything or sometimes on anything. The Secretariat and intergovernmental bodies might not be on the same page on reform. But the Secretariat has certainly the best opportunity to change itself now, substantively and significantly. This is time for the United Nations to shed its bureaucratic incrementalism: Whenever a problem surfaces, create a new unit and hire new personnel, rather than try to change the culture, improve the management process and address the root causes. Moreover, removing duplications, eliminating red tape, optimising business processes and restructuring the organisation, which are critical to reinvent the United Nations, seldom received enough attention and priority they deserved. Reform is necessary in intergovernmental bodies, but it is nowhere close to the need for reshaping and revamping the

Secretariat and its human resources management, because it has become largely anachronistic for a modern organisation.

So the Secretariat must abandon its bureaucratic incrementalism, the comfortable placebos it has chosen to treat the symptoms of its serious organisational ailment, and go for bitter but effective pills that will begin to treat the ailment itself. Private organisations as well as governments have taken a quantum leap in their human resources management and dramatically increased the productivity of their workforce. The United Nations can and should do that as well. This will create an environment of trust between the Secretariat and intergovernmental bodies, dawn a new era for collaboration between the Secretariat and member states and reinforce the utility and relevance of the United Nations as an indispensable body as ever.

We have sought to put this in perspective in this book. Therefore, this book is unique, different from other books on the United Nations.

Uniqueness of this Book

This book is different from others at least in four fundamental ways. First, the style of presentation is unique. Each chapter starts with a brief theoretical context before describing how the UN system works, what the strengths and weaknesses of the system are and what could be done to make the organisation capable of confronting the contemporary, complex challenges. The book has boxes, charts and tables to illustrate the points made it. Secondly, the information presented in the book has a rare blend of insight from the authors who have worked within the system as well as from outside for many years. Most other books, written either by complete outsiders or ultimate insiders, which are just a few anyway, present only one side of the coin.

Thirdly, this book is a critique of UN human resources managment that presents the information and analysis without any bias or prejudice to help readers to understand it in an objective fashion. This is a rarity, because most other books are done either by UN bashers or UN devotees. Fourthly, the information in the book is organised in such a manner that it should be useful to serious students of UN human resources management as well as casual readers who wish to understand the UN personnel system in leisure during their holidays. Fifthly, this book contains serious analysis almost in a handbook form to make it useful to those who seek to work with the world body, join its Secretariat as an employee, or help others to do so. No other book on the United Nations that we have come across is designed to serve such a purpose.

Scheme of the Book

The scheme is conceptualised from the prespective of bringing about reform in human resource management of the United Nations. Chapter I overviews the State of the World within which the world body operates. Chapter II provides an analysis of Basic Structures and Functions of the Secretariat. Chapter III is entitled Major Features of the International Civil Service. Chapter IV provides prespectives of major UN Entitities dealing with human resources management. Chapter V is entitled Human Resource Policy and Execution. Chapter VI provides a detailed account of the background and concept of International Civil Service, Recruitment, Selection and Appointment practices and reviews broad categories of staffing, transfer and reassignments and related strategic aspects. Chapter VII describes Types of UN Personnel. Chapter VIII deals with Position Classification, Mobility and Promotion procedures and standards. Chapter IX provides a basis for Administration of Justice for staff members working in the Secretariat. Chapter X is entitled Staff Development and Senior Management Programme. Chapter XI sketches salient features of Conditions of Service of the members of the International Civil Service. Chapter XII reviews the arangements for Human Resources Planning. Chapter XIII entitled Revitalising the UN Human Resource Management, proposes new directions and changes to support productivity, accountability and transparency. Finally, Chapter XIV presents a series of helpful ideas for prospective applicants for career opportunities in the International Civil Service. What is more, the chapters contain references from a series of best practices in human resources management, wherever appropriate.

2

United Nations: Basic Structures and Functions

Introduction

An international organisation is an organisation with international membership, scope or presence.[1] It could also be defined as an "Institution drawing membership from at least three states, having activities in several states, and whose members are held together by a formal agreement."[2] International organisations are based "on multilateral treaties between at least two sovereign nation-states. The formation of an initially fairly loose bond among the participants is generally fortified by the development of more or less stringent institutional structures and organs to pursue certain more or less clearly defined common aims in the international arena." Essentially, international organisation is an alliance of several countries.

There are different categories of international organisations. They could be general and specific. A general international organisation promotes cooperation in several areas of activities, and a specific international organisation, on the other hand, would enhance cooperation in a particular area; the latter are often called specialised international organisations. These organisations could

---

1. Penguin Publication (1998). *Penguin Dictionary of International Relations*, p.270.
2. See *Answers.com* for other definitions.

also be inter-governmental, non-governmental, or a blend of the two in which governments and non-governmental organisations are their members. These outfits can be global with membership open to all countries in the world; they could be regional, confined to nations from a particular region; and they could be selective in which like-minded countries constitute the membership.

Broadly speaking, the United Nations is a general, inter-governmental, world organisation. Its specialised agencies qualify as specific, inter-governmental, global organisations. The European Union is an example of a general, intergovernmental, regional organisation. Virtually every part of the world now has a regional or sub-regional organisation, such as the African Union, Organisation of American States, ASEAN, etc. Lion's Club and Rotary International represent non-governmental international organisations and the Red Cross, a global organisation with mixed membership.

Why United Nations?

The United Nations was established on 24 October 1945. It literally rose from the ashes of World War II. Although there are varying estimates about the war's casualties, it is widely believed that more than 55 million people—25 million military personnel and 30 million civilians—lost their lives. As is clear, the impact of the war overwhelmingly fell, as it always does, on the civilian population. The Allied countries lost nearly 44 million and the Axis powers lost another 11 million people. In that war, the Soviet Union lost more than 20 million lives and the Holocaust swallowed 5.6-5.9 million Jews.[3] The colossal loss of lives shook humanity to the core and motivated them into establishing the United Nations to prevent wars in future.

This is abundantly clear from the Preamble of the Charter of the United Nations. It says,

> We the Peoples of the United Nations Determined to save succeeding generations from the scourge of war, which twice in our lifetime has

3. See: *http://encarta.msn.com/encnet/refpages/RefArticle.aspx?refid=761563737&pn=15*

> brought untold sorrow to mankind, and to reaffirm faith in fundamental human rights, in the dignity and worth of the human person, in the equal rights of men and women and of nations large and small, and to establish conditions under which justice and respect for the obligations arising from treaties and other sources of international law can be maintained, and to promote social progress and better standards of life in larger freedom, and for these ends to practice tolerance and live together in peace with one another as good neighbors, and to unite our strength to maintain international peace and security, and to ensure, by the acceptance of principles and the institution of methods, that armed force shall not be used, save in the common interest, and to employ international machinery for the promotion of the economic and social advancement of all peoples, have resolved to combine our efforts to accomplish these aims. Accordingly, our respective Governments, through representatives assembled in the city of San Francisco, who have exhibited their full powers found to be in good and due form, have agreed to the present Charter of the United Nations and do hereby establish an international organisation to be known as the United Nations.[4]

Started small, the United Nations has grown by leaps and bounds over the years. It came into being after France, Republic of China, Soviet Union, United Kingdom and United States of America, the countries then identified as permanent members of the Security Council, as well as the majority of the 46 signatories ratified the Charter. In the first meeting of the General Assembly and the Security Council in January 1946, 51 countries participated. The ensuing process of decolonisation swelled the rank of independent states which also joined the United Nations. And the second spate of membership expansion came with the demise of the Soviet Union and break up of Yugoslavia. Today there are 192 members of the United Nations.

With time and expansion in membership, the complexity of the United Nations has also increased enormously. Its subsidiary organs and organisations have proliferated, and staff and budget have dramatically expanded. Peoples' expectations from this world body have also increased. The total number of staff that was a few hundreds at the inception has grown to more than 39,500[5] in 2008,

---

4. United Nations, Preamble of the *Charter of the United Nations*

5. See Figure 2.1 in this chapter.

and nearly 80,000 military personnel are keeping the peace around the world under the United Nations umbrella. Similarly, the UN budget of a few million dollars in the beginning has reached over 10 billion dollars a year. The Security Council and the Economic and Social Council have been expanded since, and the Trusteeship Council, having virtually no function, remains in a state of suspended animation. Non-governmental organisations have emerged as a new force to reckon with in the global arena. All these developments have contributed to the United Nations' complexity. Pressure to reform and revitalise the United Nations, in order to equip it with the capacity to confront the challenges of the 21st century, has also been mounting from all these quarters.

Evolution of United Nations

The story of the United Nations, for all practical purposes, starts with the League of Nations established by the international community in 1919, soon after World War I, under the Treaty of Versailles. Preventing war through collective security and promoting international cooperation were the principal goals of the League. But the League could not prevent the Axis powers from the acts of aggression that culminated in World War II, because it did not have its own military, and great powers were unwilling to use their armed forces in the pacifist era after World War I. So, after the end of World War II, the founders decided to establish the United Nations as a tool to prevent wars, promote human rights and improve standards of living. Although the name, United Nations, was reportedly first coined by the then US President Franklin D. Roosevelt and used in the Declaration by United Nations of 1 January 1942 to which 26 countries had pledged to continue fighting against the Axis powers,[6] the Organisation came into being only in 1945.

Conceivably, the Charter of the United Nations has been through a rigorous process of evolution. The process began in 1941 in London, home to 9 governments in exile in those days. On 12 June of that year the representatives of Great Britain, Canada, Australia, New Zealand and the Union of South Africa and of the

---

6. See the UN website: *http://www.un.org/aboutun/unhistory/*

exiled governments of Belgium, Czechoslovakia, Greece, Luxembourg, the Netherlands, Norway, Poland, Yugoslavia and of General de Gaulle of France, met at St. James's Palace and signed a declaration that said, "The only true basis of enduring peace is the willing cooperation of free peoples in a world in which, relieved of the menace of aggression, all may enjoy economic and social security. It is our intention to work together, and with other free peoples, both in war and peace, to this end."[7]

In August 1941, US President Roosevelt and UK Prime Minister Churchill met somewhere in the Atlantic Ocean and agreed on common principles to be respected in national policies including the mutually reinforcing interface between security, development and disarmament, for a better future for the world and for permanent peace. The United Nations Declaration signed on 1 January 1942 embraced this Atlantic Charter. On October 30, 1943, the foreign ministers of the USA, UK and Soviet Union and the Chinese ambassador to the Soviet Union singed the Moscow Declaration recognising the "necessity of establishing at the earliest practicable date a general international organisation, based on the principle of the sovereign equality of all peace-loving states, and open to membership by all such states, large and small, for the maintenance of international peace and security."[8]

After a meeting of Roosevelt, Churchill and Stalin in Iran, the Tehran Declaration was issued in December 1943. In the Declaration, the leaders recognised the "supreme responsibility resting upon us and all the United Nations to make peace which will command the goodwill of the overwhelming mass of the peoples of the world and banish the scourge and terror of war for many generations."[9] Subsequently, representatives of the USA, UK, Soviet Union and China fleshed out a detailed blueprint for the United Nations at Dumbarton Oaks, near Washington DC, and presented for study and discussion by the interested countries. These proposals laid out

---

7. See the UN website: *http://www.un.org/aboutun/charter/history/*

8. Ibid.

9. Ibid.

the principles and purposes of the United Nations and recommended the establishment of the General Assembly, Security Council, International Court of Justice and Secretariat; the Economic and Social Council was to work under the authority of the General Assembly. These proposals assigned the responsibility of preventing future wars to the 11-member Security Council and suggested that UN member states put their armed forces at the Security Council's disposal for that purpose. Roosevelt, Stalin and Churchill resolved the issue of voting method in the Security Council, left open at Dumbarton Oaks, in Yalta on 11 February 1945.[10]

At the San Francisco conference that year, 50 countries met to discuss establishment of the United Nations and draw up its charter. The conference considered the proposals prepared at Dumbarton Oaks by the host country, China, the Soviet Union and the United Kingdom from August to October 1944. Not included in the Dumbarton Oaks proposals, the Trusteeship Council was added later. Finally, on 26 June 1945, those countries present at the conference signed the Charter of the United Nations; Poland, not present at the conference, joined a little later; and the United Nations was duly established on 24 October 1945.

Structure

Mostly conceived at Dumbarton Oaks, the structure of the United Nations is so complex that no other international organisation can match it. The world body has six principal organs: The General Assembly, Security Council, Economic and Social Council, International Court of Justice, Trusteeship Council and Secretariat. It has also got several subsidiary bodies, functional commissions, funds and programmes, specialised agencies, departments and regional commissions.

The principal organs of the United Nations, their subsidiary bodies and entities and their interface with each other are presented in Figure 2.1.

10. Ibid.

Figure 2.1

The United Nations System

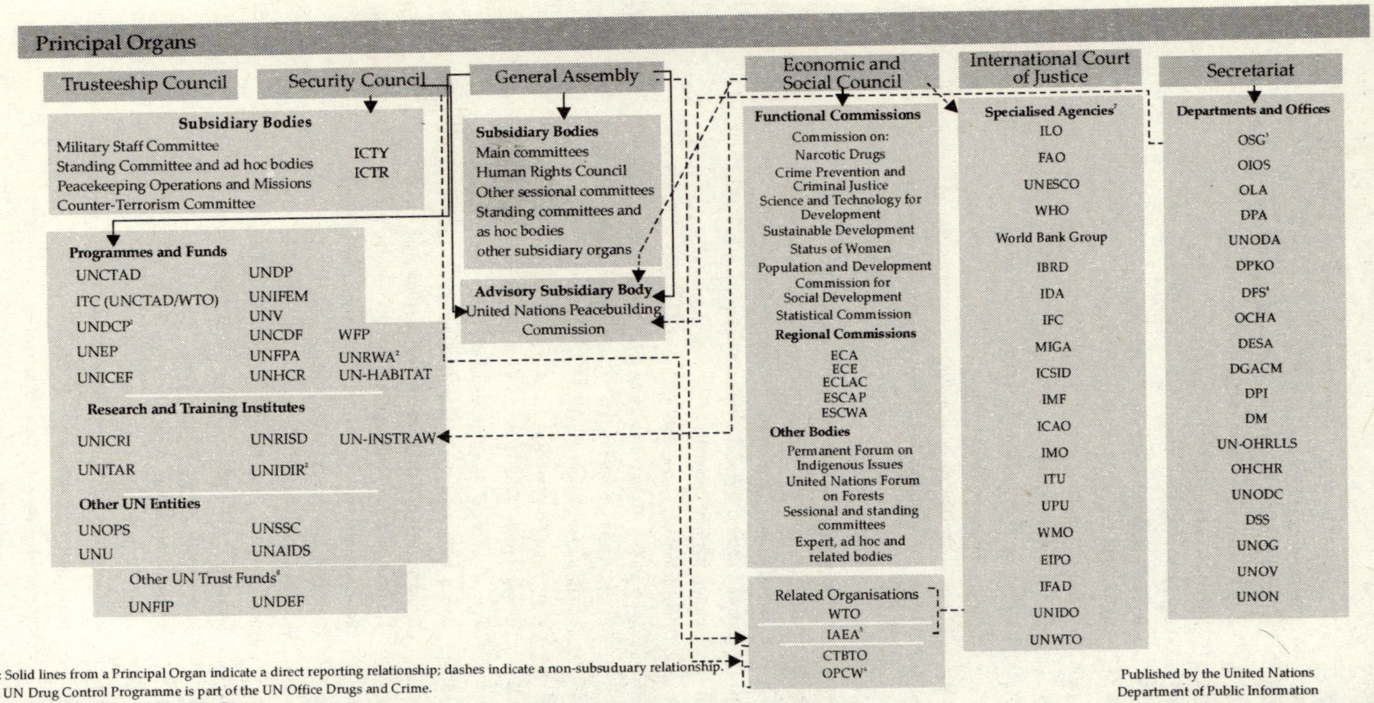

Notes: Solid lines from a Principal Organ indicate a direct reporting relationship; dashes indicate a non-subsuduary relationship.

1. The UN Drug Control Programme is part of the UN Office Drugs and Crime.
2. UNRWA and UNIDIR report only to the GA.
3. The United Nations Ethics Office, the United Nations Ombudsman's Office, and the Chief Information Technology Officer report directly to the Secretary-General.
4. In an exceptional arrangement, the Under-Secretary-General for Field Support reports directly to the Under-Secretary-General for Peacekeeping Operation.
5. IAEA reports to the Security Council and the General Assembly (GA).
6. The CTBTO Prep.Com and OPCW report to the GA.
7. Specialised agencies are autonomous organisations working with the UN and each other through the coordinating machinery of the ECOSOC at the intergovernmental level, and through the Chief Executives Board for coordination (CEB) at the inter-secretariat level.
8. UNFIP is an autonomous trust fund operating under the leadership of the United Nations Deputy Secretary-General. UNDEF's advisory board recommends funding proposals for approval by the Secretary-General.

Published by the United Nations
Department of Public Information
DPI/2470—07-49950—December 2007—3M

Legend:

ICTY:	International Criminal Tribunal for the former Yugoslavia
ICTR:	International Criminal Tribunal for Rwanda
UNCTAD:	United Nations Conference on Trade and Development
ITC:	International Trade Centre (UNCTAD/WTO)
UNDCP:	United Nations Drug Control Programme
UNEP:	United Nations Environment Programme
UNICEF:	United Nations Children's Fund
UNDP:	United Nations Development Programme
UNIFEM:	United Nations Development Fund for Women
UNV:	United Nations Volunteers
UNCDF:	United Nations Capital Development Fund
UNFPA:	United Nations Population Fund
UNHCR:	Office of the United Nations High Commissioner for Refugees
UN-INSTRAW:	United Nations International Research and Training Institute for the Advancement of Women
UNRISD:	United Nations Research Institute for Social Development
UNIDIR:	United Nations Institute for Disarmament Research
UNICRI:	United Nations Interregional Crime and Justice Research Institute
UNITAR:	United Nations Institute for Training and Research
UNOPS:	United Nations Office for Project Services
UNU:	United Nations University
UNSSC:	United Nations System Staff College
UNAIDS:	Joint United Nations Programme on HIV/AIDS
UNFIP:	United Nations Fund for International Partnerships
UNDEF:	United Nations Democracy fund
WFP:	World Food Programme
UNRWA:	United Nations Relief and Works Agency for Palestine Refugeees in the Near East
UN-HABITAT:	United Nations Human Settlements Programmes
ESCWA:	Economic and Social Commission for Western Asia
ESCAP:	Economic and Social Commission for Asia and the Pacific
ECLAC:	Economic Commission for Latin America and the Caribbean
ECE:	Economic Commission for Europe
ECA:	Economic Commission for Africa
OPCW:	Organisation for the Prohibition of Chemical Weapons
CTBTO:	Comprehensive Nuclear-Test-Ban Treaty Organisation
IAEA:	International Atomic Energy Agency
ILO:	International Labour Organisation
FAO:	Food and Agriculture Organisation of the United Nations
UNESCO:	United Nations Educational, Scientific and Cultural Organisation
WHO:	World Health Organisation
IBRD:	International Bank for Reconstruction and Development
IDA:	International Development Association

UNWTO:	World Tourism Organisation
UNIDO:	United Nations Industrial Development Organisation
IFAD:	International Fund for Agricultural Development
EIPO:	World Intellectual Property Organisation
WMO:	World Meteorological Organisation
UPU:	Universal Postal Union
ITU:	International Telecommunication Union
IMO:	International Maritime Organisation
ICAO:	International Civil Aviation Organisation
IMF:	International Monetary Fund
ICSID:	International Centre for Settlement of Investment Disputes
MIGA:	Multilateral Investment Guarantee Agency
IFC:	International Finance Corporation
UNON:	UN Office at Nairobi
UNOV:	UN Office at Vienna
UNOG:	UN Office at Geneva
DSS:	Department of Safety and Security
UNODC:	United Nations Office on Drugs and Crime
OHCHR:	Office of the United Nations High Commissioner for Human Rights
UN-OHRLLS:	Office of the High Representative for the Least Developed Countries, Landlocked Developing Countries and Small Island Developing States
DM:	Department of Management
DPI:	Department of Public Inforamtion
DGACM:	Department for General Assembly and Conference Management
DESA:	Department of Economic and Social Affairs
OCHA:	Office for the Coordination of Humanitarian Affairs
DFS:	Department of Field Support
DPKO:	Department of Peacekeeping Operations
UNODA:	Office for Disarmament Affairs
DPA:	Department of Political Affairs
OLA:	Office of Legal Affairs
OIOS:	Office of Internal Oversight Services
OSG:	Office of the Secretary-General

Courtesy: http://www.un.org/aboutun/chart_en.pdf

Principal Organs

General Assembly (GA)

GA is the apex deliberative body of the United Nations. Its membership consists of all countries that have joined the organisation. Currently it has 192 member states. The Assembly has got a very broad mandate: It can discuss and make recommendations on any question and issue covered by the United Nations' Charter—including international cooperation in such fields as political, peace and security and disarmament, economic development, social development and legal development. It considers annual and special reports from all other UN organs and a host of subsidiary bodies. Only those peace and security-related matters that are being considered by the Security Council (SC) are kept off limit for the Assembly, unless the Council requested the Assembly to take them up.

Electing members for its own subsidiary bodies and other UN organs is one of the key functions of the General Assembly as well. It elects the Secretary-General, the chief executive of the Secretariat, at the recommendation of SC. The Assembly also elects through its plenary the non-permanent members of SC, members of the Economic and Social Council (ECOSOC) and of the Human Rights Council, among others. Its Fifth Committee elects members of the Advisory Committee on Administrative and Budgetary Questions, Joint Inspection Unit, Committee on Programme Coordination, etc.

According to Article 17 of the Charter, GA considers and approves the budget of the United Nations, and the expenses so approved are borne by member states as apportioned under a formula approved by the Assembly. In addition, the Assembly is mandated to examine the administrative budget of specialised agencies and consider and approve financial and budgetary arrangements with them.[11] But the Assembly has now largely abandoned the function of considering and approving the budget of its specialised agencies.

---

11. United Nations, *Charter of the United Nations*, Article 17.

To conduct its business, the Assembly elects its own President for each session, establishes any subsidiary body it may deem appropriate and adopts its own rules of procedures. The Assembly considers and takes decisions on several key issues on its own in the plenary and works through its subsidiary bodies, primarily its six main committees on most others. Peace and security issues are the staple for the First Committee; economic development issues for the Second; social and human rights issues for the Third; political, peacekeeping and information issues for the Fourth; administrative and budgetary issues for the Fifth; and legal issues for the Sixth. All UN members would automatically be members of the main committees. Apart from these committees, the Human Rights Council, various sessional committees, standing committees and ad hoc bodies, as well as other subsidiary organs also constitute the integral parts of the General Assembly.

Each member state has one vote in the General Assembly. Usually the Assembly takes a decision by consensus, and occasionally by a majority of votes. But important questions, as described below, require a two-thirds majority:

> These questions shall include: recommendations with respect to the maintenance of international peace and security, the election of the non-permanent members of the Security Council, the election of the members of the Economic and Social Council, the election of members of the Trusteeship Council in accordance with paragraph 1(c) of Article 86, the admission of new Members to the United Nations, the suspension of the rights and privileges of membership, the expulsion of Members, questions relating to the operation of the trusteeship system, and budgetary questions.[12]

Various funds and programmes also work under the General Assembly, though rather tangentially. They include UNDP, UNICEF, UNEP, WFP, UNFPA, among others. For their operational decision-making, these funds and programmes have their own executive boards.

Security Council

SC—by far the most powerful body of the United Nations, whose decisions are obligatory on all UN members to implement—

---

12. Ibid, Article 18(2).

is responsible for maintaining international peace and security. It discharges its functions in accordance with the principles and purposes of the United Nations. Consisting of 15 members, the Council has five permanent members and 10 non-permanent members.

Evidently the UN Charter itself specifies the permanent members: The Republic of China (now replaced by the People's Republic of China), France, the Union of Soviet Socialist Republics (now succeeded by the Russian Federation), the United Kingdom of Great Britain and Northern Ireland and the United States of America. The General Assembly elects the non-permanent members for a period of two years. While electing such members, the Assembly takes into account mainly the contribution of members to the maintenance of international peace and security and also, at the same time, equitable geographical representation. These members are not eligible for immediate re-election.[13]

Out of 15, 9 affirmative votes are necessary for the Council to make procedural decisions. All other decisions require 9 members including the 5 permanent members supporting them, to be approved. The permanent members are entitled to veto power which they can exercise to block any draft resolution they do not agree with. If the Council considers that the interests of other countries are specially affected by its decisions, it can invite other countries to participate in its discussion, but without a vote, before such decisions are taken. Allowed is the Council to establish its own rules of procedures and to set up such subsidiary bodies, as it deems appropriate. It has to submit its annual report and, when necessary, special reports to GA for consideration. The Council is expected to function at all times, and all members will have to be present at all times at the seat of the organisation. Traditionally, its President rotates among its members in alphabetical order.

To maintain international peace and security, SC can ask parties to a dispute to find a pacific settlement, investigate any dispute, consider a dispute brought to its attention by a UN member, and

13. Ibid, Article 23.

recommend appropriate procedures or methods of adjustment. It can also determine the existence of any threat to peace or aggression and take measures including "complete or partial interruption of economic relations and of rail, sea, air, postal, telegraphic, radio, and other means of communication, and the severance of diplomatic relations."[14] If these measures are found to be inadequate, the Council may take action by air, sea or land forces with the assistance of the Military Staff Committee. All UN members should support such operations.

Although not provided for in the Charter, SC has devised establishing peacekeeping and political missions as a way to resolve internal conflicts which of late have emerged as major threats to international peace and security. The Council or GA has deployed political missions to prevent disputes from descending into wars. Recently the Council has begun to work with GA and ECOSOC to build peace, and the most significant manifestation of this cooperation has been the creation of a Peace-building Commission. The Council is frequently criticised for its outdated structure and opaque methods of work. Efforts to increase its membership and democratise its methods of work have been going in circle year after year at GA for over a decade with no success in sight.

Economic and Social Council

Another principal organ, ECOSOC is responsible for economic, social, cultural and human rights issues. It might undertake or initiate studies and reports regarding international economic, social, cultural, health and related matters as well as make recommendations to GA, member states and specialised agencies on those issues. Besides, the Council may recommend measures to promote human rights, prepare and submit draft conventions to GA and call international conferences in the areas of its competence.

ECOSOC consists of 54 members elected by the General Assembly for a term of 3 years, and they can seek immediate re-election. Each year, one-third members retire from the Council. ECOSOC works

14. Ibid, Article 41.

with UN specialised agencies, coordinates their activities through consultation, obtains regular reports from them and make recommendations to them, as well as furnishes relevant information to the Security Council. In addition, the Council can set up commissions in economic, social and human rights fields. On several issues, the Council works with GA as well.

Each member of ECOSOC enjoys one vote, and the Council can establish its own rules of procedures. The Council's President is elected on the basis of geographical rotation. The Council can call its meetings as necessary, and at the invitation of the Council, other UN member states, UN specialised agencies and non-governmental organisations can participate in its deliberations, but without the right to vote. With respect to such UN objectives as ensuring higher standards of living and full employment and promoting human rights, the Council works very closely with the General Assembly and member states, as well as the broader international community.

Several regional economic—in some cases economic and social—commissions work under the United Nations to collect information and provide technical assistance to member states. Africa, Europe, Latin America and the Caribbean, Asia and the Pacific, and Western Asia, each region has such a regional body. These bodies work in coordination with ECOSOC.

International Court of Justice (ICJ)

As one of the principal organs of the United Nations, the International Court of Justice carries out the responsibility of settling, in accordance with international law, legal disputes submitted by member states and of providing legal opinion at the request of the General Assembly, Security Council or any other agency authorised by the General Assembly to seek such opinion. All members of the United Nations are *ipso facto* parties to the Statute of ICJ that lays out how the Court functions. Even those countries that are not members of the United Nations could become party to the Statute on conditions stipulated by SC and approved by GA.

The Court has 15 judges elected by SC and GA, simultaneously but separately, for a period of 9 years. Through a secret ballot, the President and Vice-President of the Court are elected for a period of three years, and they could be eligible for re-election. Administrative support to the Court comes from the Registry, which is headed by a Registrar and supported by a Deputy Registrar. The Registry is entirely accountable to the Court, not to the UN Secretary-General, as is the case with most secretariats of other organs. Other staff members assist these senior officials.

Often the Court functions as Full Court, and 9 judges, excluding ad hoc judges, constitute the quorum. It has three types of chambers: The Chamber of Summary Procedures for the speedy dispatch of business, the chamber formed to deal with certain categories of cases and the chamber formed to deal with a particular case. When a state party to a dispute does not have a judge of its nationality, it can nominate an ad hoc judge for that specific case. Under the UN Charter, member states are expected to comply with the Court's verdict. If one party to the dispute fails to comply, the other may have the recourse to SC which might take appropriate measures. There is no compulsion on UN members to submit their disputes to the ICJ; they may choose to go to any other existing tribunal or may create a new one by agreement.

Trusteeship Council

As the UN Charter stipulates, the Trusteeship Council, under the authority of the General Assembly, considers reports submitted by the administering authority of trust territories; accepts petitions and examines them in consultation with such authority; organises the Council's periodic visits to trust territories; and takes other actions as necessary as per the trusteeship agreement. The Council prepares survey questions regarding political, economic, social and educational progress in those territories; and the administering authorities submit their reports in response. Three groups of countries constitute the membership of the Trusteeship Council: Permanent members of the Security Council, countries administering the trust territories, and other countries elected for 3 years in numbers equal to the other two categories combined.

Each member has a vote, and the majority of members present in voting make decisions of the Council. The Council decides its own rules of procedure, including that of electing its President. It can seek assistance from ECOSOC and UN specialised agencies in areas of their competence. As most of the trust territories have got independence by now, the Council has very few of them left to handle and remains in a state of suspended animation.

Secretariat

The Secretariat is one of the six main organs of the world body under its Charter. It consists of a Secretary-General (SG) and such staff as may be necessary and provides administrative and technical support to intergovernmental bodies. SG works as chief administrative officer of the organisation as well as of all meetings of main organs of the United Nations, except the International Court of Justice; performs other functions given to him by those organs; and presents his annual report to GA on the work of the organisation. He can bring such issues as may threaten international peace and security to SC's attention.

SG and the staff work for the United Nations. They are independent of any government or external organisation, including from the countries they come from. And all governments must respect the international character of the duties and responsibilities of the SG and the staff and refrain from influencing them in the conduct of their duties. As necessary, the Secretariat permanently appoints appropriate staffs to service other organs of the United Nations.

According to the UN Charter, GA establishes regulations for appointing SG. The existing practice is that GA appoints SG, who is also chief administrator, at the recommendation of SC and is subject to veto power by the Council's permanent members. Although SG has no term limit, none so far has served more than two terms. He in theory appoints the staff, including the Deputy Secretary-General—a post established in 1997 to assist him. While engaging the staff and determining their conditions of service, he should have the "paramount" consideration for the "necessity of securing the highest standards of efficiency, competence and integrity. Due regard shall be paid to the importance of recruiting the staff on as wide a geographical basis as possible."[15] But, in reality, the senior management team is appointed mostly on political considerations.

The Secretariat is composed of various departments, offices, commissions, tribunals, peacekeeping missions, political missions, field offices, etc. New York is home to various departments of the Secretariat. Geneva has a UN Office as well as such organisations as the Office of High Commissioner for Human Rights (OHCHR) and United Nations Conference on Trade and Development (UNCTAD). Vienna too has a UN Office and the UN Office for Drugs and Crime (UNODC). And Nairobi houses the UN Office as well as the United Nations Environment Programme and the United Nations Human Settlements Programme (UNN-Habitat).

Regional commissions for Asia and the Pacific, for Europe, for Africa, for West Asia and for Latin American countries are located in Bangkok, Geneva, Addis Ababa, Beirut and Santiago, respectively. While the Asian and West Asian ones are called economic and social commissions, others are named only as economic commissions. Stationed in The Hague, are the staffs attached to the International Tribunals for the Former Yugoslavia and in Arusha and Kigali for Rwanda. Peacekeeping operations and political missions have been deployed in many troubled spots of the globe.

Structure of Secretariat

Departments

Departments and equivalent offices, mostly based in New York, are the mainstay of the Secretariat. They are further divided into divisions, offices, branches, sections, services and units. Briefly presented below is the composition of the Secretariat's various departments.

Executive Office of the Secretary-General (EOSG): This Office provides support to the Secretary-General in carrying out his complex responsibilities. The Deputy Secretary-General, Chief of Staff at the Under Secretary-General level and other officials constitute

15. Ibid, Article 101(3).

the Executive Office of the Secretary-General. Also under this office are the Protocol and Liaison Services, Office of the Spokesman for the Secretary-General, and Global Compact Office which promotes collaboration with the private sector and helps implement projects with private sector funding.

Office of Internal Oversight Services (OIOS): Headed by an Under Secretary-General, this Office is responsible for internal auditing of UN expenses, investigation into financial and ethical wrongdoings in the Secretariat and monitoring and evaluation of performance. It also offers consultancy services to other departments and entities. OIOS is divided into Internal Audit Division, Monitoring, Evaluation and Consulting Division, and Investigations Division. Although SG appoints him/her, the head of OIOS enjoys a large measure of independence from him and directly reports to GA on substantive matters.

Office of Legal Affairs (OLA): Charged with the responsibility of providing legal opinion to the Secretary-General and helping the codification of international law, OLA is headed by an Under Secretary-General. It is organised into the Office of the Legal Counsel, General Legal Division, Treaty Section, Codification Division, International Trade Law Division, and Division for Ocean Affairs and the Law of the Sea.

Department of Political Affairs (DPA): An Under Secretary-General is in charge of DPA whose functions include providing backstopping to the Security Council and electoral assistance to member states, as well as monitoring political situation across the world to detect potential flashpoints and to exercise preventive diplomacy. Functioning under DPA are the Security Council Affairs Division, Electoral Assistance Division, Office of the Special Advisor on Cyprus, and Office of the Special Advisor on Africa. Previously separate, now the same USG is working as the Special Advisor for Cyprus and Africa as well. DPA is also responsible for several political missions at troubled parts of the world.

Department for Disarmament Affairs (DDA): This Department, under an Under Secretary-General, coordinates and promotes disarmament activities in the United Nations. It is organised around the weapons of mass destruction branch, conventional arms branch, monitoring, database and information branch and regional activities, including the regional centres for peace and disarmament. Secretary-General Ban Ki-Moon sought to downgrade this Department soon after he joined, but abandoned the effort in the face of fierce opposition from some member states.

Department of Peacekeeping Operations (DPKO): Responsible for peacekeeping operations spread around the world, this Department contains in New York the Office of Operations, Office of Logistics, Management and Mine Action Service, and Cartographic Section. Headed by an Under Secretary-General, DPKO has the largest number of staff trying to keep the peace in conflict-stricken places around the globe. It deploys military observers, military troops and civilian police, as well as administrative and technical staff to support peace efforts.

Department of Field Support: The Department is a newly created structure under an Under Secretary-General largely by breaking the Department of Peacekeeping Operations. This Department works in areas of personnel for field missions—peacekeeping operations and political missions—and operates in close collaboration with the DPKO, Department of Management and other departments.

Office for the Coordination of Humanitarian Affairs (OCHA): One of the most complex departments that has New York and Geneva hubs, this Office is composed of the Office of the Under-Secretary-General/Emergency Relief Coordinator, Deputy Emergency Relief Coordinator (including the Office of the Director, New York and Office of the AERC/Director and Deputy Director, Geneva), Executive and Administrative Offices, Donor and External Relations Section, Inter-Agency Standing Committee/Executive Committee on Humanitarian Affairs (IASC/ECHA) Secretariat, Advocacy and Information Management Branch (New York), Policy Development and Studies Branch (New York), Coordination and Response Division, Internal Displacement Division (Geneva) and Emergency Service Branch (Geneva).

Department of Economic and Social Affairs (DESA): The DESA has the Office of the Under Secretary-General, Development Policy and

Planning Office, Financing for Development Office, Office of ECOSOC Support and Coordination, Office of the Special Adviser on Gender Issues and the Advancement of Women, Division for the Advancement of Women, and Division for Sustainable Development, Secretariat of the United Nations Forum on Forests, Division for Social Policy and Development, Division for Public Administration and Development Management, Statistics Division, and Population Division. It is headed by an Under Secretary-General and grapples with economic and social development issues.

Department for General Assembly and Conference Management (DGACM): Organised around the Central Planning and Co-ordination Service, General Assembly and ECOSOC Affairs Division, Interpretation, Meetings and Publishing Division, Translation and Editorial Division, which also include the German Translation Service, DGACM is headed by an Under Secretary-General. This Department is charged with the duty of providing technical and administrative backstopping to the General Assembly and ECOSOC, translating, editing and publishing documents in six languages, and providing interpretations services to intergovernmental meetings.

Department of Public Information (DPI): Led by an Under Secretary-General, DPI is composed of the News and Media Division (the News Centre and the UN Radio), Strategic Communications Division (the DPI Updates, the Palestine and Decolonization Section, and the Information Centers Services), and Outreach Division (the Dag Hammarskjöld Library, the United Nations CyberSchoolBus, the NGO Section, the Publications Service, and the Sales and Marketing Section). This Department is the public relations arm of the United Nations.

Department of Safety and Security (DSS): Responsible for coordinating measures for the security of UN personnel and premises around the world, DSS is headed by an Under Secretary-General. The security function was upgraded into the department level after the terrorist attacks on the United States in 2001. Presently, DSS consists of the staff security training, travel advisories for all countries, and security clearance and travel notification-ISECT. This department coordinates security aspects of

UN funds and programmes and specialised agencies as well and enjoys some measure of independence from the Secretary-General.

Department of Management (DOM): Headed by an Under Secretary-General, DOM carries out the UN's personnel and financial functions. It consists of the Treasury, Office of Programme Planning, Budget and Accounts (Peace-keeping Financing Division, Programme Planning and Budget Division and Accounts Division), Office of Human Resources Management (Specialist Services Division, Operational Services Division and Medical Services Division), Office of Central Support Services (Information Technology Services Division and Facilities and Commercial Services Division). Under the Facilities and Commercial Services Division lie the Procurement Service, United Nations Postal Administration, Archives and Records Management Section and Travel and Transportation Section. DOM also has two projects right now that may run into several years: The Integrated Management Information System Project and the Capital Master Plan (renovation of the New York premises) Project.

Other UN Offices: Apart from the departments, there are several offices at the United Nations whose chiefs report directly to SG. They are the Office of the High Representative for the least developed countries, landlocked developing countries and small island developing states (OHRLL); Office of the Special Adviser on Africa (OSAA); Office of the Special Representative of the Secretary-General for Children in Armed Conflict; Office of the United Nations Ombudsman; Peace-building Support Office; and United Nations Fund for International Partnership (UNFIP), which works with the private sector to promote UN objectives. The first three are headed by Under Secretary-General, the Ombudsman and the Peace-building Support Office by Assistant Secretary-General and the Fund by a senior official. They all have their own staff who are part of the Secretariat.

Other Headquarter Duty Stations

Geneva: Outside New York headquarters, the United Nations has three more headquarter duty stations in Geneva, Nairobi and Vienna. Geneva, the second major hub after New York, houses the

UN Office in Geneva (UNOG), UNCTAD and OHCHR, and several UN affiliated organisations.

UNOG operates under Director-General, and has a structure as presented in Figure 2.2 below:

Figure 2.2

Organisation Structure of UNOG

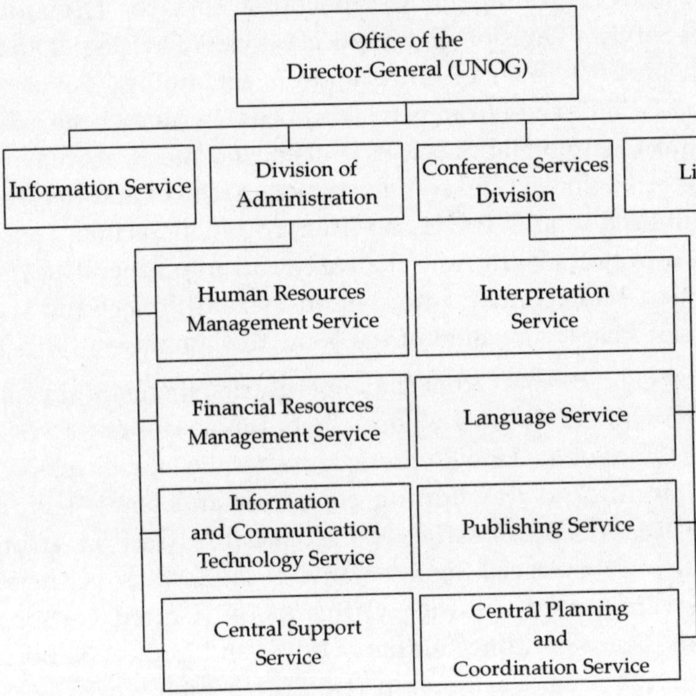

Source: United Nations.

Both UNCTAD and OHCHR are headed by Secretary-General, a post equivalent to the Under Secretary-General in the UN system. UNCTAD consists of the divisions for Africa, least developed countries, landlocked countries and small island developing states; for globalisation and development; for international trade and commodities; for investment and enterprise; and for technology and logistics. Likewise, OHCHR has had divisions for executive direction and management (policy, planning, monitoring and evaluation section, communications section, civil society unit, field security and safety unit, and donor and external relations section); for field operations and technical cooperation; for special procedures (supporting special rapporteurs, representatives, independent experts, etc.); for Human Rights Council and treaties; and for programme support and management services. Most of the Geneva, Vienna and Nairobi-based organisations also have their substantial representation in New York for the sake of coordination.

Nairobi: Kenya hosts the United Nations Office in Nairobi (UNON), UN Environment Programme (UNEP) and UN-Habitat. UNON, led by a Director-General at the level of Under Secretary-General in the UN system, has the office of the Director-General, as well as divisions for administration and for conference services, and a UN information centre. Below is the organisation chart of the UNON:

Figure 2.3

Organisation Structure of UNON

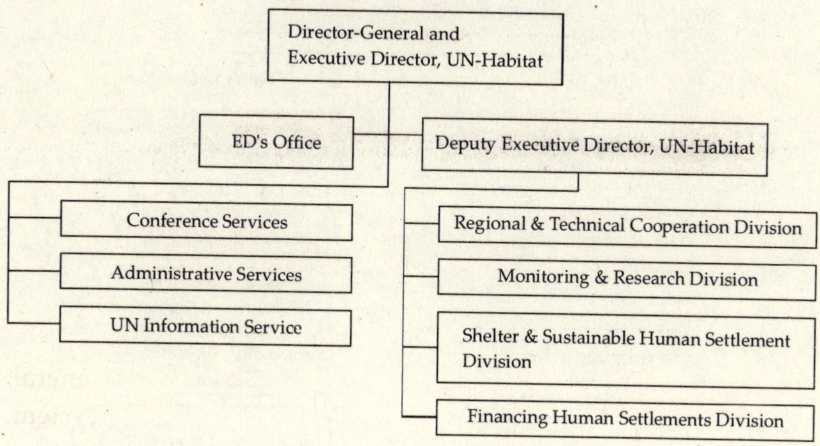

Courtesy: UNON.

UNEP has divisions for regional cooperation and representation; for environmental laws and conventions; for technology, industry and economics; for communications and public information; for early warning and assessment; for environmental policy implementation; for global environment facility coordination and for environment management group, among others. The UN-Habitat is divided into regional and technical cooperation division, monitoring and research division shelter and sustainable human settlements development division and financing human settlements division. UNON provides administrative services to the other two. Depending on their seniority, either the head of UNEP or UN-Habitat is appointed as the chief of UNON by the UN Secretary-General.

Vienna: Austria is the centre for the UN Office in Vienna (UNOV) and the Office of Drugs and Crime (UNODC). The Executive-Director of UNODC also works as Director-General (Under Secretary-General) of UNOV. The organisation structure of UNOV is presented in Figure 2.4.

Figure 2.4

Organisation Structure of UNOV

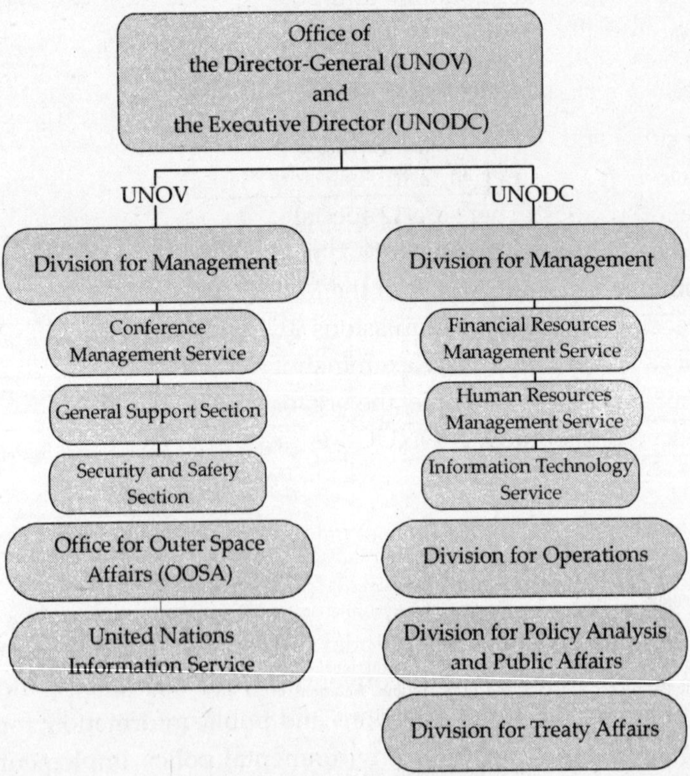

Courtesy: UNOV.

Tribunals

The Hague has, besides the International Court of Justice, the International Tribunal for the former Yugoslavia.[16] Arusha in Tanzania hosts the International Tribunal for Rwanda.[17] Both tribunals have, apart from their chambers, the Office of the Prosecutor and Registry. In order to provide administrative and technical services to the tribunals, the Office of the Registrar, with various sections under him, has been organised.

Regional Commissions

Although different regional commissions have structurally been arranged in their own ways, they are led by Executive Secretary at the level of Under Secretary-General and have organised themselves around divisions and units for thematic/sectoral programmes and for programme support. For a sample, the organisation structure of the Secretariat of the Economic and Social Commission for Asia and the Pacific has been presented in Figure 2.5.

Peacekeeping and Political Missions

As at the end of 2008, there were 16 peacekeeping missions: Seven in Africa, 1 in the America, 2 in Asia and the Pacific, 3 in Europe and 3 in the Middle East. There are 12 special political missions, 10 operating under the DPA and 2 under DPKO. Six of them are located in Africa, 3 in South and Central Asia, 3 in the Middle East. USG and ASG level staff head of most of these missions are appointed directly by the Secretary-General, rigorously examination scrutinising their capacities and competences. As a sample, the organisation structure of the largest peacekeeping operation, MONUC[18] is given in Figure 2.6.

---

16. The full form of this tribunal is the International Tribunal for the Prosecution of Persons Responsible for Serious Violations of International Humanitarian Law Committed in the Territory of the Former Yugoslavia since 1991.

17. The full form of this tribunal is the International Criminal Tribunal for the Prosecution of Persons Responsible for Genocide and Other Serious Violations of International Humanitarian Law Committed in the Territory of Rwanda and Rwandan Citizens Responsible for Genocide and Other Such Violations Committed in the Territory of Neighbouring States between 1 January and 31 December 1994.

18. UNO Mission in the Democratic Republic of the Congo, in French.

Figure 2.5

Secretariat of the Economic and Social Commission for Asia and the Pacific

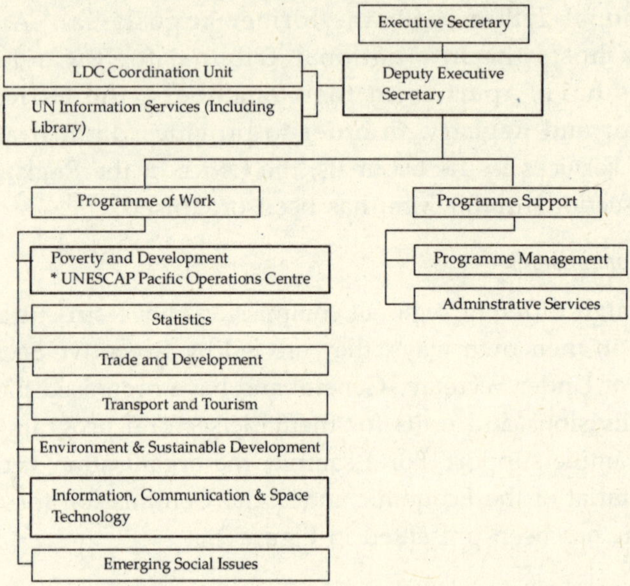

Source: UN-ESCAP.

Staff Strength

The total number of staff employed by the various departments at headquarters as well as in regional commissions, peacekeeping missions, other field locations and tribunals was 39,503 as on 30 June 2008.[19] Excluded from this figure are those 213 staffs out of whom 152 are on special leave without pay and 61 on secondment to other organisations. It also excludes over 2,006 gratis personnel, 4,275 consultants, 1,808 contractors and 194 institutional contractors, as well as those 176 locally recruited consultants and 2,260 locally recruited individual contractors who were engaged by the missions operated under the Department of Field Support in 2007. Not included in the total staff figure are also the 76,934 military personnel as on 30 June 2008 deployed in various peacekeeping missions, as well as thousands of those staff who are working for UN funds and programmes and specialised agencies.

---

19. Most of the information in this section is derived from: United Nations, *Composition of the Secretariat*, A/63/310, 29 September 2008, p.9.

Figure 2.6

Organisation Structure of MONUC

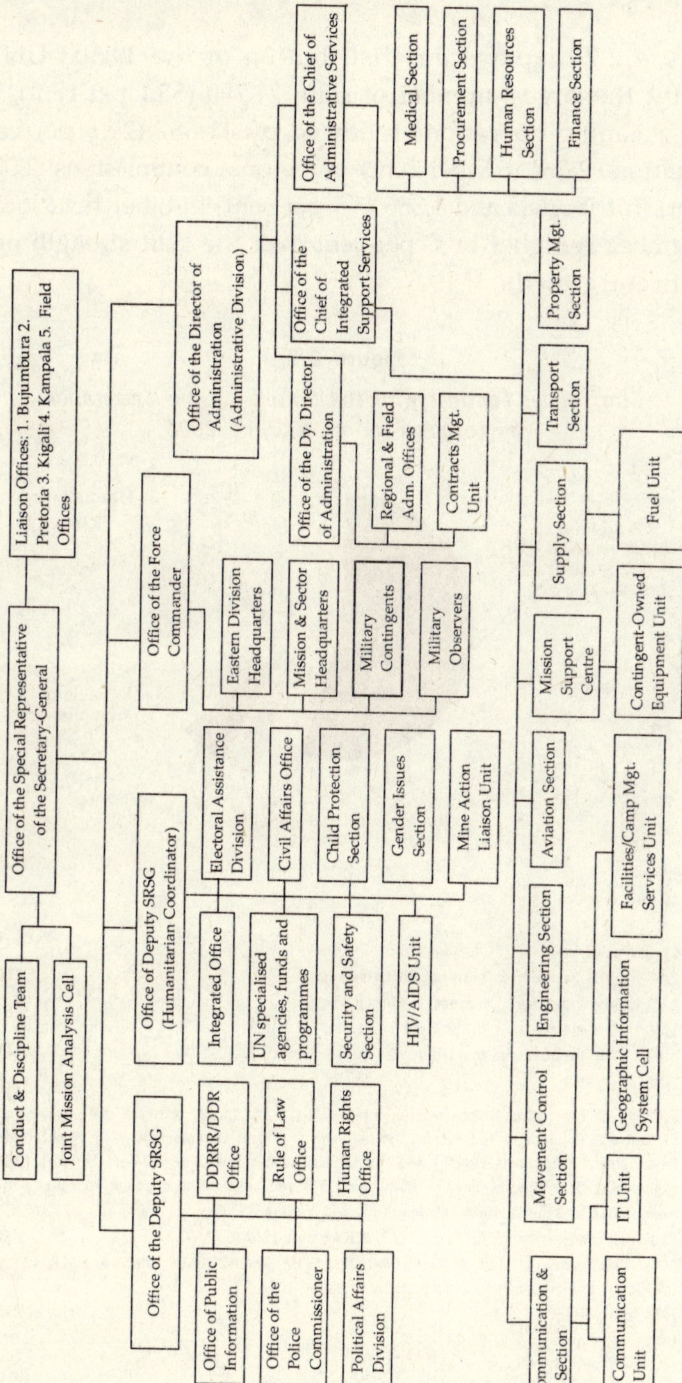

Source: MONUC (UN)

Figure 2.7 displays the distribution of the 39,503 UN staff. Evidently, the largest number of staff, 21,790 (55.1 per cent), works in peacekeeping operations followed by 11,687 (29.6 per cent) at headquarters, 2,564 (6.5 per cent) in regional commissions, 2,076 (5.3 per cent) in tribunals and 1,386 (3.5 per cent) in other field locations. This number is higher by 8 per cent over the staff strength of 2007, a significant growth.

Figure 2.7

Staff Under Contract with the United Nations Secretariat by Location as on 30 June 2008

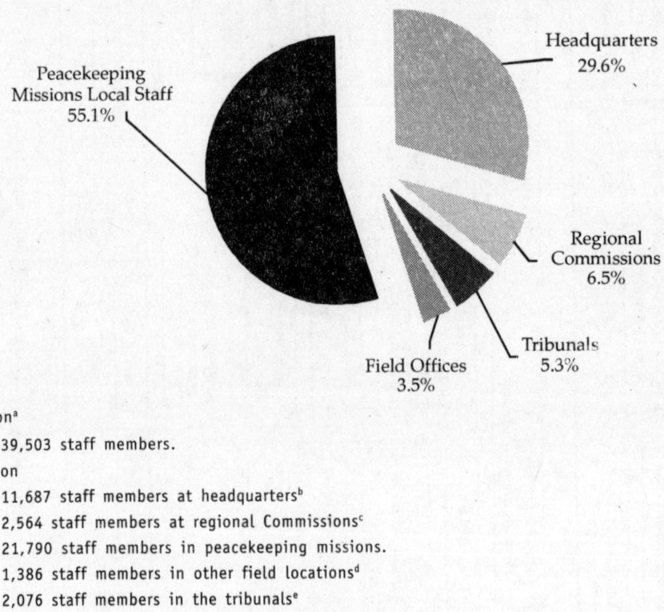

Population[a]

- 39,503 staff members.

By location

- 11,687 staff members at headquarters[b]
- 2,564 staff members at regional Commissions[c]
- 21,790 staff members in peacekeeping missions.
- 1,386 staff members in other field locations[d]
- 2,076 staff members in the tribunals[e]

Source: IMIS and FPMS

- Staff on all types of contract. Includes internationally and locally recruited staff, regardless of length of contract. Excludes United Nations international and local staff administrated by the United Nations Development Programme (UNDP) and the United Nations Office for Project Services (UNOPS). Also excludes staff on special leave without pay (152) and staff on secondment to other entities (61).
- Headquarters: Geneva, Nairobi, New York and Vienna.
- Regional Commission: ECA, ECE, ECLAC, ESCAP and ESCWA.
- Other field locations: staff of DESA, DPA, DPI, OCHA, OHCHR, ONOS, UNCTAD, UNEP, UN-Habitat and UNODC in non-headquarters duty stations.
- ICTY and ICTR.

Courtesy: United Nations.

For managerial purposes, the United Nations classifies its staff into two groups: The Professional and higher categories and the general services and related categories. Out of the active 39,503 staff, 11,293 or 28.2 per cent belonged to the Professional and higher categories and 28,423 or 71.8 per cent to the General Service and related categories. The United Nations recruits its staff internationally and locally under the 100, 200 and 300 series of its Staff Regulations and Rules. In the Professional and higher categories, 7,402 were employed under the 100 series, 1,250 under the 200 series and 2,490 under the 300 series. And in the General Service and related categories, 15,808 worked under the 100 series and 12,553 under the 300 series. Table 2.1 presents the distribution of staff across various broad categories, series, locations and periods of contract.

Procedures

The United Nations has laid out elaborate procedures for conducting its business. Its intergovernmental bodies—such as GA, SC, ECOSOC and Trusteeship Council—make policies and issue directives based on the inputs and information provided by the Secretariat and member states. Their decisions come in the forms of resolutions, decisions and directives, depending on the nature of the issue in hand. For these bodies are free to establish their own rules of procedures, they may choose to deliberate and take decisions on their own on some issues and ask for advice and support from advisory and subsidiary organs or committees on others before taking decisions. Depending on their nature, member states, the Secretariat or both, implement such decisions and directives, and the various departments play key role in this process.

To decide programmatic/substantive aspects, UNEP, UN-Habitat, and regional commissions have their own intergovernmental bodies, but their Secretariats work within the UN Staff Regulations and Rules. Similarly, the international tribunals for the former Yugoslavia and Rwanda have laid down their own procedures for the chambers, but their staffs operate under the same umbrella rules, though senior appointments are made after consultations with the Presidents of those tribunals. UN field missions—peacekeeping operations and political missions—work directly under the respective departments at UN headquarters.

Table 2.1

Staff under Contract with the United Nations Secretariat by Location, Category and Series of the Staff Rules as on 30 June 2008

	Professional and Higher Categories				General Service and Related Categories			
	100	200	300	Subtotal	100	200	Subtotal	Total
Headquarter[a]								
Contract for less than one year	618	27	348	993	230	241	471	1464
Contract for one year or more	3953	552	322	4827	5282	14	5296	10123
Subtotal	4571	579	670	5820	5512	255	5767	11587
Regional Commissions[b]								
Contract for less than one year	49	6	62	117	121	40	161	278
Contract for one year or more	662	92	60	814	1472	0	1472	2286
Subtotal	711	98	122	931	1593	40	1633	2564
Peacekeeping Missions								
Contract for less than one year	99	-	290	389	2352	3560	5912	6301
Contract for one year or more	952	1	1365	2318	4594	8617	13211	15529
Subtotal	1051	1	1655	2707	6946	12177	19123	21830
Other Field Locations[c]								
Contract for less than one year	7	28	5	40	23	3	26	66
Contract for one year or more	333	544	27	904	412	4	416	1320
Subtotal	340	572	32	944	435	7	442	1386
Tribunals[d]								
Contract for less than one year	34	-	9	43	34	24	58	101
Contract for one year or more	735	-	2	737	1188	50	12398	1975
Subtotal	769	-	11	780	1222	74	1296	2076
Total Active Staff	7402	1250	2490	11142	15903	12553	28456	39598
Other								
Staff un apacial leave without pay	81	10	2	93	56	3	59	152
Staff on document to other entites	56	2	-	58	9	-	9	67
Total other staff	137	12	2	151	65	3	68	219
Total staff under contract	7539	1262	2492	11293	15867	12556	28423	39716

Note: a Gineva, Nairobi, New York and Vienna.

b ECA, ECE, ECLAC, ESCAP and ESCWA.

c Other field locations staff of DESA, DPA, DPI, OCHA, OIAS, UNCTAD, UNEP, UN-Habitat and UNODC at non-headquarters duty statises

d ICTY and ICTR.

Courtesy: United Nations.

Observations

At its very inception, the United Nations was quite a complex organisation with challenging mandates in different areas of global life. Over the more than six decades of its existence, the world body has grown more complicated in its scope, more diverse in its activities, broader in its organisational paraphernalia and wider in its interface with its membership and partners. In some areas, like the administration of trust territories, it has also become increasingly irrelevant, for most of these territories have gotten independence. Several acute and new problems have inflicted the world body. Some of them have been around from the very beginning, others have come along with the new global issues and concurrent, expansion over the years in the organisation's structures and mandates.

Turf battle between the main organs is one of the old issues. The Security Council, on the one hand and GA and ECOSOC, on the other, have been quibbling over their territories, as SC has, some people believe, been consistently stepping on the toes of the other two by expanding its role into theirs. Another turf battle continues between GA and the Secretariat. The Secretaries-General complain about GA micro-managing the Secretariat by intervening in matters that should have been left to SG, the chief administrative officer. On the other hand, GA is unhappy that SG has been asking for more authority to deploy staff and financial resources, while he has failed to exercise those powers properly that have already been granted to him. Many small countries also fear that SG might not be able to resist if big and powerful countries lean on him to use his powers to tilt the balance in favour of the already privileged member states. On another level, various departments of the Secretariat continue to clash over scarce resources and their overlapping mandates.

Reform of the Security Council has remained a major sticking point for over a decade. The permanent members are unwilling to democratise significantly the work of the Council, while all other UN members are putting pressure for such reform. Brazil, Germany, India and Japan—G-4—are eager to join the Council as permanent members as quickly as possible. Some of their regional competitors are against such move. The United States wants to bring Japan on board as a permanent member, but not others yet. On the other hand, the United Kingdom and France want to increase the Council's permanent membership to accommodate developing countries, but do not want their status and privileges diluted. Those countries that do not find themselves eligible for a seat at the top table are clamouring for the Council's expansion only in its non-permanent membership category.[20]

A tug of war has also been going on among member states within GA. Some countries want to abandon several urgent and relevant agenda items, such as nuclear disarmament, because they feel uncomfortable discussing them and went to concentrate on non-proliferation. What is more, virtually all countries recognise that GA has too many agenda items to tackle—many of them repetitive, outdated and arcane—and that the Assembly should focus more of its energy, time and attention on topical and priority issues of the day. However, consensus ends there. Most countries have their pet agenda which they would not want to forgo. Biennialisation and triennalisation of agenda items has eased some pressure on GA but the situation is still far from optimal.

As a result, the Secretariat is saddled with overwhelming mandates and outdated administrative and budgetary systems making it difficult to cope with them. So it might not be able to do justice to several resolutions and decisions of intergovernmental bodies. Conversely, the Secretariat has also been resisting much-needed change that might prove uncomfortable to the staff, such as inculcating a robust culture of accountability, which is lacking, as Boutros-Ghali has lamented.[21] Besides, there is avoidable duplication and overlaps between various departments and organisational entities within the Secretariat, and removing them could improve its efficiency and effectiveness and reduce cost for member states. In particular, UN human resources management

20. See "Security Council Reform: An Alternative Approach" by Munir Akram in Ajit M. Banerjee and Murari R. Sharma, *Reinventing the United Nations, op. cit.*, pp.34-55.

21. Ibid, "Foreword," pp. ix-xi.

needs urgent and far-reaching reforms, as it is woefully wanting in transparency, hugely outdated in substance, disturbingly inefficient in performance and disappointingly ineffective in producing the anticipated results.

3

Major Features of International Civil Service

Introduction

Concepts of personnel administration and human resources management are often used interchangeably despite significant differences between them in their orientation. The emerging trend is to focus on human side of administration and emphasise the people-based orientation in large public organisations. Despite terminological differentiation, the concept of personnel administration or human resources management is considered to be a major institutional device to organise workforce and attain organisational goals. It is an institution that carries out the business of government or organisation which directly affects the quality of governance and management of public affairs, enterprises and civil society. Human resources are the actual executor of government policies and programmes and wielder of public service authority, irrespective of the formal depository of power. In other organisations too, the staff are the ones who carry out mandate, produce goods and deliver services.

The term civil service connotes the group of functionaries of the state who are appointed to their jobs through non-elected processes. Generally speaking, the basis for civil servants' recruitment may be patronage or merit. Patronage might be dispensed for political loyalty, family relations, or business links, with or without regard for personal competence and qualification. Merit, on the other hand, is determined through a set of objective criteria—competitive examinations or other selection techniques, academic credentials, professional expertise, experience, interviews etc.—often by some central personnel authority, at least at the professional level, if not lower. The staff so selected remain in the service usually for their working careers.

Comparative analysis of civil service systems initiatives poses some complexities. Civil service systems in most countries, developed or developing, have evolved over a period of time. In this process of evolution, they have developed specific characteristics, attributes and ethos. In fact, most of the civil service systems are embedded in the socio-political and organisational system of the specific context. The situation is further complicated by the divergence of constitutional provisions, formal laws, conventions and practices. These realities render it quite difficult to make accurate comparison between various human resources systems in general and between various civil services in particular. Nonetheless, it is also a fact that debates on personnel administration or human resources management—while differing in details and nuances among countries, organisations and institutions—indicate strikingly similar overall concerns.

In these circumstances, it is desirable to remember certain overall caveats while discussing the subject of civil service. Generally speaking, the analysis of civil service has to be understood in national and/or organisational context, and action programmes for reform or restructuring have to be designed in the specific contextuality. International discussions can serve to bring out perceptions of problems and sharing of experiences among different situations. International comparisons are also significant for the demonstration effect of specific practices particularly it they are at different stages of development.

Many debates about human resources management purport to convey a lack of clarity of the directions and modalities of the basic features. There is a tendency to use the concept with the broader jurisdiction of public management, combining both civil service and politically appointed personnel. Others use the terminology to identify bureaucracy. The latter is an organisational model not necessarily confined to public affairs. Even within the public service, clear distinction is not always made between civil service and public service workforce.

The confusion or contradiction is partly the result of changing notions of the role of the state or the organisation and scope of public affairs. The size of the workforce in the public sector has grown considerably to carry out the mandates of the state. Most states today are engaged in producing, delivering or regulating a vast array of goods and services. They use a multiplicity of organisational models to carry out these activities. Methods used to realise them have also increased significantly. They range from direct production by public officials to contractual arrangements and outsourcing. The lack of clarity about the concept of civil service becomes problematic when personnel standards have to be established for its members. The public functionaries are engaged in a variety of activities demanding different expertise, values and standards. For example, they engage in policy advice, regulation, industrial production, research and development, education or agricultural development. In many instances, public officials claim to be advisors to political leaders, committed to the due process of law. In other situations they function as managers, as in the private sector, and measure their performance in terms of productivity.

While every organisation will have to develop its own strategies for effective delivery of services, the recent trends indicate the need for at least a modicum of agreement on possible approaches and solutions. This is also important to devise and enforce consistent and effective personnel management practices. In fact, the fluidity of situation in many cases seems to be adversely affecting the system and performance of human resources and aggravating relationship between political and civil service personnel. While all the issues of civil service management are interrelated, it is important to review a set of strategic issues concerning civil or human service as a first step.

UN International Civil Service

The United Nations is a complex organisation with responsibilities in areas of peace and security, economic and social development, and humanitarian assistance. Over time, its complexity has multiplied with the phenomenal expansion in programmes and staff strength. Over the years, mandates and personnel delivering on them have increased extraordinarily. In 1949, the United Nations had 1,500 staff, of whom, 1,000 were stationed in New York. As on June 30, 2008, the organisation had 39,503 in the Secretariat, working together with nearly 80,000 military personnel and other formed units. Of those staff, almost 30 per cent are posted in four headquarters duty stations (New York, Geneva, Nairobi, and Vienna); more than 55 per cent are deployed in peacekeeping operations; more than 6 per cent in regional commissions and the rest elsewhere. For further details, see Chapter 2 of this book.

Because of the size of UN membership, the nature of the functions of the Secretariat has considerably changed, most significantly in peace and security functions, peacekeeping and peace-building activities, and in the socio-economic field. As Secretary-General Hammarskjold said in November 1968 that the UN is an instrument of multilateral diplomacy and the Secretariat has grown into an operational agency of significant dimension. The members of the civil service play a variety of roles, for example, bridge building, conflict preventer, mediator, communication facilitator, identity supporter, initiator, operator/controller/observer, expert/coordinator, and representative/negotiator.[1]

Evidently, the United Nations has evolved into a dynamic operational organisation carrying out increasingly complex mandates, which are frequently multi-disciplinary and cross-programmatic. While the world body will always require specialist expertise, there is an increasing need for multi-skilled, versatile and mobile staff, able to work across occupational groups and to manage complex integrated operations. The organisation needs to be able

1. Hammarskjold, Dag (1961). *The International Civil Service: in Law and in Fact,* (a lecture delivered at Oxford University). Oxford: Clarendon Press.

to manage its workforce as an integrated whole and more flexibility to enable it to deploy staff in accordance with operational requirements. The world body can no longer function effectively with different recruitment and development systems for headquarters and the field.[2]

The United Nations invites applications for hundreds, if not thousands, of posts/positions every year, and each opening lures a large number of applicants globally. These applicants hail from 192 member countries, numerous cultures and socio-economic backgrounds, multifarious education systems with varied scholastic standards, schools and institutions of higher learning. The volume of applicants has been increasing by leaps and bounds. The UN human resource managers have to grapple with new information everyday. As a result, HRM in the world body is in a constant flux, as it has to evolve consistently with new realities almost on a daily basis. Add to this mix the proclivity of bureaucracies to give them wide latitude for manoeuvre, and the United Nations would have one of the most fluid and intricate human resources systems in the global community.

Universal Organisation

Interestingly, the United Nations is by far the most universal organisation today. It has 192 member states, which means virtually all independent states from around the globe. Even Switzerland, which remained an observer until recently, has finally joined the world body. Evidently the United Nations has become a powerful symbol of sovereignty, freedom and identity for most new members, while it remains an important instrument of foreign policy for the old and powerful ones.

In most countries, the world body has its offices. In developing countries, the United Nations has its representation through its seven funds and programmes with several thousands of staff and nearly 20 billion dollars total budget annually. There is a network of several large, legally independent specialised agencies with headquarters

---

2. Beagle, Jan (2007). Assistant Secretary-General of OHRMs statement to ACABQ.

mostly in developed countries, with a budget of 42-45 billion annually. Besides, United Nations has its offices to liaise with host governments and to raise funds and garner resources in various countries.

International Character and Diversity

Article 100 of the Charter of the United Nations stipulates the international character of the Secretary-General and the staff of the United Nations. They are required not to seek and receive instructions from any government or authority external to the United Nations. The same Article also commits member states to respect the international character of the Secretary-General and the staff, and not to seek to influence them. The staff of the International Secretariat is protected under diplomatic immunity against any personal injury, harassment, arrest while they are on official duty, on mission or at headquarters. Specific privileges are accorded to the staff and their families at the time of appointment, and the oath of office is given to them to protect and defend the Charter of the United Nations.

Article 101 of the Charter prescribes that the UN staff should have the highest standards of efficiency, competence and integrity. It further states that, "due regards shall be paid to the importance of recruiting the staff on as wide a geographical basis as possible." In an effort to comply with the provision, the world body seeks to employ into the international civil service the nationals of countries from across the world. There are two official working languages—English and French—and four other official languages—Spanish, Chinese, Russian and Arabic—used in the United Nations. Simultaneous interpretations are given to delegations; and documents are produced in all six languages. This language diversity has been embraced in order to avoid language barriers. All this makes the international civil service and the work with the United Nations hugely multinational, multicultural and multilingual.

Uniqueness

Comparing the UN International Civil Service with its national counterparts or with private enterprises is fraught with serious problems of consistency and coherence. Yet it would be instructive to look at similarities and differences, while acknowledging the uniqueness of the world body.

The UN administration has many unique features. It also shares several features with the national civil service and with private sector enterprises. The uniqueness of the UN civil service manifests itself in different forms, above and beyond multinationalism, multiculturalism and multilingualism. In order to have a better perspective, let us have a look at the salient similarities and differences between the UN civil service and national civil services.

There are many similarities between the two. First, both operate in the public domain. Second, both the UN civil service and the national civil services provide services to peoples, largely putting equity and justice at the centre of their operation. Third, both underline the imperative for increased transparency and accountability. Fourth, both are free from the dominant motivating factor of profit and market share that drive private sector organisations. Fifth, chief executives are elected either by people or parliament in both services. Sixth, the UN General Assembly and a parliament are somewhat similar in nature and functions to the extent that both decide policy for their respective constituencies and civil services.

There are several marked differences between the UN international civil service and the national civil service as well. In order to understand the differences let us focus on the principal ones among them. First, national administrations diligently prevent aliens from joining them, while the United Nations has to maintain diversity in recruitment and placement at different levels, based on geographical representation and/or quota approved by the General Assembly.

Second, the United Nations has no public/civil service commission or similar set-up by some other nomenclature to help it recruit qualified candidates based on competitive and/or other criteria. There is however an international civil service commission at the United Nations, created with the establishment of the League of Nations which focuses on conditions of service, entitlements, allowances, leave, cost of living indexes and similar personnel management issues. Third, the UN staff do not have access to national courts, as their national counterparts do, as the ultimate resort to get their grievances addressed, although both have internal grievance redress mechanisms, in the form of ombudsman, grievance redress panels, and administrative tribunals.

From overall perspective, some of the salient traits of the UN civil service could be termed akin more to the private/corporate sector than the public sector. For instance, multinational corporations recruit persons of different nationalities depending on their areas of operation and specialisation in various functions. Like the United Nations, most private companies do not have a mechanism such as a public/civil service commission and the element of transparency that comes with a transparent recruitment and career development process. Standard personnel management issues are dealt with by the company's human resources office, as is done by the Office of Human Resources Management in United Nations.

Several authoritative sources on the UN tend to view the Security Council as a Board of Director for the United Nations. Primarily responsible for maintaining peace and security, the Council also has to recommend the candidates for the appointment of the Secretary-General, and the General Assembly acts at the recommendation of the Council. Beyond that, the General Assembly is the apex body charged with the responsibility to make policy decisions on all administrative and budgetary issues.

Moreover, the way the United Nations is functionally and structurally organised resembles, a private organisation more than a government entity. In fact this part of the world body is more or less similar to a public enterprise. But the UN international civil service's differences with the private sector are quite pronounced. The Secretary-General cannot sway the organisation the way the chief executive of a private organisation can do. And the United Nations, as already mentioned, does not work for profit, while private sector entities put profit and market share at the heart of their operations.

Obviously the Secretary-General is a poor imitation of a chief executive in the private sector. While this might be one of the major anomalies one finds in the United Nations, there are many other pertinent differences between the United Nations and the private corporate sector.

Essentially the United Nations looks like a hybrid that has imitated the management style of the private sector and the substance-lengthy decision-making process, diffused accountability, slow service delivery and myriad bureaucratic procedures leading to delays, inefficiency and red tape of the public sector. Many other unique features characterise the United Nations International Civil Service.

Although the world body is supposed to promote equality and justice, it embodies many characteristics that are inconsistent with those fundamental tenets. The Security Council has five permanent members (USA, Great Britain, France, Russia and China) with veto power that empowers them not to seek mandate from the General Assembly, the apex legislative body, while other ten rotating members have to. The permanent members with their veto power can prevent any action on a resolution if any of these members disagrees, while such action might have the broader support of the international community, as has been the case with many resolutions related to the Middle East and other sensitive places, where one or another of the permanent members of the Council has not gone with the flow.

Employment of the staff and the basis of their merit are unique and have frequently been called into question. In case of appointment of most USG and ASG, the Secretary-General might have very little freedom of action, as he has to accommodate the interest of major powers. These powers might also take significant interest in most strategic posts at the level of P5 and above. Thus, the majority of senior posts and the overwhelming majority of strategic posts go to the nationals of major powers and other developed countries. Even among developing countries the numbers are disproportionately skewed, traditionally in favour of a select few member countries. Consequently, the United Nations is frequently subjected to criticism for succumbing to political pressure and to nepotism, favouritism and cronyism in its recruitment, placement and promotion.

The UN international civil service is supposed to be independent of its member states. However the independence of staff stands on a shaky ground when the nominating countries can get their nationals hired and fired and replaced with their own. On several occasions, the Secretary-General had to helplessly contend with the blatant breach of independence of the international civil service code by the staff. The latest of such cases was that of Christopher Burnham, Under Secretary-General for Management, who had told The Washington Post, "I came here at the request of the White House. ...My primary loyalty is to the United States of America."[3] Mr. Burnham continued to serve in his post for several months after that comment and left when Washington leaned on him to quit. Independence, in that sense, remains an illusion that only lives in principle.

At the other end of the spectrum, inclusiveness in the organisation is a uniquely worthy goal in itself. However, the experience indicates that the United Nations is yet to be an inclusive and equitable organisation, and has yet to make good on its promise to ensure the broadest geographical representation in recruitment, placement and promotion.

While gender equality is its stated objective determined by General Assembly resolution, it remains a far cry in the organisation. In 2006, 63.7 per cent of the work force were men and 36.3 per cent were women, most of the latter below the P5 level.

The United Nations seeks to be a model employer. In order to do so, it provides its employees attractive terms and conditions of service that are not available to national civil services of member states. The world body uses in large part, the United States as the comparator while setting conditions of service and privileges for its staff members. In many locations, the local host country

3. Quoted from Joe Lauria's article (2007). "U.S. Seeks Even More Power at UN," posted in *The Huffington Post*, on January 23 at *http://www.huffingtonpost.com/joe-lauria/us-seeks-even-more-powe_b_39413.html*

standards particularly for field stations have also been embraced as a comparator. As a result the international civil service is considered to be one of the most attractive civil services in the world, particularly for developing countries. But the reality may say otherwise.

4

Human Resources Management

Major UN Entities

Introduction

There is no unanimity of views on the definition of human resources management (HRM). But there is a broad consensus regarding what key elements HRM encompasses, though the discipline itself is going through a process of rapid evolution. For instance, Schuler and Jackson think, HRM includes "the essential activities of resource planning, staffing, training and development, performance appraisal, compensation, safety and health, and labor relations—these comprise the traditional core of human resource management."[1]

According to Cherrington, "Human resource management is responsible for how people are treated in organisations. It is responsible for bringing people into the organisation, helping them perform their work, compensating them for their labors, and solving problems that arise."[2] In essence, HRM has to do with administrative activities associated with human resources planning,

1. Schuler, Randall S. and Susan E. Jackson (2005). "A Quarter-Century Review of Human Resource Management in the U.S.: The Growth in Importance of the International Perspective," in *Management Review* 16(1): 1.
2. Cherrington, David J. (1995). *The Management of Human Resources*. Englewood Cliffs, NJ: Prentice-Hall. p.5.

recruitment, selection, orientation, training, appraisal, motivation, remuneration, etc. HRM aims at developing people through work.

Schuler and Jackson speak of two major transformations in HRM in as many decades. First of these major changes took place when personnel administration began to be treated as HRM in the mid-1970s, in recognition of the fact that organisations not only could manage personnel policies and practices but also could, through these policies and practices, substantially influence and shape human behaviour to realise organisational objectives. Traditionally, personnel administration functions were conducted within a specified legal and institutional framework, and personnel administrators were not part of organisational strategies. In other words, this transformation essentially added the element of managing human resources to traditional personnel policies and practices, and substantially expanded the field.[3]

The second transformation took place in the last two decades or so and has further widened and enriched the discipline. It occurred when organisations began to link HRM to organisational strategies by coordinating personnel policies and practices and efforts to shape human behaviour with their strategic objectives. Incidentally, strategic HRM is directly related to strategic management which is "the process of making and implementing strategic decisions...is about the process of strategic change...is the match an organisation makes between its own resources and the threats and risks and opportunities created by the external environment in which it operates. So strategy can be seen as a key link between what the organisation wants to achieve—its objectives—and the policies adopted to guide its activities."[4] HR professionals have now grown to become "potential partners who should be involved in the strategic decision making processes of the firm."[5]

---

3. Schuler, Randall S. and Susan E. Jackson (1999). "Preface", in *Strategic Human Resource Management*. Oxford: Blackwell Publishing. p.xiv.
4. Bowman, C. and D. Asch (1987). *Strategic Management*, Basingstoke: Macmillan. p.4.
5. Schuler, Randall S. and Susan E. Jackson, *Op. Cit.*, p.2.

A third transformation has also taken place over last several years: HRM has acquired strong international dimensions with the rise and proliferation of multinational organisations and outsourcing of services and activities. Previously, organisations had the challenge of only inspiring and mainstreaming into the organisation's culture, mostly those employees and patrons who came largely from the same social, economic and political context. But now with growing globalisation, multinational organisations have to immerse their staff from different countries, cultural contexts and social milieus into their own cultures and ethos and prepare them to respond to their clients in a culturally sensitive fashion. This necessity has brought a great deal of convergence between HRM practices of multinational organisations and the United Nations.

With these changes, the environment in which HRM is to be carried out has also dramatically changed. In traditional systems, staff status, pay and perks used to be decided based on power relations and attributive considerations, rather than on merit. In professional bureaucracies, status, pay and perks predicate on the level of the assigned job, and "rank-in-job" concept dominates the HRM scene. Now most cutting-edge private sector firms have switched to strategic HRM and started linking pay, perks and status to the relative qualification of staff and their contribution to the firm's growth and profit, or call it "rank-in-man." Most government bureaucracies tend to fall into the second category, even though many have tried to borrow some elements of the third. The United Nations, by and large, is in league with governments for the sake of providing equal pay for equal work. Gradually those lines are being blurred though.

In other words, the world body is yet to fully embrace strategic dimensions in its HRM realm. You may hear much rhetoric about strategic HRM in the UN corridor, but it is not practiced much in content. Change always comes slowly in the organisation. Any major departure from the status quo is quite difficult to come by, for neither are member states ready to cough up requisite resources for such change, nor is the Secretariat willing to easily accept uncomfortable changes. One of the contributing factors to this predicament has been a lack of continuity in the leadership level of the Department of Management and the Office of Human Resources Management. Therefore, the United Nations has followed incremental reforms, piece by piece, and tried to accomplish them without major injection of new resources or innovative approaches. Notably, the organisation has been working in an environment of zero real growth in its budget for several years now.

Two contrasting pulls are discernible in the United Nations. On the one hand, member states want the global entity to perform as a public body meticulously sticking to the rulebook and accommodating the interest of the big and powerful among its members. On the other hand, the same member states also wish that the organisation would demonstrate the nimbleness of commercial enterprises and match their efficiency and productivity. Evidently, the United Nations is in a bind. Neither can it become as nimble as private organisations, because of its inherent nature and structure; nor can it address its daunting and multifarious challenges without trying hard to be one. A seemingly impossible feat to perform is marrying the strengths of both sectors while avoiding their weaknesses. Having said that, the world body must internalise the fact that only those organisations survive and flourish over time that can convert the seemingly impossible into the possible and produce encouraging results against heavy odds. It is a challenge to the UN leadership.

To be fair, the world body has tried to marry the practices of the public and the private sectors, but it has been much less successful in its efforts than many other international and regional organisations. Consequently, it is neither here nor there. Perhaps, the poor performance of the United Nations could partly be explained by the maxim that too many cooks spoil the broth. There are not only 192 countries that have to agree on each reform proposal and its nuances, it also has serious internal contradictions in the Secretariat to contend with while managing human resources.

Major HR-Related Entities

There are legislative and administrative bodies in the United Nations that directly or substantially deal with HRM issues. In the legislative realm, you have such bodies as the General Assembly (GA) and the Fifth Committee, as well as such advisory and expert bodies as the Advisory Committee on Administrative and Budgetary Questions (ACABQ), the International Civil Service Commission (ICSC), the Committee for Programme and Coordination (CPC) and the Joint Inspection Unit (JIU). In the administrative domain, there is the Secretariat—from the Secretary-General (SG) down to the Department of Management (DOM) and other departments and agencies and units under them—dealing with HRM activities.

Legislative and Expert Bodies

General Assembly

Headed by President elected from member states every year, GA is the highest deliberative and policy-making organ which, among other things, establishes staff regulations of the United Nations. Twenty-one Vice-Presidents elected for a year assist the President.[6] Article 101 of the Charter says,

1. The staff shall be appointed by the Secretary-General under regulations established by the General Assembly.
2. Appropriate staffs shall be permanently assigned to the Economic and Social Council, the Trusteeship Council, and, as required, to other organs of the United Nations. These staffs shall form a part of the Secretariat.[7]

GA is also the apex body to decide on the budget and financial resources. Article 17 of the UN Charter has authorised GA to consider and approve the budget of the organisation. It says,

1. The General Assembly shall consider and approve the budget of the Organisation.

---

6. United Nations, *Rules of Procedures of the General Assembly*, Rule 31.
7. United Nations, Charter of the United Nations.

2. The expenses of the Organisation shall be borne by the Members as apportioned by the General Assembly.
3. The General Assembly shall consider and approve any financial and budgetary arrangements with specialised agencies referred to in Article 57 and shall examine the administrative budgets of such specialised agencies with a view to making recommendations to the agencies concerned.[8]

Regulation 5.9 of the Regulations and Rules Governing Programme Planning, the Programme Aspect of the Budget, the Monitoring of Implementation and the Methods of Evaluation[9] in no uncertain terms establishes the authority of GA on financial matters. Rule 105.8 elaborates the regulation further.

Under Article 22 of the Charter, GA can establish such subsidiary organs, as it deems necessary, to carry out its work. Accordingly, it has set up a General Committee, six main committees including the Fifth Committee, as well as ACABQ, ICSC, CPC, JIU, etc., to grapple with issues relating to administration and budget. GA mainly works in plenary and through its subsidiaries. The General Committee, chaired by the President, assigns agenda items to relevant committees before the start of the new session every fall.[10] This Committee allocates all administrative and budgetary matters to the Fifth Committee for deliberation and recommendation to GA for final consideration and approval in plenary. Occasionally, GA might wish to consider and decide administrative and budgetary matters on its own, without reference to the Fifth Committee.[11] Before taking up such agenda items, GA or the Fifth Committee may seek expert advice from relevant advisory and expert bodies. ICSC covers a variety of administrative and civil service issues. On the other hand, ACABQ and CPC consider both administrative and budgetary issues as a matter of routine. JIU carries out its inspections into such issues every now and then.

---

8. Ibid.
9. United Nations, *Regulations and Rules Governing Programme Planning, the Programme Aspect of the Budget, the Monitoring of Implementation and the Methods of Evaluation,* (ST/SGB/2000/8).
10. United Nations, *Rules of Procedures of the General Assembly, op. cit.,* Rules 38 and 40.
11. Ibid, Rules 63 and 65.

Box 4.1

Regulation 5.9

No council, commission or other competent body shall take a decision involving either a change in the programme budget approved by the General Assembly or the possible requirement of expenditure unless it has received and taken account of a report from the Secretary-General on the programme budget implications of the proposal.

Rule 105.8

It shall be the responsibility of the head of the department concerned, in consultation with the Office of Programme Planning, Budget and Accounts, to ensure that a report on programme budget implications, as required by regulation 5.9, is submitted to the General Assembly prior to its adoption of any resolution or decision. The report should integrate the programme, financial and administrative implications of draft resolutions and include the following information:

(a) Modifications of the work programme that would be necessary should the proposed draft resolution, recommendation or decision be adopted, listing additions, changes or deletions to programmes, subprogrammes, outputs and activities;

(b) Indications, where applicable, of similar or closely related work being carried out elsewhere in the Secretariat and, if possible, indications of related activities being conducted in the specialised agencies of the United Nations system;

(c) In cases where it is proposed to finance such additional activities totally or partly through the redeployment of existing resources, an indication of the outputs or subprogrammes in the current work programme that would be changed, curtailed or terminated as a consequence.

As mentioned already, GA appoints the Secretary-General (SG) at the recommendation of the Security Council, and as chief administrative officer, SG appoints all other staff members. This essentially means the Assembly controls the administrative aspects of the United Nations mainly through its authority to consider and approve the world body's staff regulations and budget. This is an arrangement in many ways similar to what exist in member states: Parliament sets out personnel laws and controls the budget, and the executive branch of government appoints and manages the staff.

But this also generates and fuels the turf war between GA and SC and between GA and the Secretariat as witnessed over the last several decades.

Fifth Committee

Rightly or wrongly, the Fifth Committee is supposed to be one of the most powerful main committees of GA, as it has the handle on the UN purse strings. This Committee considers virtually all items in the administrative and budgetary agenda. The Rules of Procedure provide for the Main Committees of the Assembly.[12] Rule 96 says, "The General Assembly may establish such committees as it deems necessary for the performance of its functions." Rule 98 sets up the Administrative and Budgetary Committee (Fifth Committee). According to Rule 100, each member state is represented in the Committee.

Rules 152 and 153 set out the relationship between the Assembly, Fifth Committee and other Main Committees. Rule 152 says, GA shall establish regulations for the financial administration of the United Nations, and Rule 153 stipulates the following and gives the Fifth Committee considerable authority over financial matters and significant leverage with GA:

> No resolution involving expenditure shall be recommended by a committee for approval by the General Assembly unless it is accompanied by an estimate of expenditures prepared by the Secretary-General. No resolution is respect of which expenditures are anticipated by the Secretary-General shall be voted by the General Assembly until the Administrative and Budgetary Committee (Fifth Committee) has had an opportunity of stating the effect of the proposal upon the budget estimates of the Untied Nations.[13]

The Fifth Committee not only decides and recommends to GA, on items allocated to it, it also has jurisdiction over those programme budget implications—i.e., the involvement of additional resources—emanating from resolutions and decisions of other main committees and UN entities. The Secretariat has to present such implications before the Fifth Committee for its consideration and

12. Ibid.

13. Ibid, Rule 153.

recommendation to GA. Quite frequently, other committees and entities approve resolutions and decisions to be implemented "within the existing resources" to avoid scrutiny by the Fifth Committee. But only a limited number of small activities can be carried out within the existing funds in an already tight budgetary environment of the United Nations.

To conduct its business, the Fifth Committee elects every year a bureau—which has Chairman, two Vice-Chairmen and a Rapporteur—on the basis of geographical distribution, experience and personal competence (Rule 103). The Committee meets in formal sessions, informal sessions, and informal-informal sessions to carry out its tasks. In formal sessions, SG or his representative introduces the proposal on issues assigned to the Committee for its consideration, and ACABQ presents its views on the SG's proposal. Member states then express their position on the proposal. Although Rule 125 stipulates a simple majority of the members present and voting as sufficient for decision, the Fifth Committee seeks to make its decisions by consensus as much as possible. Actual negotiations on items before the Committee take place in informal sessions. Informal-informals are the crucial meetings in which most knotty issues are sorted out and compromises are made.

Regulations 2.4 to 2.7 of the Financial Regulations provide for budget review and approval.[14] In the budget year, SG submits his programme budget for next two years in the second year of a financial period in GA's regular session, at least five weeks prior to the opening of the session. Before that, he should have presented his programme budget to ACABQ. SG would have prepared the programme budget in accordance with the programme budget outline approved by the Committee for Programme and Coordination, a subsidiary body of the Economic and Social Council.[15] The programme budget outline contains the preliminary estimates of required resources, priorities, growth in the budget over

14. United Nations (2003). *Financial Regulations and Rules of the United Nations* (Secretary-General's bulletin), ST/SGB/2003/7, 9 May, Regulation 2.4

15. See: *Regulations and Rules Governing Programme Planning, the Programme Aspect of the Budget, the Monitoring of Implementation and the Methods of Evaluation,* (ST/SGB/2000/8), *op. cit.*

the last biennium, and the size of the Contingency Fund. Finally, the programme budget is presented to the Fifth Committee. GA gives the final approval to the budget.

The off-budget year is also known as human resources year. The Fifth Committee mostly considers human resources-related issues in the off-budget year. Nonetheless, it does consider and recommend to GA the budget for peacekeeping operations every year, even more than once a year, depending on the establishment of such operations, their expansion, reduction and extension in duration, as decided by the Security Council. The mandates of such operations run from a few months to a year and have to be frequently adjusted taking into account the continuously evolving ground realities in every mission. Each peacekeeping mission prepares its budget and presents it through the Secretariat to ACABQ and then to the Fifth Committee.

This Committee also recommends appointments of members to ACABQ, CPC, Committee on Contribution, Investment Committee of the UN Joint Staff Pension Fund, ICSC, and UN Staff Pension Committee; the GA makes the actual appointment.

In view of its heavy workload, the Fifth Committee, unlike other main committees which meet only in the fall session, convenes at least in three sessions every year.

ACABQ

One of the first few subsidiary, advisory organs of GA, the Advisory Committee on Administrative and Budgetary Questions is an independent expert body that came into existence under GA resolutions 14 (I) of 13 February 1946. The Committee has 16 members, serving for 3 years, elected on the basis of their qualification, experience and competence, with due regard to geographical distribution. Its Chairman works on a full time basis as an official of the United Nations. Initially ACABQ had 13 members, but GA resolution 32/103 of 14 December 1977 expanded the membership from 13 to 16 and amended Rules 155 to 157 of the Rules of Procedure of the General Assembly that govern ACABQ.

The revised Rule 155 provides for the number of members to be appointed by GA and their qualifications. Under Rule 156, the members are selected on the basis of broad geographical representation and personal qualification and experience; they are elected for a period of three years and retire by rotation; the experts would not retire simultaneously; and no two members could come from the same country. With regards to ACABQ's functions, Rule 157 stipulates,

> The Advisory Committee on Administrative and Budgetary Questions shall be responsible for expert examination of the programme budget of the United Nations and shall assist the Administrative and Budgetary Committee (Fifth Committee). At the beginning of each regular session at which the proposed programme budget for the following biennium is to be considered, it shall submit to the General Assembly a detailed report on the proposed programme budget for that biennium. It shall also submit, at such times as may be specified in the applicable Financial Regulations and Rules of the United Nations, a report on the accounts of the United Nations and all United Nations entities for which the Secretary-General has administrative responsibility. It shall examine on behalf of the General Assembly the administrative budgets of specialized agencies and proposals for financial and budgetary arrangements with such agencies. It shall perform such other duties as may be assigned to it under the Financial Regulations of the United Nations.[16]

ACABQ also considers the auditors' report on the accounts of the United Nations and reports to GA on them.

Regulation 3.2 (4) (5) and (6) lays out modalities for submitting the budget to ACABQ. The first provision pledges respect to the mandate and functions of the Committee; second commits the Secretariat to present the proposed programme budget, among others, to ACABQ; and the third provision calls for ACABQ to examine the proposed programme budget and submit its conclusions and recommendations to GA through the Fifth Committee for final approval of such budget. Regulation 4.8 says that ACABQ should, in addition to CPC, consider the medium term plan in accordance with its term of reference.

16. Ibid, Rule 157.

Regulation 5.7 stipulates that SG should give an advance copy of the proposed programme budget to ACABQ by the end of April, in the year prior to the budget period. According to Regulation 5.8, CPC should prepare its report on the proposed programme budget containing its programme recommendation, and communicate it to ECOSOC and ACABQ, and SG should present his statement on the subject. Although the Fifth Committee and GA have had the right to accept, curtail or reject ACABQ's recommendations, they often form the basis for the draft resolutions and decisions of the Fifth Committee among member states having divergent opinions and priorities.

Evidently, ACABQ plays a crucial role in HRM of the United Nations. It helps the Fifth Committee and GA to formulate HRM policies and determine the shape, size, composition and deployment of UN staff, through its advice on administration and budget. Currently it only scrutinises the staff and non-staff resources of the United Nations, regional commissions, peacekeeping operations and political missions, and UN funds and programme. According to the Statute of ICSC, ACABQ should be consulted by SG before he submits candidates for ICSC members to be appointed by GA.

Also in practice, ACABQ has virtually abandoned its duty of examining the administrative budget of the specialised agencies. In a perfunctory effort to fulfil its mandate, ACABQ members visit headquarters of specialised agencies every few years and hold a joint discussion on issues of common interests across the board, which might have little or no impact on the budgets of those agencies. The UN system-wide mandate of this Committee is in tatters, partly due to the heavy volume of work, partly to the reluctance of its members to travel and partly to the unwillingness of UN member states to provide it with sufficient resources.

International Civil Service Commission

ICSC, a GA subsidiary, is another key player in the HRM arena of the Untied Nations. It is an independent expert body of 15 members, elected giving due regard to geographical distribution. Established by GA resolution 3042 (XXVII) of 19 December 1972, ICSC regulates and coordinates the conditions of service of the staffs in the United Nations common system and seeks to promote and maintain high standards in the international civil service. GA resolution 3357 (XXIX) of 18 December 1974 approved the Statute of ICSC. The Commission has its own Rules of Procedures, first adopted in its first session in May 1975 and amended in its 26th session in March 1987.

Article 1 of the Statute establishes ICSC "for the regulation and coordination of the conditions of service of the Unites Nations common system."[17] That the General Assembly would appoint 15 members of the Commission—including Chairman and Vice-Chairman as full-time officials of the United Nations—and that no two members could come from the same country have been stipulated in Article 2. Qualifications of the members—they should be individuals of recognised competence and have substantial experience of executive responsibility in public administration or related fields, particularly in personnel management—have been laid out in Article 3. Article 5 spells out that the term of the members shall be 4 years and that they could be reappointed. It has also been stipulated that ICSC members must be independent and impartial.

Articles 9 through 18 of the Statue set out the functions that ICSC is supposed to perform. Under them, the Commission should recommend to GA on the broad principles of conditions of service for the staff, on salary scales and post-adjustments and on allowances and benefits. It also ought to make recommendations on the establishment of job classification standards for the staff for the work common to several organisations; on standards of recruitment, recruitment sources, selection procedures, career development and staff evaluation and on common staff regulations. ICSC should submit its annual report to the General Assembly including on implementation of its decisions, as well as establish policies and formulate guidelines regarding all matters of its responsibility.

ICSC meets at least once a year. The United Nations and other participating organisations—ILO, FAO, UNESCO, ICAO, WHO, IMO, UPU, ITU, WMO, WIPO, IFAD and UNIDO—share on pro-rata basis the cost of ICSC, namely, the salaries and allowances of the Chairman and Vice-Chairman and of the Executive Secretary and other

---

17. United Nations, *The Statute of the International Civil Service Commission*, Article 1.

staff, cost of running its secretariat, and travel and other expenses. These specialised agencies have concluded relationship agreements with ICSC. Many more organisations participate in the UN Joint Staff Pension Fund, but not in the common system as a whole.

Although ICSC is discharging its functions pretty well, it still leaves much to be desired. It has focused its attention and resources mainly on recommending the salaries based on the civil service scales of comparator countries and the recurring cost-of-living adjustments. However, it has proved unable to devote itself to a whole range of important civil service functions which their counterparts in member states have been carrying out, particularly those related to recruitment, promotion and disciplinary actions.

Joint Inspection Unit

JIU has been set up to provide an independent view, through inspection and evaluation, to help improve management and methods and to achieve greater coordination between organisations. By virtue of its broad mandate, JIU can inspect and evaluate agencies and functions and make recommendations with a view to improving HRM. First established in 1966 on an experimental basis, JIU became a regular subsidiary organ of the General Assembly when the latter, through its resolution 2924 (XXVII) of 24 November 1972, decided to continue with the Unit and approved its Statute. The Statute came into effect from 1 January 1978. By rule, JIU automatically becomes a subsidiary of the legislative bodies of all those specialised agencies which accept its Statute.

Article 1 of the Statute establishes the Unit, while Article 2 provides for not more than 11 inspectors, appointed by the General Assembly for a renewable 5-year term, on the basis of their special experience in national or international administrative and financial matters. The President of the General Assembly consults the President of the Fconomic and Social Council and Chairman of the Administrative Committee on Coordination (now renamed as UN Chief Executives Board for Coordination) before appointing the inspectors who serve in personal capacity. The inspectors represent a broad geographical distribution, and no two inspectors can come from the same country.

Laid out in Article 5 to 8 are the functions, powers and responsibilities of JIU. The inspectors would have broadest powers to investigate in all matters having a bearing on the efficiency of the services and the proper use of funds and should offer views to improve management and methods and to achieve greater coordination between organisations. They may propose reforms and make recommendations to competent UN organisations, maintaining their full independence from UN or external authorities. The inspectors constitute the officials of the United Nations and get salaries, allowances and pension benefits at the D-level of the Secretariat.

Although an inspector writes his report consulting the entities he studies and discussing the findings with other inspectors, the report bears his individual name, rather than representing the collective view of the Unit as a whole. JIU reports are often criticised for lacking depth and insight and for having no discernible impact and effectiveness to make positive changes in the organisations they inspect and report on.

Committee for Programme and Coordination

CPC was set up to review the programme of the United Nations, as defined in the medium-term plan, and to assist the Economic and Social Council in its coordination functions within the United Nations system. Although not directly involved in human resources management activities, CPC does have significant impact on these activities through it authority to examine the medium-term plan and programme budget. Now a strategic framework has replaced the medium-term plan.

CPC evolved from the Special Committee on Coordination (SCC), an ECOSOC subsidiary. ECOSOC had created it in 1962 under its resolution 920 (XXIV) with reference to the UN Development Decade, with 11 members coming from equitable geographical distribution. It converted SCC into CPC in 1966. In 1976, the number of CPC members was increased to 21 elected for 3 years. By the same resolution, ECOSOC also asked CPC to review the medium-term plan in off-budget years and programme budget in budget years and to assist the Council in its coordination functions within the UN system; it also established CPC's relationship with JIU and ACABQ.

GA increased CPC's membership from 21 to 34 in 1987. In 2003, the Assembly dropped CPC's mandate of considering the budget outline and asked SG to replace the medium-term plan, on trial basis, with a strategic framework. GA resolution 62/244 of 2007 approved CPC's recommendation to maintain the strategic framework as the principal policy directive, which will serve as the basis for planning, budgeting, monitoring and evaluation from the biennium 2010/11.

Of late, CPC has been in turmoil. Its meetings have been far from regular, timely and productive. The Secretariat believes CPC's functions extensively overlap with ACABQ's and the Fifth Committee's and its continued need should be reconsidered, as proposed by the Secretary-General Kofi Annan.[18] But member states opposed that idea and rather adjusted and strengthened CPC's mandate.

UN-Recognised Policy Groups

There are several bodies that do not constitute parts of the United Nations framework but are integral to its policy-making process and are recognised as such. For instance, there are five regional groups for Asia, Africa, Latin America and Caribbean, Eastern Europe, and Western Europe and Others. They mostly coordinate elections in the United Nations, including for administrative and budgetary policy bodies and other entities. Some of them also try to build consensus within their regions in economic, social and political fields, though with limited success. In addition, the Non-Aligned Movement works with UN intergovernmental bodies in shaping up the UN's policies and programmes in the political domain. Similarly, the Group of 77, which has nearly 130 countries, works with UN legislative bodies in deciding policies in economic and social arenas. The European Union also seeks to present its common voice on economic and social issues whenever possible. These are more or less formal groups.

The Group of 77, a framework of developing countries, is active on administrative and budgetary matters of the United Nations.

18. United Nations (2006). *Investing in the United Nations*. New York. Proposal 21.

Many negotiations plod through for days due to differences between this group and developed countries. Many others protract due to differences within the developed and developing countries themselves as well. Countries also constitute informal groups to present a common voice on issues of their agreement. Australia, New Zealand, Canada and USA, which are part of the Western European and Others Group, frequently form an informal grouping on many issues, for instance. Apart from this, several non-governmental organisations have attained consultative status with the Economic and Social Council and seek to influence ECOSOC deliberations.

Administrative Entities

As on the legislative side, several administrative bodies have roles to play in the HRM of the United Nations. Some involve directly, others indirectly and yet others tangentially. Some perform line functions, and others staff or advisory functions. Some of these functions happen to be purely administrative and some purely technical-legal and others in-between. The main players on the administrative side of the HR continuum have been presented in this section.

Secretary-General

SG performs two key functions, among others. As chief diplomat of the United Nations, he must promote the realisation of the world body's principals and purposes in such areas as peace and security, economic and social development, human rights and humanitarian assistance. As chief administrative officer of the organisation, SG must ensure that the United Nations runs smoothly, efficiently and effectively and that it is able to deliver on its mandates.

According to Article 101 (1) of the Charter of the United Nations, "The staff shall be appointed by the Secretary-General under regulations established by the General Assembly." In regard to HRM, SG is the ultimate authority in the organisation, as every personnel decision is made and every action is taken by him or in his name. He selects candidates for recruitment, appoints them, and places them; he also transfers, trains, promotes, rewards, and retires them; departmental action against or dismissal of the erring staff also takes place under his name; and he is also substantially involved in the administration of justice, as the first point of appeal, under the existing staff rules and regulations. All UN staff members are under the authority of SG and accountable to him.[19]

To assist SG, the General Assembly has—by its resolution 52/12B of 9 January 1998—created a post of Deputy Secretary-General, as an integral part of the Office of the Secretary-General. SG is supposed to appoint DSG, the second in command at the Secretariat, in accordance with Article 101 of the Charter and in consultation with member states. DSG's term is set to be co-terminus with SG's. As mentioned in the resolution, DSG assists SG in managing the Secretariat's operations, acts for him in his absence at headquarters, and represents him in official activities and functions, among other things.

Executive Office of the Secretary-General (EOSG)

EOSG supports SG in discharging his duties, including those related to human resources. In charge of daily operations of EOSG is the Chef de Cabinet of SG, an USG level official. Important policy matters, including those related to personnel issues, go to SG for clearance and approval and trek down to the respective departments and units to be implemented by them or to be forwarded to the legislative bodies for policy decisions. A designated officer in EOSG presents personnel matters to SG for his consideration and approval and transmits his decisions to the concerned departments and bodies for execution. The Office of the Spokesperson of EOSG announces all senior appointments. A new Ethics Office has also been appended to EOSG a couple of years back, particularly after the rampant corruption was ferreted out in the Oil-for-food programme in Iraq.

Department of Management

Headed by an Under Secretary-General, the Department of Management (DOM) stands at the centre of all human resources management activities. The Office of the USG (OUSG) supports him. Under the USG, there are four Assistant Secretaries-General (ASGs), each for Office of Human Resources Management (OHRM); Office of Programme Planning, Budget and Accounts (OPPBA); Office of

19. See *UN Staff Regulations and Rules 2003* for further details.

Central Support Services (OCSS); and Office of Pandemic Influenza Preparedness Coordinator for the UN System in New York (OPIPC). The Capital Master Plan (CMP) is headed by a D-level staff.

OHRM is the principal locus of all activities related to personnel issues. Under the ASG, apart from her office (OASG), there are three divisions: Division for Organisational Development, Operational Services Division and Medical Services Division. The self-explanatory organisational chart of DOM, and particularly of OHRM, is as follows:

Figure 4.1

Department of Management

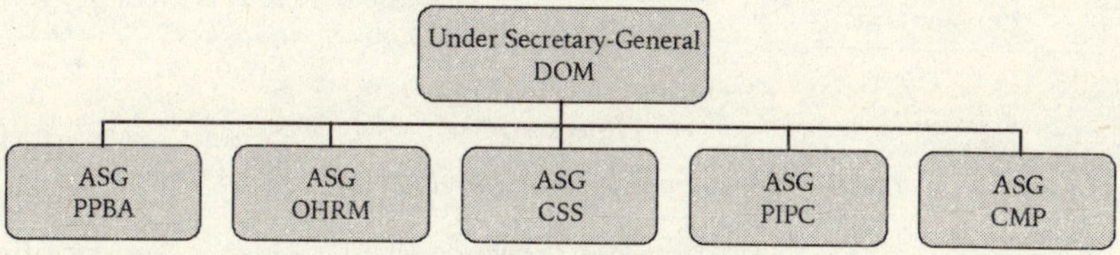

PIPC and CMP offices have been created for the specific ad hoc purposes. Other three are of more permanent nature. The organisation of the Office of the Under Secretary-General is presented in the following chart and other HRM related units in the subsequent charts:

Figure 4.2

Office of the Under Secretary-General, DOM

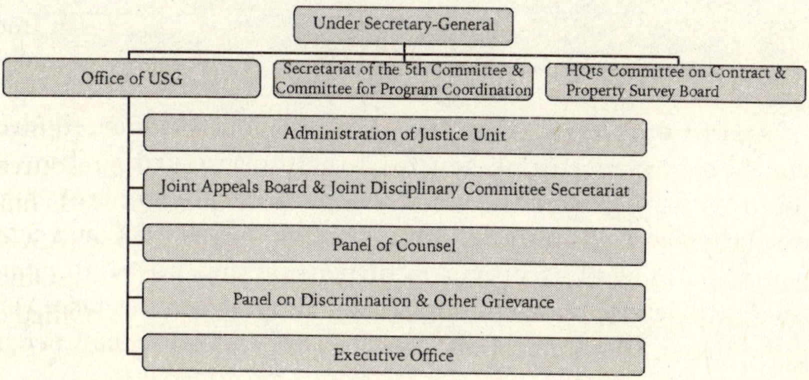

Figure 4.3

Office of Human Resources Management, DOM

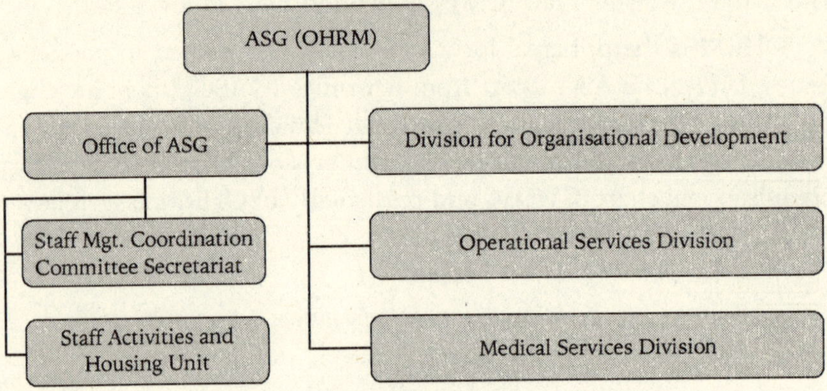

Figure 4.4

Division for Organisational Development, OHRM

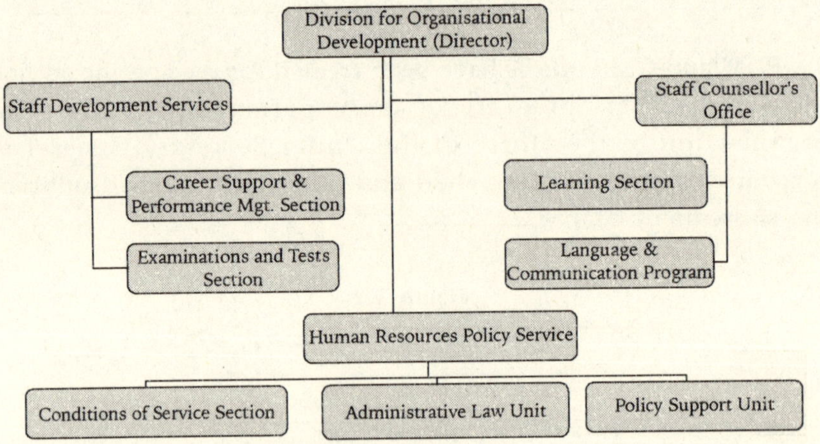

Apart from OHRM, the Office of Programme Planning, Budget and Accounts performs several functions regarding human resources management. Included among them are administration of salaries and allowances, compensation and claims, and staff insurance, as well as provision of pension and post-retirement benefits. Likewise, the Office of Central Support Services takes care of the travel, communication, procurement and other staff needs.

Figure 4.5

Operational Services Division, OHRM

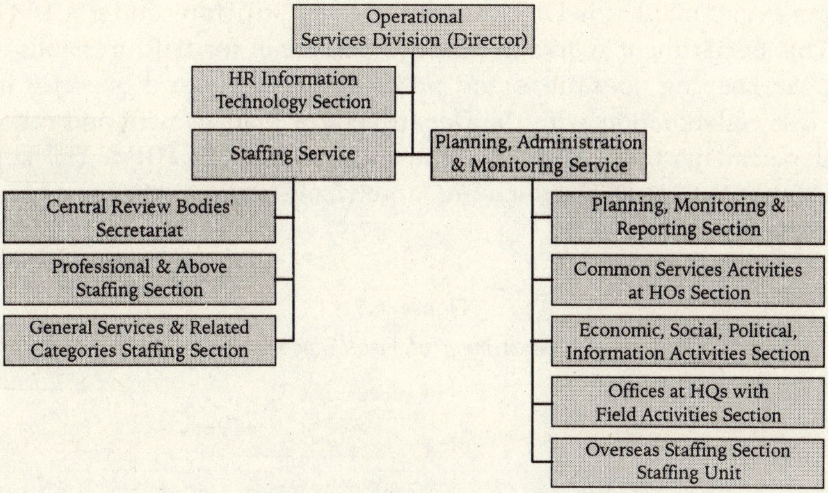

Figure 4.6

Medical Services Division, OHRM

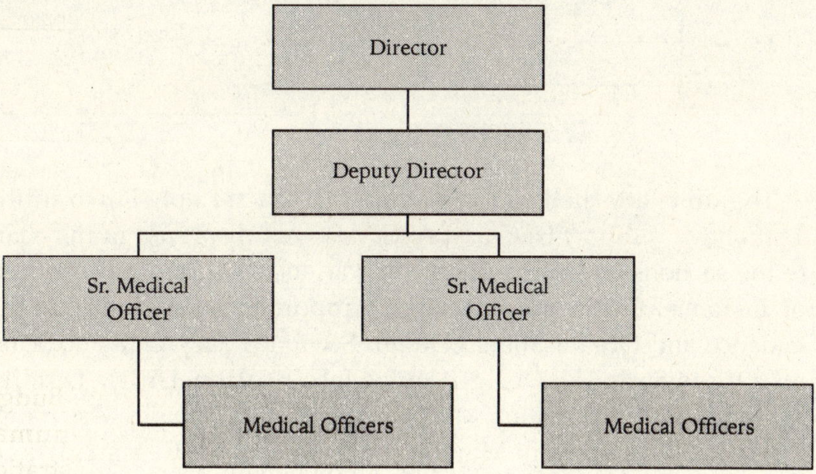

Department of Field Support (DFS)

Another department that deals directly and significantly with personnel matters is DFS, a newly created structure under a USG. This Department works in areas of personnel for field missions—peacekeeping operations and political missions—and operates in close collaboration with the Department of Management and other departments that get involved in issues related to HRM. The key components of DFS, which are largely self-explanatory, have been presented below:

Figure 4.7

Department of Field Support

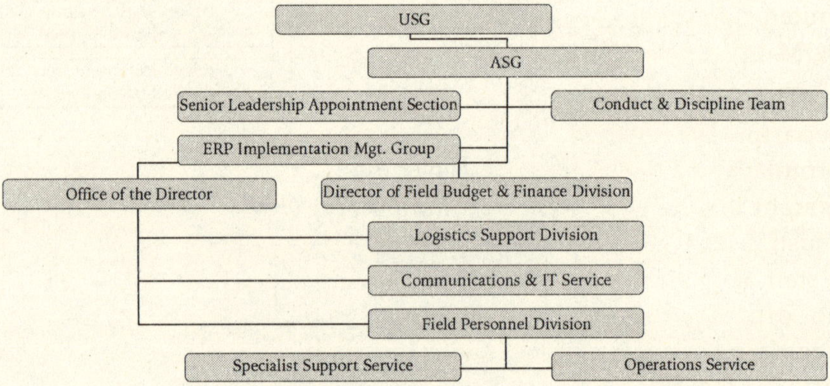

The units attached to their offices, which are not shown in the Chart above, support USG and ASG. Also not displayed in the chart are the sections and units under the various divisions and services. For instance, under the Specialist Support Service, there are the Guidance and Organisational Design Section (Policy Guidance Unit and Organisational Design and Classification Unit); Quality Assurance and Information Management Section (Quality Assurance Unit and Information Management Unit and Registry); and Recruitment, Outreach and Career Development Section (Recruitment and Outreach Unit and Career Development and Succession Plan Unit). The Special Entitlement and Travel Unit with teams assigned to tasks related to various geographical regions is the main entity under the Operations Service of the Field Personnel Division.

Other Departments and Entities

Many other departments and entities of the United Nations are also engaged in human resources-related functions in a considerable way. Each department has to assess its own human resources requirements, formulate justifications to create new posts, write vacancy announcement to advertise the post once created, help DOM in the selection process, place the new recruits or promotees, work out the succession plan, and so on. Moreover, some perform limited administrative/personnel functions, while others help DOM to carry out its responsibilities properly and effectively in the area of personnel administration. For instance, the Department of Safety and Security carries out some human resources management functions with respect to the security personnel working with the United Nations at headquarters and out in field locations, and helps DOM in others.

The Office of Legal Affairs provides legal support to the Department of Management on personnel matters, including the formulation of staff rules, and represents the United Nations in cases brought to the adjudication and appeal bodies in the administration of justice. The Office of Ombudsman seeks to address minor grievances of staff and refers the major ones to the appropriate departments of the organisation. Cases where thorough investigation into irregularities have to be made go to the Office of Internal Oversight Services for investigation. For investing pension funds and administering pension, there is the UN Joint Staff Pension Fund.

In addition, headquarters locations outside New York, regional commissions and field offices—including the tribunals, peacekeeping operations and political missions—have their own divisions or sections for the management of human resources. These frameworks work within their own scope of operation, in line with the UN staff regulations and rules established by GA and elaborated by SG through administrative instructions. For the administration of justice, there are joint appeals boards and grievances committees composed of management and staff representatives. These mechanisms will be replaced by new entities—UN Dispute Tribunal and UN Appeals Tribunal, for instance—when the new system of administration of justice just introduced becomes fully operational.

Observations

The Gingrich Task Force had this observation to make about HRM in the United Nations, in 2005:

> The Human Resources Department does not utilise basic standard management practices. The existing performance appraisal system is ineffective. Supervisors appraise their own staff, but there is no 360-degree appraisal to enable staff to provide feedback about their supervisors; and the Human Resources Department has no system in place to rate the performance of managers or to provide an independent assessment of employees' performance. In any case, the Human Resources Department is headed by an assistant secretary-general who is outranked by the under secretaries-general, whose performance her department ought to be evaluating. Among the reforms announced by the United Nations in May 2005 is the establishment of a management performance board intended to systematically assess the performance of senior managers. The board is to be chaired by the deputy secretary-general and include two under secretaries-general and one former senior official, with the heads of the Department of Management and the Office of Internal Oversight Services serving as ex officio members. There is no system for developing staff careers within the United Nations as all positions are filled through open competition. The internal justice system available to staff who are threatened with termination for poor performance is, as one senior official candidly told us, "royally screwed up," contributing mightily to the personnel problems by making it difficult to fire staff for cause.[20]

Most of these comments remain valid today, though there might be differences as to what remedies should be applied to the problems of HRM. In this section, we have tried to point out the root causes of HRM problems in the world body and sought to suggest measures to resolve them.

Lack of a Dedicated, Independent Recruitment Entity: One of the most serious lacunas in the United Nations is the lack of a dedicated and independent entity that can imbibe and absorb new HRM methods and practice and implement them uniformly across the organisation in recruitment and selection and in other critical aspects of HRM. Most member states have such an entity to promote a semblance of

20. United States Institute of Peace (2005). *American Interests and UN Reform, Report of the Task Force on the United Nations*. Washington DC. p.48

order in recruiting, placing, firing and training staff and taking disciplinary action against them; so does the European Commission's European Personnel Selection Office, to a limited extent. Unfortunately, the United Nations does not have such an entity, partly because of fear that it would limit the discretionary power of senior executives and partly because member states are often reluctant to put their money where their mouth is. It is high time that the United Nations set up such an entity to streamline and upgrade its HR functions and to bring uniformity in their standards across the system. Such an entity could go a long way in addressing several root causes of HRM problems faced consistently by the United Nations.

Weak Leadership: The United Nations is not one of those organisations in which leadership is able to drive it along its vision. SG usually has very limited effective control over the organisation and over his staff; many a time, he is subject to pressure, and even defiance, from his deputies. SG usually comes from a small country with limited political and economic clout. On the other hand, most Under Secretaries-General come from big and powerful countries and want to operate without many strings or conditions attached. On a different plane, although DOM is the principal locus for all human resources management activities of the United Nations, it enjoys limited leverage—at least not as much as smooth and robust HRM would entail—with other departments.

To remedy this situation, SG should establish an advisory committee of eminent persons that would help him select senior executives based on their merit and geographical distribution, neutralise the undue political influence of member states, and create an environment in which he could drive the organisation's administration.

Duplication and Overlap: Duplication and overlap in HRM functions is a major drag for the United Nations, and it takes place on different levels. There is certainly much duplication between the work of ACABQ and CPC on the legislative side. Occasionally, JIU also joins in aggravating duplication and overlap in terms of investigation it carries out of HR activities. On the administrative side, the Department of Management and the Department of Field Support essentially perform the same functions, one for non-peacekeeping staff and the other for peacekeeping and field staff.

The Department of Safety and Security has its own HRM activities pertaining to security staff. What is more, each department is engaged in several HRM activities, even though several departments might be working under the same roof. To avoid such duplication and overlap, SG should appoint a high-level external panel to carry out an in-depth study of the departments and their processes to streamline their functions, integrate them where possible, and remove unnecessary duplication and overlap, and should implement the panel's report.

This issue has been further elaborated in the next chapter, with examples, particularly in reference to the Secretariat.

Lack of Independent Administration of Justice: Finally, administration of justice has been the Achilles heel for the United Nations. There is no independent, objective, and expert entity to which the staff could go to get their grievances addressed and to which they could file their appeals against those disciplinary actions and dismissals which they deem unjustified. It is a shame that the world body that preaches justice to others does not have one for its own staff. As of now, the organisation has a primitive and far-from-democratic justice system that lacks teeth and confidence of staff. The existing joint appeals and grievance committees are neither independent nor objective; and they are so weak that often their verdict against the Secretariat and in favour of the staff, especially if they come from smaller and less powerful countries, are largely ignored.

The United Nations must institute an efficient, effective and independent system of administration of justice. And the recommendations of the Redesign Panel will go a long way in this sphere.[21] In a welcome development, the General Assembly has finally crafted a new system of justice taking into account the Redesign Panel's recommendations and SG's report on them. The new system has been introduced from 1 July 2009. We will discuss this issue at length later in a separate chapter.

---

21. United Nations (2006). *Report of the Redesign Panel on the United Nations System of Administration of Justice*, New York. July the Panel was constituted as per GA resolution 59/283.

5

Human Resources Management Policy and Execution

Introduction

Organisations may look different from outside and from inside. They could look different from outside but could be similar from inside. By the same token, they could look similar from outside but may be different from inside. Their defining parameters include their mission, motto, brand, business ethos and culture as well as their governance, management structures and staff configurations. However, the fundamentals of HRM policies tend to be more similar across most organisations than different, more so among entities of the similar nature, size and scope, though we should not rule out significant differences across organisational constellation due to their own specific organisational mission and operational needs.

Policy is a plan or course of action, of a government, political party, or business, intended to influence and determine decisions, actions, and other matters. HRM policy has to do with the plan or course of action regarding the management of human resources. There are several issues that constitute the integral part of this policy. Principal among them include: Selection, recruitment, placement, pay and perks, children's allowances, leaves, job performance and training, as well as rules governing the conduct of staff, promotion, administration of justice, separation, retirement, pension and post-retirement services.

In other words, HR policies cover all those areas that happen to be within the ambit of traditional personnel administration plus those new elements and emphases that have been added to the discipline by evolution—human resources management and strategic angles, as have been described in the previous chapter of this book. These policies must be able to make clear to the employees about, among other things, the organisation's nature, terms and conditions of service, code of conduct, reward and punishment regimes, disciplinary processes, as well as measures, strategies and procedures for their implementation. In modern times, with the concept of strategic HRM gaining ground, HR policy makers and implementers increasingly participate in the processes designed to formulate strategic goals and objectives of an organisation and, once approved, in their implementation.

Modern HR policies have become progressively intricate and entangled over time. Several factors have contributed to this development. Key among them include the growing competition between firms and organisations for competent managers and leaders; increased mobility of the people across various organisations and problem of retention of competent staff; rising imperative to be inclusive and equitable with respect to racial, ethnic, geographical, cultural and religious diversity in workplace; growing recognition of and awareness about sexual harassment; burgeoning concept of sharing gains with employees; enhanced use of information technology and sophisticated means of communication, etc. These complexities add new challenges to HRM, especially in large, multifaced and professional organisations.

Although many commonalities may exist among organisations of simliar sizes, scales and complexity, each organisation starts with unique characteristics or acquires them as it evolves. From this perspective, any generalisation across organisations is fraught with serious problems. Yet we can find several common elements, typical to large organisations, including in the areas as presented in Box 5.1.

Box 5.1

Sample Areas of HRM Policies

- Needs assessment
- Development of job description
- Vacancy announcements
- Affirmative action
- Selection and recruitment
- Classification and placement
- Attendance and hours of work
- Compensation and allowances
- Leaves of absence
- Confidentiality
- Staff development and training
- Mobility
- Vacations/Holidays
- Health and safety provisions
- Communications protocol
- Conflict of interest and ethics
- Job Performance and evaluation
- Promotion and career progression
- Affirmative action
- Grievances and dispute resolution
- Sexual harassment and other unacceptable acts
- Discipline and/or termination
- Pension and post-retirement benefits
- Jury and other civic duties
- Miscellaneous

While these areas are, by and large, common to all big organisations, what draws a line between traditional and modern outfits is the purpose, orientation and emphasis with which they seek to realise organisational goals and objectives. For example, you may take a new recruit on board to fill a vacant post that is assigned a routine work. Or you may recruit someone to occupy a specific niche. Rather than letting go of a superb employee because for a while s/he could not be present during the set working hours, you give them flexible working hours. Holidays could be treated as the days off from work as a matter of routine or as part of a productivity and incentive package. In other words, while the scope of personnel administration and HRM might not look different in their appearance, there is a huge difference the way these common areas could be applied on the ground.

As already discussed, the primary responsibility of formulating broad HR policies rests with the apex policy-making body of an organisation or of parliament of a country. The HR department of the respective entity helps the policy-making body to formulate policies and, once approved, implements them. But this department alone cannot carry out those functions without the support and assistance from other departments of the same organisation and from specialised outside agencies. It has to rely on other departments, where the bulk of actual staff activities exists, for the formulation and execution of most HR policies—from carrying out needs assessment for new posts to developing job profile to ascertaining the qualifications and experience necessary for staff to training, transferring, promoting and retiring staff members. In many cases, HRM departments remain under obligation to seek advisory opinion from concerned departments within the organisation's umbrella or from specialised independent agencies outside. As an example of the latter, in most countries, government must by law obtain the opinion or recommendation of the public service commission in regard to formulating all HR policies and carrying out their execution.

Apart from this, seeking expert support from outside agencies and through outsourcing for the formulation and execution of HR policies has come increasingly in vogue in the corporate world, and now quite frequently in the public sector as well. There are consulting agencies that specialise in a whole gamut of HR policy elements—starting from writing vacancy announcements to hunting for talents to addressing post-partum stress after the retirement of the staff. As well, outsourcing has become another raging phenomenon in which HR services are sought from across the world where they are more affordable. Even small operations have been increasingly resorting to outsourcing to save the cost of doing business. Revolution in information technology has made it possible to connect one end of the world to another within a fraction of a second and made outsourcing an increasingly attractive option.

An organisation consists not only of a formal chain of command and lines of reporting, but also of informal linkages and channels of communication that have a significant bearing on its operation. Therefore, the actual situation may reflect a much more complex web of relationships—both formal and informal—within and without an organisation than a flow chart can demonstrate. Nonetheless, the following brutally simplified figure gives some idea about the formal interface in an organisation:

Figure 5.1

Inside and Outside Bodies Involved in HR Policy-Making and Implementation

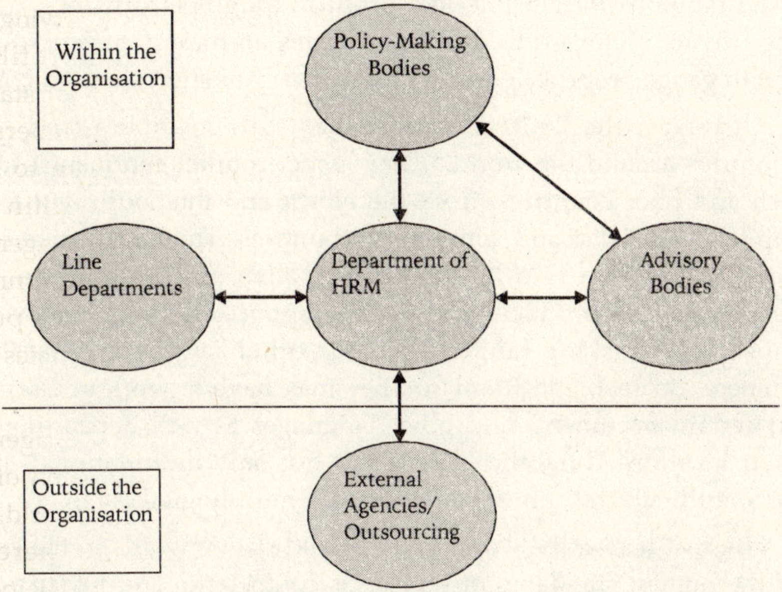

Within the department of HRM, there would be a defined chain of command and a set of procedures for the formulation and implementation of HR policies. In the following section, we will look at the UN specific formulation and execution of HR policies.

UN HRM Environment

The United Nations' HRM environment is very delicate, complex, fragmented and interesting. But it remains largely a traditional organisation in its HRM domain. Occasionally staff members may strut around words like "strategic," but they often are no more than rhetoric, which does not translate into action for three reasons: One, the Secretariat often uses grandiose words to tell the world that it is in tune with time and to have more leeway in HRM from the intergovernmental bodies, rather than to bring change that might be uncomfortable to the staff. Two, the intergovernmental bodies are unwilling to give more slack to the

Secretariat than it already enjoys unless the latter proves its capacity to deliver on those matters over which it already exercises authority. Three, in public organisations like the United Nations—where there is no tangible bottom line like profit to judge performance, as in the private sector—due process becomes an important measuring rod to gauge propriety of action and efficacy of efforts and outcome.

Anyway, the United Nations has staff members from 187 countries around the world.[1] They come from all continents, from rich and poor countries, from the North and the South and from capitalist, socialist and communist countries. These staff members have to work in two languages—English and French—in the Secretariat and produce reports and support meetings in, besides those two working languages, four other languages—Arabic, Chinese, Spanish and Russian. They may have to work in German on certain documents and other languages as well depending on their location. Thus, the UN staff is not only multinational, it is also multicultural, multi-religious and multilingual.

By its Charter, the world body should not only hire on the basis of the highest standards of efficiency, competence and integrity, in doing so it also should pay due regard to the widest possible geographical distribution of its staff members. Of late, striking a gender balance in its workforce has become another challenge for the organisation to pursue vigorously. Out of the global civilian workforce of the United Nations of 39,503 on 30 June 2008, 25,928 (65.6 per cent) were men and 13,575 (34.4 per cent) were women. Among the 15,219 locally recruited staff in the field missions administered by the Department Field Support, the ratio was more sharply skewed in men's favour with only 17.9 per cent being women.[2]

If this configuration is not already mind-boggling enough to some, here are some more facts that would spin the head of even the generally UN-savvy persons. The United Nations appoints its staff members under the 100 series, 200 series and 300 series. All these series have their own staff rules. Although they differ from

1. See Chapter 1 of this book.

2. United Nations (2008). *Composition of the Secretariat*. New York. p.18.

each other in many ways, the fundamental principles and regulations and rules governing all these series are not very dissimilar. These provisions work under the broad elements of the Charter of the United Nations and the Convention on the Privileges and Immunities and build on them. Presented below are the main points and policy areas included in the Staff Regulations and the Staff Rules under the 100 series.[3] It should be noted that GA resolution 63/250 has asked SG to evolve one set of staff rules in the future. These regulations find their origin in the UN Charter, as do national ones in their constitutions.

Key Features of Staff Regulations

The UN Charter, its Staff Regulations and Staff Rules govern the nature and conditions of service for the UN staff members. As we have seen in the previous chapter, the General Assembly (GA) establishes staff rules under which the Secretary-General (SG) administers and manages the staff members. We will have a brief look at the principal features of the UN Staff Regulations and the Rules under them that elaborate the regulations further. Additionally, measures to uphold ethics and to protect whistle blowers have also been put in place following the Volcker Committee's report after the investigation into the Oil-for-food scandal.[4]

Charter Provisions: Naturally, the UN Charter is the source of the UN Staff Regulations and Staff Rules. Article 8, Articles 97 through 101 and Article 105 of the UN Charter, set down the basic conditions regarding the appointment and work of SG and other staff members. These provisions stipulate that the United Nations not place any restrictions on the eligibility of men and women to participate in any capacity in its principal and subsidiary organs; the Secretariat would have the SG who works as the chief administration officer and other staff, as necessary; SG would act as Secretary to all inter-governmental principal organs of the United Nations except the International Court of Justice. Specifically Article 105 of the Charter says,

3. See for details: United Nations (2003). *Staff Regulations, ST/SGB/2003/5* of 7 February and *Staff Rules, ST/SGB/2002/1* with amendments contained up to *ST/SGB/2006/1.*

4. See United Nations (2008). *Investing in the United Nations.* New York. Box 5.1.

1. The staff shall be appointed by the Secretary-General under regulations established by the General Assembly.
2. Appropriate staffs shall be permanently assigned to the Economic and Social Council, the Trusteeship Council, and, as required, to other organs of the United Nations. These staffs shall form a part of the Secretariat.
3. The paramount consideration in the employment of the staff and in the determination of the conditions of service shall be the necessity of securing the highest standards of efficiency, competence and integrity. Due regard shall be paid to the importance of recruiting the staff on as wide a geographical basis as possible.

Convention on Privileges and Immunities: Article V of the Convention stipulates that privileges and immunities granted to the staff are for the interest of the organisation rather than for their individual benefits, and that the organisation would cooperate with member states in the administration of justice and observance of police regulations. The Staff Regulations specifically address the issues given in Box 5.2.

Box 5.2

Key HR Policy Areas of the United Nations (100 Series Staff Members)

Duties, obligations and privileges	Staff relations
Classification of posts and staff	Separation from service
Salaries and related allowances	Disciplinary measures
Appointment and promotion	Appeals
Annual and special leave	Joint appeals boards
Social security	General provisions
Travel and removal expenses	

Duties, Obligations and Privileges: The Staff Regulations stipulate that UN staff members are international civil servants with their responsibility being exclusively international; that they would be appointed in accordance with Article 101 of the Charter; that these regulations apply to all series of staff members; and that they would enjoy the immunities and privileges for the benefit of the organisation. Staff members are subject to SG's authority; should not accept instructions from any external entity; should discharge their functions and conduct themselves only in view of the organisation's interest; should work without their views and convictions influencing their work; should work impartially; and should maintain confidentiality. Moreover, staff members cannot accept honours, decorations, gifts or favours from any government; if received from a non-governmental organisation, they should accept only with the SG's approval.

Regarding the conflict of interest, the Staff Regulations say that staff members should not be actively associated with the management of or hold a financial interest in any profit making business or concern, and those at the Assistant Secretary-General (ASG) level and above should make financial disclosure about them and their children. No staff member can accept outside occupation or employment without prior approval. The organisation's property and assets should not be used for purposes other than official, and information should be provided to the investigator looking into a possible misuse of funds, waste or abuse. Moreover, staff members should follow directions and instructions from SG and from their supervisors, comply with local laws, and honour their private legal obligations. Disciplinary action can be instituted against those staff members who fail to comply with their obligations and standards of conduct set out in the Charter, as well as the Staff Regulations and Financial Regulations and the rules thereunder.

Prohibited for staff members are any acts of discrimination or harassment, including sexual and gender-related, as well as physical or verbal abuse at workplace or in connection with work. They should not interfere with or disrupt any meeting and official activity of the organisation, nor should they threaten, intimidate or otherwise interfere with the ability of other staff members to discharge their duties. Nor should staff members misrepresent their functions or position to anyone else; alter, destroy, misplace or render useless official documents, records or files; and seek to influence member states or organs of the United Nations to change the decision of SG or any unit of the organisation in their favour. Staff members should not offer or promise any favour, gift, remuneration or any other benefit to another staff member or to a third party to influence the course of action or decision, or accept such favours from others.

Staff members are accountable to SG, and the whole of their time should be at his disposal. Their performance is assessed through a performance appraisal mechanism. SG determines the hours of work and decides holidays for each duty station. Staff members could be sent on loan or transferred to another organisation by him.

Classification of Posts and Staff: Consistent with the principles laid down by the General Assembly, SG decides on the classification of posts and staffs based on the nature of work and responsibilities.

Salaries and Related Allowances: SG establishes salaries for various posts and groups, and the increments thereof, for staff members; terms and conditions for educational grant; dependency allowances; and language allowances. Post adjustment is given to staff members assigned to a duty station for one year or more, and a promoted staff is placed at the lowest step of the higher level salary—and two steps above that if his increments in the lower post had reached that lowest step. If a staff member assumes a higher responsibility for more than three months, he is entitled to the salary applicable to the higher level. General Service staff members in trades and crafts get an overtime allowance for work in excess of the required hours of work. Night work attracts a night differential, but it cannot overlap with the overtime payment. The organisation deducts a certain percentage from the salary as staff assessment and applies it to pay the taxes of those staff members who are subject to them in their home countries and uses such proceeds from others to reduce the contribution of member states on a pro-rata basis. It also deducts a certain amount from the salary to contribute to the pension fund. During mission assignments, staff members get a mission subsistence allowance in lieu of the mobility and hardship allowances, which are paid in certain situations.

Appointment and Promotion: Selection of staff members should happen without discrimination against race, sex or religion. Paramount in appointment and promotion considerations is the necessity for securing the highest standards of efficiency, competence and integrity. The General Assembly appoints SG at the recommendation of the Security Council and SG appoints all other staff members in accordance with Article 101 of the UN Charter. USG and ASG are appointed for a period of 5 years, subject to further renewal, and other staff members are appointed temporarily for a fixed term, indefinitely or permanently. For an appointment of one year and more, SG should seek the advice of the Appointment and Promotion Board, which has 7 members and an appropriate number of alternate members at the Principal Officer level. Appointment and promotion committees are constituted at the level of the Second Officer or above. Close relatives of a staff member cannot be appointed as long as there is an equally qualified non-related candidate. Central review bodies advise SG on candidates before their final selection for appointment.

GA resolution 63/250 has asked SG to appoint the staff only in three categories under one set of staff rules: temporary, fixed-term and continuing. If implemented, this will reduce and simplify the types of appointments in the United Nations.

Preference is given to internal candidates—from the Secretariat and staff members of other international organisations—if they are equal in competence to external candidates. According to the Staff Regulations, appointments to P-1 and P-2 posts and posts requiring language competencies are made exclusively through competitive examinations. Those who seek promotion from the General Service level to the Professional level have to take competitive tests as well. Before appointment, the selected candidates have to go through a medical check to establish that they have no ailments that could hamper their work.

Annual Leave and Special Leave: SG allows staff members to have annual leave and special leave in exceptional cases—for studies, extended illness, childcare and other important reasons. Home leave is generally given to go to home country, once every two years, with pay and travel expenses paid by the organisation if the staff member stays in his country at least for 7 days excluding the travel time; special leave is generally without pay, but in exceptional cases it could be given with full or partial pay. Special leave is not granted to work with government in a political office or diplomatic post.

Social Security: Staff members who work for the United Nations for six months or more at one stretch or combined are eligible to participate in the UN Joint Staff Pension Fund. Sick leave is provided for varying durations depending on the length of service or type of appointment, and needs to be certified by a designated Medical Officer if it is for longer than three consecutive working days and up to 7 days a year. Staff members get 16-week maternity/paternity leave with full pay starting up to six months prior to the expected delivery date. The United Nations provides compensation for the death, injury and illness, as well as for the loss of personal effects, attributable to the performance of official duties. And staff members might be required to participate in a medical insurance scheme.

Travel and Removal Expenses: The United Nations pays travel expenses of internationally recruited staff members and their spouses and dependent children at the time of initial appointment. It also bears expenses for travelling on official business, changing the duty station, home leave once every two years, family visit in non-family postings and separation from service. Expenses are also given when travel is authorised on medical, safety or security reasons. Covered are carrier fare on the most direct and economical route, terminal expenses, transit expenses, travel subsistence allowance according to locations of travel, and other necessary expenses. Generally the United Nations itself purchases tickets for staff members and their family members, and family members get subsistence allowance at half the rate of staff members.

Staff members get an assignment grant for 30 days—could be extended up to 90 days at 60 per cent—at the applicable daily subsistence allowance rate for those having an appointment of a year and longer, and a lump sum for a shorter duration. They also get an additional allowance equal to one month's net base salary if they are entitled to removal cost and two months' net base salary if not eligible for removal cost. The United Nations also foots the bill of excess baggage in air travel and unaccompanied baggage shipment. Internationally recruited staff members get removal cost for their household effects at the time of initial appointment, transfer and separation if the service period is expected or completed, as applicable, is two years and more. A ceiling of 4890-KG weight has been set for the removal cost.

Staff Relations: It is incumbent on SG to establish staff representative bodies to maintain continuous contact and communication with the staff to involve them in identifying, examining and resolving issues relating to staff welfare, including the conditions of work, general conditions of life and other personnel policies. These bodies should provide for equitable representation to all staff members. SG should also set up joint staff-management machinery having 3-7 staff members and equal number of his representatives to advise him on personnel policy and staff welfare. Accordingly, several UN locations have such staff representative bodies established, and staff members select their representatives through elections. And the joint staff-management machinery has also been set up in various UN duty stations.

Separation from Service: Termination of appointments occurs when staff members resign, when they reach the retirement age (60 for those appointed before 1 January 1990 and 62 for those appointed afterward), or when SG decides to terminate their service. SG can terminate a permanent staff's appointment during the probationary period; he can also terminate a permanent appointment after the probationary period has been completed if the post has to be abolished, if the staff strength has to be reduced, if the staff's performance is unsatisfactory and/or if the staff is incapacitated for reasons of health. Fixed term appointments can be terminated at the end of such term or at any time in the interest of the organisation, and other appointments could be terminated at the end of the term or at any time.

When SG terminates an appointment, the staff member gets a notice to that effect and an indemnity payment at a specified rate, plus up to 50 per cent more if the circumstances warrant it. Staff members resigning their posts should give 3-month prior notice. SG also gives the notice of termination at least 3 months in advance for permanent appointment and 30 days for temporary appointment. A repatriation grant is given to staff members—and their spouses and dependent children—after the termination of their appointment if they have served for a year or more to go to their home countries, and such grant must be used within two years of separation. Retired staff members also get compensation for up to 60 days of accrued annual leave.

Disciplinary Measures: SG might summarily dismiss a staff member for serious misconduct, and impose other disciplinary measures on those staff members whose conduct is unsatisfactory. He can establish administrative machinery with staff participation to advise him on disciplinary cases. Disciplinary measures consist of written censure, loss of salary in steps-in-grade, deferment of grade increment, suspension without pay up to three months, fine, demotion, separation from service with or without notice, and summary dismissal. No disciplinary measures can be taken without the due process, including giving notice to the staff member and opportunity to defend himself and referring the matter for advice to the Joint Disciplinary Committee (JDC). Such measures might be taken without referring to JDC when it has been mutually agreed to waive that step, or when a staff member is summarily dismissed. SG establishes JDCs with his representatives and that of the staff members at main UN locations; the Office of Legal Affairs would also be present in JDC. Appeals against JDC decisions on cases of gross financial negligence should go to the UN Administrative Tribunal, not to the executive head and SG. A staff member can be suspended up to three months during an investigation into misconduct.[5]

Appeals: According to the Staff Regulations, SG should establish administrative machinery with staff participation to advise him in

5. When the new system of administration of justice that is being introduced from the middle of 2009 becomes fully functional, there will be two—informal and formal—systems of dispute resolution. The Ombudsman and the Mediation Division will constitute the central pillars of the informal system and the Internal Justice Council and the United Nations Dispute Tribunal will replace the existing dispute resolution mechanisms as the formal system.

case of any appeal by a staff member against any administrative decision "alleging the non-observance of their terms of appointment, including all pertinent regulations and rules." The UN Administrative Tribunal hears such cases and passes its judgment. The Staff Rules under the Staff Regulations mandate SG to establish Joint Appeals Boards at various UN locations that have equal members of SG's and the staff's representatives. A staff member seeking appeal should request his executive head through a letter, and give copy to SG, for the review of the administrative decision. If the staff member gets a response, he can appeal against such letter and the original decision. On the other hand, if SG or his deputy does not respond within a month, the staff member could file an appeal against the original decision. SG takes the final decision on appeals within a month of receiving recommendation from JAB, and it is communicated to the staff member in question, who may then exercise his right to make an application to the UN Administrative Tribunal, which has its own statute. Under the new system being introduced from the middle of 2009, a United Nations Appeals Tribunal will be established to look into the appeal cases, as part of the new system of administration of justice. This will be the last entity in two tier formal dispute resolution process—UN Dispute Tribunal and UN Appeals Tribunal.

General Provisions: These include miscellaneous issues. Among others, the liability of staff members to pay in part or in full the damage done by them, the liability to have insurance for those who drive vehicles, and the beneficiary of staff benefits if a staff member dies.

Challenges

Challenges are synonymous to the United Nations. They exist not only in its key functions of maintaining peace and security; promoting economic development and social progress; and providing humanitarian assistance and protecting human rights. They also abound in human resources management. In fact, no other organisation can compete with the United Nations in terms of challenges in the HRM area. The main ones among them include complexity, competition, multiculturalism, the need to balance among merit, geographical distribution, and gender requirements; a lack of clarity in rules and regulations; political influence in recruitment, promotion, mobility and disciplinary measures; duplication and overlaps; haphazard distribution of staff in the pyramid; multiple sources of funding; diffused responsibility and lack of individual accountability and the need to continually renew the world body.

Complexity

If there are people from 187 countries working under the banner of one organisation in far-flung nations of the globe, that environment must perforce be an inordinately complex to work in. The United Nations is almost like a world government, having virtually all elements, institutions and frameworks of government. It has people working in such diverse areas as outer space, drugs and crime; election and the environment; military, police and civilian administration; library, archives, media, and information technology; human habitat and animal habitat; air travel and sea transport; construction and demolition; military mobilisation and peace building; arms procurement and disarmament; human rights promotion and humanitarian assistance delivery; and so on.

To manage all these diverse areas and handle them within one set of HR regulations and rules under one institutional roof without discordant commotion and chaos is bound to be extraordinarily hard, if not entirely impossible. Even more improbable would be to implement those rules in a systematic fashion in as diverse societies and cultures and countries as one can imagine and keep the institution unwaveringly focused on its objectives, coherent in its approach and cogent in its pursuit. What is more, the world body lacks the power of enforcement which national governments enjoy. It has to carry out its functions and mobilise its human resources mostly through inspiration and persuasion, which make its tasks incredibly delicate and involved.

Competition

For qualified and experienced staff, the United Nations has to compete with other entities today: State institutions, commercial enterprises, non-governmental organisations and international organisations. They in many cases offer better conditions of service than the United Nations. State institutions offer permanent contracts, security and stability; commercial enterprises offer much better salaries and perquisites; non-governmental organisations offer the chance for people to do what they like and enjoy freedom from many obligations the more formal organisations impose on them; and other international organisations—such as regional frameworks or the World Bank—provide more attractive conditions of service to their staff members in many respects.

It was different when the United Nations was first established. Most people joined the organisation as staff driven by their idealism and commitment to peace, in the aftermath of the colossal loss of life in World War II, the most devastating of all wars in human history. They wanted to rid the world of wars and to dawn permanent peace and progress through the United Nations. For such people, there was no other comparable organisation having such lofty objectives, and they joined as staff regardless of how much it paid or what kinds of facilities it offered. Working with the United Nations was a matter of pride, a duty, and a dream which could not be surpassed by any material consideration. Even today many people join the world body with the same sense of pride, duty and dream. But for many others, it has become just another employer and another place to work, partly because the United Nations has lost its halo by failing to rise to peoples' expectations, partly because peoples have, now living in relative peace for so long, forgotten the context in which it was created; and partly because it is not offering permanent contracts and other lucrative conditions of service to its staff anymore.

To attract and then retain the best and the brightest in UN employment is not always easy. Enlisting such people from the wealthy countries, many of whom offer better salaries and perquisites, has become an increasingly onerous challenge for the United Nations. The world body still attracts talents from the developing countries due to relative salary differentials, but employing the best ones is not always an available option due to the imperative to maintain the quota system, geographical distribution, gender balance, desirable range, etc. Salary comparisons have been presented in a separate, later chapter.

Multiculturalism

The world body, a universal organisation, must be inclusive. Though it is one of the most multicultural organisations on earth, it is still far from accommodating all 192 members in its workforce. Multicultural workplaces have become a common feature of an increasingly globalised and democratised world. Elsewhere too, the concepts of inclusiveness and social justice have caught up, and organisations of similar sizes have been trying to accommodate staff from different ethnic, racial and cultural backgrounds. Multinationals too strive to have staff from all countries of their operations.

For the world body, multicultural workforce has created many administrative and managerial challenges. Staff members from different countries bring diverse cultures, values, beliefs, ideologies, attitudes, gestures, symbols, symbolism, and work orientation to the United Nations. In such an environment, it is not always easy and smooth to build teams and make them work seamlessly in a coherent chain of command to produce common goods and deliver services efficiently and effectively to realise the organisational mission.

Merit and Geographical Distribution

Merit *versus* equitable geographical distribution has always been a subject of fierce debate in the United Nations. The UN Charter itself has sown the seed of this perennial debate. Article 101 of the Charter gives paramount consideration to "securing the highest standards of efficiency, competence and integrity." In the same breath, it also underlines the imperative to recruit on "as wide a geographical basis as possible." Although these two concepts are not necessarily paradoxical, the lines of argument that are pursued in heated, politically charged debates between the wealthy and developing countries to their advantage seem to make them mutually exclusive.

The wealthy states often argue that merit must be the paramount consideration. They are right. Merit is something without which an organisation can hardly function reasonably, let alone perform effectively and realise its goal. At the same time, they also imply that candidates from their countries are better trained and more appropriately equipped to take up the daunting tasks of the world organisation. This argument is questionable. Indeed, the developed countries often have better educational institutions, and their citizens might have travelled the world more widely. But the fact remains that the officials from the wealthy nations lack the grasp of the socio-economic realities and cultural sensitivities of the developing states that they are trying to help. You need to have a grip on local realities more than good education if the United Nations were to succeed in its missions of resolving conflicts and spurring development.

On the other hand, the developing nations argue that their wealthy friends are undermining the concept of geographical balance and preventing the United Nations from being a more equitable and just organisation. They are right too. The developed world has less than 30 per cent of the world population but it has 50 per cent share in the senior posts, (D-1 and above) in the United Nations among the posts subject to geographical distribution in 2008. If you include those senior posts that are outside the purview of geographical distribution—essentially, only posts in the Professional category funded by the regular budget are subject to geographical distribution, and that excludes all peacekeeping posts and positions under the Support Account at headquarters and in the filed as well as those that are under various other sources of funding—the developed country share in those posts and positions rises much higher. For instance, 51.5 per cent posts were outside this framework in 1994,[6] and 52.1 per cent in 1999[7] and it remains in the same range today. This is a highly skewed distribution of senior posts by any

6. See Bouayad-Agha, Fatih and Homero L. Hernandez (1996). *Comparison of Methods of Calculating Equitable Geographical Distribution within the United Nations Common System* (Joint Inspection Unit, United Nations, Geneva), Interagency Comparative Summary, p.viii.

7. Kudryavstev, Eduard V. (2000). *Senior-Level Appointments in the United Nations, its Programs and Funds*, (Joint Inspection Unit, United Nations, Geneva), p.2.

standard. What is more, cultural barriers are the most difficult ones to overcome. UN officials from countries with similar cultural backgrounds and socio-economic realities might be better equipped and better placed to win the confidence of the states that need help.

A better marriage between merit and relevant experience is in order. It is both desirable and feasible. Merit must be emphasised because it is absolutely critical for the United Nations to perform well; and geographical distribution is equally vital to make the organisation more inclusive and just and to bring more relevant experience and sensitivity to tackle problems in the developing countries. These two requisites, rather than being mutually exclusive, could be mutually complementary if treated judiciously and properly. You hire the best from both groups of countries, and let them work together and allow them to compete and excel. That will serve the Untied Nations and humanity better than chasing our own tail in a circular sprint.

Merit and Gender

Merit and gender balance have been another area of debate in the corridors of the United Nations. Women remain woefully underrepresented in the world body, particularly in senior posts. For instance, from D-1 and above, there are only 120 women out of 346 posts (34 per cent) subject to geographical distribution. "In the two most senior grades of the Secretariat—Under-Secretary-General and Assistant Secretary-General—women represent 18.5 per cent of the total of 124 staff. Female representation in the Director levels is 27.4 per cent of 559 staff (23.7 per cent at the D-2 level and 28.5 per cent at the D-1 level)."[8]

The debate is not about whether we should have one or both, for there is no difference in opinions across the board that we need both. It is about the way these two requirements seemed to be pursued. We must start with the point that merit, together with geographical distribution, is a requirement stipulated by the UN Charter. General Assembly resolutions have added and reiterated

8. United Nations (2008). *Composition of the Secretariat* New York. September. p.18.

the need for gender balance, a valid goal.[9] What has attracted serious arguments is the actual or perceived implementation of the resolutions. The authors have in their previous capacities had personally witnessed some of the heated exchanges between the two rival camps in various UN fora.

One camp—consisting of countries mostly from the developing world and the transition economies—argues that the rich countries are trying to aggravate further the already skewed distribution of senior posts in their favour by sneaking in more of their women citizens in the name of gender balance, as the developing countries do not have as many qualified women to choose from. This camp does want to strike gender balance, but it does not want to do so at the expense of geographical distribution, in which there is still a long distance to cover. The other camp—composed mainly of the developed countries and some better off developing countries with fairly good representation of their nationals in the UN system—stress merit and gender balance over geographical distribution.

Geography and Gender

With some back and forth, geographical distribution of staff in the UN system has marginally improved over time. Still on 30 June 2008, 5 countries remained completely unrepresented. In posts subject to geographical distribution, 16 countries remain unrepresented, a decline from 18 countries in June 2007; and 24 underrepresented, an increase from 19. The United States as well as 9 developing countries—mostly those where UN offices exist or missions are currently deployed—are over-represented and have had more than 1,000 staff members from each. As already discussed in this chapter's preceding paragraphs, the complaints of the developing countries about geographical distribution are yet to be addressed to their satisfaction.

While overall gender imbalance remains a serious problem, women have surpassed the number of men in P-1 and P-2 (in which 60 and 52.8 per cent respectively were women) as on 30 June 2008.

9. For a series of UN resolutions on gender balance, visit: *http://www.un.org/womenwatch/osagi/gmresolutionsthrdcomm.htm*

Elsewhere women trail behind men. Although the United Nations has not presented information in its report as to what percentage of women come from which categories of countries, anecdotal evidence suggests that the majority of women at the D1 level and above are from the developed world. As already discussed, developing countries entertain the fear that their wealthy partners from the North are trying to improve gender balance at the cost of equitable geographical representation.

Political Influence and Career Progress

By far the most thoroughly politicised organisation in the world is the United Nations. It is like an entity with 192 shareholders who have equal voting strength but differing degrees of political clout. Staff members from smaller developing countries often complain that they are passed over by their counterparts from the wealthy countries and powerful developing nations in appointment, promotion and other opportunities. They argue that less qualified candidates from wealthier/bigger countries usually enter the organisation at a much higher level than those coming from weaker states. There is some truth to it. It has been observed that, at the top echelons and strategic posts, nationals from the same country fill the slot consecutively. This tendency has further grown in the past several years, despite the fact that GA resolution 47/226 has prohibited it.[10] The staffs from weak nations also contend that powerful member states push their candidates quickly up the ladder. As a result, there exist an utter and boiling frustration among those qualified and capable staff members from weaker countries who get passed over by external or internal candidates from stronger nations, often with lesser or less relevant competence and experience.

Promotion is equally fraught with serious problems and resultant resentment. Staff members confide that, if you do not have the right political connections, you might rot in the same post for 20 years. On the other hand, if one is very well connected, he can leapfrog the steps quickly and make it to the top in no time. The

10. See GA resolution 47/226, Section A.1, para 1.

authors of this book have witnessed first hand several cases of these two extremes. While the best and brightest should be rewarded for their better performance, political influence giving preference to certain nationals over others only creates a deep sense of injustice and frustration in the entire workforce and hampers collective performance of the organisation.

Political influence also plays an important role with respect to mobility and disciplinary measures. Although the poor Secretary-General has been entrusted with the responsibility of Chief Administrative Officers and all staff members work on his charge, he is hardly in a position to manage human resources as he sees fit. As mentioned already, when Kofi Annan was SG, one USG openly and publicly expressed his allegiance to the President of his country, flouting the Charter provision entailing that all staff members remain neutral. But Mr. Annan could not sack or reprimand the USG and this staff left UN only when his capital leaned on him to quit.

Problems have also been witnessed in mobility. SGs want the authority to transfer staff across the system in the same manner as governments enjoy with respect to transferring their employees. However, member states, in particular the wealthy and big ones who ought to foot the bulk of the bill emerging from more robust mobility provisions, have prevented them from having such authority at all. Rather, the General Assembly has authorised SG to move around 50 posts every year on an experimental basis, but SG could not exercise that authority for two reasons: One, he has not often been able to lean on USG and ASG to release their subordinates because he wields very little control over most, if not all, of them; so they would only release willingly those staff members for transfer who were poor performers or non-performers. Two, senior officials resent and resist selective mobility, which is unlike the mandatory and near universal mobility practiced in governments. So SG has asked GA to suspend the managed mobility programme in his report contained in A/63/208.

Also in administration of justice at the United Nations, political influence always plays a significant role. Those with links to power may go scot-free or get a milder punishment for the same negligence or lack of performance than someone who enjoys no such links.

Duplication and Overlaps

The United Nations is fraught with too much of debilitating fragmentation, avoidable duplication and unnecessary overlaps in its administrative machinery. This has been the case partly because the world body has always pursued the policy of incrementalism, adding one element at a time without really having a comprehensive view of the whole gamut of tasks and their distribution across the organisation and its constituent units; and partly, because every senior manager wants to have his own empire from the centre to the field. There are hundreds of staff members who are doing the same or similar tasks under different departments and entities of the Untied Nations. This level of duplication and overlap would have been completely intolerable for any government and would have long been eliminated, most of it. Unfortunately, at the United Nations, this is not only tolerated, this has become the *modus operandi*.

For instance, you have political officers doing political monitoring and reporting on the same set of countries at the Departments of Political Affairs and of Peacekeeping Operations; you have economic analysts doing the same job in the UN regional commissions and in the Department of Economic and Social Affairs (DESA); moreover, the UN regional commissions have been duplicating the work of other regional organisations without adding any value; DESA is duplicating the work of the World Bank. The Departments of Field Support and of Management have mind-boggling duplication and overlaps in their functions. One step removed, the United Nations Development Program and the United Nations Children's Fund have so much avoidable duplication and overlaps. These are only a few examples of rampant duplication and overlap within the organisation and without. All this also makes pinpointing responsibility and accountability, which is the subject of the next point, nearly impossible. Here is a sample.

Haphazard Distribution of Staff Members

By design or default, the United Nations has had the most haphazard distribution of staff members across the staff architecture,

Box 5.3

Example of Duplication and Overlaps between DPKO and DPA

Department of Peacekeeping Operations	*Department of Political Affairs*
Office of Operations (Political Units)	(Political Units)
Africa Division	
Africa I	Africa I Division
Africa II	Africa II Division
Asia and Middle East Division	Asia and the Pacific Division
Europe and Latin America Division	Americas and Europe Division
	Division for Palestinian Rights

to the point of looking absurd. In the Professional and higher categories, there are 68 USGs, and one step below only 66 ASGs; 1308 P-2s, and 3190 P-3s, and only one P-1. No big difference exists in numbers between P-3s and P-4s. The largest concentration of staff members is found at P-3 and P-4 levels. Evidently such a chaotic distribution could not have been deliberately designed; it is an anomaly accumulated over time by rabid incrementalism that is the hallmark of the United Nations. The following figure demonstrates the distribution of Professional and higher category staff members:

Figure 5.2

Distribution of Staff in the Professional and Higher Categories by Level as on 30 June 2008

(Population: 9,892 of 39,503)[a]

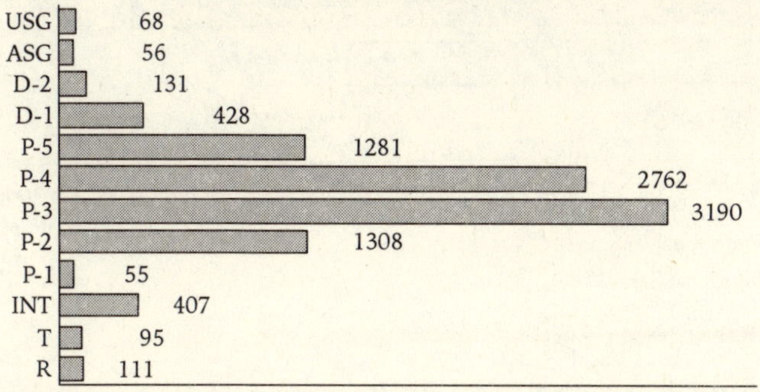

Note: a Excludes 1,250 staff appointed under the 200 series of the Staff Rules.

INT (interpreters), R (revisers) and T (translators) are staff on "when actually employed" contracts.

Courtesy: United Nations.

Equally absurd is the distribution of the General Service category staff members. Evidently there are only 185 G-1 staff members, whereas just one step above, the number of G-2 staff members is 3740. The biggest concentration of staff in this category is seen at G-4 level, followed by G-3 and G-5 levels. There are no ratios and common principles, neither is any logic with which this kind of staff distribution could reasonably be explained.

With this kind of arbitrary staff distribution, no staff member can anticipate their career paths and their future prospects in the system. This encourages staff members to give up and leave or to pull the political strings to advance their career. This type of staff distribution is a sure recipe for chaos, resentment and frustration in the house, and the United Nations has all of them.

Figure 5.3

Distribution of Staff in the General Service Category by Level as on 30 June 2008

(Population: 22,938 of 39,503)[a]

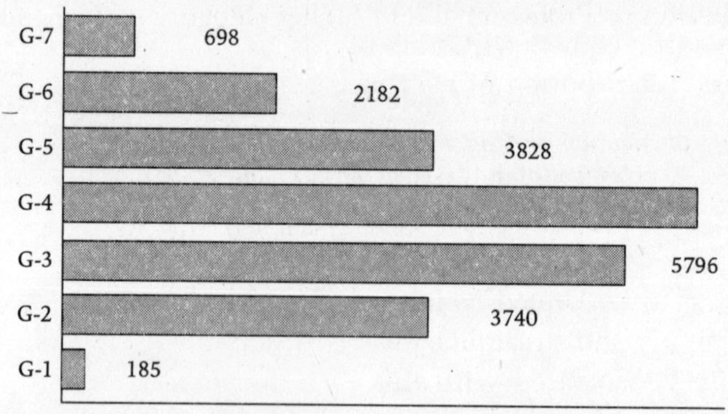

Note: a Excludes 5,423 staff (4,076 Field Service category, 331 Security category, 175 Trades and Crafts category, 36 language teachers, 787 national officers, 8 conference typists and 10 public information assistants).

Courtesy: United Nations.

Deficient Recruitment System

The Joint Inspection Unit, in its report of 1995, had found that United Nations recruitment suffered from many shortcomings and deficiencies. They included the absence of objective, uniform criteria guiding recruitment, absence of planning, obsolete methods of recruitment, long delays in recruitment, regularisation and absence of spouse recruitment program.[11] Not much has changed in the recruitment system though much water has flowed down the Hudson River. In addition, there is still no independent entity dedicated to recruiting and promoting the best fit to vacancies, to apply basic norms of HRM uniformly across the system, and to bring order in the UN personnel firmament.

Multiple Sources of Funding

One of the problems the United Nations has is that its staff members work under several sources of funding. Some are recruited under the regular budget and many under the peacekeeping budget, both of which are mandatory contributions; and a sizeable number of posts are funded under extra-budgetary resources, which are voluntary contributions from member states and from private organisations—such as the one donated by Ted Turner, the largest shareholder of CNN. Yet other posts are jointly funded by the United Nations and other entities under the UN umbrella. If you include people working under extra-budgetary resources also, the number of staff members will climb from 39,503 to 55,984 as on June 30, 2008. The distribution of staff members by funding sources is presented in Table 5.1 in the following page.

Figure 5.4 demonstrates the distribution of 55,984 staff members within the UN system organisations.

All these sources of funding make for a chaotic HRM environment in the United Nations. Sufficient efforts are yet to be made to simplify and streamline the sources of funding and address the problems associated with this phenomenon. In fact, extra-budgetary resources coming from different sources have been on the rise, spelling more chaos and complications in the HRM sector of the world organisation.

---

11. United Nations (1995). *Inspection of the Application of United Nations Recruitment, Placement and Promotion Policies*, a JIU Report. New York. p.21.

Table 5.1

Staff of the Secretariat and Related Entities in the United Nations System by Category and Source of Funds as on 30 June 2008

Entities	Regular Budget				Extrabudgatory Resources				Total
	Professional and Higher Categories	Project Personal	General Service and Related Categories	Subtotal	Professional and Higher Categories	Project Personal	General Service and Related Categories	Subtotal	
United Nations Secretariat	3304	17	4790	8111	3995[a]	1171	13921[b]	19087	27198
ICTY					413		609	1022	1022
ICTR					324		629	953	953
UNDP[c]					1924[d]	1128	3478	6530	6530
UNFPA					498		1221[e]	1719	1719
UNHCR[f]	89		131	220	1902[g]		4262	6164	6384
UNICEF					1357[h]	3734	5272	10363	10363
UNITAR					3	25	7	35	35
UNJSPF					59		118	177	177
UNOPS					82	579	298	959	959
UNRWA[j]	101		11	112	47		5	52	164
UNU					26	42	46	114	114

contd...

contd...

Entities	Regular Budget				Extrabudgatory Resources				Total
	Professional and Higher Categories	*Project Personal*	*General Service and Related Categories*	*Subtotal*	*Professional and Higher Categories*	*Project Personal*	*General Service and Related Categories*	*Subtotal*	
ICJ	44		56	100					100
ICSC					20		21	41	41
ITC[k]					71	53	101	225	225
Total	3538	17	4988	8543	10721	6732	29988	47441	55984

Note: a. Includes 2328 staff in the Professional and higher categories serving in field missions administered by DFS and 21 Professional staff against revenue-producing accounts.

b. Includes, 7845 local staff and 3606 staff in the General Service and related categories serving in field missions adminstrated by DFS and 69 General Service staff against revenue-producing accounts.

c. Includes staff charged to the UNDP core budget, funds managed by UNDP and UNDP supplementary funds.

d. Includes national officers.

e. Includes junior professional officers.

f. Latest availables data, as at 30 June 2007.

g. Includes national and junior professional officers.

h. Includes professional staff and national officers occupying posts funded by regular budget resources.

i. Includes professional staff and national officers occupying posts funded from project funds.

j. Excludes area personnal.

k. A number of posts in the International Trade Centre are financed jointly by the United Nations from this regular budget and by the World Trade Organization.

Courtesy: United Nations.

Figure 5.4

Staff of the Secretariat and Related Entities of the United Nations with an Appointment of One Year or More as on 30 June 2008 (Population: 55,984)

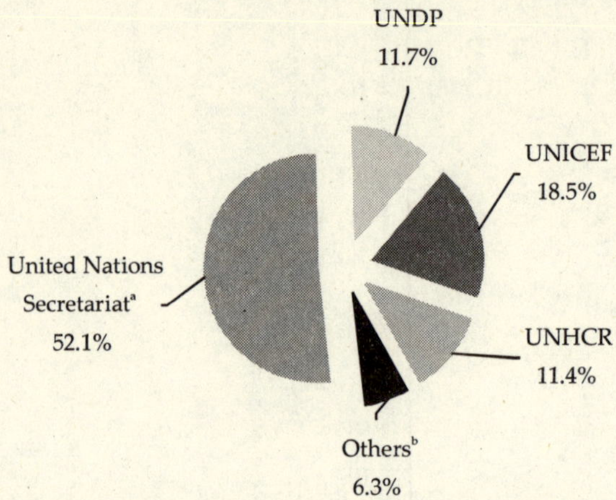

Note: a includes ICTR and ICTY.
b includes ICJ, ICSC, ITC, UNFPA, UNJSPF, UNRWA, UNU, UNITAR and UNOPS.

Courtesy: United Nations.

Problems of Transparency, Responsibility and Accountability

The United Nations presents a body of stark contrasts in its transparency. On the one hand, you have the General Assembly whose discussions and decision-making are highly transparent. On the other, you have the Security Council and the Secretariat that work in a highly opaque environment. Even the non-permanent members of the Council are unaware what decision is being made until one is made. Similarly, even staff members have no idea how and on what basis the Secretariat makes its administrative decisions, particularly related to human resources management.

Moreover, the responsibility architecture of the United Nations is excessively diffused. In the General Assembly, 192 countries are involved in making decisions; in the Security Council you have 15 members, in ECOSOC, 54. While the decisions of the Security Council are mandatory on all UN members, other bodies' decisions are not. In paper, SG may have full control over the Secretariat; but in reality, he is one of the weakest Chief Administrative Officers in the world who has no writ large over his own subordinates.

So neither SG nor other senior managers would want to be pinned down by a rigorous and robust accountability framework.

No wonder why accountability is the weakest pillar of the United Nations. The Comprehensive Review on Governance and Oversight, a report prepared and presented by a high level panel, has identified several problems with respect to governance. Among them, the key ones relate to insufficient transparency in nominations and appointments to executive management, incomplete communication of ethics and the code of conduct, and inadequate executive management accountability.[12] Each and every SG has given lip service to the need for enhancing accountability and holding staff members to account but resisted efforts to introduce concrete measures to inculcate the culture of accountability. No SG has ever convincingly answered the question as to why they have not done that.

In view of the unbending resistance from the Secretariat, ACABQ asked SG in 2006 to clearly define institutional accountability and individual accountability and to offer their precise definition and implementation. Under pressure, SG cited various problems in defining accountability.[13] The furthest the Secretariat is willing to take accountability is to "to explain and justify." Evidently, no one in the UN wants to be held to account for their failure. It is so partly because holding someone accountable is unpleasant; partly a lack of transparency and clear line of responsibility does not help holding anyone accountable; and partly because the system is so set up that there is no direct link between performance and incentives and disincentives. This leaves a wide room for impunity and ad hocism and encourages non-compliance to rules and non-performance on the job.

Having strong accountability machinery with transparent and concrete measurements would invariably call for a strong link between performance and positive and negative incentives, carrot

12. United Nations (2006). *Comprehensive Review of Governance and Oversight within the United Nations, Funds, Programs and Specialized Agencies,* Volume III, A/60/883 Add. 1. New York. June, pp. 91-92
13. See: United Nations (2006). *Investing in the United Nations for a Stronger Organization Worldwide: Detailed Report—Accountability,* of ACABQ, A/60/909. New York.

and stick if you will. If you make someone accountable to failure, then you must also reward him for success. This will apparently narrow the scope for administrative flexibility that senior managers of the United Nations have exercised all along. And no one who has enjoyed unfettered power and grip on the organisation would want to see his hands tied by a system that would make him accountable, as long as he is not forced to do so by policy making bodies. At any rate, a lack of accountability culture is a serious problem at the United Nations, as the former SG Boutrous-Ghali has lamented;[14] and such culture must be introduced.

GA must, therefore, insist that the Secretariat put in place a robust transparency and accountability mechanism. Establishment of an independent and permanent panel, which keeps an eye on the senior management, could be the starting point.

Fluidity of Regulations and Rules

The UN Staff Regulations and Rules are so broad and fluid that no one can expect that similar cases would end up with similar outcomes. Staff members are mostly unable to predict their future, reasonably chart their career paths, and anticipate timeframes for promotion and career advancement. There is no certainty whether a post is filled through transfer, promotion or external recruitment, because there are no clear career streams. So UN programme managers exercise significantly more discretionary power than their counterparts in governments and regional organisations. Governments usually decide the proportion of people who could fill the available posts from different routes. But such clarity does not exist in the United Nations, except for a miniscule number of junior programme officers.

The world body must strive for more stability and clarity in its staff regulations and rules, their consistent implementation across the system. It should also have a clear apportionment of vacancies for filling them through transfer, promotion and external recruitment considering the need to provide career opportunity for

---

14. Banerjee, Ajit M. and Sharma, Murari R. (2007). *Reinventing the United Nations.* New Delhi: Prentice-Hall. See foreword by Boutros Boutros-Ghali.

the existing staff and the imperative to inject new blood to ensure the organisation's continued vitality in the long run.

Need to Renew HRM

Of all the HRM challenges, continuously renewing and reinventing the organisation is the most formidable because it has to do with thinking, walking and working human beings who are acutely aware of their surroundings and alternative opportunities. Those entities that cannot reinvent themselves get atrophied, lose their relevance and go out of existence, sooner or later. Reform and reorganisation is the way to keep an organisation relevant and capable of rising up to the unfolding challenges. The United Nations is no exception to this general rule.

Unanticipated changes have occurred in the world since the establishment of the world body in 1945, including in the HRM environment. Conflicts have become more numerous and more complicated as many nations began to have civil wars and insurgencies. Development and humanitarian challenges have grown. A few hundred staff members at the United Nations' inception have grown close to 120,000 if you include the blue helmets deployed in peacekeeping and political missions around the world. UN workplaces have gone more multinational; mandates have proliferated; and responsibilities UN staff members have to grapple with have become more diverse and complicated. With all this, HRM policies have also become hugely more intricate.

But reform, to update the organisation in general and its HRM in particular, has been slow in coming. In the HRM sector, some efforts were confined to rhetoric only—like injecting new blood into the organisation; some were harped merely to create new senior posts to accommodate some cronies and countries, without regard to the need and coordination nightmare they were bound to create; and others were to expand SG's authority and sphere of influence. So these reform endeavours could not bear fruit. After projecting himself for long as Reform Secretary-General, Kofi Annan in his last reform report admitted, "Previous reform efforts, while generating some significant improvements, have sometimes addressed the symptoms rather than the causes of the Organisation's weaknesses, and have failed to adequately address new needs and requirements."[15]

Conclusion

The former SG Kofi Annan's 2006 report aptly lays out the problems facing HRM:

> The existing human resources management framework was designed for a stable, largely Headquarters-based environment, whereas currently more than half of our 30,000 staff members are serving in the field. The Organisation's increasingly complex mandates require a new skills profile, that will enable it to respond in an integrated way to new needs in areas as diverse as humanitarian assistance, peacekeeping, electoral assistance and drugs and crime. It needs to be able to recruit and retain leaders, managers and personnel capable of handling large, complex multidisciplinary operations with increasingly high budgets. Too many staff turn away from the United Nations, frustrated by the lack of a career path across the full range of opportunities in our global Organisation.[16]

In that report, Mr. Annan identified the areas of reform where the General Assembly needed to take action. Those areas are presented in Annex A-5.1 to this chapter. The report itself is discussed in more detail in a separate chapter, together with other reform proposals.

---

15. United Nations (2006). *Investing in the United Nations,* (New York), see the Summary.

16. Ibid, para 22.

Annex A-5.1

Proposals Requiring General Assembly Action and Support

(Contained in the Report Investing in the United Nations)

To ensure that the Organisation hires the best people and gets the best from them:

- Modifying the existing requirements in the system of recruiting, promoting and placing United Nations staff.
- Explicit authority for the Secretary-General to move staff members according to organisational need.
- Broadening current mobility requirements and approving a simplified contract system.
- Investing more in staff development and training programmes.
- Aligning benefits for United Nations staff in the field with those of the United Nations funds and programmes.

To equip the Organisation with up-to-date information and communications technology:

- Creating a Chief Information Technology Officer.
- Commitment to developing a fully integrated global ICT management support system, subject to the results of the current feasibility study.

To ensure that the Organisation gets the best value for money spent on services:

- Reviewing guidance on alternative service delivery and agreeing to the preparation of cost/benefit analyses in certain administrative areas.

To ensure transparent and efficient financial and budgetary management:

- Shortening of the cycle for review and adoption of the Organisation's programme budget.
- Giving greater budgetary discretion to the Secretary-General in consolidating peacekeeping accounts for separate field operations.
- Introducing improvements in the system of financial management—including delegation of financial authority with a clear framework of controls.
- Increasing capacity for performance monitoring and evaluation.

To improve the Secretariat's accountability to Member States:

- Approving improved reporting mechanisms to intergovernmental bodies.
- Agreeing to identify ways to improve interactions with the Secretariat on management issues.

To ensure that change is carried through in a resolute and sustained manner:

- Supporting the creation of change management capacity.
- Continuing support to the change management process.

6

Making of International Civil Service

Introduction

The ultimate goal of human resources management is to recruit, retain and reward those people who can best contribute to realising organisational objective and get the best out of them.

Human resource configuration depends on the organisation's objective, nature, culture, size, orientation, location, and the level of specialisation and diversification. Different organisations have different mix of elements in their human resources management. We will endeavour to examine some of the key steps and processes of HR—recruitment, selection and appointment—in this chapter in some detail.

Multinational organisations employ people from different backgrounds and varied disciplines in several countries depending on their needs and objectives and on the laws and rules applicable to the countries concerned. What staff and in how many categories are employed depend on several factors, including the nature, scope, tradition, and complexity of work an organisation does as well as the circumstances in which it was born. Old organisations would have a lot of hiring principles and practices that were in vogue at the time of their establishment. Newer entities would have more modern foundations of human resources management. For example, lifelong employment with defined benefits, once in vogue in most countries, has given way to more flexible employment that allows the organisation to bring staff through lateral entry and the employees to look for greener pastures.

Government organisations have all along been more uniform and consistent in providing defined benefits and job security than private enterprises. Their employment practices too have been more inclusive and transparent. Often governments have a central authority that keeps a tab on other government organisations with respect to maintaining fundamental consistency in selection, appointment and promotion, among other things. Due to diplomatic immunities and privileges, governments can largely maintain such consistency even outside their national boundaries.

The United Nations, conceived as a universal organisation, has to be inclusive and uniform in its HR practices, as well as fair and just to all its member states. Therefore, the international civil service, collectively the UN staff, has to be not only balanced in its representation from different countries but also be seen as such. Conditions of service for staff members regardless of their origin and location of work have to be generally similar, though there might be some location-specific differences from place to place. Staff members should be able to work in all countries of the world, unimpeded, to realise the principles and purposes of the United Nations, and enjoy some immunities and privileges for this reason.

Background: International Civil Service

For more than six decades, a slow but complex process has gradually progressed towards an International Civil Service. Since the days of the birth of the League of Nations to the early 1970s, a growing number of young men and women from a number of ex-colonial and independent nations were recruited for service in the Secretariat. People from across cultural boundaries, linguistic demands, ideological walls, professional and general staff have come to join talents, experience and competencies in support of global missions. Perceptions prevail among critics that an international merit system where individuals can be selected on the basis of excellence and outstanding qualifications, where national origin would be incidental, where assignment anywhere in the international arena might be expected, has not been fully realised. Critics point out to the continuing influence of geographical distribution, political patronage, family connections, insider information, nepotism as well as corrupt practices that continue to prevail in recruitment, which impact on the credibility of the organisation.[1]

Origin of Concept

Secretary-General U Thant, in his opening statement to the special committee for the Review of the United Nations Salary System in June 1971, stated that the concept of the International Civil Service is the product of the Committee of Experts of 1949 appointed by Secretary General Trygve Lie. The committee underlined that international recruitment and an international system of pay should serve as the modus operandi of the international civil service. A number of current features of the system presently in use originated from that committee.

As already mentioned, the legal basis of the concept is set out in Articles 100 and 101 of the Charter of the United Nations[2] and the corresponding provisions of the constitutions of the specialised agencies. Article 100 lays down the principles of international responsibility, independence and impartiality. It provides that, in the performance of their duties, members of the Secretariat are only responsible to the organisation. The article requires of the staff not to seek or receive instructions from any government or from any other authority external to the organisation and to refrain from any action which might adversely reflect on their status as international civil servants. Under the same Article, each member state undertakes to respect the exclusively international character of the Secretariat and responsibilities of member states of the Secretariat and not to seek to influence its staff in the discharge of their responsibilities.

In implementation of these principles, the General Assembly has established regulations for the Secretariat's administration. Article I

1. Macy, John W., Jr. (1971). *Public Service: The Human Side of Government*. Harper Row. p.273-274.
2. United Nations, *Charter of the United Nations*: See *http://www.un.org/aboutun/charter/chapter15.shtml*

of the Staff Regulations specifies that staff members are subject to the authority of the Secretary-General (SG) and to any of the activities assigned by him or offices of the United Nations, that they are responsible to him in the exercise of their functions, that although they are not expected to give up their national sentiments or their political or religious convictions, they must bear in mind the reserve and tact incumbent upon them by reason of their status; and that they may not accept any gift or remuneration from any government.

Article 101, paragraph 3, of the Charter prescribes the principles of competence and of geographical distribution by stating that: "The paramount consideration in the employment of the staff and in the determination of the conditions of the service shall be the necessity of securing the highest standards of efficiency, competence and integrity. Due regard shall be paid to the importance of recruiting the staff on as wide a geographical basis as possible."

These two principles together are fundamental to the human resources management of the United Nations. From the outset, the General Assembly has taken the view that they are mutually complimentary. If the Secretariat has to meet the test of competence in its international context, it must reflect, and profit from the assets of all cultures of the world. In practice this means that its conditions of service must be such as to attract and retain persons from every member country.

The Secretariats of the United Nations and of the specialised agencies have thus been conceived as a corps of officials—imbued with the spirit of international cooperation and responsive to the needs of the community of nations as defined by the deliberative organs of various UN organisations—who are appointed by, and responsible to the chief administrative officer of their respective organisations; for example, SG in case of the United Nations. Although much of what they do is not unlike the task assigned to officials of national civil services, the circumstances in which they work and the manner in which they carry out their duties set them apart to a certain extent as a distinctive service.

There is no doubt that the staff is multinational but the overall predominance of personnel, particularly at the higher levels, continues to reflect the world situation at the time the United Nations was established over 60 years ago, when more than half of its present members were not independent. The basic concepts of global mobility and inter-organisational interchangeability, so essentially part of the concept of an international civil service, exist perhaps largely in theory. In this sense, officials of international organisations are international civil servants, as international civil service maybe said to exist, whether the conditions of service are 'common' or not. Equally, however, the existence of common conditions and entitlements would not by themselves produce a unified civil service analogous to a national civil service, fully integrated and centrally administered with appropriate delegation of authority to the constituent departments.

A deliberate review is required to define precisely what is meant by an international civil service. Despite the work done by the academics and professionals from and within the common system, the recent unparallel growth in the tasks and personnel of the United Nations family, many basic organisational and structural defects have developed. This is substantially because the original concepts formulated when the League of Nations was founded and the United Nations established have changed very little. A critical review is due to re-examine some of the basic ideas in relation to the changed tasks and personnel requirements of the 21st century and to adapt them to the dramatically different and constantly changing times in which the world body now has to operate to deliver timely and meaningful results.[3]

Recruitment, Selection and Appointment Practices

Staff Recruitment and Selection

Selection is "the elimination of candidates whose values, interests, needs and liabilities, having been carefully analysed, fail

3. United Nations (1971). *Report of the Special Committee for the Review of the United Nations Salary System*, General Assembly, 26 Session, 28 September, statement of the Secretary-General, opening session, 1 June 1971, p.8; *Report of the Special Committee*, Official Records, General Assembly 1: 20.

to satisfy the requirements for a particular role."[4] Steps in the selection process include writing the job description and establishing the selection criteria, receiving applications and selecting candidates for interview, checking references and credentials, selecting best candidates, implementing the job offer and acceptance, and notifying unsuccessful candidates.[5] Blundell and Murdock say, "The overall aim of the recruitment and selection process in an organisation should be to obtain the quantity and quality of employment required by the Human Resources Plan, in accordance with organisational requirements and within the law."[6]

The recruitment and selection process should be integral to a human resource plan to align them with organisational goals and requirements to meet them. The main stages of recruitment and selection are given in Figure 6.1.[7]

There are no uniform arrangements across the board for the recruitment and selection of employees. Most governments and international organisations have specialised agencies to help them recruit and select the best candidates available, objectively and without bias, in order to fill various vacancies. Some states even have constitutional bodies for the purpose. In some other governments and private organisations, the concerned departments themselves, in coordination with their personnel departments, undertake the recruitment and selection process. Either way, the agency responsible for hiring staff announces vacancies, tests and interviews candidates, and recommends the successful candidates for appointment. In many countries, such selection agencies conduct written and oral tests—some of them give IQ tests as well—and check the background and medical report of candidates before selecting them for appointment. They announce successful candidates and forward their names to the relevant department of government for appointment.

---

4. Guillory, Robert D, *Staff Selection*, McNeese State University; See: *www.nationalforum.com*

5. Ibid.

6. Blundell, B. and Alex Murdock (1997). *Managing in the Public Sector*. Oxford: Butterworth-Heinemann p.84.

7. Ibid, p.85.

Figure 6.1

Main Stages of Recruitment and Selection

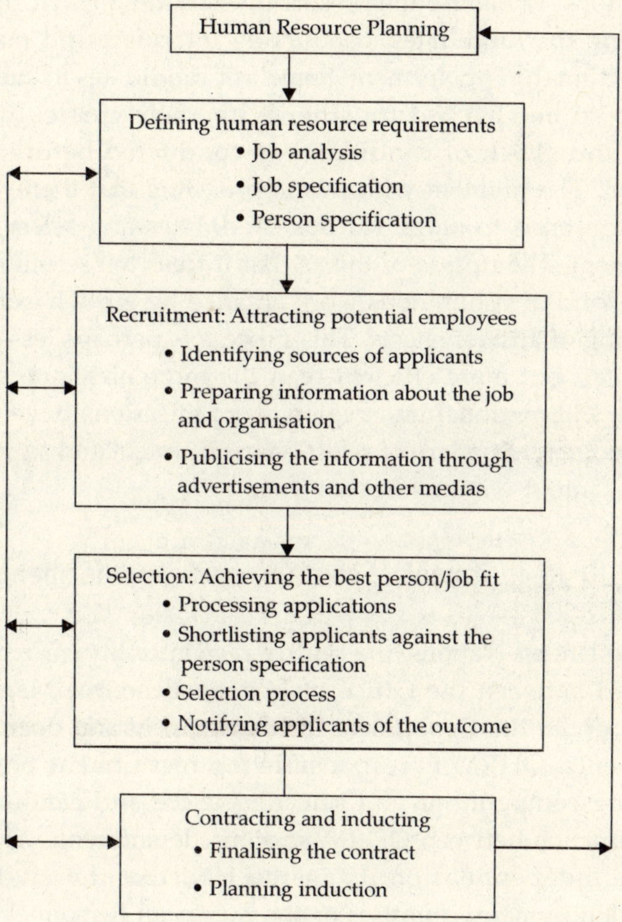

This process allows for the broadest participation of qualified candidates and for quite a uniform set of standards on which they could be tested and vetted. Therefore, it is also equitable, fair and just. At the same time, this process of selection is quite difficult to manage; you have to administer tests all over the country and get a huge number of test answers examined. It also largely focuses on a narrow set of criteria on which selection is made. If the United Nations were to organise such written tests worldwide, it could be a recurring, enormous and expensive undertaking.

A number of countries have abandoned written examination for selecting candidates to fill their vacancies, so have most private organisations. Evidently they resort to examining curriculum vitae, shortlisting the candidates, conducting interview and making the final selection for appointment. Some ask candidates to submit their write-up to be checked together with their curriculum vitae. Background check of candidates is conducted before they are appointed. The problem with this approach is that there would be no uniform basis to judge various candidates and select them for appointment. The upside of this is that it frees the selection agency from the kind of voluminous work entailed by written examination and scoring of answer sheets. This process is perhaps less equitable and less fair but more efficient than the more elaborate system of selection. International and regional organisations have followed a slightly different pattern of selection, recruitment and appointment. And the United Nations has its own.

UN Recruitment, Selection and Appointment

In the United Nations, the central responsibility for recruitment is divided between the Office of Human Resource Management (OHRM) under the Department of Management and operating line departments. OHRM is responsible for recruitment policy; and organising competitions and selecting successful candidates is a shared function between OHRM and line departments. There is no separate independent entity in the UN, like the civil service commission in many countries or the European Personnel Selection Office of the European Commission. In addition, the line departments in consultation with the OHRM recruit some very large categories of substantive and professional staff based on evaluation of resumes, applications, references, and competitive interviews. The essence of recruitment and selection process is two-fold: Firstly, a person who wants to enter as a staff of the United Nations, whether as an administrator or a specialist or professional, must demonstrate by objective and impartial tests that the person has the necessary qualifications; and secondly, if there is competitive examination, the person must stand high enough in order of merit amongst the candidates available.

The United Nations works neither as government nor as a private company. It has many similarities and differences with government and with the private sector. A country has parliament, government, departments, regional and local offices; so has the United Nations; in democratic societies, government is accountable to the legislature; the Secretary-General and his team are supposedly accountable to the General Assembly and other policy-making bodies of the United Nations; parliament exercises legislative oversight over government; so does the General Assembly, though more poorly; parliament has specialised and constitutional agencies to help check government; so does the General Assembly in the form of the Office of Internal Oversight Service, Board of Auditors, and so on.

Moreover, both government and the General Assembly do not pursue profit. Both have elaborate rules and procedures to follow, and their performance is measured as much by the application of due process as by their efficiency and effectiveness in delivery. And both are accountable to taxpayers and people, governments directly and the world body indirectly. Obviously these are the main, though not exhaustive, similarities between the United Nations and government.

On the other hand, there are several important differences between the United Nations and government as well. Unlike the elected parliaments which represent people in a country, the General Assembly is a legislative body consisting of government representatives. In democratic national parliaments, you have ruling and opposition parties but not in the General Assembly. In a Westminster system of government, the chief executive has to prove his majority in the legislature; but SG in the United Nations stays in his post for 5 years, once elected, just like the president in a presidential system, although he has no such powers as an executive president enjoys. Regional assemblies in a country are in charge of their own local affairs; but the UN regional commissions, though they are deliberative bodies, exercise virtually no legislative power on administrative aspects. Most local offices in a state report to the provincial government; the peacekeeping and political missions out in the field report directly to the UN Secretariat. Government has the right to tax while the world body relies on government contributions. The culture of accountability is yet to be as strong in the United Nations as it is in various democratic governments.

There are also similarities and differences between the United Nations and private sector. Both are not governments, neither have they the right to tax. Both are organisations and have no power to govern. On the other side, the private sector consists entirely of private units and outfits, whereas the world body is a conglomeration of governments. The world body is an intergovernmental body, while private organisations are not. And it does not enjoy the same kind of organisational and operational flexibility as private sector bodies do.

These similarities and differences have their direct bearing on their HRM realms. Put differently, the HRM of the United Nations is similar to that of government and private organisations in many important respects and dissimilar in many others. Consequently, HRM in the world body is unique in many ways: In selection and recruitment of staff, in training and promotion of staff, in pension and other facilities for staff and in the majoring rods against which performance of UN employees is assessed. We will see similarities and dissimilarities between the United Nations, governments and private organisations specific to recruitment and selection process in the ensuing paragraphs.

Recruitment and Selection Process

Let us proceed with the process beginning with how a position is created and classified and see how a vacancy is announced, applications are accepted and qualifications are analysed before moving to selection and appointment.

Creation of posts: In the United Nations, the line department that needs new posts has to write to the Office of Human Resources Management (OHRM) of the Department of Management (DOM) underlining, among other things, the functions of new posts, their duties and responsibilities, their qualifications and other requirements, and their sources of funding, their proposed levels and classification, as well as justifications for creating such posts. Once OHRM and the line department agree on the details, the Office of Comptroller and Financial Management does the costing of the posts to submit to SG for approval. Upon endorsement by SG, these proposed posts are included either in the Peacekeeping Support Account or the regular budget to be examined by ACABQ and then the Fifth Committee and the General Assembly plenary, in that sequence, for their approval. When approved, these new posts/ positions go for advertisement.

Among other organisations, the European Commission Staff Regulations are quiet about how new positions are created in its various organisations, giving the room to every agency to create positions as they need. In the US government, the Office of Personnel Management has that jurisdiction for senior executive posts; the concerned departments create lower level positions based on the guidelines stipulated by the OPM.

Advertising: Clearly, the selection process in the United Nations begins publicly with a vacancy announcement. This notice contains information on the vacant post, such as minimum and desired academic qualification, necessary experience, language requirements, and type and location of the post, and so on. In keeping with time, the United Nations has gone high-tech in its vacancy announcements. It places them on the Galaxy e-staffing system, a portal specifically designed for the purpose. Galaxy has been a remarkable advance for an otherwise traditional organisation, but a significant failure to achieve its objectives. It offers facilities to fill and file applications for posts on-line, but lacks capacity to process information and shortlist those candidates who meet the basic criteria. It is, therefore, that the Secretariat is trying to either add such facilities to Galaxy or to replace the system with a new one that can also perform the required additional functions.[8]

Although many a time, the Secretariat has proposed to do away with the conventional form of advertising vacant posts, many

8. For further details, see United Nations (2008). *In-Depth Evaluation of the Office of Human Resources Management*, an OIOS report, 22 September. pp. 11-12.

member states have forced it to continue to produce and distribute hard copies of vacancy announcements through its information centres and offices around the world. Occasionally, it advertises vacancies in reputed newspapers and magazines as well. Candidates can submit their applications, in addition to the Galaxy system, through mail, email, fax, and in person. A real vacancy announcement of the United Nations, as posted in the Galaxy system, has been reproduced in Annex A-6.1 to this chapter. Its hard copies come in a similar form and shape. Those published in newspapers and magazine might come in an abridged form.

Basis of selection: The UN Staff Regulations stipulate the terms and conditions for selection, appointment and promotion of staff members of the United Nations and the staff rules add procedural details.[9] As stated already in the previous chapters, the United Nations should comply with Article 101 of the UN Charter. Accordingly, Article IV of the Staff Regulations reiterates and elaborates the basis on which staff members should be selected, appointed and promoted. Regulation 4.2 reiterates the Charter provision that staff members should be appointed, transferred or promoted in view of securing the highest standards of efficiency, competence and integrity, paying due regard to wide geographical basis. Regulation 4.3 states that "selection of staff members shall be made without distinction as to race, sex or religion. So far as practicable, selection shall be made on a competitive basis." Regulation 4.4 more specifically outlines the procedural part of the selection process. It says:

> Subject to the provisions of Article 101, paragraph 3, of the Charter, and without prejudice to the recruitment of fresh talent at all levels, the fullest regard shall be had, in filling vacancies, to the requisite qualifications and experience of persons already in the service of the United Nations. This consideration shall also apply, on a reciprocal basis, to the specialised agencies brought into relationship with the United Nations. The Secretary-General may limit eligibility to apply for vacant posts to be filled by staff members appointed for one year or longer under the 100 series of the Staff Rules to internal candidates,

9. See: United Nations (2003). *Staff Regulations and Staff Rules 100.1 to 112.8 (revised)*, ST/SGB/2008/1, (New York).

> as defined by the Secretary-General. If so, other candidates shall be allowed to apply, under conditions to be defined by the Secretary-General, when no internal candidate meets the requirements of Article 101, paragraph 3, of the Charter as well as the requirements of the post.

As stated above, the highest standards of efficiency, competence and integrity form the bedrock of a merit system, which happens generally to be the universal considerations for staff selection. To meet its requirements, the United Nations selects its staff through competitive methods. The world body has specific recruitment criteria for junior professionals and professionals. It says,

> Junior professionals (P1/P2) and professionals (P3) are recruited through National Competitive Recruitment Examinations. The examinations are organised as a matter of priority in countries that are inadequately represented among the staff of the Secretariat. The examinations are administered in a number of occupational groups, including administration, economics, electronic data processing, finance, legal affairs, library, political affairs, public information, social development, and statistics. In order to qualify for P1/P2 positions, a candidate must possess a first level university degree and be 32 years of age or younger. For P3 positions, a candidate must possess an advanced university degree, four years of professional experience, and be 39 years of age or younger. Fluency in either English or French is required for both P1/P2s and P3s. All those who meet these criteria and believe in the purposes and ideals of the United Nations are encouraged to apply.[10]

There are also competitive examinations for language positions (translators, editors, interpreters, proofreaders, etc.) as well as for General Services posts.[11] In most other cases, the world body selects its employee by examining applicants' curriculum vitae and interviewing a few candidates that meet all requirements. Selection of staff generally depends on the system of desirable ranges. Box 6.1 presents the method of calculation of the midpoint and ranges. In the latest report of the Secretary-General, he has calculated the system of desirable ranges based on 2,797 staff members in posts subject to geographical distribution. These staff members are out

---

10. *https://jobs.un.org/elearn/production/home.html*

11. Ibid.

of those 12,328 appointed by the Secretary-General under the 100 series of the Staff Rules for a period of at least one year to posts subject to geographical distribution in the Professional and higher categories funded under the regular budget.[12] Thus most staff members are excluded from the calculation of the system of desirable ranges.[13] The methodology of deriving weighted ranges has been given in Annex A-6.2 to this chapter.

Selection System Elsewhere

To put it in perspective, let us have a comparative look at the UN's hiring practices *vis-à-vis* some intergovernmental organisations, countries and private sector organisations. The European Commission hires its staff on merit basis through competition. Once in every five years, the European Parliament organises an internal competition on the basis of qualification and test for each function group at AST6 level or higher and AD9 level or higher; but exceptions could be made for the senior-most posts—AD14 to AD16—and for posts that need special qualifications.[14]

In the United Kingdom, Article 2 of the Civil Service Order in Council 1995 (as amended) stipulates that no person should be appointed unless the selection is made on the basis of fair and open competition and unless the candidate meets the prescribed qualifications; Article 3 allows for exceptions in some cases—such as when the appointments are made directly by the Crown and ministers in positions of their trust.[15] There might be tests and

12. United Nations (2008). *Composition of the Secretariat*, (New York), p.38.
13. *Ibid*, p. 36-37: The following are not included in the system of desirable ranges: staff appointed to the secretariats of subsidiary programs, funds and organs with special status in matters of appointment; staff appointed to the International Tribunal for the Former Yugoslavia and the International Criminal Tribunal for Rwanda; staff appointed to peacekeeping posts, posts specifically funded for other field mission service or posts financed under the support account for peacekeeping operations; staff appointed to posts with special language requirements; staff in the Field Service and the General Service and related categories of staff (such as Trades and Crafts, security officers and public information assistants) who are locally recruited; staff appointed to posts for service limited to UNEP, UN-Habitat or the United Nations Office on Drugs and Crime; staff appointed to posts financed on an inter-agency basis; staff appointed to technical cooperation project posts; national officers at United Nations information centres; staff on special leave without pay; and staff on secondment to other organisations.
14. Article 29 of the *EEC Staff Regulations: http://eur-lex.europa.eu/LexUriServ/site/en/consleg/1962/R/01962R0031-20060701-en.pdf*
15. *www.civilservicecommissioner.org*

Box 6.1

System of Desirable Ranges

Method of calculation of the midpoint and ranges

1. Three factors are used to calculate the midpoint of the desirable range: the membership factor, the contribution factor and the population factor.
2. The membership factor is defined by the number of member states and is the same for each member state. It accounts for 40 per cent of the base figure and is equal to 6.5 posts for each member state, which is the total number of posts for this factor (40 per cent of 3,100 = 1,240 posts), divided by the number of member states (192).
3. The contribution factor is based on the most recent scale of assessments agreed by the General Assembly; the number of posts allotted for each member state varies proportionally. The contribution factor, which is different for each member state, represents the total number of posts for that factor (55 per cent of 3,100 = 1,705 posts) divided by 100 and multiplied by the member state's most recent assessment percentage.
4. The population factor is based on the proportion of each member state's population as compared with the global population of all member states. The figures are based on United Nations statistics (population and vital statistics report) for each country. This factor is equal to the total number of posts for the population factor (5 per cent of 3,100 = 155 posts) divided by the total population of all member states and multiplied by the population of the relevant member state.
5. Once the three factors have been calculated, the midpoint of the range is derived by adding the individual member state's share of the membership factor, the contribution factor and the population factor. The upper and lower limits of each range are determined by adding or subtracting 15 per cent from the midpoint of the range. The General Assembly, in its resolution 42/220 A, specified that that flexibility must cover a minimum of 4.8 posts and that the upper limit of the range should be not less than 14 posts.

Courtesy: Composition of the Secretariat, 2008, p.50.

assessments to look at the candidate's writing skills, communication skills, numeracy, interpersonal and analytical skills and decision-making abilities.[16] In the United States, which is a key comparator for the United Nations, they have competitive and excepted categories of selection in the civil service. Very few posts require written examination now. The competitive category is subject to US civil service laws and the Office of Personal Management's jurisdiction.

On the other hand, the excepted service categories have their own qualification requirements. Veterans belong to the latter category, so do virtually all employees of the Federal Bureau of Investigation and the Central Intelligence Agency. Other agencies might have a mix of these two categories.[17]

Evidently the United Nations and these two governments have rather traditional methods of selecting their staff, compared to the private sector, which presents a sharply different scenario. This sector may occasionally resort to traditional methods of hiring but most of the time, it deploys much more innovative and broad range of methods and approaches to recruit its employees. Employees might be recruited on the basis of curriculum vitae, headhunting, networking, job fairs, and performance as interns, among other things; an interview could cap the process of hiring. For instance, IBM aims to hire 40 per cent of its new recruits from among its interns and coops; it also hires through career fairs, recruitment conferences, recruitment campaigns at universities, etc. In doing so, IBM should abide by affirmative action requirements.[18]

Dedicated agency: The United Nations does not have a dedicated agency, or a central personnel agency, for carrying out the selection and recruitment of staff. The Department of Management, in coordination with the relevant line department, conducts the process of selection. In contrast, the European Commission has the European Personnel Selection Office to do the job. Among

---

16. *http://careers.civil-service.gov.uk/index.asp?txtNavID=141&635132=*

17. *http://www.usajobs.gov/infocenter/howjobsgetfilled.asp*

18. See IBM website: *http://www-03.ibm.com/ibm/history/documents/pdf/hr.pdf*

governments, some have such an agency but others do not. For instance, the United States has the Office of Personnel Management which helps implement civil service laws by working with various government departments. In the United Kingdom, the Civil Service Commissioners provide guidance to departments for the selection of senior civil servants and chair the selection process; they also carry compliance audit for other posts.[19] Selection of other posts is made by the departments and agencies themselves. Private sector enterprises do have their HRM departments, but no specialised agency of their own for recruitment and selection; they quite frequently outsource talent hunting and short-listing of candidates.

Hiring practices and preferences: Different organisations have adopted different hiring preferences and practices. The United Nations, as we have seen under the 'Basis of selection' in this chapter above, gives priority to internal candidates: First it looks at the qualified internal candidates, if there are no appropriate internal candidates, then OHRM considers candidates from other UN system organisations; only if none of these two categories have a candidate that meets qualification and experience requirements, external candidates are considered. In other words, the world body usually short-changes external candidates, who might be more qualified than their internal competitors, because their dossiers are not even looked at if reasonably qualified internal candidates are found.

According to the existing system, heads of departments and offices are responsible for making selection decisions after the central review bodies have ensured that the process has been observed and all candidates, both internal and external, have been evaluated against the requirement of the post. Some of the recent changes include, among others, strengthening compliance with the mandates of geographical representation and gender balance, as well as giving priority to serving staff and rostered candidates who were successful in a National Competitive Recruitment Examination—NCRE—for vacancies at the P-3 level. Another change was to allow the OHRM to place candidates from the NCRE roster on P-2 posts that have been vacant for three months.

19. Civil Service Commissioners, *http://www.civilservicecommissioners.org/What_we_do/*

The European Commission has had similar preferences for internal candidates over external, as the United Nations. The European Personnel Selection Office announces vacancies and does the selection of staff for its institutions. These institutions inform the Selection Office when they have to fill up the posts. Priority is given to filling vacancies by transfer and by promotion from an assistants' function group (AST) to an administrators' function group (AD). If vacancies could not be filled through those means, they are notified to the staff of the other institutions and/or an international competition is organised.[20]

However, governments have had slightly different provisions; they usually apportion the number of vacancies to be filled through promotion, through transfers and through hiring from outside. In those countries where vacancy announcement attracts thousands of applicants, governments organise competitive written examinations, and interviews for those who succeed in written tests, to select staff. In other countries where the volume of applications per job is quite limited, such as in developed countries where there are good alternatives in the private sector, selection agency picks up staff by examining curriculum vitae of applicants and interviewing short-listed candidates.

As already mentioned, the United States gives additional points to veterans in their hiring decisions, something several other countries also do. On the other hand, private sector firms do promote or transfer internal staff to fill vacancies in order to motivate the staff already on board. They also liberally hire outsiders if they find highly qualified candidates who could contribute to their bottom line, which is their primary driving force. Increasingly, they have also started hiring minorities and women to meet the requirements of law and to behave as responsible corporate citizens.[21]

As in the United Kingdom and the United States, the United Nations hires bulk of its staff, *viz.*, other than those who have to

20. EEC *Staff Regulations, op. cit.*, Article 29.

21. See IBM website, *op. cit., http://www-03.ibm.com/ibm/history/documents/pdf/hr.pdf*

be recruited through competitive examinations under the existing rules, through looking at CVs, though it gets thousands of application for each vacancy, unlike those advanced countries that receive limited applications for each opening. On the other hand, the United Nations seeks, to a certain extent, to emulate business corporations in recruitment and selection but does a poor job of it. Corporations use, among others, personal connection and network to hire employees.

By rule, the world body has to follow an open and transparent procedure for hiring the staff. Hiring a relative of a UN staff is discouraged. Although no one with some authority in the UN corridor would admit that they select people on the basis of their personal links or networking, in most cases that is how people join the UN civil service. And the selection process, in most cases through CVs and interviews, provides ample opportunity for it. Competitive written examinations are organised, as many developing countries with high volume of applicants do; but they are largely confined to countries which are unrepresented or underrepresented in the UN bureaucracy. And some staffs so selected are left in lurch for long without appointing or placing them.

Broad Categories of Staffing

Posts in the United Nations International Civil Service can be broadly put into four categories by the nature of appointment and responsibilities: Political/Policy, Substantive/Technical, Managerial and Support Services.

Political/Policy: Normally the departments and major units in the Secretariat are headed by a USG or by an ASG. These officials are part of the Secretary-General's cabinet, and they are political appointees. They lead various departments, offices and missions. Most of these high level posts go to the nationals of the permanent members (P5) of the Security Council as well as to large contributors to the United Nations and otherwise big and powerful countries. The UN corridor has been full of murmurs that some departments have been treated as monopolies of a few countries. What is more, some countries have been able to get their nationals to head multiple departments and offices in the Secretariat in New York alone. For instance, US citizens head the Department of Political Affairs, Department of Field Service and Office of Ombudsman. UK nationals preside over the Departments of Humanitarian Affairs and of Safety and Security. This practice is of fairly recent origin.

SGs have paid hardly any attention to the professional competence of candidates proposed by powerful governments for particular posts resulting in some technical departments headed by persons who have little or no knowledge and experience in the area of their responsibility. Heads of departments should have demonstrated professional competence in their area, and be able to provide leadership to generate new ideas in their respective fields. In short, this exemplifies the misuse of political clout by powerful countries.

Substantive/Technical: Recruitment to mid-level and senior posts/positions (P5-D2) in substantive, specialised and professional categories is done by internal promotion, lateral transfers and external hiring, in accordance with the Staff Rules. These posts/positions demand advanced education and a minimum 5-year experience at high technical and substantive levels, demonstrated research, analytical ability and other requirements. The revised selection system was introduced and implemented in May 2002 (as revised) with the following elements:

- Delegation of authority for selecting staff to heads of departments.
- Establishment of central review bodies for monitoring and maintaining accountability.
- Rostering of qualified short listed candidates.
- Use of generic job profiles.
- Introduction of competency-based interviews as part of the evaluation of candidates.

As mentioned before, the United Nations has introduced a Galaxy e-staffing system which has improved access to potential applicants worldwide. Since the introduction of this staffing tool, the average number of applications increased from 50,000 per year to about 350,000, which are received from 192 member countries. The Galaxy system has helped to fill vacancies and prepare vacancy announcements. The time taken to fill vacancies is now reduced from 275 days to 174 days. Galaxy is available both in English and French, as these are two working languages of the Secretariat. The UN website provides information, policies and procedures in all six languages. The time required for advertising a post has also been reduced from 60 to 45 days. For posts P-3 to D-1 levels, the average time taken for vacancy announcements in Galaxy is 45 days.[22]

As mandated by the General Assembly, the selection of personnel for posts is done through a competitive process. For posts at the P-3 and higher levels, the staff selection system requires that candidates meet the published requirements for a post. Vacancy announcements state the requirements, such as experience, education, languages and skills, as well as the competencies that candidates must have in order to be qualified and suitable to carry out the functions of the advertised posts. A competency-based interview conducted by a panel is required before a candidate can be recommended. This type of interview is designed to establish whether a qualified candidate has the required set of behavioural skills to be successful.

Virtually all posts in this group are of strategic importance, as they provide inputs to policy-making, prepare work programmes, supervise staff, network with governments and other organisations, research, analyse, prepare and supply information to senior managers, help draft resolutions, prepare budgets, prepare answers to questions raised in legislative bodies, and other important matters. These staff constitute more than 52 per cent of the entire professional staff—P-5 and above. Majority of them are permanent appointments drawn mostly from the 100-series and some from the 200-series. Their recruitment and selection is an issue of great significance and

22. United Nations (2008). *In-depth Evaluation of the Office of Human Resources Management*, Report of OIOS, A/62/221, September 22, Section IV.

concern to the organisation. Therefore, recruitment and selections to these posts must be made more rigorous and competitive.

Managerial: This group consists of those senior officials working in administrative areas below the levels of USG and ASG and above the Support Services category. There are three major practices of recruitment in this broad category. For people from P-4 to D-2, the hiring practices are the same as the substantive/technical group, in accordance with the Staff Rules.

(a) National Competitive Recruitment Examination (NCRE): Recruitment to P-2 and P-3 posts are made through NCRE. Particularly, P-2 level, non-language posts under the regular budget are junior professional posts, and the objectives of the national competitive recruitment system at this level stand to be: [23]

- To provide qualified professionals for the organisation;
- To improve geographical representation;
- To strengthen gender balance.

The first two objectives are in relation to Article 101 of the Charter of the United Nations to secure the highest standards of efficiency, competence and integrity. Overall assessment done of the programme in 2008 indicates that the professional skills and knowledge of the staff recruited through National Competitive Recruitment Examination (NCRE) is excellent. Half of the managers indicated that a significant number of candidates on the roster could have been appointed at P-3 level, either immediately or after the compulsory probationary period, as they were already well qualified. On an average, NCRE candidates are appointed to P-2 posts. In fact within four years, half of the staff members were promoted from P-2 to P-3, and a similar proportion of those P-3 staff were promoted to P-4 in the following four years.

NCRE is offered annually to all member states that are unrepresented, underrepresented, or in danger of being unrepresented. In the period 2001-2005, a total of 366 staff members were recruited

---

23. United Nations (2008). *Review of the National Competitive Recruitment Examination as a Recruitment Tool*, Note by the Secretary-General (on JIU Report), A/62/707, February 15, p.4.

based on national competitive examinations drawn from the NCRE roster; 14,133 candidates from 58 members states had applied, 3,515 were convoked and 221 were successful. Experience has shown that candidates are most often selected within the first two years after they were placed on the roster. Candidates are not taken off the roster unless they have indicated their non-availability, they refused offers of employment with the UN, or they can no longer be traced.

Competitive examinations have been held for 22 occupational groups, and in a given year usually 7 to 8 occupational groups are covered by the NCRE system. The occupational groups include the following:

Table 6.1

Occupational Groups

Administration	Architecture and Engineering	Associate Radio Producer
Demography	Economics	Finance
Human Rights	Humanitarian Affairs	Information Technology
Legal Affairs	Library	Nursing
Photography	Political Affairs	Public Administration
Publishing and Printing	Science and Technology	Security
Social Affairs	Statistics	Urban Development
Web Designers and Developers		

It is to be noted that the number of occupational groups is increasing; some occupational groups are becoming more specialised. This results in increasing pressure from programme managers who are interested in recruiting specialists so that they can take up assignments with the shortest possible period of training and development. Therefore, more specialised examinations are conducted. One example is the former occupational group of information and technology, which has been fragmented and now includes a new specialised group for web designers. Staff members recruited at entry level through NCRE get permanent contracts, and such specialised recruitment goes against the established human resource policy of the United Nations which foresees a versatile, competent, and mobile staff working in different duty stations, in different areas and in similar but not necessarily identical jobs throughout their career.

Clearly, the over-specialisation of occupational groups creates short-term problems as well, including more demands for examinations and more resource commitments, more candidates on the roster and more administrative burdens. It is essential that the proliferation of occupational groups should be carefully analysed and addressed so that attempts to further narrow specialisation at entry level is avoided. There are alternative ways of doing the occupational grouping system.

The overall assessment indicates that the system is a cost effective recruitment tool comparing favourably to the fees paid to specialised head hunting companies. Since the number of participating member states and applicants has significantly increased over the last several years, to the present number of 40 countries, followed by a centralised process, it requires a huge and complex logistical operation. The examination and tests section of OHRM has ensured the smooth running of the operation of NCRE on an increasing scale; the announcements, the convocations and the examinations have taken place without significant problems. The system has elaborated and implemented a complex set of measures ensuring security, confidentiality and impartiality and respect of cultural and linguistic diversity throughout the process. There have been hardly any significant number of reported cases of leakage of the test questions or violations of the rules set forth for the purpose.

Nonetheless, the greatest weakness of the system is reported to be in the placement of candidates, because the system was not fully based on an analysis of actual organisational needs and was not linked to workforce planning. Candidates were identified regardless of actual needs for staff, resulting delays in placement and increase in candidates on the roster. The number of listed roster candidates increased to 485 persons at the end of 2006. The evaluation done by inspectors noted that the entire NCRE process is excessively lengthy. It took an average of over 200 days to complete the examination part alone, and the final placement takes an additional six months to three years. This long processing and waiting time is unusually slow to meet the urgent and changing needs of a global body. The inspectors opined that it is also damaging to the reputation of the United Nations.[24]

(b) General Service to Professional Examination: The other component of this category consists of those who get promoted from the General Service (G) to the Professional Category (P) through internal recruitment based on examination. This examination system was first used in 1979 from General service staff to Professional level placement. Until 1999, 30 per cent of P-2 posts were reserved for G to P examination every year. In 2000, the number of posts were reduced to 10 per cent. Subsequently the percentage of P-2 posts for successful candidates was raised to 25 per cent, and a roster system was introduced to allow high scoring but unplaced candidates to apply for posts not subject to geographic distribution. It was also decided that each year up to three successful G to P candidates could be placed in P-2 posts in duty station with chronically high vacancy rates. From all accounts and reports, it appears that G to P examination for placement has not proved to be satisfactory, and it has impacted on the morale and productivity of General service staff. During 2004-05, 40.2 per cent of vacant P-3 posts were filled through promotions and 5.7 per cent through lateral moves. The remaining 54.1 per cent were filled through recruitment when the central review committees were satisfied that there were no suitable candidates.[25]

Support Services: As already mentioned elsewhere in this book, there are 22,938 General Service and related staff employed by the United Nations as on 30 September 2008. The GS category has 7 grades of salary levels, the largest concentration of these staff is in G-4 and G-3 levels. The recruitment and selection of such staff is decentralised to operating departments/offices, based on roster and vacancy announcement which spells out education, experiences, languages and skills as well as competencies that candidates must have in order to qualify to carry out the functions assigned to them.

---

24. United Nations (2008). *Report of the Evaluation of National Competitive Examination, op. cit.*, August.

25. United Nations Secretariat (2008). *Information Circular*, ST/IC/2008/52, September 24.

The service conditions and entitlement follow a set of standard procedures. The related categories include the field service staff, trades and crafts, security, conference typists and information assistants.

Appointments

As has already been mentioned in the preceding chapter, the United Nations appoints its staff members in the 100, 200, and 300 series. And Article IV of the Staff Regulations sets out the manner in which SG appoints staff members. According to Regulation 4.1, "Upon appointment, each staff member, including a staff member on secondment from government service, shall receive a letter of appointment in accordance with the provisions of annex II to the present Regulations and signed by the Secretary-General or by an official in the name of the Secretary-General." The annex II to the Regulation lays out the key elements to be mentioned in the letter of appointment.

Appointment of USG and ASG: Regulation 4.5 stipulates the nature and tenure of USG, ASG and other staff members. It says,

> (a) Appointment of Under-Secretaries-General and Assistant Secretaries-General shall normally be for a period of five years, subject to prolongation or renewal. Other staff members shall be granted either permanent or temporary appointments under such terms and conditions consistent with the present Regulations as the Secretary-General may prescribe;
>
> (b) The Secretary-General shall prescribe which staff members are eligible for permanent appointments. The probationary period for granting or confirming a permanent appointment shall normally not exceed two years, provided that in individual cases the Secretary-General may extend the probationary period for not more than one additional year.

As the point(b) above stipulates, there could be two major types of appointment for other staff members—permanent and temporary.

Permanent Appointments: According to the Staff Rule 104.13, for a permanent appointment, a staff member must have completed his probationary service, or gotten such service waived or completed 5 years of service under a fixed-term appointment. Recommendation for a permanent appointment must be reported to the Appointment and Promotion Board before submitting it to SG. The Board forwards its recommendation to SG, advising either the extension of the probationary period up to a year or eligibility for appointment. All appointments of more than a year that have been endorsed by the Appointment and Promotion Committee unanimously could go directly to SG for final decision. Those that have failed to get unanimous endorsement should be sent to the Appointment and Promotion Board for review, and SG should take the Board's view into account while making the final decision. In case of the General Service category, the task of the Appointment and Promotion Committee is carried out by subsidiary panels for the purpose. Chiefs of UN funds and programmes make permanent appointments applicable only to their own specific organisations, but following similar procedures.

Temporary Appointments: Temporary appointments could—according to Staff Rule 104.12—be of three types: probationary, fixed-term, or indefinite. Probationary appointment—which would be normally for two years but which SG could reduce or waive or extend up to a year in exceptional circumstances—is granted to persons under the age of 50 who are "recruited for career service." At the end of such a period the staff member could either be appointed permanently or separated from the service.

Fixed-term appointment could be for a period of up to 5 years without the expectation of renewal or conversion into permanent appointment. However, the United Nations gives reasonable consideration to such a staff member if he or she is a good performer and is under the age of 53.

Indefinite or continuing appointment applies to those staff members who are not granted permanent or fixed-term appointments. This type of appointment does not have specific expiration date and does not offer any expectation of conversion into other types of appointments. The UNHCR and other agencies designated by SG have mostly this type of staff members.

Other Types of Temporary Appointments: In addition to the standard types of appointments described above, the United Nations also grants several other kinds of temporary appointments. It accepts gratis personnel offered by member states at their own cost (1,952 type I gratis personnel and 45 type II, in 2007),[26] hires consultants individual contractors and institutional contractors to do specific short-time assignments,[27] and retains retired staff members (979 persons in 2006-07).[28] These people working for the United Nations do so under the contract signed between the two parties. Even though there is very little stomach among most member states for these types of assignments, some of these people, many of whom retired UN civil servants and other influential persons, continue to get appointed, some for a long-time, while many candidates who have been selected through NCRE have for an inordinately long-time been waiting for placement.

Local and International Appointments

Appointments could be put under, local and international rubrics as well (Rule 104.6 and 104.7). Those staff who have been recruited into the Trades and Crafts category or the General Service category from within the area of the duty station would be deemed local appointments. But they remain no longer local appointments when they are reassigned to a post deemed to have been filled from outside the area of the duty station or when they are reclassified into the Professional category. All other staff would have been internationally recruited and appointed.

Reappointments

Under Rule 104.3 of Article IV of the Staff Regulations, the United Nations can re-employ a former staff member, and such a staff member gets a new appointment. However, if he is employed within 12 months of separation from service or longer period, if he had retired or left on account of disability, he can be reinstated. If he is reinstated, it would be mentioned in the letter of appointment,

26. United Nations (2008). *Gratis Personnel Provided by Governments and other Entities*, A/63/310/Add. 1, August 19.
27. For details, see: United Nations (2008). *Consultants and Individual Contractor*, A/63/310/Add.3, August 21.
28. For details, see: United Nations (2008). *Employment of Retirees and Retired Former Staff, and Extension of Staff beyond the Mandatory Age of Separation*, A/63/310/Add.2, August 20.

and the gap would be charged to the previously accrued annual leave and the rest would be treated as special leave without pay; in this case, his seniority is maintained. A re-employed staff member must return all monies he might have received as part of the termination package—including termination indemnity, repatriation grant and payment for accrued leave—at the time of separation or retirement.

Transfers and Reassignments

The United Nations follows a similar process of recommendation through the Appointment and Promotion Committees or the Appointment and Promotion Boards, as applicable to new appointments, whenever staff have to be reassigned or laterally transferred for a year or more.

Promotion

Promotion decisions are taken more or less along the same line as appointment decisions. For the staff who have passed the competitive examination, the recommendation of the Appointment and Promotion Committee or Board is not necessary. Other candidates should have completed the minimum years of service in the grade and found appropriate for promotion before the view of the Board is sought.

The Secretary-General should, pursuant to Regulation 4.6, ask for medical standards to be met before he appoints all staff members described above. In other words, those who are selected for appointment must have medical check and meet the minimum standards of health.

Staff Appointment in Governments and Private Sector

As the United Nations draws much from governments and the private sector, it would be relevant here to see cursorily how others make their appointments. Evidently, governments make several categories of appointments. They include, but are not limited to, permanent appointments, appointments on fixed-term contracts, appointments for project duration, and temporary appointments to fill the vacancies for the time being. Those who seek permanent appointment in the civil services have to often go through a rigorous process of vetting as described in this chapter elsewhere. Unlike in the United Nations, entry of new staff into government is allowed only at certain levels or grades. The rest of the vacancies are filled through promotions.

Most of the appointments in the UK civil service are made on permanent basis. There are also temporary and part-time appointments.[29] The civil service is divided into three broad professional groups: Corporate services delivery, operational delivery, and policy delivery.[30] And it has several professional entry routes[31] and occupational areas.[32] But they do have a graduate induction scheme which allows new graduates to join the civil service as a group. There is a Senior Civil Service with three pay bands plus Permanent Under-Secretary in various departments; below that level, each department has its own grades and pay structure,[33] which essentially means there is no uniform structure below the Senior Civil Service. The Civil Service Commissioners have to approve all appointments, except those that are for less than 12 months, that are for less than 24 months in the case of secondment, and that are directly appointed by the Crown and ministers to assist them.[34]

The US civil service consists of the General Schedule, Scientific or Professional Positions, and Senior Executive Service. The General Schedule has 15 grades, the scientific or professional positions and senior level positions—both non-executive positions—have two grades (old G-16 to G-18 grades) and the Senior Executive Service has 5 grades levels.[35] In the Senior Executive Service, there are two types of positions—career reserved and general—and four types of appointment—career, non-career, limited term (up to 3 years) and

---

29. *http://careers.civil-service.gov.uk/index.asp?txtNavID=141&635132=*

30. *http://careers.civil-service.gov.uk/index.asp?txtNavID=137&635132=*

31. *http://careers.civil-service.gov.uk/index.asp?txtNavID=136&635132=*

32. *http://careers.civil-service.gov.uk/index.asp?txtNavID=137&635132=*

33. See *http://www.civilservice.gov.uk/documents/doc/pay_reward/CSPayGuidance2007-08.doc*

34. Civil Service Commissioners, *Civil Service Commissioners' Recruitment Code, http://www.civilservicecommissioners.org/web-resources/resources/b0adccaa9dc.doc*

35. *http://www.opm.gov/oca/08tables/indexSES.asp*

emergency (up to 18 months).[36] In the GS category, there are permanent, temporary, part-time and other types of appointments.

According to Article 31 of the EU Staff Regulations, candidates are appointed from AST 1 to AST 4 and AD 5 to AD 8; where appropriate, competition can also be organised to fill posts from AD 9 to AD 11, and in exceptional circumstances, in AD 12, not exceeding 20 per cent of the total vacancies per year. Article 35 identifies active employment, secondment, leave on personal grounds, non-active status, military service and parental leave or family leave as the various administrative statuses of its staff rather than categorising them on the basis of their length or purpose of service. Probationary period is 9 months in European Union institutions.[37]

Commercial entities widely differ in their hiring practices and appointments, though permanent appointments have become increasingly rare with change in time and business environment. Even Japanese companies that used to hire staff for life have begun to change their practices. Most US companies do not provide pension benefit anymore, something that was common only a few decades ago. They all now seek to reduce legacy costs. In the era of globalisation, they have to, unlike the United Nations, abide by local laws and practices of various countries in which they have their operations. Take the example of the General Electric, a multinational company. The GE 2006 Citizenship Report says,

> GE maintains constructive statutory and contractual relationships with hundreds of employee representatives throughout its global operations. The employee representative arrangements take various forms, but can be generally described as trade unions or works councils. Relationships with these employee representatives are structured based on applicable laws in the countries where GE operates.[38]

What has become increasingly common as a trend is the flexibility in employment and mobility of staff. Private companies might have different types of appointments: Permanent, fixed-term

36. *http://www.opm.gov/ses/about_ses/overview.asp*

37. *http://eur-lex.europa.eu/LexUriServ/site/en/consleg/1962/R/01962R0031-20060701-en.pdf*

38. General Electric, *GE 2006 Citizenship Report*, p.79.

contract, part-time, time-sharing, and work-from-home, to name a few. Permanent appointment in a company might no longer mean the same thing as permanent appointment with government. Such an appointment with a company might in most cases simply mean that the staff may work until the company fires him or her. Employees often look out for greener pastures and move whenever they can, and employers kick them out whenever the business environment is bleak.

Feedback from Internal Evaluations

There has been a departmental evaluation of the status of the process of recruitment and selection in OHRM. A summary of salient issues are reflected below:[39]

- It has been reported that current staff selection process does not facilitate strategic talent management, despite recent improvements. The organisation's staff selection process needs to be credible in the eyes of staff, management, and other stakeholders.
- Despite improvements made through Galaxy-based staff selections for recruitment and promotion, some steps in the process have consistently taken longer than others, such as evaluation, interviewing and creating the recommended list.
- Perceptions persist that staff selection process takes too long. A majority of Secretariat managers including those in peace-keeping missions rated the timeliness as "very poor". Managers cited the length of the staff selection process as negatively impacting their ability to fulfil departmental mandates.
- The IT systems for human resources functions do not support efficient processing of human resources transactions. IT systems users do not report high levels of satisfaction. Several problems with both IMIS and Galaxy involve transferring employee scripts. When staff members transfer between duty

39. See: United Nations (2008). *In-depth Evaluation of the Office of Human Resources Management*, Report of OIOS, A/62/221, September 22.

stations, their electronic data cannot be transferred without human intervention.

- Promotion outcomes associated with the current Secretariat staff selection process are not highly effective from the perspective of managers and staff.
- Feedback from Secretariat staff on promotional opportunities was also not favourable. Over half of Secretariat staff rated staff selection process as "poor". Fifty-one per cent of Secretariat staff members did not believe that hard work and skills development would result in promotion. However, analysis of Galaxy data indicated that for the first 5-year period between 2002 and 2007, approximately 78 per cent of staff selections resulted in the selection of internal candidates. And 22 per cent resulted in selection of external candidates. The data indicated that internal candidates are getting favourable consideration for promotion and lateral movement.
- Over half of Secretariat staff rated transparency of the selection process as "very poor", and only 2 per cent as "excellent". The majority of Secretariat staff reported that they did not perceive the selection process resulting in selection of most qualified candidate.
- The analysis of Galaxy recruitment, promotion and lateral movements data for 2003-2007 shows gender differences. The proportion of newly recruited males at the Director level was significantly higher than that of females. The pattern is generally the same at the P-5 level with recruitments and promotions more likely to go to men. The trend changes somewhat at the P-3 level.
- Secretariat managers, staff and other stakeholders cite the need for clearer human resources policies. They report that policies are not interpreted in a consistent manner even within OHRM. Human resources officers and executive officers commented that the policies are not practical, not flexible enough to accommodate different circumstances and not clear enough to hold managers and staff fully accountable.

- A multitude of weaknesses are identified in current delegation of authority. Most human resources officers and executive officers reported that the delegation of authority from OHRM to their department is working only "somewhat effectively". Ratings from peacekeeping officers were even lower. Human resource management staff in offices away from headquarters were also more likely to rate this negatively. The United Nations office at Geneva identified significant problems with the delegation of authority framework.
- Very limited OHRM monitoring of human resources processes are being performed. Examples of the risk of not having sufficient monitoring include the hiring of unqualified staff and improper payment of entitlements. In addition, accountability tools, human resource action plans and senior management compacts are not adequate. The survey indicated that there is a lack of familiarity with either the compacts or the action plan. A lack of monitoring and effective accountability mechanisms increases five significant organisational risks: (a) inefficient human resources processes; (b) actions in line with Secretariat-side human resources rules; (c) demoralising of high performing staff; (d) departments not to be able to achieve their mandates because they do not have the proper human resource capacity to do so; and (e) increased organisational liability.[40]

Challenges and Responses

From the ground we have covered in this chapter, it is abundantly clear that the United Nations' recruitment, selection and appointments are highly deficient and problematic. More so at a time when the United Nations has to compete increasingly with governments and private organisations to tap the pool of talented people, which is always scarce. Until few years ago, many people were driven to join the world body out of their commitment to

40. *Courtesy:* United Nations

world peace, humanitarian assistance, the development of poor countries, and the desire to travel and interact with people from different cultures and countries. Various factors have played a role in changing the environment. One of them is the rise of non-governmental organisations that are involved in promoting grass-roots efforts to promote the same objectives as that of the United Nations. Another is the globalisation wherein multinational companies have been offering competitive opportunities to work around the world and quite lucrative package of salaries and benefits. Yet another is the opportunities being provided by a greater number of countries to their citizens to go abroad and work for common good under their development assistance programmes and peace facilitation efforts.

As the work environment changed, governments and multinational have adapted their selection and appointment practices to suit the needs of time. However, change does not come easy in the United Nations. Every country would like to mould the United Nations to its vision and priorities as much as possible. The world body has the most developed and most underdeveloped members and many in-between, and it must seek to accommodate them all as much as possible and still maintain a robust multicultural workforce that can effectively deliver and help it meet its principles and purposes. The former Secretary-General Kofi Annan used to joke, he had 192 masters and pleasing them all was a tough call.

One of the key interests of member states, regardless of their state of development, is to get as many of their people into the United Nations Secretariat as possible, get them at policy-making and other strategic posts, and get them promoted as quickly as possible. This makes the United Nations face gargantuan and numerous challenges in its HRM sector. We have mentioned in the preceding chapter the main systemic problems the world body has to grapple with. Here we wish to highlight more specific problems related to selection, recruitment and promotion of staff members. And the most significant of these problems is a lack of new approaches and innovative methods.

Hunt for Talent: The United Nations has been slow in embracing new approaches to selection, appointment and promotion of staff members, something into which the corporate world and, to a certain extent, even some branches of government, particularly in the wealthy countries have made significant inroads. Hunting for the right talent in the market has been almost a *modus operandi* for big corporations. They send their people to schools and colleges and training institutions to locate bright people and develop links with them in order to attract them when they come out of school. Even military departments send their teams to schools and colleges to lure young students to join their services often with offers of scholarship. The United Nations has, however, not walked down this route vigorously. Occasionally its funds and programmes have enlisted services of consultants to find appropriate candidates to fill vacancies, but that is quite rare. At least for strategic posts, talent hunt could be a good route to purse, but it has to be inclusive, fair and just.

Reaching Out: In spite of the United Nations' high visibility, there are millions of qualified people who have never thought of the organisation as a place to get a job and build a career. At the other extreme, there are, across the world, millions of highly qualified and experienced people who have always dreamt of working for the United Nations but have never got the opportunity or know-how about how to get into it. The world body has not done enough to reach out to the un-reached and give fair considerations to all those who are interested to join it. Its information centres and radio and television programmes have an extremely limited coverage. Its Galaxy portal does not have the functionalities to collate and compare required qualifications and experiences with that of applicants, and it is a pity that thousands of applications go unnoticed and un-vetted, raising a serious doubt about the world body's commitment to inclusiveness, justice and fairness. A robust and sustained information dissemination campaign needs to be launched using the library system, as well as print and electronic media to reach out to those who are yet to become familiar with the United Nations as a place to work. And the organisation must put in place an open and transparent system whereby it is able to vet all candidates that apply for jobs and shortlist those who meet all requirements. If many low-resourced governments can do so, the United Nations must be able to follow suit.

Outsourcing: The private sector has gone into outsourcing in a big way, and even governments have been going down that route for non-strategic activities. Corporations not only outsource components and services from within the country, they do so across the world. Even small and medium size firms have resorted to this device to cut costs and increase their bottom line. But staff members of the United Nations have opposed the idea of outsourcing tooth and nail. Of course, some outsourcing has taken place in the language area, such as translation and editing, but not much has happened in other areas of UN operation. When the former Secretary-General Kofi Annan proposed broader outsourcing in his last report, staff members went into open revolt, and management-staff relations at the United Nations hit the nadir. The world body must find a way to do its work as efficiently and economically as possible and go for outsourcing and privatisation, while protecting as much staff interest as possible, of non-strategic activities to get more done with less.

Improving Electronic Processing: Computers and modern means of communication have revolutionised the workplace everywhere, and the United Nations is no exception to this general trend. Every four years, the world body replaces its computers, whether necessary or not and spends millions of dollars. The discarded computers are often given to member states, and their schools and colleges, and they work fine for many years. The world body also has put in place capacity redundancies and developed alternate locations for business continuity in times of disasters. However, the United Nations has not been able to improve sufficiently its electronic data processing systems. Its Galaxy system largely works as a vacancy announcement and application submission portal, but cannot process information to help develop a shortlist of qualified candidates. The IMIS that is in place has not been satisfactory either, as it does not offer many of the functionalities which human resources management requires.[41] The electronic data processing system at the Secretariat lacks capacity to do all those things an ERP system is expected to do. Evidently, there are misguided priorities in the UN house, and efforts must be made through concerted efforts to get its priority right. Greater investment is needed to modernise this sector with commensurate reduction in staff costs.

Balancing Experience and Energy

The United Nations suffers from a serious and overarching problem—a lack of balance between experience and energy. An organisation needs experience to do things in a mature and informed way and tide over its problems; at the same time, it also needs energy and innovation, which come more from the fresh blood and younger generation. Many countries, including a least developed Nepal, have found a way to accommodate these two cardinal needs in their civil service—injecting new blood and securing reasonable room for career progression of the existing staff—by filling vacancies through new intake and through promotion. But it is a pity that the world body seems sleeping at the switch and letting time slip away. A thorough review of recruitment practices is long overdue to overcome this deficit and to strike a healthy balance between maturity and energy, as well as experience and new blood, for the organisation's continued good health.

This problem is evident from statistics. The average age of its workforce was 45.5 in 2008 and those below 30 were only 2.8 per cent holding 100-series appointments of one year or more.[42] Suffice it is to say the world body is fast losing touch with the younger generation, and this is very unhealthy for the long-term relevance of an important organisation. The following figure displays the age distribution of the 100-series staff members appointed for a year and more.

41. United Nations, *In-Depth Evaluation of the Office of Human Resources Management, op. cit.*, pp 11-12.

42. United Nations, *Composition of the Secretariat, op. cit.*, p. 27.

Figure 6.2

Distribution of Staff Holding a 100-series Appointment of One Year or Longer by Age as on 30 June 2008

(Population: 12,328)

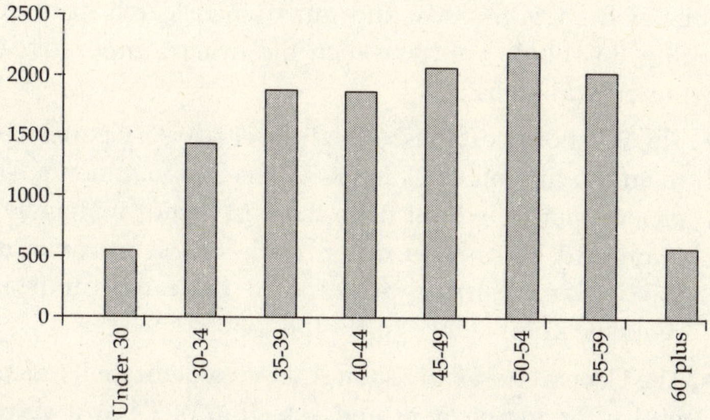

Courtesy: United Nations.

Removing Cronyism and Nepotism: Cronyism, favouritism and nepotism are rampant in the United Nations. If there was any value of merit ever in the world body, those days are gone. In principle, the world body discourages employment of relatives, but it is really rare to find someone who has joined the United Nations without direct intervention from someone senior within the organisation—a close relative or a strong benefactor. In other words, you rarely get selected for a job and promoted to a higher position unless you are very well connected with someone powerful within the United Nations or in a powerful member state.

You should not be surprised to know that the big and powerful countries impose most senior appointments. Quite frequently, senior managers lack the competencies they need in the area of their assignment, and this becomes extremely demoralising for the substantive staff, and the performance of such departments suffers badly. There is no rigorous, reliable and independent selection process for P4 and above staff recruitment and selection either. This has undermined the United Nations and its capacity to deliver. To remedy this situation, Bhouraskar has proposed that a small expert panel should be set up to identify posts requiring the highest professional credibility and recruit individuals only from those countries that can provide such persons with excellence without any interference from member countries.[43] Taking into account the findings of the OIOS study and our own research in the context of writing this book, we have seen the urgent imperative for the following critical steps:

- The SG should establish a high-level advisory panel of experts to advise him on USG and ASG level appointments. This will ensure that he would have the best senior managers on his team and be able to mitigate the pressure on him from particular countries to appoint their nationals lacking requisite competence to do the job.
- The General Assembly should set up a dedicated, independent entity for recruitment and selection of P4 and above staff members of the United Nations without delay. This will help the United Nations get the best pool of talents selected through a rigorous and meticulous vetting process, will free SG from staffing pressures and worries, will improve the overall performance of the Secretariat, and will repair the damage done to the organisation due to allegations of nepotism, favouritism and cronyism in staff hiring that have been haunting the world body for a long time.

Simplifying Appointments: It is absurd that the United Nations continues to maintain several types of appointments under 100, 200 and 300 series, to make its human resources management unnecessarily complex and undesirably convoluted. If the European Commission has been able to simplify its appointments in 2004, the United Nations can certainly do so. Although the Fifth Committee has in principle agreed to simplify appointments in its resolution on human resources management,[44] there is a long way before the

---

43. Bhouraskar's Digambar (2007). "Rationalization of UN Functions and Staffing: Economic and Social Field" in Ajit, M. Banerjee and Murari R. Sharma (eds.), *Reinventing the United Nations*. pp. 132-134. Prentice-Hall.
44. United Nations (2008). *Human Resources Management*, Report of the Fifth Committee, A/63/639. December 30.

goal is achieved, as it has been in discussion for a long time without actually being approved and implemented. We see the critical need to simplify the staff appointment system without delay. Although GA resolution 63/250 has approved several reforms, they do not go far enough.[45]

45. See GA resolution 63/250, published on 10 February 2009.

Annex A-6.1

UN Vacancy Announcement

Administrative Officer, P-4

Deadline for Applications: 12 December 2008

Date of Issuance: 13 October 2008

Organisational Unit: Office of Human Resources Management

Duty Station: New York

Vacancy Announcement Number: 08-ADM-DM OHRM-419015-R-NEW YORK (G)

This is a recirculation of VA# 417910. Those candidates who applied previously need to reapply if they are still interested.

Remuneration

Depending on professional background, experience and family situation, a competitive compensation and benefits package is offered.

More Info

United Nations Core Values: Integrity,
Professionalism, Respect for Diversity

Responsibilities

Under the supervision of the Director, Learning, Development and Human Resources Services Division in the Office of Human Resources Management, the incumbent will be responsible for the following duties: The incumbent provides assistance and advice as necessary to the Director in the management of human and financial resources of the Division. S/he will prepare donor proposals for funding, and support the design, development, implementation and monitoring of fund raising projects to mobilise resources for learning activities. The incumbent will provide advice to the Director on the financial administration of the Division. He or she will initiate and conduct studies to improve budget reporting systems and cost-effective utilization of programme resources; monitor and control budgetary allocations through regular reviews; provide effective monitoring reports and data; identify deviations from plans and propose corrective measures; and establish and maintain a set of sound policies, procedures, standards and tools which are consistent with UN policy and practice in order to ensure proper accounting, financial management and control. The incumbent will assist and, as necessary, advise the Director in the management of the organisational training budget. S/he will work in close collaboration with departments/offices, offices away from Headquarters and peacekeeping missions to: assess training requirements; monitor implementation of training plans and expenditures of allocated funds; analyse IMIS and other expenditure reports; provide on-going advice on improving effectiveness of training implementation of plans; and take steps to ensure that funds are appropriately utilised. The incumbent will supervise a staff team, providing expert guidance and leadership to more junior staff. S/he will also provide advice to others on human resources administration, financial administration and management information issues and practices.

Competencies

Professionalism–Knowledge of programming, budgeting, financial management and fundraising activities. Knowledge of management reform policy issues. Knowledge of the UN system, organization and inter-relationships. Knowledge of UN human resources policies, procedures, practices, regulations and rules. Knowledge of UN financial rules and regulations. Takes responsibility for incorporating gender perspectives and ensuring the equal participation of women and men in all areas of work. Planning and organising—Develops clear goals that are consistent with agreed strategies; identifies priority activities and assignments; adjusts priorities as required; allocates appropriate amount of time and resources for completing work; foresees risks and allows for contingencies when planning; monitors and adjusts plans and actions as necessary; uses time efficiently. Client Orientation—Considers all those to whom services are provided to be "clients" and seeks to see things from clients' point of view; establishes and maintains productive partnerships with clients by gaining their trust and respect; identifies clients' needs and matches them to appropriate solutions; monitors ongoing developments inside and outside the clients' environment to keep informed and anticipate problems; keeps clients informed of progress or setbacks in projects; meets timeline for delivery of products or services to client. Creativity - Actively seeks to improve programmes or services; offers new and different options to solve problems or meet client needs; promotes and persuades others to consider new ideas; takes calculated risks on new and unusual ideas;

thinks "outside the box"; takes an interest in new ideas and new ways of doing things; is not bound by current thinking or traditional approaches. Communication—Speaks and writes clearly and effectively; listens to others, correctly interprets messages from others and responds appropriately; asks questions to clarify, and exhibits interest in having two-way communication; tailors language, tone, style and format to match audience; demonstrates openness in sharing information and keeping people informed.

Qualifications

Education

Advanced university degree (Masters Degree or equivalent) preferably in business administration, human resources management, finance, or a related field. A first level university degree with a combination of qualifying experience may be accepted in lieu of the advanced university degree.

Work Experience

At least 7 years progressively responsible experience in administration, human resources, finance or related field. Experience in the United Nations system is required. Experience in developing and implementing fundraising strategies and activities is required.

Languages

English and French are the working languages of the United Nations Secretariat. For this post, fluency in oral and written English is required; knowledge of a second official UN language an advantage.

Other Skills

Proficiency in the utilisation of Microsoft Office (Word, Excel, and PowerPoint) and IMIS is required.

The United Nations shall place no restrictions on the eligibility of men and women to participate in any capacity and under conditions of equality in its principal and subsidiary organs. (Charter of the United Nations—Chapter 3, article 8.) English and French are the two working languages of the United Nations Secretariat. The United Nations Secretariat is a non-smoking environment.

The united nations does not charge a fee at any stage of the recruitment process (application, interview meeting, processing, training or any other fees). The united nations does not concern itself with information on bank accounts.

Please note that applications received after the deadline will not be accepted.

How to apply

All applicants are strongly encouraged to apply online as soon as possible after the vacancy has been posted and well before the deadline stated in the vacancy announcement. Because applications submitted by United Nations (UN) staff members are considered first, provided the eligibility requirements set out in ST/AI/2006/3 are met and the application is submitted in a timely fashion, staff members should apply within 15-day or 30-day mark.

Online applications will be acknowledged where an email address has been provided. If you do not receive an e-mail acknowledgement within 24 hours of submission, your application may not have been received. In such cases, please go to "My UN" page and check the status of your application by clicking on "View Application History", and resubmit the application, if necessary.

1. To start the application process, applicants are required to register by opening a "My UN" account. Go to Login, and Register as a User. Fill in the form and choose a User Name and Password.
2. After opening the account, applicants may apply for vacancies using the Personal History Profile (PHP) provided. Once the PHP has been completed for a particular vacancy, it can be saved and used for future applications. The PHP may be up-dated, when necessary, for future applications.
3. In completing the PHP, please note that all fields marked with an asterisk must be completed.
4. UN staff members must submit scanned copies of their two latest Performance Appraisal System (PAS) reports at the time of application to the appropriate Human Resources Office (HRO)/ Personnel Office (PO) to the email address below, clearly indicating the vacancy announcement number. In case you have no access to the digitising equipment, please submit hard copies of the two latest PAS reposts to the relevant HRO/PO via fax.

E-mail: *staffing@un.org,*

Fax: 1-917-367-0524

Please see the Frequently Asked Questions, if you encounter problems when applying.

Annex A-6.2

Methodology for Deriving Weighted Ranges

Grade	*(1) Number of Staff*	*(2) Percentage of Total*	*(3) Base Weighted Number of Staff*	*(4) Salary(a)*	*(5)=(3)x(4) Weighted Base Figure*
USG	28	1.00	31.03	190	5896
ASG	23	0.82	25.49	173	4410
D-2	67	2.40	74.26	142	10545
D-1	228	8.15	252.70	129	32598
P-5	529	18.91	586.31	107	62735
P-4	788	28.17	873.36	88	76856
P-3	713	25.49	790.24	72	56897
P-2	421	15.05	466.61	58	27063
Total	2797	100.00	3100.00		277000

Note: (a) Gross annual salary, in United States dollars, divided by 1,000. Salary scale effective 1 January 2008.

7

Types of United Nations Personnel

Introduction

Organisations are organic bodies, though their structures might be mechanical. They have their own life, mission, strategy, goals, motto, and way of doing things, for they are made of people. Large ones among them—be they commercial, non-governmental, governmental, or intergovernmental—would generally have different types of personnel belonging to various occupational groups. At the top they would have policy level people who decide strategic and policy matters; supervise the smooth operation of the entity; and execute, monitor, and evaluate the execution of policies made by policy-making bodies. Below that level come senior managers who assist the policy level people in policy formulation; they also help their seniors in policy implementation. Under the senior officials would be working middle managers and junior managers. At the bottom, organisations have auxiliary staff who carry out secretarial, clerical and support duties. There might be technical people at some or all levels depending on the nature of business.

Interestingly, each sizeable organisation is a universe onto itself. It has its own structure and hierarchy, decision makers and implementers, supervisors and subordinates, formal and informal communication channels, managers and experts, generalists and specialists, clients and community. Even though the multiplicity of levels and diversity of personnel could be a common feature of all large organised entities, the nature of business they transact, the mission and strategy they embrace, the scope of operation they cover, and the goal they pursue, determine their exact structures and hierarchies. Growing organisations would generally have flexible structures, while stable ones more rigid. All these factors determine their staff configurations; an engineering firm would have more engineers than administrators; an apparel trading firm would have more salespeople than information technologists; a department of defence would have more military officers than civilian; and so on. But they would all have some support staff and some policy makers, senior managers and junior managers, though they might have different technical qualifications and competencies.

Hierarchies exist in all big organisations to delegate authority and assign accountability. They could be tall or flat—having many layers or few—depending on the nature of their work. Research and legal organisations tend to have relatively flat hierarchies, with few levels of largely similar types of staff and a broad span of control. On the other hand, administrative and managerial bodies are relatively tall with many layers and diverse staff and narrow span of control for each supervisor.

The scope of work determines the organisation structure. For instance, local bodies would have jurisdiction limited to a relatively small area and a small staff with few layers; national organisations spread their structural tentacles throughout the country and tend to have many layers of staff coming from different disciplines; multinational companies and some government departments—foreign ministries or foreign aid outfits—work in several countries, have their structures in all areas of their operations and might have very diversified and highly stratified staff population.

Every medium and large organisation would have people with different specialisations and expertise to do its job in the best possible manner in a competitive environment. They have to compete for talents, skills, and space; commercial firms also have to fight for market share and profit. And each employee must find a niche and career path for himself in the organisation he chooses. So you have various occupational and functional groups in which employees work under different types of contracts and arrangements.

United Nations

The United Nations has had its various entities spread throughout the globe and its personnel working at several levels and different types of jobs. The General Assembly is the political master of the world body with respect to its budgetary and administrative policies. In some aspects, the Security Council works as the executive body of the organisation, but the Secretary-General (SG) is its undisputed chief administrative officer. Although everyone working for UN, including SG, is generically called a staff member, there are clearly differences—nuanced or stark—among them. Such differences might exist in occupational groups and types of personnel working for it—professionals and generalists, permanent and fixed-term, male and female, etc. We will shed light on these various types of staff in this chapter.

Staff Strength

Let us get started with the staff strength. The United Nations—quite large with 39,503 staff working for it as at 30 June 2008—is a medium size organisation on a global scale. At 30 June 2007, this number stood at 36,579 staff.[1] The details of the 2007 figures have been produced in Annex A-7.1 to this chapter.

If all UN organisations participating in the Common System were included, the number of staff would go much higher. As of 31 December 2008, such combined number stood at 81,384 staff, an increase from 75,282 at the end of December 2007.[2] In addition, there were also 6,066 National Professional Officers on the same date. Evidently, the Common System also includes several UN specialised agencies. For more detailed breakdown of the staff belonging to the Common System, see Annex A-7.1 through A-7.6 to this chapter.[3]

1. United Nations (2007). *Composition of the Secretariat*. New York. 31 August, pp.11-12
2. United Nations (2007). *2007 CEB Personnel Statistics* as at 31 December, taken from the website: *http://hr.unsystemceb.org/statistics/archives/stats/2007*
3. You might note that there is discrepancy between the figures presented in the Composition of the Secretariat Report and the ones in the statistical tables annexed to this chapter. That is because of the national professional officers and some other factors which are included in the report but separately treated in the statistical tables.

These figures do not include military troops and other formed unit peacekeepers, who now number around 80,000 people. If they too were added, the total number of people working for the world body would be around 160,000 people. This number is not really big compared to most governments and many multinational organisations. The United States federal government employs 2.7 million staff out of whom 2.5 million are full-time, US local governments employ another 1.9 million, 1.5 million of them working full-time.

Table 7.1

Summary of US Public Employment

Item	*All Governments*	*Federal Government (Civilian)*	*State and Local Government*
	1	*2 (Dec. 2007)*	*3 (Nov. 2008)*
Number of total employees	22,117,543	2,730,050	19,387,493
Full-time	17,144,814	2,462,127	14,682,687
Part-time	4,972,729	267,923	4,704,806

Courtesy: For federal employees: *http://ftp2.census.gov/govs/apes/07fedfun.xls*
For state employees: *http://ftp2.census.gov/govs/apes/07stlall.xls*

In the United Kingdom, which has only one-fifth of the US population, the total full-time equivalent civilian staff number on 30 September 2006 was 520,000.[4] Besides, most sovereign countries employ thousands of armed forces that operate outside the civil service's purview. The European Commission employed 24,607 staff as of October 2008.[5] In the private sector, the General Electric Co, a US multinational company, employed 327,000 people as of December 2007.[6]

Occupational Groups

For its classification needs, the UN International Civil Service Commission uses the Common Classification of Occupational Groups (CCOG).[7] According to ICSC, "The CCOG is an occupational

4. UK Office for National Statistics (2007). *Civil Service Statistics 2006*. London. p.3.
5. *http://ec.europa.eu/civil_service/docs/bs_sexe_age_en.pdf*
6. General Electric (2007-08). *Investing and Delivering in Citizenship*. GE Citizenship Report. p.68.
7. *http://icsc.un.org/resources/pdfs/ppd/ccog/ccogv.pdf*

dictionary which lists the various occupations that exist in the organizations, groups these occupations and sub-occupations into larger fields of work, families and occupational groups on the basis of similarity of functions, gives detailed definitions for each of the groups, sub-groups and occupations and provides an alpha-numeric coding for each entry in the system to facilitate data collection and sharing on a system-wide basis."[8] First promulgated by ICSC in 1979, CCOG can be applied to both professional and non-professional jobs.

The basic idea used for the classification is this: One ought to first identify jobs by the level and nature of work and to assign a number. Then they should establish job families and identify them with a code and identify the fields of work and give a number to each field. For instance, CCOG has assigned 1 to professional, managerial and technical work and 2 to support work related to professional occupation, code A to administrative specialists and B to architects and engineers, 05 to computer information systems specialists, and b to systems development specialists. So when you see a classification code 1.A.05.b, you would know it is talking about a systems development specialist on the professional, managerial and technical level.[9] Analytical chemists are identified by classification 1.J.02.a and so on.

In other words, there might be several broad levels of responsibilities, several hundred job families, and different areas of specialisation within each of them. In the Secretariat, there are two broad levels of responsibilities: Professional and higher categories and General Service and related categories. In each broad level, you then have different job families, fields of work, and areas of specialisation. If you take the broader UN Common System, the classification scheme becomes even wider and more complex.

The United Nations is not alone in such an involved classification scheme, however. In fact, some governments have even more complex and broader classification systems. For instance, the

8. ICSC website: *http://icsc.un.org/resources/pdfs/ppd/ccog/ccogi_ii.pdf*

9. For further details, see ICSC website: *http://icsc.un.org/resources/pdfs/ppd/ccog/ccogv.pdf*

United States has five levels of responsibilities—professional, administrative, technical, clerical and other kinds of work; it then has duties—major *vs.* minor, regular *vs.* part-time, project duties, and trainee duties; and occupational series with their separate codes, such as 0201 is human resources management and 0341 is administrative officers; these series run into several hundred and sub-groups into thousands.[10] But some organisations have made their erstwhile complex classifications much simpler now. The European Commission is one of them. We will discuss this issue further in the relevant chapter of this book.

Staff Distribution

For analytical purpose here, we will continue to stick to the staff strength of 39,503, which has been included in the SG's report, Composition of the Secretariat 2008. Many remarkable differences are apparent among the UN staff members, who have appointments in different series and durations; who have been financed by different sources of funding; and who belong to different categories and so on. Table 7.1 displays the distribution of 39,503 UN staff members by locations, by entities, by the series of appointment, by geographical distribution and other categories, and by the duration of appointment, as at 30 September 2008.[11]

Staff Members by Locations

UN staff members work at different locations around the world. As mentioned already, the United Nations operates from four headquarters duty stations, five regional commissions, near three dozen field missions and two tribunal locations, excluding the International Court of Justice based in The Hague. New York, Geneva, Vienna and Nairobi constitute the headquarters duty stations. Santiago, Geneva, Addis Ababa, Beirut, and Bangkok are homes too regional commissions. There are several field offices—peacekeeping, peace-making, and political missions—around the world under the Departments of Peacekeeping Operations and of Political Affairs. One tribunal is located in The Hague

---

10. For details, see the US Office of Personnel Management, Introduction to the Position Classification Standards, 1991 or website: *http://www.opm.gov/fedclass/gsintro.pdf*

11. United Nations (2008). *Composition of the Secretariat*. New York. 30 June. p.12.

Table 7.2

Staff under Contract with the United Nations Secretariat by Location, Category and Series of the Staff Rules as on 30 June 2008

(Population: 39503)

	Professional and Higher Categories				*General Service and Related Categories*			
	100	*200*	*300*	*Subtotal*	*100*	*200*	*Subtotal*	*Total*
Headquarters[a]								
Contract for less than one year	618	27	348	993	230	241	471	1464
Contract for one year or more	3953	552	322	4827	5382	14	5396	10223
Subtotal	4571	579	670	5820	5612	255	5867	11687
Regional Commissions[b]								
Contract for less than one year	49	6	62	117	121	40	161	278
Contract for one year or more	662	92	60	814	1472	0	1472	2286
Subtotal	711	98	122	931	1593	40	1633	2564
Peacekeeping missions								
Contract for less than one year	59	-	290	349	2352	3560	5912	6261
Contract for one year or more	952	1	1365	2318	4594	8617	13211	15529
Subtotal	1011	1	1655	2667	6946	12177	19123	21790
Other field locations[c]								
Contract for less than one year	7	28	5	40	23	3	26	66
Contract for one year or more	333	544	27	904	412	4	416	1320
Subtotal	340	572	32	944	435	7	442	1386

contd...

...contd...

	Professional and Higher Categories				*General Service and Related Categories*			
	100	*200*	*300*	*Subtotal*	*100*	*200*	*Subtotal*	*Total*
Tribunals[d]								
Contract for less than one year	34	-	9	43	34	24	58	101
Contract for one year or more	735	-	2	737	1188	50	1238	1975
Subtotal	769	-	11	780	1222	74	1296	2076
Total active staff	7402	1250	2490	11142	15808	12553	28361	39503
Other								
Staff on spcial leave without pay	81	10	2	93	56	3	59	152
Staff on recomdment to other entities	56	2	-	58	3	-	3	61
Total other staff	137	12	2	151	59	3	62	213
Total staff under contract	7539	1262	2492	11293	15867	12556	28423	39716

Note: a Geneva, Nairobi, New York and Vienna.

b. ECA, ECE, ECLAC, ESCAP and ESCWA.

c. Other field location: staff of DESA, DPA, DPI, OCHA, OHCHR, OIOS, UNCTAD, UNEP, UN-Habitat and UNODC at non-headquarters duty stations.

d. ICTY and ICTR.

Courtesy: United Nations (2008). *Composition of the Secretariat.*

and the other in Arusha in Tanzania. The following table shows the distribution of the UN staff at various locations:

Table 7.3

UN Staff by Location

Location	*Professional & Higher*	*General Service and Related*	*Total*	
Headquarters	5,820	5,867	11,687	29.6%
Regional commissions	931	1,633	2,564	06.5%
Peacekeeping missions	2,667	19,123	21,790	55.2%
Other field locations	944	442	1,366	03.5%
Tribunals	780	1,296	2,076	05.3%
Total	11,142	28,361	39,503	100%

Source: United Nations (2008). *Composition of the Secretariat.*

Evidently, 52.2 per cent of the Professional and higher staff and 20.7 per cent of the General Service and related staff worked out of headquarters duty stations (New York, Geneva, Nairobi and Vienna). Both told, their share in the total staff strength stood at 29.6 per cent. But the largest concentration of staff happened to be in peacekeeping missions, having 55.2 per cent of the total staff. The total number of staff increased by 2,924 over the 2007 reporting period, and 2,452 increased in peacekeeping operations alone (see Annex A-7.1). The above information, for a better visual comprehension, has been presented in the form of a pie chart in Figure 7.1.

Staff by Series

The UN staff can also be divided along the 100-series, 200-series, and 300-series of appointments. It would be easier to understand what 100-series staff are all about by starting with the 300-series and 200-series. The 300-series staffs are specifically appointed for short-term service and for limited duration. Those hired for short-term service work for up to 6 months, and they fill the gap created by such factors as the peak-time excess demand, the absence of a staff due to leave or vacancy and the need to provide service to a conference, or meet some other short-term demand. Those recruited for limited duration of up to 3 years—and rarely extended more than 4 years—work for peacekeeping operations, humanitarian missions or technical cooperation in field missions or emergency operations.[12]

Figure 7.1

Distribution of Professional and General Service Staff Members

Professional Category and Above

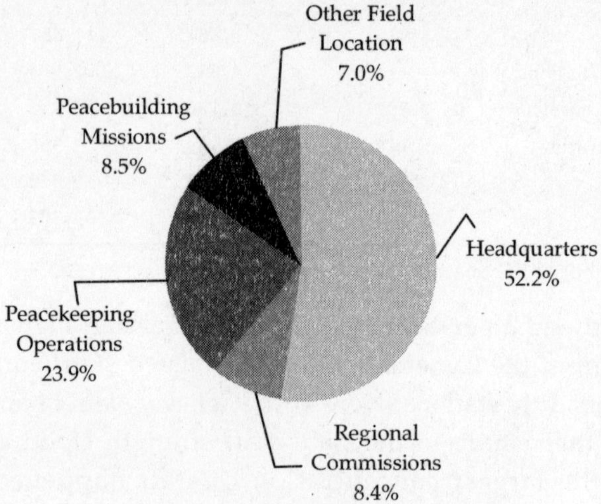

General Service and Related Categories

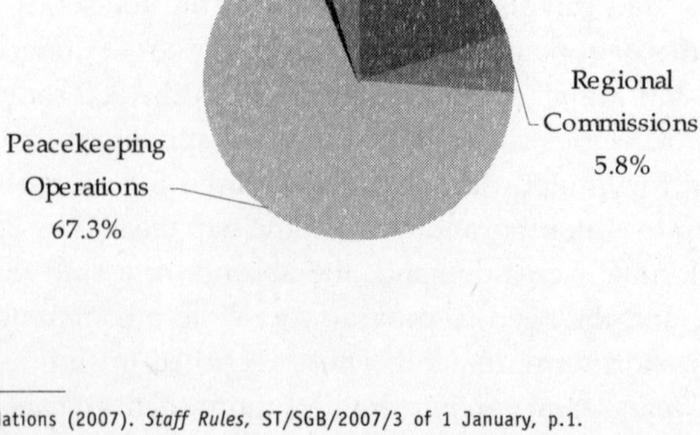

12. United Nations (2007). *Staff Rules,* ST/SGB/2007/3 of 1 January, p.1.

On the other hand, the United Nations recruits the 200-series staff for service with technical assistance projects, though with several exceptions.[13] All other staff members, whose job is of more permanent in nature, are appointed under the 100-series. Curiously, these series have to do with the UN Staff Rules that start with 100.1 for the 100-series, with 200.1 for the 200-series and 300.1 for the 300-series. The distribution of staff among the three series is presented in the following table:

Table 7.4

Staff by Various Series

Location	*Number of Staff*			
	100-series	*200-series*	*300-series*	*Total*
Professional and higher categories	**7,402**	**1,250**	**2,490**	**11,142**
Headquarters	4,571	579	670	5,820
Regional commissions	711	98	122	931
Peacekeeping missions	1,011	1	1655	2,667
Other field locations	340	572	32	944
Tribunals	769	-	11	780
GS and related categories	**15,808**	-	**12,553**	**28,361**
Headquarters	5612	-	255	5867
Regional commissions	1593	-	40	1633
Peacekeeping missions	6946	-	12177	19123
Other field locations	435	-	7	442
Tribunals	1222	-	74	1296
Total	**23210**	**1250**	**15043**	**39,503**

Source: United Nations (2008).

In the professional and higher categories, the largest number belonged to the 100-series, followed by 300-series and 200-series. Similarly, 100-series General Service and related staff outnumbered the 300-series staff, and there were no 200-series staff in this group. The tribunals recorded a sharp decline in staff numbers in 2008 over 2007; so did the USG and ASG levels, as their number declined by 8 posts; elsewhere there was a general tendency for staff numbers to increase.

13. United Nations (2002). *Staff Rules*, ST/SGB/2002/2 of 1 January.

Staff by Types of Appointment

The UN staff can be categorised in terms of the types of their appointment as well. Out of the 39,503 staff under discussion, 10.9 per cent were under permanent appointments; 46.8 per cent under fixed-term contracts; 35.1 per cent under limited duration contracts; 3.2 per cent under 200-series contracts; 1.5 per cent under when-actually-employed contracts (interpreters, revisers and translators); 1.4 per cent under short-term contracts; 0.4 per cent under indefinite contracts; and 0.7 per cent under probationary period. By levels, Directors have had the largest proportion, 27.7 per cent, of the permanent appointments, followed by the Professionals (P1-P5) at 19.4 per cent, and the General Service staff at 7.2 per cent.

Based on those percentages, the number of staff in those categories could be calculated as follows:

Table 7.5

Numbers of Staff by Types of Appointment

Types of Staff	*Number*	*Percentage*
Permanent	4,306	10.9
Fixed-term	18,487	46.8
200-series	1,264	3.2
Short-term	553	1.4
Limited duration	13,866	35.1
Indefinite	158	0.4
When actually employed	593	1.5
Probationary	276	0.7
Total	39,503	100

Note: Converted into numbers from the percentages, so they might not add up.

Source: Calculated by the Authors.

Figure 7.2 displays this distribution of posts and positions by the types of appointment.

Staff by Nationality and Subject to Geographical Distribution

Out of 187 member states represented by the staff in the Secretariat, 176 states have staff in posts subject to geographical distribution, and 178 states have their nationals appointed to the 100-series posts. And 5 countries have no nationals serving in the United Nations. In 2007, 183 member states were represented, and 9 countries had no staff in the Secretariat; among those countries having their nationals as UN staff, 174 countries occupied posts subject to such distribution. In other words, there has been a slight improvement in the national representation status. Generally, only posts under the regular budget are subject to geographical distribution. For the sake of establishing a basis for calculation, the United Nations has used only 2,797 posts. And out of them, only 1,428 (or 51.1 per cent) are permanent appointments.

Figure 7.2

Staff Distribution by Type of Appointment as on 30 June 2008

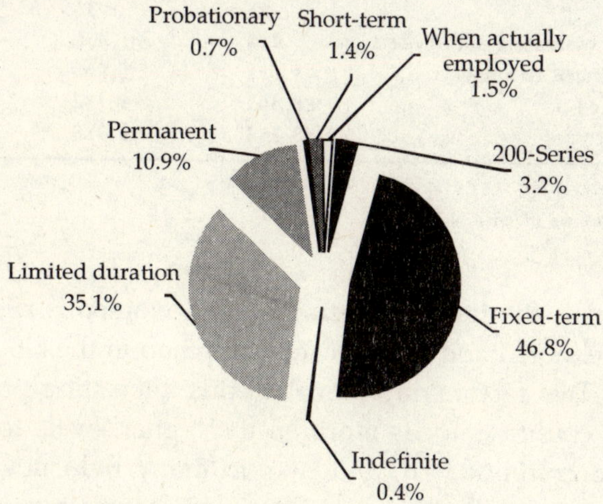

Courtesy: Composition of the Secretariat, 2008, p.21.

Staff by Gender

Although the General Assembly has asked SG to strike a gender balance in the Secretariat's global staff, that objective is yet to be achieved. As on 30 June 2008, there were 25,928 (65.6 per cent) men and 13,575 (34.4 per cent) women. Among the locally recruited staff of 15,219 in field missions, women constituted only 17.1 per cent. In terms of various levels, men outnumbered by 5 to 1 at the highest echelons, as only 18.5 per cent were women at the level of USG and ASG combined. At P-1 and P-2 levels, however, women outnumber men: At P-1 level, 60 per cent staff are women and at P-2 level, 52.8 per cent. The following table shows the distribution of women at various levels:

Table 7.6

Share of Women in the UN Staff (30 June 2008)

Levels	*Total Numbers*	*Women*	*Percentage*
USG and ASG	124	23	18.5%
D2	131	31	23.7%
D1	428	122	28.5%
P5	1,281	398	31.1%
P4	2,762	1,003	36.3%
P3	3,190	1,317	41.3%
P2	1,308	690	52.8%
P1	55	33	60%
Interpreters, translators and revisers	613	339	55.3%
Total Professional & higher*	9,892	3,956	40%
GS and related	28,361	9,132	32.2%
Total*	38,253	13,088	34.2%

Note: * Excludes 1,250 staff appointed under the 200-series out of 39,503 staff. Figures are rounded.

Source: United Nations.

Obviously, the ratio between men and women is slightly better in the Professional and higher categories than in the GS and related categories. Two factors might explain this interesting phenomenon: One, most countries focus more on the higher levels to have their nationals accommodated; and two, in many field missions, such as peacekeeping operations, which are by nature more dangerous than stable UN offices or missions, women prefer to stay out due to the high risks involved. And this illustrates why only 17.1 per cent of locally recruited staff in field missions happened to be women. In 2007, 65.2 per cent of the global Secretariat staff were men and 34.8 per cent women. Evidently, women lost some ground in 2008.

Appointments by Types of Funding

Although no real difference exists in terms of work between those staff who are funded under the regular budget and those outside it, there are significant differences in terms of certain benefits they receive from the United Nations. A majority of posts under the regular budget are permanent or for a long period, whereas positions under other sources of funding—peacekeeping support account, extra-budgetary resources, etc.—are fundamentally temporary, either under fixed-term, short-term, limited duration or indefinite appointments. There could be temporary posts under the regular budget as well, but permanent posts exist only under the regular budget. Therefore, those people who want to have a permanent appointment must compete for posts that are within the purview of the UN regular budget.

Of the total 4,306 permanent appointments, 3,294 posts (76.5%) were under the regular budget and the remaining 1,012 (22.5%) under other resources in 2008. Moreover, 37.4 per cent staff in regular budget posts and 3.5 per cent in other posts have had permanent appointments. As the following table demonstrates, the General Service and related category had the smallest number of permanent appointees, and the largest percentage went to Directors. It should be noted here, as we have mentioned already, USG and ASG are appointed for five years and their term, in principle, is coterminous with that of SG, though some from the previous administration have been retained by the new SG for the time being.

Table 7.7

Appointments by Types of Funding

Levels	*Posts*	*Permanent Appointments*	*Other Appointments*	*Total*
Directors	559*	27.7%	72.3%	100%
Professionals	9,209*	19.4%	81.6%	100%
General Service and Related	22,938**	7.2%	92.8%	100%

Note: * Excludes staff under the 200-series.

** Excludes staff in the field service, security, trades and crafts, language teachers, national officers, conference typists and information assistants.

Source: United Nations.

Appointments by Levels

As at 30 September 2008, General Service and related category staff (G1-G7) constituted the largest chunk (71.8 per cent) of the total staff strength. Of the remaining staff, 26.6 per cent were Professionals (P5-P1), 1.04 per cent were Directors (D2 and D1) and 0.3 per cent were senior managers. These data are shown in Figure 7.3.

Figure 7.3

Secretariat Staff by Category as on 30 June 2008

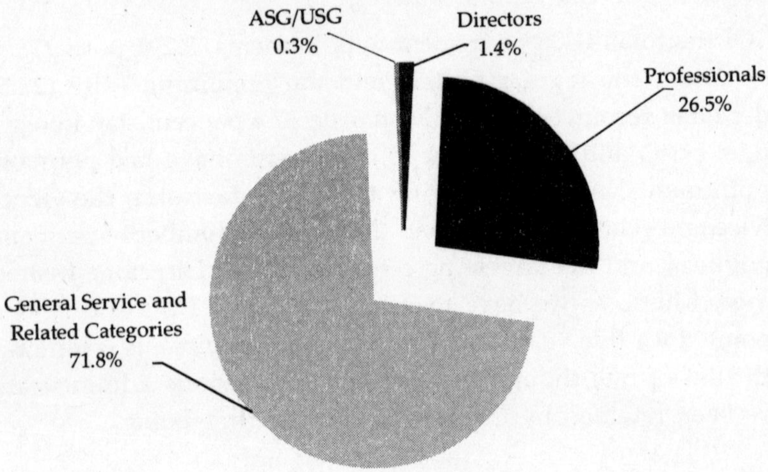

Courtesy: United Nations (2008). *Composition of the Secretariat.*

This structure militates against the conventional pyramid structure that has generally ruled the roost of staff distribution in hierarchical large organisations across the world. From that perspective, the staff distribution of the global body seems extremely haphazard to the naked eyes. If there was any profound logic to this type of staff distribution, it is far from apparent, and no one has tried to explain it with some degree of rationale so far. Figure 7.4 displays the numerical distribution of the posts in Professional and Higher Categories.

SG, DSG, USG and ASG constitute the senior managers of the UN. As already mentioned elsewhere in this book, the General

Assembly appoints the SG at the recommendation of the Security Council. In turn, SG appoints the DSG, USG and ASG for 5 years at a time, or in a manner that their term is coterminous with his own. In other words, there is no provision for their permanent appointment, like other staff members of the UN. These senior appointees are members of the SG's cabinet, if you will, who are in charge of a department or a major functional area. They, in theory, serve at the discretion of SG, as the secretaries of various departments in the United States do at the discretion of the US President.

Figure 7.4

Distribution of Staff in the Professional and Higher Categories by Level as on 30 June 2008

(Population: 9,892 of 39,503)[a]

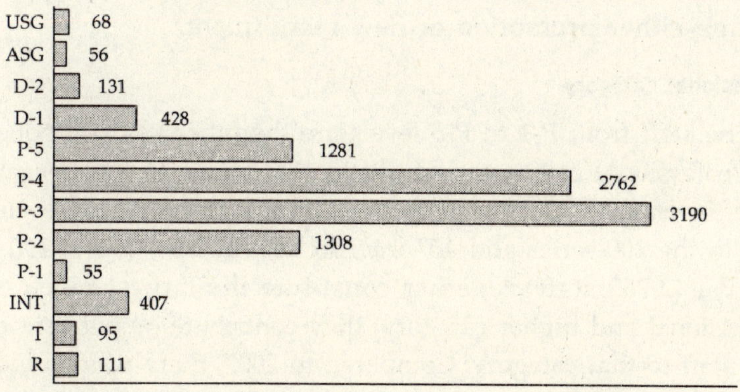

Note: a Excludes 1,250 staff appointed under the 200 series of the Staff Rules.

INT (interpreters), R (revisers) and T (translators) are staff on "when actually employed" contracts.

Courtesy: United Nations (2008). *Composition of the Secretariat.*

Senior Managers

Only one post of DSG has been established in the UN, and it is under the regular budget. There are also 124 USG, and ASG, a decline from 132 in 2007, besides SG and DSG, as on 30 September 2008.[14] USGs are heads of departments, chiefs of headquarters locations and leaders of most peacekeeping missions and political

14. United Nations (2008). *Composition of the Secretariat,* (New York).

missions; and under them would be several ASGs. ASGs are in charge of some of those missions as well. Likewise, UN funds and programmes—UNDP, UNICEF, WFP, etc.—are headed by a USG and have several ASG working for them. Some organisations like UNHCR are in theory temporary; they are also headed by USG and have several ASG under them.

Directors

Director level staff members—D1 and D2—are another important building block of the UN Secretariat architecture. They assist USG and ASG in managing the department or functions in different aspects and responsibilities. Each department or function has several of these senior professional staff. There were 509 Directors, 131 of them at the D-2 level and 428 at the D-1 level. In 2007, their number was to the tune of 549, out of whom 132 were at the D-2 level and 417 at D-1 level. These senior professionals could be appointed through either promotion or new recruitment.

Professional Category

The staff from P-1 to P-5 levels are the other key component of the Professional category and above. According to the *Composition of the Secretariat,*[15] there were 8,596 P level staff members, excluding 1250 in the 200-series and 407 interpreters. In 2008, P-3 (3,190 staff) and P-4 (2,762 staff) together constitute the largest block of the professional and higher category; they contribute 60 per cent of the total staff to that category. Compared to 2007, there was an increase of 436 staff in this category, excluding 1,139 staff appointed under the 200-series and 603 revisers, interpreters and translators. As mentioned elsewhere, the P-1 and P-2 level professionals are hired exclusively through competitive examination, and the P-3 professionals generally, not exclusively, through such examinations. Other posts could be filled through both—promotion and new intake.

General Service and Related Category

There were 22,938 General Service staff members on 30 September 2008. In other categories, additional 5,423 staff—4,076 in the Field

15. Ibid.

Service category, 787 national officers, 331 in the Security category, 175 in Trades and Crafts category, 36 language teachers, 10 public information assistants, and 8 conference typists—were engaged. All told, the total number of staff in this category stood at 28,361. In 2007, this number was 21,281 GS staff and 4,715 other staff, bringing the total to 25,996 staff. There was a remarkable decline in staff numbers in the tribunals as they have been striving to phase out and a significant hike in peacekeeping operations. The following chart presents the GS category staff (excluding the related categories):

Figure 7.5

Distribution of Staff in the General Service Category by Level as on 30 June 2008

(Population: 22,938 of 39,503)[a]

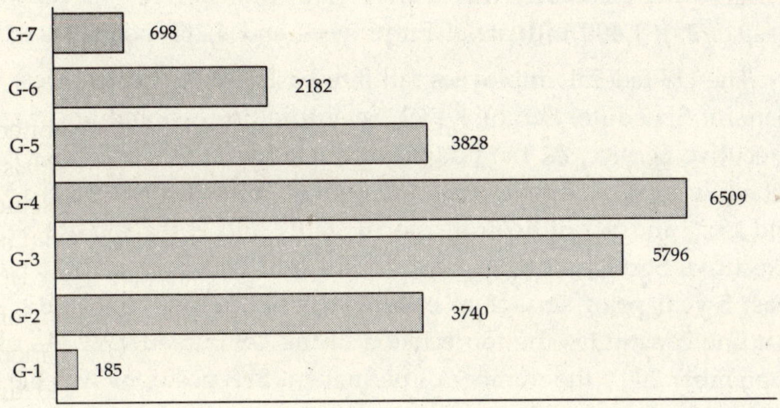

Note: a Excludes 5,423 staff (4,076 Field Service Category, 331 Security Category, 175 Trades and Crafts Category, 36 language teachers, 787 national officers, 8 conference typists and 10 public information assistants).

Courtesy: United Nations (2008). *Composition of the Secretariat.*

Other Types

Although not an integral part of the international civil service, several other categories of people also work under the roof of the United Nations. In 2007, over 2006 gratis personnel (1,952 type I and 54 type II), 4,275 consultants, 1,808 contractors and 94 institutional contractors worked for the world body. In addition, 176 locally recruited consultants and 2,260 locally recruited individual contractors were also engaged in the field missions. As the name itself suggests, the gratis personnel come free of cost to the United Nations. Almost 85 per cent of the type I gratis personnel in the above number were interns, and most of the rest came from member states on secondment. The United Nations hires consultants for special assignments and contractors for specific services.

Staff Distribution Elsewhere

Let us have a look at how the staff strength is distributed in some countries and organisations *vis-à-vis* the United Nations, for comparison. In the United Kingdom, 4,750 belonged to the Senior Management (Senior Civil Service); 249,130 to Other Management (Grades 6 and 7, Senior and Higher Executive Officers, and Executive Officers); 229,580 Administrative (Administrative Officers and Assistants); 1,400 Industrial Employees and 4,260 not reported.[16]

The US federal employees fall into basically four categories: The General Schedule, Senior Level, Scientific/Professional and Senior Executive Service. At the bottom of the ladder, there are 15 General Schedule grades. Above them are Senior Level (formerly GS-16, 17 and 18),[17] and Scientific/Professional staff;[18] and at the top are Senior Executive Service staff, at least 70 per cent of whom must have at least 5-year prior service to ensure experience and continuity. The last one constitutes the top echelon of the US bureaucracy. As of 30 September 2007, the number of permanent SES positions was 8,096.[19]

In the European Commission, there are two functional groups: administrators' group (AD) and assistants' group (AST). But these two groups are starkly different from the Professional and General service categories in the United Nations. AST start at Grade 1 and goes up to Grade 11 and covers executive, technical and clerical duties; and the AD starts at Grade 5 and goes up to Grade 16, Direct-

16. *http://www.statistics.gov.uk/downloads/theme_labour/Civil_service_tables_2007.xls*
17. *http://www.opm.gov/ses/recruitment/slpositions.asp*
18. *http://www.opm.gov/ses/recruitment/stpositions.asp*
19. *http://www.opm.gov/ses/recruitment/allocate.asp*

General, the highest level, and covers administrative, advisory, linguistic and scientific duties.[20] The previous B and C groups were integrated into AST effective 2004. Grades 9 to 14 are treated as middle management. Apart from permanent officials, there could be staff under temporary, contract and secondment appointments.[21]

Private firms are organised quite differently, though. Here is the example of the General Electric Company. At the top of the management pyramid sits Chairman and Chief Executive Officer, at the Corporate Executive Office, who plays pivotal role in shaping policies and implementing them and driving the organisation. To help him, there are scores of corporate executives and business executives. Then each firm under the GE umbrella has its own chief and senior management team. Under them are middle and junior level managers and support staff. The GE management comprises of people from such career paths as engineering, finance, human resources, information technology, marketing, operations, quality and sales.[22]

Observations

Compared to other contemporary organisations, the United Nations appears stuck in a time warp. Many of the features the world body has in place in its personnel management configuration today is the continuation of what it was around the time of its inception. In the meantime, many other international organisations, including the European Union, have been reviving themselves in response to needs of time. Indeed, reform has been slow in coming in the UN house for reasons we have already discussed at some length. What is more, in some areas, the United Nations is under pressure to accommodate reluctantly some of the powerful member states, and in others, it has also circumvented the wish and decision of member states. Fear of anything new is always there, and that has been benumbing the world organisation, more than anything else. We will discuss some of the key concerns below.

---

20. European Commission, *Staff Regulations (2004)*, Article 5, p. 1-5 and 1-6
21. *http://ec.europa.eu/civil_service/job/sne/index_en.htm*
22. *http://www.gecareers.com/GECAREERS/html/us/ourPeople/paths.html*

Post and Person

In the United Nations, post and person are taken to be almost synonymous. In national bureaucracies, persons and posts are treated separately, and persons tend to have no specific claim to their particular posts. Employees can be transferred from one department to other, from one duty station to another, and even one state to another in a federal state, as long as the level is commensurate. Therefore, the level becomes more important for them, rather than the post or place.

But in the United Nations, transfers across departments, agencies and duty stations are few and far between, and over time, the staff tend to develop a very strong sense of ownership in their posts and in their place of initial appointment, if it is perceived to be good. And this makes change extremely difficult, not only in terms of staff mobility but also in terms of adopting new business plans and improving working procedures.

Posts and Positions

Multiplicity of sources of funding has created a weird distinction between posts and positions in the United Nations. Those posts funded with regular budgets are called posts, and those funded with other sources are deemed positions. Clearly this is an unnecessary hairsplitting that irritates those people who are occupying positions, rather than posts. No effort has been made to remove this simple and debilitating anomaly. Although many member states do have the old, hackneyed system of drawing obvious lines among employees working together on the basis of their types of employment, many others have done away with such avoidable irritants to give a semblance of equal dignity to all categories of staff working at the same levels. The United Nations should try and become a leader in making the workplace more conducive, if not ideal.

What is more, the world body needs to look at the possibility of removing the distinction between the regular and peacekeeping staff under the support account. The support account has given the Secretariat flexibility to overcome its staff shortage. In that sense, it has been a useful tool. At the same time, support account positions funded with the peacekeeping budget from various missions have also given the Secretariat the room to pad its staff strength and the flexibility which can be used in unwarranted manners—such as disingenuously shifting the cost from one source to another to remain within the ceilings set by member states and evading scrutiny of expenditures where member states want to see deep cuts.

Upward Mobility

Unfortunately, no other bureaucracy could be as haphazard and chaotic as the United Nations is in terms of staff upward mobility. There is no real and predictable system of mobility through promotion and job enrichment, due mainly to three reasons: One, the distribution of posts is patently asymmetrical, to say the least, and yields very little room for a smooth system of career advancement. For instance, among G1-G7 posts/positions, G4 has the highest numbers; and the levels below and above it have fewer posts/positions. Similarly, in the Professional and higher category, P4 has the largest number of posts/positions, whereas those below and above it have fewer. As a result, the organisation has had battalions of stagnated, frustrated and under-performing staff. With the majority of staff in this state of affairs, it cannot succeed in achieving its principles and purposes. What aggravates the situation further is that there is no horizontal mobility either to give staff the chance to re-energise themselves in a new place and environment.

Two, there is no firmly established career path from lower category to higher. The United Nations has adopted a system of taking fresh recruits, on the basis of political influence and pressure, virtually at all levels in P4 and above. This provides for no reliable, let alone predictable, basis for promotion and career planning for the staff. Moreover, there is no solid set of bases—such as educational qualification, performance, publication, and so on—for promotion whenever it takes place, and it makes promotion dependent on the mercy of personal liking or disliking of managers, rather than on the performance of the staff. These two factors combined, the long-serving staff having no political backing from powerful states or influential managers find themselves mired in a swamp of stagnation and disappointment.

Three, except in the rare cases, no Professional staff could aspire to become USG and ASG; and the G to P ratio is so small that very few openings are available for General Service staff to get into the Professional category. When people join the United Nations staff, or the staff of any other organisation, most of them dream to rise to the senior most echelons some day. Very few do; many of them rot pretty much very close to where they had started, thanks to political patronage, a lack of direct link between promotion and performance and the absence of a systematic and credible route to the top.

Personnel of Other Types

Despite tremendous opposition from the majority of member states, the United Nations Secretariat has clung to the practice of hiring cronies of senior managers as consultants, taking staff from member states on secondment as gratis personnel other than interns, contracting out work that could be done in-house, and doing those many things in-house which could be done economically and better outside. Some of these practices contravene the spirit of the United Nations Charter and some create avoidable burden on the organisation. For example, gratis personnel—those who hold any position of responsibility, and most of them do—are not part of the international civil service, nor are they loyal to the United Nations. These people do enjoy the capacity to influence the work of the world body in a way that undermines the Charter principle of neutrality and loyalty to the United Nations.

While the majority of the staff work hard in the United Nations, a sizeable number of them insist on hiring consultants to do the job they are supposed to do. In many cases, expert consultants might be able to do a better job and would be needed for specific tasks. In such cases, the need for UN staff should have been lessened. In other cases, it is simply an unmistakable symptom of cronyism—to keep the retired colleagues engaged and reduce, if not shirk, the work of the incumbent staff. Some contractors also fit this description. While we see the need for occasional services of experts as consultants and contractors, the United Nations has used them quite liberally and without full justification for tasks that could be easily performed by the existing staff members, to patronise friends and cronies. Such abuse of resources must stop forthwith.

Sadly, no SG has shown the guts to take up these issues head on for the fear of being unpopular, despite the repeated urgings of member states. He ought to bear in mind that he is not there to win a popularity contest; he is there to lead the United Nations effectively through improved management and delivery.

Way Forward

The entrenched incrementalism is a bane that is responsible for the haphazard growth of the United Nations. Incrementalism promotes a piecemeal approach, and as a result, the world body sees a tree but misses the whole forest. The organisation must break out of this trap, have a comprehensive look at its organisation and staff structure to rearrange and streamline them, find ways to better link its HRM to organisational objectives, and strive to improve its efficiency and performance accordingly. Increasing a few hundred staff in response to a seemingly new demand is not the best answer. Let us not forget, the Thatcher government in the UK was able to bring about structural and cultural change in the British civil service and improve its performance by reducing the work force from 650,000 to 533,000 between 1983 and 1994[23], and turn around the moribund British society into a vibrant, confident and growing country.

What the United Nations needs is better HRM and improved staff performance within a much-simplified and streamlined system. Equally important is the imperative to strike a balance between the old and the new to keep the world body alive and effective not only for now but also far into the future. It is entirely possible to develop such a structure. For instance, the European Union has—though it too has many shortcomings—embraced a much simpler but more effective system, at least for the core staff, even if it is equally weak in injecting new blood. So have done many member states of the United Nations. This is time for the United Nations to bring strategic change in its HRM.

---

23. Blundell, B. and Murdock, Alex (1997). *Managing in the Public Sector,* (Butterworth-Heinemann, Oxford) p.47.

Annex A-7.1

Staff under Contract with the United Nations Secretariat by Location, Category and Series of the Staff Rules as on 31 December 2007

	Professional and Higher Categories				*General Service and Related Categories*			
	100	*200*	*300*	*Sub-total*	*100*	*300*	*Sub-total*	*Total*
Headquarters*								
-Contract for less than one year	461	13	371	845	200	349	549	1,394
-Contract for one year or more	3,789	526	305	4620	5,225	14	5,239	9,859
Sub-total	4,250	539	676	5,465	5,425	363	5,788	11,253
Regional commissions**								
-Contract for less than one year	54	10	62	126	108	60	168	294
-Contract for one year or more	672	107	84	863	1,463	0	1,463	2,326
Sub-total	726	117	146	989	1,571	60	1,631	2,620
Peacekeeping missions								
-Contract for less than one year	103	1	448	552	227	2,829	3,056	3,608
-Contract for one year or more	869	3	1,070	1,942	5,917	7,871	13,788	15,730
Sub-total	972	4	1,518	2,494	6,144	10,700	16,844	19,338
Other field locations***								
-Contract for less than one year	10	20	2	32	13	0	13	45
-Contract for one year or more	312	459	32	803	384	6	390	1,193
Sub-total	322	479	34	835	397	6	403	1,238

contd...

...contd...

	Professional and Higher Categories				*General Service and Related Categories*			
	100	*200*	*300*	*Sub-total*	*100*	*300*	*Sub-total*	*Total*
Tribunals****								
-Contract for less than one year	34	0	4	38	17	35	52	90
-Contract for one year or more	762	0	0	762	1,258	20	1,278	2,040
Sub-total	796	0	4	800	1,275	55	1,330	2,130
Total active staff	7,066	1,139	2,378	10,583	14,812	11,184	25,996	36,579
Other								
-Staff on special leave without pay	84	10	4	98	84	1	85	183
-Staff on secondment to other entities	52	2	0	54	1	0	1	55
Total other staff	136	12	4	152	85	1	86	238
Total staff under contract	7,202	1,151	2,382	10,735	14,897	11,185	26,082	36,817

Note: *Geneva, Nairobi, New York and Vienna.

**ECA, ECE, ECLAC, ESCAP and ESCWA.

***Other field locations: staff of DESA, DPA, DPI, OCHA, OHCHR, OIOS, UNCTAD, UNEP, UN-Habitat and UNDOC at non-headquarters duty stations.

****International Tribunal for the Former Yugoslavia and International Criminal Tribunal for Rwanda.

Annex A-7.2

Number of Staff by Organisation, Location and Project

Organisation	Headquarters				Other Established Offices				Project				Total		
	Prof	*GS*	*Total*	*% Total*	*Prof*	*GS*	*Total*	*% Total*	*Prof*	*GS*	*Total*	*% Total*	*Prof*	*GS*	*Total*
UN	4374	5215	9589	30	4123	17782	21905	70	0	0	0	0	8497	22997	31494
UNDP	568	296	864	16	1317	3170	4487	84	0	0	0	0	1885	3466	5351
UNFPA	193	121	314	24	298	689	987	76	0	0	0	0	491	810	1301
UNOPS	36	31	67	13	233	223	456	87	0	0	0	0	269	254	523
UNHCR	487	344	831	18	1066	2722	3788	82	0	0	0	0	1553	3066	4619
UNICEF	464	398	862	14	1129	3960	5089	86	0	0	0	0	1593	4358	5951
UNITAR	0	0	0	0	26	4	30	100	0	0	0	0	26	4	30
UNRWA	60	5	65	39	90	9	99	59	3	0	3	2	153	14	167
ITC	131	110	241	99	2	1	3	1	0	0	0	0	133	111	244
ICSC	0	0	0	0	20	19	39	100	0	0	0	0	20	19	39
ICJ	43	53	96	100	0	0	0	0	0	0	0	0	43	53	96
UNJSPF	0	0	0	0	59	108	167	100	0	0	0	0	59	108	167
UNU	21	18	39	39	34	26	60	59	2	0	2	2	57	44	101
ILO	464	503	967	42	204	442	646	28	252	454	706	30	920	1399	2319
ITCILO	73	111	184	98	0	1	1	1	2	0	2	1	75	112	187
FAO	1000	1013	2013	60	271	699	970	29	170	184	354	11	1441	1896	3337
WFP	491	352	843	22	842	2232	3074	78	0	0	0	0	1333	2584	3917
UNESCO	666	716	1382	64	328	445	773	36	0	0	0	0	994	1161	2155
WHO	985	784	1769	33	797	1799	2596	48	462	606	1068	20	2244	3189	5433

contd...

...contd...

Organisation	Headquarters				Other Established Offices				Project				Total		
	Prof	*GS*	*Total*	*% Total*	*Prof*	*GS*	*Total*	*% Total*	*Prof*	*GS*	*Total*	*% Total*	*Prof*	*GS*	*Total*
PAHO	205	212	417	54	155	124	279	36	39	33	72	9	399	369	768
UNAIDS	99	79	178	50	0	0	0	0	174	1	175	50	273	80	353
ICAO	234	331	565	79	71	80	151	21	0	0	0	0	305	411	716
UPU	89	88	177	100	0	0	0	0	0	0	0	0	89	88	177
ITU	312	489	801	97	21	0	21	3	5	0	5	1	338	489	827
WMO	133	143	276	95	6	6	12	4	0	4	4	1	139	153	292
IMO	147	148	295	92	0	0	0	0	9	16	25	8	156	164	320
WIPO	441	488	929	99	7	1	8	1	0	0	0	0	448	489	937
IFAD	255	249	504	98	7	1	8	2	0	0	0	0	262	250	512
UNIDO	200	309	509	76	37	52	89	13	42	26	68	10	279	387	666
IAEA	998	1104	2102	96	48	32	80	4	0	0	0	0	1046	1136	2182
UNWTO	42	59	101	100	0	0	0	0	0	0	0	0	42	59	101
Total	13211	13769	26980	36	11191	34627	45818	61	1160	1324	2484	3	25562	49720	75282

Note: 1. Attached are the annual statistical tables on the staff of the organisations in the United Nations common system with appointments for a period of one year or more as on 31 December 2007.

2. The tables exclude information on National Professional Officers.

Source: United Nations (2007). *2007 CEB Personnel Statistics* as on 31 December.

Annex A-7.3

Number of Staff by Category and Source of Funds as at 31 December 2007

Organisation	Regular Budget				All Other Funds				Total		
	Prof	GS	Total	% Total	Prof	GS	Total	% Total	Prof	GS	Total
UN	3071	3989	7060	22	5426	19008	24434	78	8497	22997	31494
UNDP	0	0	0	0	1885	3466	5351	100	1885	3455	6861
UNFPA	0	0	0	0	491	810	1301	100	491	810	1301
UNOPS	0	0	0	0	269	254	523	100	269	254	523
UNHCR	79	101	180	4	1474	2965	4439	96	1553	3066	4818
UNICEF	0	0	0	0	1593	4358	5951	100	1593	4358	6861
UNITAR	0	0	0	0	26	4	30	100	26	4	80
UNRWA	105	11	116	69	48	3	51	31	153	14	187
ITC	72	85	157	64	61	26	87	36	133	111	244
IC&C	0	0	0	0	20	19	39	100	20	19	38
ICJ	43	53	96	100	0	0	0	0	43	53	98
UNJ&PF	0	0	0	0	59	108	167	100	59	108	187
UNU	57	44	101	100	0	0	0	0	57	44	101
ILO	659	934	1593	69	261	465	726	31	920	1399	2818
ITCILO	56	91	147	79	19	21	40	21	75	112	187
FAO	978	1506	2484	74	463	390	853	26	1441	1896	3887
WFP	632	326	958	24	701	2258	2959	76	1333	2584	3817
UNESCO	785	887	1672	78	209	274	483	22	994	1161	2166

contd...

...contd...

Organisation	Regular Budget				All Other Funds				Total		
	Prof	*GS*	*Total*	*% Total*	*Prof*	*GS*	*Total*	*% Total*	*Prof*	*GS*	*Total*
WHO	985	1970	2955	54	1259	1219	2478	46	2244	3189	5488
PAHO	315	314	629	82	84	55	139	18	399	359	788
UNAIDS	0	0	0	0	273	80	353	100	273	80	868
ICAO	245	319	564	79	60	92	152	21	305	411	718
UPU	62	72	134	76	27	16	43	24	89	88	177
ITU	333	489	822	99	5	0	5	1	338	489	827
WMO	120	135	255	87	19	18	37	13	139	153	282
IMO	130	112	242	76	26	52	78	24	166	164	320
WIPO	442	489	931	99	6	0	6	1	448	489	887
IFAD	229	237	466	91	33	13	46	9	262	250	612
UNIDO	235	356	591	89	44	31	75	11	279	387	888
IAEA	950	1042	1992	91	96	94	190	9	1046	1136	2182
UNWTO	42	58	100	99	0	1	1	1	42	59	101
Total	10625	13620	24245	32	14937	36100	51037	60	26602	49720	75282

Source: United Nations.

Annex A-7.4

Number of Male by Category and Organisation Location as on 31 December 2007

Organisation	Headquarters				Other Established Offices				Project				Total		
	Prof	GS	Total	% Total	Prof	GS	Total	% Total	Prof	GS	Total	% Total	Prof	GS	Total
UN	2471	2239	4710	23	2873	13212	16085	77	0	0	0	0	5344	15451	20795
UNDP	275	63	338	13	879	1381	2260	87	0	0	0	0	1154	1444	2598
UNFPA	78	23	101	17	157	329	486	83	0	0	0	0	235	352	587
UNOPS	22	13	35	12	171	91	262	88	0	0	0	0	193	104	297
UNHCR	267	89	356	12	676	1821	2497	88	0	0	0	0	943	1910	2853
UNICEF	204	136	340	11	615	2251	2866	89	0	0	0	0	819	2387	3206
UNITAR	0	0	0	0	13	0	13	100	0	0	0	0	13	0	13
UNRWA	34	2	36	34	63	6	69	64	2	0	2	2	99	8	107
ITC	84	20	104	98	2	0	2	2	0	0	0	0	86	20	106
ICSC	0	0	0	0	13	6	19	100	0	0	0	0	13	6	19
ICJ	22	18	40	100	0	0	0	0	0	0	0	0	22	18	40
UNJSPF	0	0	0	0	37	41	78	100	0	0	0	0	37	41	78
UNU	19	6	25	40	27	8	35	56	2	0	2	3	48	14	62
ILO	268	155	423	40	126	167	293	27	143	208	351	33	537	530	1067
ITCILO	46	17	63	98	0	0	0	0	1	0	1	2	47	17	64
FAO	655	291	946	55	225	289	514	30	149	108	257	15	1029	688	1717
WFP	265	83	348	15	532	1508	2040	85	0	0	0	0	797	1591	2388
UNESCO	325	249	574	62	201	158	359	38	0	0	0	0	526	407	933
WHO	556	217	773	28	489	895	1384	51	332	233	565	21	1377	1345	2722

contd...

...contd...

Organisation	Headquarters				Other Established Offices				Project				Total		
	Prof	GS	Total	% Total	Prof	GS	Total	% Total	Prof	GS	Total	% Total	Prof	GS	Total
PAHO	109	44	153	48	104	17	121	38	28	14	42	13	241	75	316
UNAIDS	45	12	57	36	0	0	0	0	103	0	103	64	148	12	160
ICAO	154	65	219	73	59	20	79	27	0	0	0	0	213	85	298
UPU	71	35	106	100	0	0	0	0	0	0	0	0	71	35	106
ITU	202	144	346	94	16	0	16	4	5	0	5	1	223	144	367
WMO	94	37	131	94	6	2	8	6	0	1	1	1	100	40	140
IMO	87	57	144	92	0	0	0	0	7	5	12	8	94	62	156
WIPO	250	175	425	99	5	0	5	1	0	0	0	0	255	175	430
IFAD	141	46	187	98	3	0	3	2	0	0	0	0	144	46	190
UNIDO	147	126	273	73	29	25	54	15	33	12	45	12	209	163	372
IAEA	774	432	1206	96	42	13	55	4	0	0	0	0	816	445	1261
UNWTO	25	20	45	100	0	0	0	0	0	0	0	0	25	20	45
Total	7690	4814	12504	29	7363	22240	29603	68	805	581	1386	3	15858	27635	43493

Source: United Nations.

Annex A-7.5

Number of Female by Category and Organisation Location as on 31 December 2007

Organisation	Headquarters				Other Established Offices				Project				Total		
	Prof	GS	Total	% Total	Prof	GS	Total	% Total	Prof	GS	Total	% Total	Prof	GS	Total
UN	1903	2976	4879	46	1250	4570	5820	54	0	0	0	0	3153	7546	10699
UNDP	293	233	526	19	438	1789	2227	81	0	0	0	0	731	2022	2753
UNFPA	115	98	213	30	141	360	501	70	0	0	0	0	256	458	714
UNOPS	14	18	32	14	62	132	194	86	0	0	0	0	76	150	226
UNHCR	220	255	475	27	390	901	1291	73	0	0	0	0	610	1156	1766
UNICEF	260	262	522	19	514	1709	2223	81	0	0	0	0	774	1971	2745
UNITAR	0	0	0	0	13	4	17	100	0	0	0	0	13	4	17
UNRWA	26	3	29	48	27	3	30	50	1	0	1	2	54	6	60
ITC	47	90	137	99	0	1	1	1	0	0	0	0	47	91	138
ICSC	0	0	0	0	7	13	20	100	0	0	0	0	7	13	20
ICJ	21	35	56	100	0	0	0	0	0	0	0	0	21	35	56
UNJSPF	0	0	0	0	22	67	89	100	0	0	0	0	22	67	89
UNU	2	12	14	36	7	18	25	64	0	0	0	0	9	30	39
ILO	196	348	544	43	78	275	353	28	109	246	355	28	383	869	1252
ITCILO	27	94	121	98	0	1	1	1	1	0	1	1	28	95	123
FAO	345	722	1067	66	46	410	456	28	21	76	97	6	412	1208	1620
WFP	226	269	495	32	310	724	1034	68	0	0	0	0	536	993	1529
UNESCO	341	467	808	66	127	287	414	34	0	0	0	0	468	754	1222
WHO	429	567	996	37	308	904	1212	45	130	373	503	19	867	1844	2711

contd...

...contd...

Organisation	Headquarters				Other Established Offices				Project				Total		
	Prof	GS	Total	% Total	Prof	GS	Total	% Total	Prof	GS	Total	% Total	Prof	GS	Total
PAHO	96	168	264	58	51	107	158	35	11	19	30	7	158	294	452
UNAIDS	54	67	121	63	0	0	0	0	71	1	72	37	125	66	191
ICAO	80	266	346	83	12	60	72	17	0	0	0	0	92	326	418
UPU	18	53	71	100	0	0	0	0	0	0	0	0	18	53	71
ITU	110	345	455	99	5	0	5	1	0	0	0	0	115	345	460
WMO	39	106	145	95	0	4	4	3	0	3	3	2	39	113	152
IMO	60	91	151	92	0	0	0	0	2	11	13	8	62	102	164
WIPO	191	313	504	99	2	1	3	1	0	0	0	0	193	314	507
IFAD	114	203	317	98	4	1	5	2	0	0	0	0	118	204	322
UNIDO	53	183	236	80	8	27	35	12	9	14	23	8	70	224	294
IAEA	224	672	896	97	6	19	25	3	0	0	0	0	230	691	921
UNWTO	17	39	56	100	0	0	0	0	0	0	0	0	17	39	56
Total	5521	8955	14476	46	3828	12387	16215	51	355	743	1098	3	9704	22083	31787

Source: United Nations.

Annex A-7.6

Number of National Professional Officers by Organisation Location as on 31 December 2007

Organisation	*Headquarters*	*Other Established Offices*	*Project*	*Total*
UN	0	505	0	505
UNDP	0	1112	0	1112
UNFPA	0	337	0	337
UNOPS	0	94	0	94
UNHCR	0	271	0	271
UNICEF	0	2250	0	2250
UNU	0	8	0	8
ILO	0	99	209	308
FAO	0	112	7	119
WFP	0	438	0	438
UNESCO	0	84	0	84
WHO	0	133	271	404
PAHO	0	32	3	35
UNAIDS	0	0	57	57
WMO	0	3	1	4
IMO	0	0	7	7
UNIDO	0	16	17	33
Total	0	5494	572	6066

Source: United Nations.

Annex A-7.7

Number of National Professional Officers by Source of Funds as on 31 December 2007

Organisation	*Regular Budget*	*Other Sources*	*Total*
UN	1	504	505
UNDP	0	1112	1112
UNFPA	0	337	337
UNOPS	0	94	94
UNHCR	1	270	271
UNICEF	0	2250	2250
UNU	8	0	8
ILO	97	211	308
FAO	108	11	119
WFP	0	438	438
UNESCO	53	31	84
WHO	268	136	404
PAHO	28	7	35
UNAIDS	0	57	57
WMO	3	1	4
IMO	0	7	7
UNIDO	16	17	33
Total	583	5483	6066

Source: United Nations.

8

Position Classification, Transfer, Performance Appraisal, and Promotion

Introduction

Right man at the right place, competition, good performance, and fair pay are strategic elements that contribute to the success of organised entities and progress of employees working for them. To promote these values, position classification, transfer, performance appraisal and promotion are vital and so is a link between performance and pay. These factors are integral and interrelated parts of human resources management in all modern organisations.

Position classification is essential to place the right employee at the right place and ensure equal pay for equal qualification and work. Transfer, or mobility, of staff is critical to put the best staff at the best place, to keep them motivated and to help them acquire different skills needed to assume positions of leadership in the future. Performance appraisal constitutes the lynchpin for decisions related to transfer and promotion. And promotion is one of the key ways to reward good performance, to keep the staff motivated, to meet the need for self-realisation, and to groom managers and leaders.

Position Classification

Position classification and job classification are used interchangeably. According to the United Nations' International Civil Service Commission (ICSC), job classification is "a system in which jobs are given a grade level according to their relative worth to the organisation, arrived at on the basis of a predetermined standard."[1]

Position classification is not only an organisational necessity but also a functional imperative. A properly devised classification works as a control mechanism and as a tool for human resources planning. It also assists management in developing an administrative hierarchy and in making a proper division of work among various levels in terms of their relative importance and skills requirements. Another strategic use of the classification is to help institutionalise pay and conditions of service and entitlements based upon objective criteria so as to prevent arbitrary standards.

Hence, position classification is critical to carry out orderly human resources management in a large organisation with many employees. Every individual that joins an organisation is different. Rarely any two persons could be identical—let alone hundreds and thousands of people that work for a large organisation—in their qualification and experience, in their capacity to learn and perform, in their ability to work in teams and lead, in their competence to innovate and invent, and in their aptitude and orientation. Everyone, even within the same occupational group brings in different qualifications, competencies, attitude and orientation. Ensuring that every one of the employees doing the same level and nature of work are treated as equally, fairly and justly as possible is far from easy and smooth. When you have hundreds of occupational groups—all governments and some big organisations have had a large number of such groups—the task of ascertaining equal pay for equal work becomes infinitely tangled.

Governments and large organisations, including the United Nations, have tried to address this issue through a system of position classification. The system began in earnest in the early part of the 20th century with Frederick F. Taylor, the father of scientific management, who believed that work could be divided in small tasks, and there was a best way for workers to do each task.[2] This

1. *http://icsc.un.org/resources/FAQ/default.htm*

2. Taylor, Frederick W. (1919). *The Principles of Scientific Management.* New York: Harper and Brothers Publishers.

system caught up with governments when the US Congress adopted the Classification Act of 1923 for the US federal government.

Steps in Classification

Job description, analysis, evaluation and classification are sequential and interlinked steps of position classification. Actually, job description is the fodder to job analysis; without a thorough job analysis, job evaluation would be impossible; and no job classification is possible without job evaluation. The following figure presents this interface graphically:

Figure 8.1

Job Description, Analysis, Evaluation and Classification

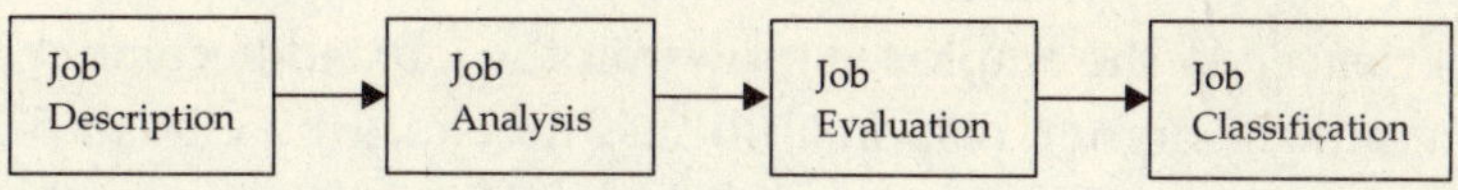

In other words, position classification has four steps: Checking job description, analysing it, evaluating it and assigning the job to a proper level and grade. Job description includes, among other things, job profile, job environment and job requirements. It encompasses the job title, responsibilities of the job in question, supervisory interface with other employees and qualification and skills required for the job. The next step, job analysis, has to do with the listing of tasks to be performed, determining how frequently each task is done, assessing the relative importance of each task and estimating the difficulty in doing them. Job evaluation entails comparing the job in question with all other jobs in the organisation in terms of its contribution to the employer and its level of difficulty *vis-à-vis* other jobs, and figuring out qualification and other elements relative to other positions. In other words, job evaluation is:

> the analysis of the component parts of a job; the comparison with other jobs in similar disciplines; discussion with experts in the occupational field, the job holder and the supervisor, to name a few of the methods used... Finally, from this information, the job analyst applies specialized training to focus on the significant elements that are to be taken into account in the job evaluation process.[3]

3. Ibid.

Systems

There are two systems of position classification: Rank-in-job and rank-in-person. In the rank-in-job, the post is classified at a certain level and grade of job, and irrespective of qualification and experience, the employee who occupies that post or position and draws the salary and benefits associated with it. This system gives not much flexibility to managers to place or pay the staff based on their merit and contribution to organisational objectives. If the employee has more qualification and can contribute to the organisation more, the position itself has to be upgraded or the employee has to be promoted to a higher position if it is vacant. On the other hand, the rank-in-person determines the level and grade of man in the hierarchy, based on qualification and experience. As the employee grows on the job and becomes capable of handling higher responsibilities, he could be elevated in his position or pay. The employee can take his position upward along with his growth. This system offers considerably more flexibility to managers.

Position classification ensures fairly reasonable equality of work and pay in a large organisation or in government, even though perfect equality might be an ideal difficult to achieve. Therefore, it is essential. At the same time, such classification also limits the flexibility, of managers, which they may wish to exercise when the employee can take higher responsibility and contribute more to the organisation or vice versa.

Basis for Position Classification in UN

Article 13 of ICSC's Statute and Rules of Procedure has mandated the Commission to "establish job classification standards for all categories of staff in fields of work common to several of the organisations. It shall advise the organisations on the development of consistent job classification plans in other fields of work."[4]

Regulation 2.1 of the UN Staff Regulations provides for the classification of posts and staff. It says, "In conformity with principles

4. United Nations (1987). ICSC, *Statute and Rules of Procedure*. New York, p.5.

laid down by the General Assembly, the Secretary-General shall make appropriate provision for the classification of posts and staff according to the nature of the duties and responsibilities required."[5] The principal objectives of job classification in the United Nations are two-fold: To ensure equal pay for equal work and to link the salaries paid to the service provided. Evidently, the United Nations has opted for the rank-in-job approach to classification rather than the rank-in-person approach. Ranking, grade description and point factor rating constitute the key elements of job evaluation.[6]

Under the existing provisions, requests for classification or reclassification should be submitted to the Assistant Secretary-General (ASG), OHRM, at headquarters or the head of office, if the authority has been delegated to him in the field service category. And in case of the GS category in headquarters locations outside New York and at regional commissions, such requests should go to the chiefs of their human resources offices. Two analysts, independently of each other, carry out classification analysis before a job classification is approved.[7]

The United Nations has—as we have discussed in the previous chapters—two broad categories of staff: Professional and higher and General Service and others. The ICSC has, in its 12th session in 1980, defined professional work in the United Nations as follows:

> Professional work is analytical, evaluative, conceptual, interpretive and/or creative and thus requires the application of the basic principles of an organized body of theoretical knowledge, such as a field of science, learning or specialized discipline. It is intricate and involves a level of difficulty and complexity requiring the identification and consideration not only of the interrelationships between its constituent elements, which are of a varied and diverse nature, but also the broader context and perspective within which it is performed, including its impact on, and interrelationship with, the larger objectives and programmes of the Organization. It requires judgment in analysing and evaluating problems and in decision-making involving discretionary choices between alternative courses of action.

---

5. United Nations Staff Rules (2002). ST/SGB/2002/1 of 1 January, p.11.
6. *http://www.un.org/Depts/OHRM/salaries_allowances/classif.htm*
7. *http://www.un.org/Depts/OHRM/salaries_allowances/classification/classifs.htm*

> Professional work requires the understanding of an organized body of theoretical knowledge which is of a level equivalent to that represented by a university degree. While this knowledge is customarily and characteristically acquired through formal education, it may, in some fields of learning or specialized disciplines, be acquired through other training, self-study, or practical experience.[8]

By a subsequent decision, the Commission also defined the GS work:

> General Service work is procedural, operational or technical in nature and supports the execution of the programmes of the organization. It ranges from simple, routine or repetitive duties based on following detailed instructions to varied and complex assignments requiring identification and consideration of alternative course of action based on extensive and in-depth practical knowledge of a specific subject area. The assignments are generally performed on a continuing basis. The knowledge of the subject field and higher-level skills are generally developed through long experience and familiarity with applicable procedures, regulations and precedents or projects of the Organization in a narrow technical field or in an administrative support activity.[9]

The Commission in its 10th session in August 1979 first approved a Common Classification of Occupational Groups (CCOG) applicable largely across the UN system.[10] It included four levels of categorisation: (a) the occupational groups such as professional, managerial, technical and related workers; (b) the occupation family such as architects, engineers, etc.; (c) the fields of work such as civil engineers; and (d) the occupation or specialty such as sanitary engineers.[11] Unlike the OPM's method, which is discussed a little later, ICSC has, for the classification of Professional posts, three tiers of standards and six factors and point-factor rating system for the Master standards.[12]

---

8. United Nations, *ICSC Compendium*, Section 1.8.10, p.1.
9. Ibid: 2.
10. *Note:* ICSC works not only for the United Nations *per se*, it also works with the specialised agencies of the United Nations. The classification thus applies to all those participating in the common system.
11. United Nations, *ICSC Compendium*, *op. cit.*, Section 1.8.20, p.2.
12. Taken from: *http://www.opm.gov/compconf/postconf00/universl/salmons1.pdf;* also see for details: *http://icsc.un.org/resources/pdfs/ppd/benchmark/hrm.pdf#search=|vacancies|*

ICSC Classification Standards for Professional Posts

Tier I	Master Standard: Point-factor evaluation system: Applies to all jobs in all organisations of the common system
Tier II	Occupational standards: Typical duties depicted at each grade level and accompanied by a narrative explanation of the ratings of the Master Standard to each grade
Tier III	Benchmark job descriptions Descriptions of actual jobs within an organisation which are identical to those profiled in the Tier H standards

Weight Assigned to Factors in Master Standard

Factors	*Weighting*	
Supervisory Responsibility	**300**	Measures management responsibility of the job in terms of the numbers of staff supervised.
—Responsibility for support	150	
—Responsibility for professional staff	150	
Difficulty of Work	**800**	Measures the mental demands of the job in terms of the number of the complexity of the work and degree of individual contribution required.
—Individual contribution	500	
—Complexity of assigned work	300	
Work Relationships	**850**	Measures the skill required in work relationships and the importance of contacts to the organisations' programmes.
—Skill of contacts inside the organisation	225	
—Skill of contacts outside the organisation	100	
—Importance of contacts inside the organisation	225	
—Importance of contacts outside the organisation	300	
Impact of Work	**600**	Measures importance of decisions and proposals on the organisation's objectives and the consequences of errors on such objectives.
—Effect on work	400	
—Consequences of errors	200	
Independence of Work	**700**	Measures the degree to which guidelines apply to the work and the amount of supervisory assistance and control given.
—Application of Guidelines	300	
—Supervisory control over incumbent	400	
Professional Knowledge Required	**700**	Measures the theoretical knowledge and practical experience required by the job.
—Theoretical knowledge required	300	
—Practical experience required	300	
—Language knowledge required	100	

Tier I: Master Standard (Point-factor rating system)

Point Range	*Grade Level*
800-969	P-1
970-1319	P-2
1320-1669	P-3
1670-2039	P-4
2040-2479	P-5
2480-2939	D-1
2940-3339	D-2
3340-3679	ASG
3680-3799	USG

Application of Classification

The Committee of Experts, appointed by SG, had for the first time proposed the classification for the United Nations. The General Assembly modified and adopted that classification in January 1951, which continues till today with certain adjustments. The classification scheme is as follows:[13]

a) Director category, with 2 levels:
   - Director (D-2) with 6 steps;
   - Principal Officer (D-1) with 9 steps.

b) Professional category, with 5 levels:
   - Senior Officer (P-5) with 13 steps;
   - First Officer (P-4) with 15 steps;
   - Second Officer (P-3) with 15 steps;
   - Associate Officer (P-2) with 12 steps;
   - Assistant Officer (P-1) with 10 steps.

c) General Service category, with 5 levels:
   - Principal Level with 7 steps;
   - Senior level with 8 steps;
   - Intermediate level with 9 steps;
   - Junior level with 9 steps;
   - Messenger level with 9 steps.

13. United Nations (1951). *Report of the Committee of Experts*, January.

It was the conviction of the Committee that a sound and properly administered classification and salary system should have the following objectives:

a) Equality of treatment throughout the Secretariat in terms of posts and individuals.
b) Reasonable opportunities for promotion.
c) A maximum degree of security and career prospects.
d) Flexibility in the use of staff and their assignment: and
e) Simple and economical personnel and salary administration, which does not impair effective budgetary control.

Bearing these objectives in mind, the Committee proposed that all classified posts be grouped under four categories whose basic duties would be as follows:

- The Director and Principal Officer category comprising policy making and administrative posts.
- The Substantive Service category comprising of professional personnel, general administrative, information, legal, economists, language, library, and other relevant occupational groups.
- The Special Service category—comprising such groups of special administrative and executive personnel such as accounting, procurement, printing, presentation, and other posts involving primarily 'service functions', although requiring certain recognised certification and standards with three levels.
- The General Service category comprising the clerical and secretarial staff, messengers, telephone operators, security guards, machine operators, and other groups of personnel whose posts involve essentially clerical and routine administrative duties with five levels.

The 1956 Salary Review Committee approved this service structure. The 1971 Salary Review Committee mentioned that the distinction between the categories related to:

- The nature of the posts they contain;
- The manner in which the posts are filled (international as against largely local or regional recruitment); and

- The method of determining the conditions of service for the staff so recruited.

The Committee examined the following possible modifications:

- Re-establishing a single grading structure,
- Reverting to the idea of a special category,
- Dividing the present professional category into two groups distinguished on the basis of liability of transfer,
- Creating a separate language service category.

The Administrative Committee on Coordination, which later became the Chief Executives Board for Coordination, a club of chief executives of UN system organisations, examined the above modifications and considered that the professional or international category should continue to provide posts:

- Having functions concerned with the substantive programme and managerial activities of the organisations, general administration and language services;
- For the performance of which a university or professional background, or equivalent experience was required;
- For which recruitment should, by the nature of the organisations, be on a global basis with appropriate geographical distribution.

The International Civil Service Commission examined and agreed to these provisions.[14]

Currently, there are, two principal categories of staff in the United Nations and 17 levels, if the post of Deputy Secretary-General is treated as a separate level and if trade and craft staff are excluded. P1-P5, D1, D2, ASG, USG, DSG and SG constitute the Professional and higher categories. The General Service and related categories consist of G1-G7 levels. The posts in the Trades and Crafts categories are separate from them.

In the existing classification scheme, as we have previously mentioned in this book, any post starting with 1 belongs to the

14. United Nations (1951). *Report of Committee of Experts*. January.

Professional and higher categories and with 2 to the General Service category. Capital letters—A, B, C, etc.—are used for specialist occupations; 01, 02, 03 to specialist groups; and small letters—a, b, c. etc.—to subgroups. For instance, if you come across a post identified as 1.A.02.a, it would mean the post belongs to the Professional category, to the Administrative specialist occupation, to the Management and programme specialists group and to the Management and organisational subgroup. Other posts are also identified accordingly.[15]

While ICSC has recognised the need to reclassify posts based on the change in the nature and responsibility of work, it discourages reclassification for personal promotion of the incumbent staff, though he or she may apply on a competitive basis to the position when it is reclassified due to job enrichment—extension in depth or breadth or rise in the level of responsibilities.

SG or his designated official can propose to classify or reclassify posts, as the need arises. In case posts are proposed in the budget, they come with the approval of the budget from the policy making—intergovernmental—entities of the world body. Generally, these entities defer to SG with respect to GS posts and P level posts. But in D1 and above, these entities—the ACABQ, Fifth Committee and GA plenary—take active interest and debate before they approve or disapprove of a proposed classification or reclassification.

US Government

No discussion on job classification will be complete without looking at how the United States federal government does it. In fact, the USA was the first country to adopt an elaborate and comprehensive system of job classification in the public sector. The United Nations relies on the US system, as we have already mentioned, as the residual source of information and complementarity and as the chief comparator country. The US system also helps the reader to understand clearly what classification is and how it works.

Under chapter 51, title 5 of the Classification Act of 1949, the US federal government has had 23 broad white collar occupational

15. See for further details at: *http://icsc.un.org/resources/pdfs/ppd/ccog/ccogiv-1.a.pdf#search=|vacancies|*

groups and 34 trades, crafts and labour groups, both groups with their constituent components. The Act establishes equal pay for equal work; provides definition of each grade in the General Schedule (GS1-15); and directs the Office of Personnel Management to prepare standards to place positions in their proper levels and grades; as well as states that OPM should define classes of various positions in terms of duties, responsibilities and qualification requirements and establish official class titles.[16]

OPM has identified 9 primary factors to ascertain equality across a broad spectrum of positions in the US federal government. These factors are widely used by other governments and international organisations. A job analyst assigns points to each factor and determines as to what level the position belongs, based on the total points. Such standards and established guidelines help the job analyst to ensure that job evaluation and assignment of a position to a level and grade is consistent across the board.

In the General Schedule, OPM has laid out the primary elements to be considered for placing positions in various grades. They are first converted into points, and then the point ranges determine the grades and commensurate salary and other perquisites. The primary elements for factor evaluation are presented in Box 8.1.

The classifier assigns points to every element to ascertain factor evaluation, depending on the level of understanding and expertise required to do the job in question. Take knowledge, or factor 1, for instance. It has 9 levels. If a position requires simple, routine or repetitive tasks requiring step-by-step instructions (level 1) but no prior training or experience, it would be assigned 50 points. The knowledge of basic or commonly used rules, procedures or operations that typically require some previous training or experience (level 2) commands 200 points, and so on. At the top, the mastery of the professional field to generate and develop new hypotheses or theories (level 9) secures 1850 points. Factor 2 has 5 levels and carries 25-650 points depending on the level. Other factors also have different levels and commensurate values for each level of skills required. The following table demonstrates the distribution of points for each factor:

16. OPM (1995). *Introduction to the Position Classification Standards*, TS-134. Washington DC. July. p.2.

Box 8.1

Primary Elements of the Factor Evaluation System[17]

Factor 1 - Knowledge Required by the Position

- Kind or nature of knowledge and skills needed.
- How the knowledge and skills are used in doing the work.

Factor 2 - Supervisory Controls

- How the work is assigned.
- Employee's responsibility for carrying out the work.
- How the work is reviewed.

Factor 3 - Guidelines

- Nature of guidelines for performing the work.
- Judgment needed to apply the guidelines or develop new guides.

Factor 4 - Complexity

- Nature of the assignment.
- Difficulty in identifying what needs to be done.
- Difficulty and originality involved in performing the work.

Factor 5 - Scope and Effect

- Purpose of the work.
- Impact of the work product or service.

Factor 6 - Personal Contacts

- People and conditions/settings under which contacts are made.

Factor 7 - Purpose of Contacts

- Reasons for contacts in Factor 6.

Note: In some FES standards the point values for factors 6 and 7 are combined into a matrix chart. The levels of each factor are described separately.

Factor 8 - Physical Demands

- Nature, frequency and intensity of physical activity.

Factor 9 - Work Environment

- Risks and discomforts caused by physical surroundings and the safety precautions necessary to avoid accidents or discomfort.

17. Ibid: 42.

Table 8.1

Distribution of Points for Factors and Levels[18]

Factor	*Levels in Each Factor*	*Points Lowest-Highest*
1 Knowledge Required by the Position	9	50-1850
2 Supervisory Controls	5	25-650
3 Guidelines	5	25-650
4 Complexity	6	25-450
5 Scope and Effect	6	25-450
6 Personal Contacts	4	10-110
7 Purpose of Contacts	4	20-220
8 Physical Demands	3	5-50
9 Work Environment	3	5-50

Once all elements have been rated and totaled, this gives the point range and determines the GS grades, as follows:

Table 8.2

Grade Conversion Table

GS Grade	*Point Range*
1	190-250
2	255-450
3	455-650
4	655-850
5	85-1100
6	1105-1350
7	1355-1600
8	1605-1850
9	1855-2100
10	2105-2350
11	2355-2750
12	2755-3150
13	3155-3600
14	3605-4050
15	4055-up

European Commission

The classification system, as applied in the European Commission, another regional/international organisation, is much

18. For further information on what level in each factor roughly corresponds to what grade in Professional, Administrative, Technical and Clerical and assistance works, see OPM (1991). *The Classifier's Handbook*, TS-107. Washington DC. August p.14-17.

simpler than that of the United Nations. In the new classification system adopted in 2004, there is a unified structure of two categories, having altogether 16 grades: AD and AST. AD (administrator function group) consists of the middle management (9-14 grades) and senior management (15 and 16 grades), and embraces the old A and LA categories. On the other hand, AST (assistant function group) comprises 1-11 grades and absorbs the former B and C categories. Category D is slated to be phased out. Evidently there is an overlap in 9-11 grades between the two new groups, something that does not happen in the United Nations. In terms of salaries, all grades have 5 steps, whereas the world body has more steps in many cases.

Under the old system, created in 1962, the Commission had four categories: A, B, C, and D, each having up to 8 steps. The following table shows the broad classification of staff under the old system,[19] later merged into the new two categories.

Table 8.3

Categories of Staff in the European Commission

Categories	*Grades*	*Steps*
A	8 Grades A8-A1	Up to 8
LA	6 Grades LA8-LA3	Up to 8
B	5 Grades B5-B1	Up to 8
C	5 Grades C5-C1	Up to 8
D	4 Grades D4-D1	Up to 8

At the bottom of the pyramid, D category staff performed menial and service duties, and C category officials carried out secretarial and clerical duties. B category people had to have at least an advanced level of secondary education and were responsible for executive duties, mostly in administration, budget and library. And A category—including the Language group (LA)—needed a university degree and relevant professional experience; out of them, from A8, the lowest rung in this category, to A6 were at the lower echelons;

19. *http://ec.europa.eu/reform/2002/chapter02_en.htm#5_2*

A5-A3 at the middle management and A2 and A1, the highest, at the senior management level.

Private Sector

Job classification is not confined to governments and international organisations alone. Private companies also pursue job classification, and F.M. Taylor was the first one to introduce it in the private sector. For instance, the General Electric, one of the largest commercial enterprises, employs 327,000 people from different occupational streams: Engineering, Finance, Human Resources, Information Technology, Marketing, Operations, Quality, and Sales. GE has hundreds of job classifications in each stream. At GE, their job number, industry focus group, and business segment identify jobs. And under each segment, the company has several job classifications. Thus, GE has 32 job classifications, down from 84 in 1987, for its autoworkers alone.[20]

At the International Business Machine too, there are at least 22 services[21] and hundreds of job classifications. It has professional and non-professional categories of jobs. Job identification code, job unit, job area, job category, and job role are used to classify jobs.

Mobility

Background

Mobility is the movement of an employee from his erstwhile job to a job that is in a different department, agency or location within the same classification or outside the classification but in the same salary range. It could be broadly of two types: Position transfer and lateral transfer. In the position transfer, the employee moves between departments, agencies, and locations within the same classification, level and grade. In lateral transfer, the employee moves between two different classifications but in the same salary range. Transfer could also be voluntary and mandatory. When the employee seeks a transfer on his own, it would be voluntary. On the other hand, a transfer initiated by the employer is involuntary.

---

20. See Ruben, George (1988). "Work stoppage at General Electric Ends–Developments in Industrial Relations", in *Monthly Labor Review*, June.

21. See *https://jobs3.netmedia1.com/cp/search_results.jsp*

Transfer could also be temporary to fill the gap in the interim or permanent to fill the post on a long-term basis. It could also be mutual—between two interested employees of the same level and grade—with the employer's approval.

Provision of moving cost may differ depending on the nature of transfer. Some employers do not pay the moving cost to the employee, and his family, who seeks voluntary or mutual transfer requiring the movement of accommodation due to distance. The transferred employee might be eligible for a daily subsistence allowance, in lieu of locally applicable post adjustment (allowance), for temporary transfers of short durations.

Mobility in UN

Managed mobility is relatively of recent origin in the United Nations. Since 2002, the world body has been trying to implement a managed mobility programme, apart from a voluntary one, to develop a more versatile, multi-tasked and experienced staff and to ensure that the Secretariat has a more integrated approach to achieve its objectives. On an experimental basis, SG has been authorised to move 50 staff every year under the managed mobility programme; and those UN staff members who have worked at one place for more than 5 years are encouraged to move to a new function, office or duty station.

Mobility or lateral move has been mandatory for promotion, except in certain situations when it is waved.[22] All staff should generally spend at least 2 years in a post before they become eligible for movement, and they, up to and including D2, are expected to move periodically to new functions throughout their careers.[23] But several exceptions apply to this as well.

The UN experience with staff mobility has so far largely failed. Let us have a brief look at the recent experience with the mobility programme.

- From February 2006 to July 2008, only 100 staff members moved between duty stations under the managed and voluntary mobility programmes, and only 39 of them were

22. United Nations (2002). *Staff Selection System*, ST/AI/2002/4 of 23 April p.6.

23. Ibid: 2.

at the Professional and higher category. And no one moved from a headquarters post to a field post.[24] The managed reassignment programme has not resulted in a more mobile Secretariat staff: concerns exist about its effectiveness. Significant challenges are evident in the OHRM efforts to achieve desired outcomes, including work-life issues, such as the difficulty faced by dual carrier families, the need to maintain institutional capacity, limitation of human resources IT systems, including inaccurate employee records.

- Participation in the managed reassignment programme has been very low. Many participants in the managed reassignment programme cited negative experiences such as "deeply disappointing"; "traumatic" and "unrealistic". Many of the respondents also reported that the mobility programme has had a negative impact on their careers.

Table 8.4, which demonstrates the voluntary and mandated movement of staff between duty stations, speaks for this failure.

Table 8.4

OHRM Mobility Programme's Participation and Result

	Volumtary Reassignment Programme		*Managed Reassignment Programme*	
	No. of Participants in the Programme/ No. of Participants Assigned to a New Post	*Percentage of Participants Assigned to a New Post*	*No. of Participants in the Programme/ No. of Participants Assigned to a New Post*	*Percentage of Participants Assigned to a New Post*
P-2	35/13	34	65/38	58
P-3	68/0	0	44/16	36
P-4	46/0	0	31/7	23
P-6	13/0	0	97/20	21
P-7	3/0	0	37/10	27
Total	165/13	8	274/87	32

Source: Ibid: 17.

Seventy per cent of Secretariat managers share the perception expressed by the staff. The Office of Human Resources Management

24. United Nations (2008). *In-depth Evaluation of the Office of Human Resources Management.* A report by OIOS. 22 September pp.16-17.

finds it time consuming and expensive.[25] What is more notable is the fact that no one has moved from field station to headquarters where the quality of life and educational opportunities for staff children tend to be much better than in field offices. And no assessment has been made of the benefits of the mobility programme for the organisation's work. So the jury is still out on this issue in terms of the world body.

Evidently, SG has not been able to shift staff around, as warranted. There seem to be several reasons for it. Staff resistance is one of them; those staff who are serving in more desirable duty stations would not want to move to a hard duty station. At the same time, those staff working in less desirable places would certainly crave and push for their transfer to a better place if such prospects existed. Unwillingness of senior managers to part with their good subordinates is another; they would often release non-performers and underperformers for transfer. The experimental and limited nature of the extant mobility programme does not inspire much confidence either.

Therefore, the Secretariat believes SG should be given more latitude and broader authority for effective staff mobility. Member states seem to think otherwise. Those member states which want more staff mobility in the United Nations are not convinced that more authority to SG might translate into greater mobility without his greater commitment to enforce it; those countries that are reluctant about mobility on reasons of added cost or otherwise only find their position vindicated by the failure of the experimental mobility programme.

Although all member states have managed mobility programmes for their civil servants, they have refused the same provision for the United Nations. Additional cost entailed by mobility is certainly a key factor in this entrenched reluctance. Human and political factors could be equally important. Member states might also have soft corner towards those of their nationals who might be serving in attractive duty stations or strategic

25. United Nations, *In-depth Evaluation of the Office of Human Resources Management*, *op. cit.*, pp.17-18.

functional areas. The failure of this programme has become so obvious that SG has asked for its suspension, as mentioned already, and the General Assembly has sidestepped the issue by asking SG to promote voluntary staff mobility (see: GA resolution 63/250).

Mobility Elsewhere

It will be instructive to have a look at how mobility has been treated in the European Commission. The Commission introduced new provisions for mobility and promotion in 2004. It has recognised the need for mobility to help keep its staff abreast with the changing technology and skill requirements. As the environment in which the Commission has to work has changed, the Commission needs to maintain dynamism and freshness within the house by removing routineness and monotony associated with long stay in one position or line of work and to prevent national influence on the staff. Several elements constitute this policy:

- A non-binding benchmark of two to five years for all officials is introduced;
- Mobility is compulsory for 'sensitive' jobs (e.g., those dealing with the award of contracts, determining rights and obligations, award subsidies, etc.);
- Directorates-General are allowed to implement structured mobility programmes;
- Greater transparency and objectivity is sought in filling vacant posts;
- Support on mobility matters is provided by a Central Career Guidance Function and local careers officers in the individual DGs;
- Detachments to other institutions are facilitated, so are secondments to another EU institution or to an organisation devoted to furthering the EU's interests and two-way exchanges of staff between the Commission and Member States in the interests of the individual or of the service.[26]

At the Commission, mobility has become a norm at senior levels since 1999. Senior managers must move to another post after five—

26. *http://ec.europa.eu/reform/2002/chapter02_en.htm#2*

and in exceptional circumstances, seven—years. It has two fundamental objectives: To prevent bureaucratic stasis and to resist national influence on senior managers from their respective countries. A sense of stasis begins to creep up after prolonged work in one position, and change brings new dynamism and opportunity to do something new. It is also necessary that no senior official is influenced by the nation s/he comes from or have worked on for long. Mobility also helps senior managers to acquire experience and expertise in various areas of European Union activities.

The US federal government allows staff to have location-to-location transfers and inter-agency transfers without breaking their service. For such transfers, the eligible career or career-conditional staff must apply for a vacancy in a competitive service position in a different agency at the same, or a higher or lower grade; they must meet the minimum qualification requirements; and unless veteran or otherwise preferences apply, selection for such transfers is made on the basis of merit. The staffs retain their status—career or career-conditional—after such transfer. So, it is hard to justify the US reluctance towards allowing the United Nations to embrace a broad mobility provision.

Based on this, it is imperative for SG of the United Nations to have broader authority than he now enjoys in shifting staff and non-staff resources around for better overall performance of the organisation. Such increased power must also be accompanied by increased accountability, another vital necessity for the United Nations to espouse.

Performance Appraisal

Background

Performance appraisal is the "process of identifying, measuring and developing human performance in organisations."[27] Organisations use performance appraisal for several purposes. Key among them include justifying the salary, recommending a raise in pay, identifying training needs and removing staff weaknesses, granting bonus or

27. Schneier, Craig Erick and Richard W. Beatty (1979). "Integrating Behaviorally-Based Methods", *The Personnel Administration* XXIV: 66 July.

recognition for good performance, and providing promotion; it could also be used to determine who should be laid-off in times of staff cuts—those with bad performance go first. Through such appraisals, the supervisor periodically reviews the performance of his subordinates in order to find strengths and weaknesses and to decide whether the employee needs improvements in his performance, and deserves a bonus or a raise, as well as to set future targets.

Although performance appraisal has been around for nearly 2000 years, it was formally introduced in 1813 and became popular after the Second World War.[28] Business organisations adopted it *en masse* by the 1950s. Two trends have been witnessed in the performance appraisal system. One, "appraisal methods have evolved from trait and essay approaches to such behavioural and result-oriented methods as Behaviorally Anchored Rating Scales (BARS) and Management by Objective (MBO)... A second trend is that the number of uses of PA in organisations has increased during the past 30 years."[29]

While performance evaluation is used quite widely, it has also become the main source of dissatisfaction among employees and an irritant between supervisors and supervisees. Supervisors do not want to rate their subordinates poorly, nor subordinates appreciate bad appraisals; supervisors often lack accountability for their ratings; and not least, performance evaluation standards are far from objective.

Performance Appraisal at the UN

Performance appraisal is integral to UN human resources management. Started in 1980, the matter has gone through a process of evolution, though it appears to have been far behind any commercial and government organisation or the European Commission. The four categories of performance appraisal objectives, as approved by ICSC in 1980, are presented in Annex A-8.1 to this chapter. Another major milestone was hit when ICSC in its 26th session in July 1987 recommended that:

---

28. Murphy, Kevin R. and Jeanette Cleveland (1995). *Understanding Performance Appraisal*. Sage International. p.3.

29. Ibid: 5.

(a) the organisations should take into account the performance appraisal principles and associated guidelines and regularly appraise the performance of all staff members at least up to and including staff at the D-1 level; (b) the organisations should also take into account the principles and associated guidelines concerning appropriate consequences for different performance levels; (c) where necessary, the organisations should actively set targets to have their performance appraisal systems consistent with the performance appraisal principles and guidelines as soon as reasonably possible, but in any event no later than 1 July 1992; (d) the organisations should send their performance appraisal and recognition of merit plans, systems and forms to the ICSC secretariat for appropriate consultations.[30]

In 1994, ICSC asked to add two more elements to the UN performance appraisal regime:

(a) a stronger focus on the importance of a performance-related management environment in which senior management set the tone in reinforcing the credibility of performance appraisal and management; (b) greater emphasis on the need for full transparency and understanding of the system at all levels; stronger insistence on the need for objective and rigorous appraisal of performance at all levels; introduction of the concept of competencies (i.e., generic standards of knowledge, skills and abilities applicable to job groups) as a complement to task-based performance appraisal schemes.[31]

Based on these sets of guidelines and subsequent developments in this area, SG has issued on 20 March 2002 the latest administrative instructions on a performance appraisal system.[32] The objective of the system is to promote a culture of high performance and continuous learning; empower managers and hold them accountable for managing and motivating their staff; encourage a high level of staff participation in planning, delivery, and monitoring of work; and recognise successful performance and address underperformance in an equitable and fair manner. The annual performance cycle also provides for a mid-year assessment to identify shortcomings and improve on them and is supposed to be linked to individual work plans that encourage continuous learning, team

30. *http://icsc.un.org/resources/pdfs/general/compend/9-70.pdf*

31. Ibid.

32. United Nations, *Performance Appraisal System*, ST/AI/2002/3, p.1.

work and career development plan. As laid out, the first reporting officer—read the supervisor—makes the first assessment of performance and the second reporting officer—the supervisor of the first reporting officer—does the second evaluation.

There are five levels of performance rated in the United Nations. The staff member who:

- Consistently exceeds performance expectations.
- Frequently exceeds performance expectations.
- Delivers fully successful performance.
- Partially meets performance expectations.
- Does not meet performance expectations.

Those who are rated in the first three categories receive consideration for the renewal of fixed-term appointments and for selection at the same or higher level post. The fourth rating for consecutive two years might result in withholding of the salary increment in the same grade, and the last one in administrative action including transfer, non-renewal of contract, or termination of service.[33] The prescribed performance evaluation form is produced in Annex A-8.2.

Nonetheless, the Office of Internal Oversight Service found no strong link of the Secretariat Performance Appraisal System (e-PAS) to participation in learning programmes, and strategic development of staff skills and career paths. For example, it says, "staff performance appraisal information is not consistently considered during the staff selection process..."[34]

To address these issues and others, the General Assembly has, by its resolution 63/250, asked SG to introduce the 360-degree performance appraisal system and to strengthen the link between performance appraisal and career progression. This evaluation system has been outlined in the following section.

Performance Appraisal in Other Organisations

The United Nations can learn much from the performance appraisal systems, as practiced in its member states and other

33. Ibid: 6.

34. Ibid: 20.

international organisations. For instance, OPM in the United States, which is the UN's main comparator country, supports the use of multiple rating sources as an effective method for performance appraisal of civil servants.[35] It also believes that not all the sources should be tapped by every agency of the federal government. The following table shows the multiple rating sources, also known as the 360-degree assessment:

Figure 8.2

Multiple Performance Rating Sources

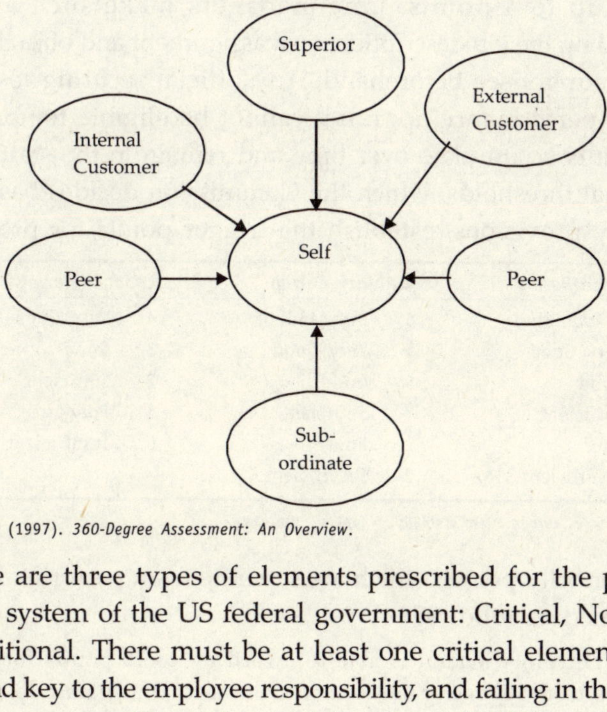

Courtesy: OPM (1997). *360-Degree Assessment: An Overview.*

There are three types of elements prescribed for the personnel appraisal system of the US federal government: Critical, Non-critical, and Additional. There must be at least one critical element directly related and key to the employee responsibility, and failing in this element should be unacceptable to the employer. It might differ from agency to agency or job to job. The non-critical elements could be related to individual, group or organisational performance. On the other hand, the additional elements might include objectives, goals, programme plans, work plans and other methods of expressing performance.

35. OPM (1997). 360-Degree Assessment: An Overview. September p.1.

The European Commission has made performance appraisal as the kingpin of promotional decisions for its staff. There are no automatic promotions along the hierarchical ladder, something that shears the staff of any initiative and motivation to improve their performance. Now every employee has to earn a promotion, and they have to do it through merit points in the performance appraisal, which has to be done of every employee annually. And priority points are assigned as the promotion procedure unfolds.

Appraisal is done on the basis of three criteria, having 20 points: performance up to 10 points, ability to perform up to 6 points, and conduct up to 4 points. Line managers make such appraisals predicated on the job description, task assignment and objective agreed with the supervisee beforehand. Any official securing less than 10 points in performance appraisal cannot be eligible for promotion. These points accumulate over time and remain in the staff's dossier. The annual thresholds, which the Commission decides based on the budgetary provisions, establish the trigger points for promotion.

Performance Rating		*Ability Rating*		*Conduct Rating*	
9-10	Outstanding	6	Outstanding	4	Very Good
7-8	Very Good	5	Very Good	3	Good
6	Good	4	Good	2	Sufficient
5	Sufficient	3	Sufficient	1	Poor
3-4	Poor	2	Poor	0	Insufficient
0-2	Insufficient	0-1	Insufficient		

Source: http://ec.europa.eu/reform/2002/chapter02_en.htm#2

The priority points, which are separate from performance points, are assigned as follows:

1. The Director-General is able to award up to 10 points for special services to the Directorate-General from a total available to him/her of 2.5 times the number of staff. Half of these points goes to the 15 per cent or so officials rated as above average, each of these receiving between six and ten points. The other half goes to the rest of the staff concerned, individuals receiving between zero and four points each. In this way the Director-General can accentuate differences in appraisals.

2. Up to two additional priority points per official may be awarded by the Promotion Committees (in each DG) from a quota allocated

> to them of 0.25 times the number of staff. The Promotion Committee assesses activities performed in the interest of the Commission, e.g. participation in a selection board. The Committee can award one or two points maximum per official.[36]

For the middle management (9-14 AD grades), performance is assessed on the basis of the objectives; an added element of quality control is assessed in the appraisal. The rest of the promotion procedure for this level of management is the same as set out above for the higher echelons of EC organisations.

Appointments are considered in the order of transfer, promotion from among those who have been taking part in the compulsory training or who have passed a written examination, and promotion, all within the institution. Separate procedures could be followed for grades 14-16. Chapter 3 of the EC Staff Regulations provides the procedure for promotion. Every staff advances to the next step in the same grade after two years. Article 45 says,

> Promotion shall be exclusively by selection from among officials who have completed a minimum of two years in their grade after consideration of the comparative merits of the officials eligible for promotion. When considering comparative merits, the Appointing Authority shall in particular take account of the reports on the officials, the use of languages in the execution of their duties other than the language for which they have produced evidence of thorough knowledge...and, where appropriate, the level of responsibilities exercised by them.

Only up to 20 per cent vacancies in the AD category can be filled with AST category staff through promotion. Promotees in the EC are generally placed in the first step of the promoted grade. In case of 9-16 grades, promotees are put in the second step of the higher grade to which they have been promoted.

In the private sector, performance appraisal is done to assess the core competencies identified by the organisation. The key elements of appraisal are those that are applied to such personnel decisions as promotions and rewards. GE has a forced distribution system of appraisal: Supervisors have to rank 10 per cent of their subordinates

36. Ibid.

as top performers, 10 per cent as low performers and the rest in the middle; and their compensation is based on the ranking.[37] Under Jack Welch, the now retired long-time charismatic CEO, who was a strong advocate of performance evaluation, GE also exercised successfully the policy of "rank and yank" under which employees are ranked in three groups—top 20 per cent, middle 70 per cent and bottom 10 per cent—and those at the bottom were let go.[38] Such appraisal is done on the basis of goals and expectations worked out between management and the employee and agreed to by the latter. This is something from which the United Nations can learn a lot and adapt to meet its performance evaluation requirements with a view to improving its human resources management.

Promotion

Background

Promotion is a means to motivate employees, reward superior performers, and provide greater responsibility to them.[39] Elevating internal candidates to higher levels is a way to reward high performers and to manage talent within the organisation. It is also a form of selection. The initial selection has to do with picking up candidates from outside, while promotion with selection of existing employees for a higher post.

Two basic conditions have to be met for promotion. First, there should be a post for it. Second, employee must fulfil qualification and experience standards determined by the organisation in advance. Pergamit and Veum describe several theoretical models of staff promotion: economic, revealed ability, human capital and job match. In the economic model, promotion is deemed as a prize to be won based on the productivity of employee. The employee who makes the highest contribution to the organisation from his level or grade gets promotion. An employee might be promoted based on the revealed-on-the-job ability to perform. Encouraging that ability and retaining the employee is the objective of such promotion. On the

37. *http://www.swlearning.com/management/hrm_news/perform_0404_001.html*
38. Welch, Jack with Suzy Welch (2005). *Winning*. New York: Harper-Collins. Chapter 3, pp. 37-51.
39. Pergamit, Michael R. and Jonathan R. Veum (1995). "What is a Promotion?", *BLS Working Paper* 264, (US Department of Labor) p.3.

other hand, the human capital model views promotion as a way to reward the added value of the employee through training. In the job match model, promotion is an optimal response of the organisation after learning the employee's productivity.[40]

Promotion might take different forms. It could, among others, be an upgrading of the employee's existing post without any change in responsibilities; a movement to a higher post and higher responsibility; an appointment in a newly created higher position; and an upward movement due to reorganisation and adjustment. In most cases, if not all, higher post, higher responsibility and higher salary are the common features of promotion; in many cases it might only involve a higher salary, and nothing more, such as when the rank-in-person approach is pursued, and the man or woman holding a position continues to carry it even after the promotion. In the following section, we will discuss promotion concepts as applied to the United Nations in its generic context.

Promotion in UN

Article IV of the UN Staff Regulations provides for appointment and promotion. Regulation 4.2 says, "The paramount consideration in the appointment, transfer or promotion of the staff shall be the necessity of securing the highest standards of efficiency, competence and integrity. Due regard shall be paid to the importance of recruiting the staff on as wide a geographical basis as possible." Rule 104.14 of the Staff Regulations offers details about the Appointment and Promotion Board and the Appointment and Promotion Committees that approve appointments and promotions. For the GS and other categories, subsidiary panels could be established. Particularly with respect to promotion, Rule 104.14 f (iii) stipulates:[41]

a. The selection of staff members qualified for promotion, except for staff having successfully passed a competitive examination, in accordance with staff rule 104.15;
b. Minimum periods of service in the grade, as a normal requirement for consideration for promotion, shall be established

40. Ibid: 3-5

41. *http://www.sas.undp.org/documents/Staff_Rules_100_English.pdf*

by the Secretary-General upon recommendation by the Appointment and Promotion Board.

In the United Nations, both in initial selection, except for some entry-level posts, and in promotional selection, internal candidates get huge preference over external applicants. Section 7.1 of the Staff Selection System clearly mentions that:

> In considering candidates, programme managers must give first priority to lateral moves of candidates eligible to be considered at the 15-day mark...If no suitable candidate can be identified at this first stage, candidates eligible at the 30-day mark...Other candidates shall be considered at the 60-day mark, where applicable.[42]

Those candidates whose appointment is not limited to service with a particular office get first priority in selection for lateral move to a vacant post. Next in line come those internal candidates who are not limited to service with a particular office. In addition, certain categories of internal candidates get precedence over external candidates. Only then external candidates are considered. According to OIOS, the following staff selections, which demonstrate a clear bias against external candidates, resulted from 2003 to 2007:[43]

- 3,232 staff were promoted to higher posts,
- 588 were external candidates with previous appointments,
- 214 were selected through lateral movement
- 393 were selected from external initial candidates
- 62 were selected from the roster, both external and internal.

No wonder why the number of fresh candidates joining the United Nations is meager, and the workforce is aging fast. OIOS says that, in the five year period between 2002 and 2007, 78 per cent staff selection took place from among internal candidates, and only 22 per cent came from outside. The rostered candidates were left out in calculating the percentages because it was difficult to determine whether they were external or internal.[44] What is not clear from the OIOS report is whether or not the external candidates with previous appointments had their appointments

42. United Nations, *Staff Selection System, op. cit.*, p.9.

43. Ibid, taken from the note to Table 1 in p.9.

44. Ibid: 13.

with the UN agencies or non-UN agencies. If all or most of them had their previous appointments with the United Nations or its specialised agencies, then the actual share of external candidates in the total selections dips down to a paltry 12 per cent. Despite that, 38 per cent staff who participated in the survey rated the staff selection process as poor or very poor.[45]

If the staff dissatisfaction is anything to go by, the above statistics of high ratio of promotion of internal candidates apparently means the staff have complaints about more than promotion, though it is near the top of the reasons for dissatisfaction. The high share of internal candidates for higher post offers promotional prospects for those employees that are already on board and boosts their motivation. However, it is unfortunate that this also makes the world body inherently biased against external candidates and new blood, and might seriously undermines its long-term health and vitality. Striking a balance between motivating internal staff through improved promotion and career advancement prospects and recruiting young and talents new employees from outside has been a perennial challenge for the United Nations.

Promotion Elsewhere

However, other international organisations and many countries have been able to grapple with this challenge in a much more balanced manner. For instance, the European Commission has a policy of hiring new blood at the entry level and promoting internal candidates as the need arises. So there is a constant infusion of the youth into the organisation at the entry level.

In the United States, promotion involves several steps, and it virtually starts as soon as an employee joins his job. The new employee needs to sit down with his supervisor to discuss his career objectives, interests and training needs and map out his individual development plan (IDP) with long-term and short-term strategies. The employees seeking promotion must meet the acceptable level of performance and requisite qualifications—education, experience, and certain time in the grade. Once such requirements are met, promotion takes place in two ways: Promotion within the career

45. Ibid.

ladders and the merit promotion programme. In the first category, the supervisor recommends his staff for promotion which takes place within the department concerned. OPM also conducts competitive examinations for merit-based promotions from within the civil service and without.[46] Positions with career ladder promotions are non-competitive, and all others are competitive. Certain departments have special promotion programmes—for instance, the US State Department's Mustang Career Mobility Programme—for talented civil service career personnel.

All big private organisations have had their own promotion policies, requirements and procedures. For instance, the General Electric Co. conducts various training and development programmes and encourages higher education for its employee. About the staff promotion, GE says:

> We recruit hard-working, self-motivated people, and support their growth in an environment that allows them to reach their full potential. We do this by operating as a meritocracy, making significant investment in training, providing challenging assignments to develop breadth and depth, giving frequent feedback, and rigorously measuring performance from the very beginning of a career. Our people must be experienced and motivated. They must understand their industries and GE's expectations for their performance. Our teams must be willing to learn and change. Personal growth is key to a successful career at GE.[47]

At the International Business Machine, you come across a flexible career path, as the organisation has many opportunities in different areas. You may choose an individual development plan: Move vertically and deepen your field of expertise, or move laterally to broaden the range of your skills. Or you may pursue the management field and prepare for growth in that area as well.[48] The following are the areas identified by IBM as key competencies for professional progress:[49]

46. *http://careers.state.gov/civil-service/development.html*
47. *http://www.ge.com/citizenship/priorities_engagement/operational_excellence_co.jsp*
48. *http://www-03.ibm.com/employment/us/cd_career_dev.shtml*
49. *http://www-03.ibm.com/employment/us/li_values.shtml*

- Adaptability
- Client Focus
- Taking Ownership
- Communication
- Drive to Achieve
- Teamwork and Collaboration
- Creative Problem Solving
- Passion for the Business
- Trustworthiness

IBM looks the following competencies for professional growth at the company.

Figure 8.3

Competencies for Professional Growth at IBM

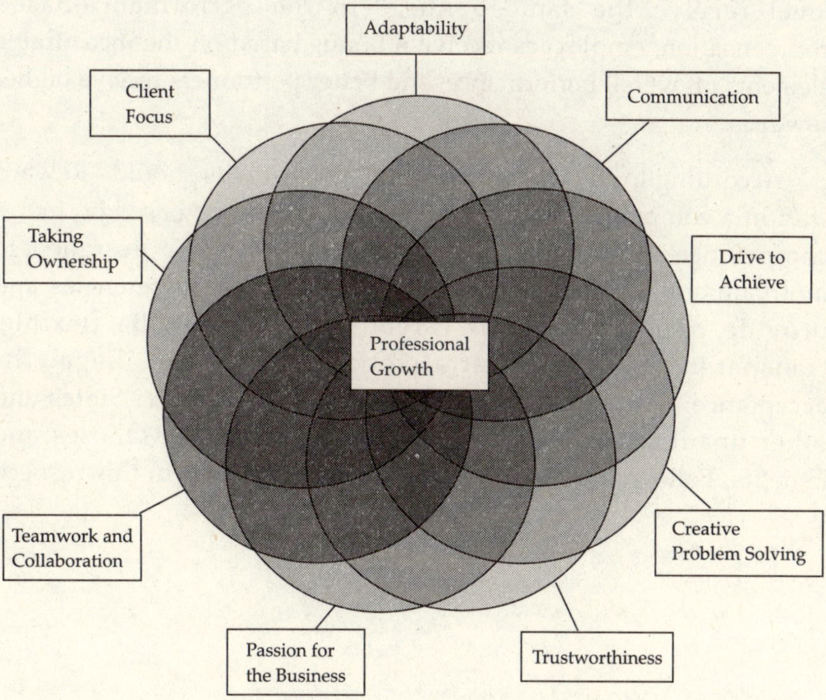

The United Nations can learn from the US government as well as from EC, GE and IBM to improve its performance evaluation system significantly. Particularly notable is IBM's professional growth concept and GE's rank and yank programme.

Compensation

Background

Compensation mainly consists of pay and benefits. It could be status-based, merit-based or performance-based. Most widely used system is the status-based, which pays employees at a level prevailing in the industry. Employee-related factors determine the status, and economic elements help ascertain compensation in this system. Under the merit-based compensation, employees are paid a fixed one-time bonus on the basis of their pay, and all employees of the same level receive the same bonus.[50] In the performance-based compensation, employees receive a bonus based on the measurable elements of overall performance, and better performers receive higher rewards.[51]

According to ICSC, compensation and benefits should "Reward staff in a competitive and equitable manner and be based on merit, competence, responsibility and accountability; Be designed to motivate and encourage staff to develop skills competencies and provide opportunities for career advancement; Be flexible, transparent, and administratively simple; Make illegal the acceptance of supplementary payments from Member States and other unauthorised sources."[52] It consists of both salaries and benefits. Following is the chart ICSC has developed in this respect:

50. For details, McAdams, Jerry L. (1996). *The Reward Plan Advantage*. San Francisco Jossey-Bass Inc., pp.92&97.

51. Lawler, Edward E. (1990). *Strategic Pay: Aligning Organizational Strategies and Pay Systems*. San Francisco Jossey-Bass Inc., p.71.

52. *http://icsc.un.org/resources/pdfs/ppd/hrmframe/ICSC_hrm_eng.pdf*

Figure 8.4

Compensation and Benefits

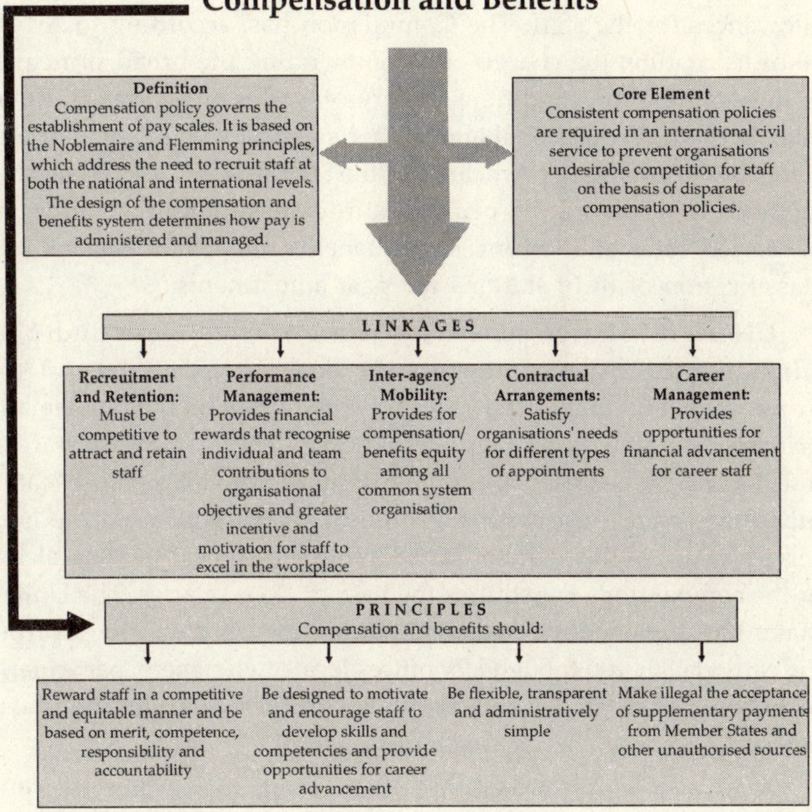

Compensation at UN

The UN Staff Regulation 3.1 sets out the provision of salaries. It says, "Salaries of staff members shall be fixed by the Secretary-General in accordance with the provisions of Annex A-8.1 to the present Regulations." Regulation 3.2 lays out educational allowances, 3.3 staff assessment and 3.4 dependency allowances. The UN Staff Rule 103 and its sub-rules 103.0 through 103.24 provide for the salary scales of various categories and sub-categories of staff, non-resident allowances, language allowance, post adjustment allowance, salary increment at promotion, special allowances, overtime, night differential, salary advances, retroactivity of payments and other payments and allowances.

Based on these regulations and rules, ICSC considers and recommends to the General Assembly the increments in salaries and allowances for the staff. The Commission has, according to Article 10 of its Statute, the charge of recommending the broad principles of determining the conditions of service, scales of salaries and post adjustment of Professional and higher staff, allowances of staff and staff assessment. As per Article 11 of the Statute, ICSC also establishes methods of applying the principles in determining the conditions of service, rates of allowances and benefits other than pension and classification of duty stations for post adjustments.[53]

UN staff salaries consist of two elements: base and post adjustment. ICSC recommends the base or floor salary of the Professional and higher staff, and it is predicated on the Noblemaire principle—which essentially says the UN should pay its staff as much as might be necessary to recruit them from all member states, including from those with the highest salary scales. So the civil service salary of the member state having the highest salary scales—or the comparator—constitutes the base or floor salaries. The United States has remained the main comparator for UN staff salaries from the early days, even though UN offices located elsewhere, particularly in Europe, such as ICJ and Tribunal for Former Yugoslavia, also take into account the local salaries.

At the General Service and related categories, the salary is determined on the basis of the Flemming principle, which means the salary should reflect the best prevailing conditions found locally for similar work.[54] Of course, salaries and allowances have to be approved by the policy-making intergovernmental bodies before they can be implemented. UN staff get post adjustments to preserve their purchasing power based on the cost of living adjustments on top of the floor salaries.

The salary scales of the Professional and higher and GS and other categories of UN staff have been produced in Annex A-8.3 to this chapter. The GS salaries, which differ from place to place

53. United Nations, *ICSC Statute, op. cit.*, pp. 3-4.

54. *http://icsc.un.org/resources/FAQ/default.htm*

depending on the best prevailing local conditions, are shown only for New York. Besides, there are scales for the Deputy Secretary-General and for the Trades and Crafts groups which are not shown in Annex A-8.3.

Of late, UN salaries have not been very attractive to many talented people from the advanced countries, though they are still quite tempting to equally bright people from the developing world. Even though US civil service salaries are taken as the comparator for the world organisation, many other countries are now paying their civil servants more than America. However, the world body cannot and should not discriminate against competent people from the developing countries simply because the pay structure in their countries is not comparable to their wealthy partners. So, the issue of UN salaries remains a thorny and unresolved one.

Presented in Annex A-8.4 is the sample of EC salaries, as included in the Staff Regulations, for the sake of comparison. Appropriate cost-of-living adjustments have been made in the basic salary schedule. US civil service salaries would be close to that of the United Nations, as the world body takes the US federal pay as its comparator. Private sector organisations often keep their salary scales confidential.

Observations

As we have seen in the previous sections of this chapter, the United Nations is a mixed bag of problems and progress in several key areas of human resources management discussed in this chapter. It has made several attempts to improve these areas of HRM, but progress has been less than consistent and far from encouraging. We wish to describe the key problems facing the United Nations, in this section.

Job Classification

Problems abound in the job classification of the United Nations. The system leaves much to be desired on many counts and looks pretty poor compared to what OPM does in the US federal government, even though this is also far from perfect. For instance,

UN parameters for the classification are fewer and less precise than that of OPM; there are no objective, consistent and reliable standards for classifying a job at various levels; so they do not necessarily reflect the essence and significance of a post to the organisation. And the point-ranging system is quite rudimentary, to say the least, and leaves much discretionary power in the hands of classification analysts and gives room for cronyism in many cases.

Otherwise, it might be difficult to explain why posts doing similar work in different places are often classified in different levels and categories. Quite often, certain posts are created and placed at a certain level to accommodate friends and colleagues of senior managers or the nominees of powerful countries, more often at senior levels. It is quite common to promise someone informally of a senior level post and then try to carve out duties and responsibilities to fit the post. Such a top-down and politically driven process undermines the credibility of job classification, engenders frustration among the staff and adversely affects the overall performance of the unit concerned and organisation as a whole. Quite frequently, fairly junior level staff from powerful member states land jobs at the top echelons of the United Nations. And this takes a heavy toll on the staff morale. Such things happen because the process of selection of candidates is so subjective and job classification in the United Nations is so highly amenable to political manipulations.

One of the prerequisites for the United Nations to revitalise its HRM is to have a realistic and objective job classification system. Work and not the qualifications of potential candidates should determine the levels of posts.

Mobility

The United Nations has made a mockery of the principle of staff mobility, even though it is being widely practiced throughout the world with highly positive effects and without many difficulties. There are four reasons for it. First, the nature of work across the world body, which is engaged in a wide variety of activities, might not be the same in different posts and locations to make mobility easy and seamless. Second, not all staff are equally eager to move from place to place due to family or work reasons. Particularly those working in influential units and departments, "lucrative" posts and good locations do not want to move to less attractive units, posts or locations.

Third, cronyism and political influence always comes in the way of mobility. Those who are close to power would not want to move to less desirable posts and less attractive places. Fourth, member states have been unwilling to give teeth to the managed mobility programme in the UN system and to foot the bill of an organisation-wide mandatory mobility programme.

We need to address these deficiencies. Doing so is critical, because a lack of staff mobility in the United Nations has undermined its ability for too long to embrace the much-needed dynamism, initiative, fresh perspective and innovation. It has also prevented the staff from acquiring multi-tasking skills to develop leadership capacities.

Performance Appraisal

Nothing could be more shocking than to find out that performance appraisal is not even considered to select candidates for training and promotion in the United Nations. Performance appraisal is largely a perfunctory exercise. If staff performance at the existing levels and expected performance at the higher level are not the kingpins of staff promotion, then the promotion system in the United Nations could be nothing but a ludicrous farce. What is more, the existing performance appraisal method is highly subjective and devoid of measurability in concrete terms. It is a pity that the United Nations, which preaches to member states about improving their HRM, has such a very poor state of personnel administration and even poorer state of the performance appraisal system.

The United States, GE and IBM impart valuable lessons for the world body to learn to improve its performance appraisal system.

Promotion

In the United Nations, promotion has remained a random result of an uncertain system, rather than an expected outcome of a systematic process of human resources management. We have already mentioned the ailments related to job classification, mobility and performance that have a direct bearing on promotional decisions. In the organisation, the staff cannot draw a lesson by observing the promotion pattern and prepare them for such an outcome other than the fact that most promotees come from within the system because of the high preference given to internal candidates. The rest lies in the hand of powerful countries or senior managers. A more competent person might rust in his position without any promotion for decades, whereas those who find favour with big countries and big bosses get fast-track elevations in their jobs.

The promotion system of the United Nations needs to be thoroughly changed to link it to training and performance and to ensure that a balance is struck between experience and new blood as well as the imperative to motivate the existing staff and infuse new vigour and innovative streak of external candidates. The current virtually non-system might work to the advantage of senior managers, but it has been hurting the organisation and its long-term viability.

Lessons to be Learned

As we have noted in the various paragraphs, the United Nations can learn much from its member states, from the European Commission, and from the private sector to improve its job classification system, mobility, performance appraisal and promotion. There have been many efforts to poorly imitate better systems, but seldom have they been sincere and systematic and serious. Of course, not everything suitable for governments and other organisations could address the requirements of the United Nations due to its unique nature, but there is much out there that could be beneficially adopted and adapted to improve UN staff performance. The Secretary-General should take an urgent initiative to repair the broken UN system.

Annex A-8.1

ICSC-Approved Performance Appraisal Objectives, 1980[55]

(a) Work-related objectives

- provide a control for work done;
- improve productivity;
- improve efficiency;
- help in assigning work;
- determine if the objectives of the job are met by the staff member;
- plan future work assignments.

(b) Career development objectives

- identify training needs;
- provide an opportunity to indicate career goals and aspirations;
- identify career possibilities within the organizations;
- identify strong and weak points and encourage finding remedies for weak points;
- determine career potential;
- plan developmental (promotional or lateral) assignments.

(c) Objectives of communication

- permit a dialogue between the supervisor and the subordinate;
- provide adequate feedback on performance;
- clearly establish what is expected of the staff member in terms of performance and future
- work assignments;
- provide motivation and job satisfaction through open discussion of performance;
- let employees know where they stand within the organization in terms of their performance.

(d) Administrative objectives

- check if the job description is up-to-date;
- serve as a basis for allocating merit awards;
- determine if an annual increment is to be awarded;
- serve as a basis for determining transfers;

- determine successful or unsuccessful completion of probationary assignment;
- serve as a basis for promotion or demotion;
- serve as a basis for extension or termination of contract in case of satisfactory or unsatisfactory service;
- serve as a basis for termination in case of reductions of staff;
- provide information for future employers

55. See United Nations, A/35/30 para. 275

Annex A-8.2

United Nations Performance Evaluation Report

Before filling out the report, please read attached guidelines (P.91/A) and refer to Administrative Instruction ST/AI/240/Rev. 1

SECTION I—To be completed by the Executive Officer

Name (Last, first, middle) Entry Date of UN Service Type of Appointment

Functional Title In this Function since

Department of Office/Bureau or Division/Section/Unit

Category and Level at this Level since period covered by this report

SECTION II

PART A—To be completed by the staff member

1. Describe the main assignments you have accomplished during the reporting period:
2. Indicate any training undertaken during the reporting period, including type and duration:
3. Indicate what guidance and counseling you have received in the performance of your duties:

PART B – To be completed by the first reporting officer

1. If you deem it appropriate, give your comments or clarification on the staff member's statements in part A above:
2. Indicate to what extent you have discussed with the staff member his/her performance during the reporting period

SECTION III—To be completed by the first reporting officer

In assessing the staff member's performance below, please bear in mind the staff member's level of duties and responsibilities so as not judge him/her inappropriate standards or by personality traits unrelated to his/her work Every 'A' or 'F' rating must be supplemented by a statement under "Comments", giving on explanation or examples illustrative of the rating. A report will not be considered complete unless such comments are given in respect of each 'A' or 'F' rating.

RATINGS: A: Excellent; B: Very Good; C: Good; D: Fair; E: Somewhat below standard; F: Unsatisfactory Enter in the column below the rating which most nearly describes the staff member's performance.

Rating Specially important Relevant Not applicable Comments

1. Competence (knowledge and skills the staff member possesses in his/her field of work).

2. Quality of work accomplished.
3. Quantity of work accomplished.
4. Ability to meet schedules and routine when required; skillful use of time and resources to achieve maximum efficiency.
5. Initiative (demonstrated aptitude to produce new ideas and/or bring about constructive innovation).
6. Ability to work independently or with minimal supervision
7. Effectiveness in maintaining harmonious working relations.
8. Sense of responsibility and dependability as regards working hours.

Rating Specially important Relevant Not applicable Comments

9. Effectiveness in planning and organization of work.
10. Skill in producing a solution (ability to identify problems, power of analysis and soundness of recommendations and decisions).
11. Ability to negotiate and persuade.
12. Effectiveness in supervision (ability to motivate, maintain and direct a productive work unit). Indicate below the number and level of staff under his/her supervision.

(NOT APPLICABLE TO LANGUAGE STAFF)

13. Written and oral expression in working language(s) (ability to communicate in a clear, concise and effective manner). If the staff member works in more than one language, rate each separately by entering the rating followed by the initial of each language in parentheses.
14. i. Linguistic knowledge and ability in official languages.

    ii. Accuracy and style.

Note: Rate each language separately by entering the rating followed by the initial of each language in parentheses.

15. Comment on the staff member's attitude to the United Nations.
16. Indicate any assignment(s) which the staff member performed in a particularly effective way. Signature: Date: Name and Title:

SECTION IV

To be completed by the second reporting officer

A. Before completing this section, please discuss the staff member's performance with the first reporting officer and, if you deem it necessary, with the staff member. If discussion with the first reporting officer cannot be held, please give an explanation.

B. Keeping in mind the requirements of the post, please check one of the following statements describing the staff member's performance. 1. ▯ An Excellent Performance 2. ▯ A Very Good Performance 3 ▯ A Good Performance 4. ▯ Fair 5 ▯ A Performance that does not fully Meet Standards 3 ▯ A Unsatisfactory Performance should you have checked statement 1 or 6 above, please elaborate. Otherwise comments are optional.

C. I you disagree with the first reporting officer's evaluation in Section III, give your comments:

Signature:

Date: Name and Title:

SECTION V

This section is to be completed by the head of the department or office or a director designated by him/her. (The making of comments under (ii) is optional.)

(i) I take note of this report (Place a mark here)

(ii) My comments are as follows:

Signature:

Date: Name and Title:

SECTION VI

After the sections above have been completed, the staff member must sign the original of the report and be given a copy thereof. The signature merely acknowledges that the staff member has read the report and received a copy; it does not necessarily indicate agreements with the evaluations contained in this report.

I have read this report and received a copy thereof. I understand that I may, if I wish, submit a written explanation or rebuttal within one month of receipt of this report in accordance with administrative instruction ST/AI/240/Rev.1.

Date: Signature of staff member:

NB: If rebuttal is submitted, this report must not be filed in the Official Status File until such time as the rebuttal procedure is completed (see ST/AI/240/Rev. 1, para. 12).

Annex A-8.3

Salary Scale for the Professional and Higher Categories Showing Annual Gross Salaries and Net Equivalents after Application of Staff Assessment

(in United States dollars)

Level		STEPS														
		1	*II*	*III*	*IV*	*V*	*VI*	*VII*	*VIII*	*IX*	*X*	*XI*	*XII*	*XIII*	*XIV*	*XV*
								Effective 1 January 2008								
USG	Gross	189,929														
	Net D	136,454														
	Net S	122,802														
ASG	Gross	172,546														
	Net D	125,155														
	Net S	113,332														
			*	*	*	*	*									
D-2	Gross	141,524	144,528	147,534	150,566	153,709	156,854									
	Net D	104,736	106,779	108,823	110,868	112,911	114,955									
	Net S	96,219	97,944	99,663	101,375	103,084	104,784									
						*	*	*	*	*						
D-1	Gross	129,304	131,944	134,579	137,219	139,859	142,496	145,135	147,775	150,431						
	Net D	96,427	98,222	100,014	101,809	103,604	105,397	107,192	108,987	110,780						
	Net S	89,129	90,689	92,245	93,797	95,346	96,892	98,432	99,971	101,505						
												*	*	*		
P-5	Gross	106,907	109,153	111,399	113,641	115,888	118,131	120,378	122,622	124,868	127,112	129,356	131,601	133,847		
	Net D	81,197	82,724	84,251	85,776	87,304	88,829	90,357	91,883	93,410	94,936	94,462	97,989	99,516		
	Net S	75,432	76,789	78,141	79,493	80,842	82,187	83,532	84,873	86,213	87,550	88,885	90,216	91,547		

contd...

...contd...

Level		STEPS														
		1	II	III	IV	V	VI	VII	VIII	IX	X	XI	XII	XIII	XIV	XV
														*	*	*
P-4	Gross	87,790	89,836	91,882	93,926	95,974	98,019	100,071	102,235	104,403	106,566	108,734	110,899	113,066	115,232	117,400
	Net D	67,709	69,182	70,655	72,127	73,601	75,074	76,548	78,020	79,494	80,965	82,439	83,911	85,385	86,858	88,332
	Net S	63,052	64,394	65,734	67,071	68,408	69,744	71,079	72,411	73,742	75,073	76,401	77,729	79,056	80,381	81,705
															*	*
P-3	Gross	71,729	73,622	75,518	77,410	79,306	81,197	83,090	84,986	86,881	88,774	90,669	92,560	94,457	96,349	98,242
	Net D	56,145	57,508	58,873	60,235	61,600	62,962	64,325	65,690	67,054	68,417	69,782	71,143	72,509	73,871	75,234
	Net S	52,408	53,662	54,918	56,171	57,427	58,679	59,932	61,188	62,440	63,694	64,944	66,195	67,443	68,693	69,943
													*			
P-2	Gross	58,401	60,097	61,790	63,485	65,179	66,871	68,567	70,257	71,953	73,649	75,340	77,038			
	Net D	46,549	47,770	49,989	50,209	51,429	52,647	53,868	55,085	56,306	57,527	58,745	59,967			
	Net S	43,662	44,769	45,872	46,978	48,082	49,188	50,312	51,432	52,557	53,679	54,799	55,924			
P-1	Gross	45,493	46,942	48,386	49,836	51,440	53,068	54,699	56,326	57,951	59,581					
	Net D	36,849	28,023	39,193	40,367	41,537	42,709	43,883	45,055	46,225	47,398					
	Net S	34,760	35,840	36,921	38,001	39,080	40,159	41,240	42,307	43,369	44,431					

Note: D = Rate applicable to staff mamebers with a dependent spouse or child.

S = Rate applicable to staff members with no dependent spouse or child.

* = The normal qualifying period for in-grade movement between consecutive steps is one year, except at those steps marked with an asterisk for which a two-year period at the preceding step is required.

General Service Category—Annual Salaries and Allowances

(in United States dollars)

Level		STEPS										
		I	II	III	IV	V	VI	VII	VIII	IX	X	XI
						Effective 1 August 2008						
7	(Gross)	68599	71491	74384	77277	80170	83062	85955	88848	91741	94633	97526*
	(Gross Pens)	66252	68946	71643	74338	77033	79730	82425	85121	87816	90512	93208*
	(Total Net)	52333	54329	56325	58321	60317	62313	64309	66305	68301	70297	72293*
	(Net Pens)	52333	54329	56325	58321	60317	62313	64309	66305	68301	70297	72293*
	(NPC)	0	0	0	0	0	0	0	0	0	0	0*
6	Gross	61420	64030	66641	69251	71861	74471	77081	79691	82301	84912	87522*
	(Gross Pens)	59813	62152	64490	66850	69283	71716	74149	76583	79016	81449	83882*
	(Total Net)	47380	49181	50982	52783	54584	56385	58186	59987	61788	63589	65390*
	(Net Pens)	47380	49181	50982	52783	54584	56385	58186	59987	61788	63589	65390*
	(NPC)	0	0	0	0	0	0	0	0	0	0	0*
5	(Gross)	55226	57427	59628	61962	64323	66684	69045	71406	73767	76128	78488*
	(Gross Pens)	53949	56065	58181	60296	62413	64528	66658	68861	71062	73264	75465*
	(Total Net)	42867	44496	46125	47754	49383	51012	52641	54270	55899	57528	59157*
	(Net Pens)	42867	44496	46125	47754	49383	51012	52641	54270	55899	57528	59157*
	(NPC)	0	0	0	0	0	0	0	0	0	0	0*
4	(Gross)	49739	51731	53723	55715	57707	59699	61813	63949	66086	68222	70358*
	(Gross Pens)	48673	50589	52503	54418	56333	58248	60162	62077	63993	65907	67884*
	(Total net)	38807	40281	41755	43229	44703	46177	47651	49125	50599	52073	53547*
	(Net Pens)	38807	40281	41755	43229	44703	46177	47651	49125	50599	52073	53547*
	(NPC)	0	0	0	0	0	0	0	0	0	0	0*
3	(Gross)	44726	46534	48342	50150	51958	53766	55574	57382	59191	61071	63010*
	(Gross Pens)	43863	45599	47336	49073	50809	52546	54282	56019	57756	59496	61229*

contd...

contd...

Level		STEPS										
		I	II	III	IV	V	VI	VII	VIII	IX	X	XI
	(Total Net)	35097	36435	37773	39111	40449	41787	43125	44463	45801	47139	48477*
	(Net Pens)	35097	36435	37773	39111	40449	41787	43125	44463	45801	47139	48477*
	(NPC)	0	0	0	0	0	0	0	0	0	0	0*
2	(Gross)	40238	41873	43508	45143	46778	48414	50049	51684	53319	54954*	
	(Gross Pens)	39541	41114	42686	44260	45832	47405	48977	50549	52122	53694*	
	(Total Net)	31776	31986	34196	35406	36616	37826	39036	40246	41456	42666*	
	(Net Pens)	31776	31986	34196	35406	36616	37826	39036	40246	41456	42666*	
	(NPC)	0	0	0	0	0	0	0	0	0	0*	
1	(Gross)	36312	37732	39153	40597	42076	43554	45032	46511	47989*		
	(Gross Pens)	35626	37048	38469	39890	41312	42734	44155	45577	46998*		
	(Total Net)	28760	29854	30948	32042	33136	34230	35324	36418	37512*		
	(Net Pens)	28760	29854	30948	32042	33136	34230	35324	36418	37512*		
	(NPC)	0	0	0	0	0	0	0	0	0*		

New York (USA)

Dependency Allowance:		*Language Allowances (to be included in pensionable remuneration):*	
Child	US$2,083 net per annum. 1/	First language	US$ 2,148 net per annum.
		Second language	US$ 1,074 net per annum.
	US$2,217 net per annum. 2/		
Except for the first dependent child of a single, widowed or divorced staff member	US$2,879 net per annum. 1/		
	US$3,246 net per annum. 2/		
Dependent spouse	US$3,336 net per annum. 1/		
	US$3,562 net per annum. 2/		
Secondary dependent	US$1,257 net per annum. 1/		
	US$1,307 net per annum. 2/		
	US$1,318 net per annum. 3/		

1/ Payable to staff who become eligible on or after 1 September 2006.

2/ Payable to eligible staff on board and already in receipt of amount prior to 1 September 2006.

3/ Payable to eligible staff on board and already in receipt of amount prior to 1 June 2004.

Increments: Salary increments within the levels shall be awarded annually on the basis of staisfactory service.

* Long-service step.

Step XI at levels G-3 to G-7, Step X at level G-2 and Step IX at level G-1 are long-service steps.

The qualifying criteria for in-grade increases to the long-service step are as follows:

(a) The staff member should have had at least 20 years of service within the United Nations Common System and five years of service at the top regular step of the current grade.

(b) The staff member's service should have been satisfactory.

Gross: Gross salaries have been derived through the application of staff assessment to Total Net salaries.
Gross salaries are established for purposes of separation payments and as the basis for calculating tax reimbursements whenever UN salaries are taxed.

Gross Pens: Gross Pensionable salaries have been derived through application of staff assessment to Net Pensionable salaries.
Gross Pensionable is the basis for determining Pension Fund contributions under Article 25 of UNJSPF Regulations and for determining Pension benefits.

Total Net: Total net remuneration is the sum of the non-pensionable component and the net pensionable salary.

Net Pens: Net Pensionable is that part of net salary which is used to derive to the Gross Pensionable Salary.
Net Pensionable salary is the Total Net salary less the Non-pensionable component, i.e. 100 per cent of total net salaries.

NPC: Non-Pensionable Component is that part of net salary excluded friom application of staff assessment in determination of the Gross Pensionable salary.
The Non-Pensionable Component has been established at 0 per cent.

Annex A-8.4

Salary Schedule of EC Staff[56]

(COLA not included)

Each staff category has a basic salary scale, divided into steps.

University graduates, without professional experience, may be recruited to the basic grade of AD (administrator) career.

Officials in AST (assistant) career are also recruited to the starting grade or level.

Examples of basic monthly salary, allowances, benefits and deductions, are available in the

- *Staff Regulations* Salary is subject to a weighting factor which varies according to the cost of living in the areas concerned.

Grades	*Steps*				
1.05.2004	*1*	*2*	*3*	*4*	*5*
16	14822,86	15445,74	16094,79		
15	13100,93	13651,45	14225,11	14620,87	14822,86
14	11579,04	12065,60	12572,62	12922,41	13100,93
13	10233,93	10663,98	11112,09	11421,25	11579,04
12	9045,09	9425,17	9821,23	10094,47	10233,93
11	7994,35	8330,28	8680,33	8921,83	9045,09
10	7065,67	7362,57	7671,96	7885,41	7994,35
9	6244,87	6507,29	6780,73	6969,38	7065,67
8	5519,42	5751,35	5993,03	6159,77	6244,87
7	4878,24	5083,24	5296,84	5444,21	5519,42
6	4311,55	4492,73	4681,52	4811,77	4878,24
5	3810,69	3970,82	4137,68	4252,80	4311,55
4	3368,02	3509,54	3657,02	3758,76	3810,69
3	2976,76	3101,85	3232,19	3322,12	3368,02
2	2630,96	2741,52	2856,72	2936,20	2976,76
1	2325,33	2423,04	2524,86	2595,11	2630,96

9

Administration of Justice

Introduction

It is said justice is the maintenance or administration of what is just especially by the impartial adjustment of merited rewards and punishments. Justice may take many forms: It could be utilitarian in nature in which punishment is aimed at increased future social benefits, such as reduction in crimes. It could be retaliatory, in which crime and punishment are equal—eye for an eye. It could be retributive in which punishment is not only proportionate but also morally just. And it could be distributive in which power, wealth and benefits could be allocated among the stakeholders.

Justice could be internal and external. Internal justice is the process and mechanism established by most large organisations to redress staff grievances, undertake disciplinary measures and hear appeals on administrative verdicts. In contrast, external justice is sought with and given by a competent legal entity—tribunal or court—that works outside an individual organisation. All societies and organisations confront situations in which one party or another to a dispute seeks justice.

It is therefore that the administration of justice is one of the pillars of an organisation. With the growth of human rights at workplace and the organised labour, this pillar has been gaining increasing attention in all kinds of organisations—business, government and international. There was a time when employers could simply fire the employees they did not like, and not a single legal murmur could be heard about it. Not any more. There are more workers' rights to defend today than anytime before, and employees do not accept management's adverse decisions as a work of their fate. Conversely, employers do not hesitate to file a legal case if their employees harm them or damage their business.

The field of labour rights has greatly expanded overtime. It has happened with the spread of democracy around the world, improved education and awareness across the board, rise of international organisations committed to human rights and dignity, and the deepening concept of a welfare state. The United Nations has been at the forefront of creating new rights or bringing them to light from the shadow of society. More than anything, the Universal Declaration of Human Rights and subsequent treaties and covenants formulated under the auspices of the United Nations have enriched the field of human rights. Regional organisations have contributed their bit to the expansion of this landscape. The International Labor Organization continuously churns out fresh resolutions creating or strengthening labour rights. Governments have not stayed behind in this race, not only by accommodating some of the internationally and regionally agreed rights, but also by adding several of their own. In many cases, some states have forced global and regional organisations to embrace new rights to make them universally accepted and implemented.

With this expansion of their rights, employees have more cases and more areas to protect their rights in. Now employees fight for their various rights. Today's workforce is more educated and enlightened. It has acquired new skills and techniques to make and fight their case, and learned how to use the administration of justice structures to its advantage. New products and services in the legal field—such as fighting for compensation without fee but taking a cut from the award—have also empowered labour to fight cases that would have otherwise been inconceivable. Now protection and enforcement of labour laws has become a big business and a large sub-sector in the legal domain.

Organisations face both civil and criminal cases. Cases relating to sexual harassment, discrimination, undue departmental action and willful negligence etc. are what might be called civil cases. On the other hand, cases pertaining to scandals, corruption, criminal negligence, serious personal harm, or destruction of property through vandalism, arson, larceny, etc., might give rise to criminal cases. Management as well as employees, depending on the real or perceived harm, might raise such cases. Each organisation has its own unique rules and regulations pertaining to such cases, and they would generally like to deal with them as quickly, as amicably, and as least disruptively as possible from the comfort of their own organisation.

So an internal system of justice becomes vital for all organised bodies.The general process of internal justice has been demonstrated in the figure below.

Figure 9.1

Administration of Justice

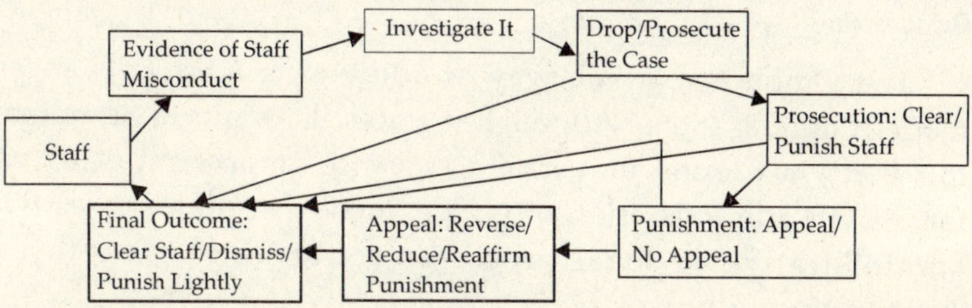

Only when internal redress mechanisms have been exhausted and when one of the parties to dispute is not satisfied with the outcome, the external administration of justice comes into play. And such a system of justice—i.e., resorting to the national court system, or regional and global courts, where applicable—is common to both employers and employees in government and the private sectors. Regional and international organisations have different sets of provisions. Some regional entities, such as the European Commission, have their own supra-national courts whose verdicts are binding on all member states. However, there is no international court so far whose verdicts are writ large on global organisations or their member states. Although the International Court of Justice, a principal organ of the United Nations, is there, it has no mandate over the United Nations in cases arising from management-employee disputes.

Administration of Justice in United Nations: Existing Provisions

Like other organisations, the United Nations has its own administration of justice. This pillar has, however, remained one of the weakest links in the UN human resources management chain. Let us have a brief look at the existing provisions in this domain.

The administration of justice in the United Nations involves three key elements: Addressing grievances, taking up disciplinary measures, and handling appeals against the administrative decisions emerging from the implementation of disciplinary measures. Although there is no mention of Ombudsman in the UN Staff Regulations and Rules, Article X of the Staff Regulations provides for disciplinary measures and Article XI for appeals.

Ombudsman

The Ombudsman is a way of addressing staff grievances in modern organisations. Although it traces its origin to Scandinavia, this body has found universal acceptance on account of its value for a swift administration of justice, mostly in minor cases where administrative or legal processes could be too lengthy and cumbersome to purse.

In the United Nations, the Ombudsman is of fairly recent origin, in fact, less than a decade old. The Secretary-General's Bulletin ST/SGB/2002/12 sets out the terms of reference for the Office of the Ombudsman.[1] It says, "The Office of the Ombudsman is established in the Office of the Secretary-General to make available the services of an impartial and independent person to address the employment-related problems of staff members. The Ombudsman shall be guided by the Charter, the Staff Regulations and the Staff Rules, as well as by the principles of justice and fairness."

1. *http://daccessdds.un.org/doc/UNDOC/GEN/N02/639/98/PDF/N0263998.pdf?OpenElement*

With respect to the nature of issues the Ombudsman is entrusted to handle, the bulletin clarifies further, "The Ombudsman shall have authority to consider conflicts of any nature related to employment by the United Nations. The term 'conflict' is to be construed in its broadest sense and includes, *inter alia,* matters pertaining to conditions of employment, administration of benefits, managerial practices, as well as professional and staff relations matters."

The Ombudsman, though working under the Office of SG, is supposed to maintain his neutrality and independence in handling the cases of grievances. He maintains confidentiality of all his communications with staff and can advise staff members of various options and avenues available to them to get their grievances addressed or refer them to such bodies as may be competent to handle such cases. The Ombudsman may also request the Joint Appeals Board to extend the normal time limit for filing an appeal within the framework of the Staff Rule 111.2. Apart from this, the Ombudsman has remained aloof from the whole scheme of administration of justice in the United Nations. The Redesign Panel report, which we have discussed later in this chapter, has sought to integrate the Ombudsman in the administration of justice's framework.

Disciplinary Measures

Regulation 10.1 stipulates, "The Secretary-General may establish administrative machinery with staff participation which will be available to advise him or her in disciplinary cases." And Regulation 10.2 lays out, "The Secretary-General may impose disciplinary measures on staff members whose conduct is unsatisfactory...may summarily dismiss a member of the staff for serious misconduct."[2]

The United Nations Staff Rules further elaborate the Staff Regulations. Rule 110.1 deals with misconduct which is defined as the failure of a staff member to comply with their obligations under the UN Charter, Staff Regulations, Staff Rules or administrative instructions or observe the standards of conduct expected of an international civil servant. It says,

2. *http://www.sas.undp.org/documents/Staff_Rules_100_English.pdf*

> Failure by a staff member to comply with his or her obligations under the Charter of the United Nations, the Staff Regulations and Staff Rules or other relevant administrative issuances, or to observe the standards of conduct expected of an international civil servant, may amount to unsatisfactory conduct within the meaning of staff regulation 10.2, leading to the institution of disciplinary proceedings and the imposition of disciplinary measures for misconduct.

Under Rule 110.2, charges of misconduct are investigated. During the investigation, SG might suspend the staff member so charged with full or part pay, which would be paid if he is cleared of the charges. It stipulates:

(a) If a charge of misconduct is made against a staff member and the Secretary-General so decides, the staff member may be suspended from duty during the investigation and pending completion of disciplinary proceedings for a period which should normally not exceed three months. Such suspension shall be with pay unless, in exceptional circumstances, the Secretary-General decides that suspension without pay is appropriate. The suspension shall be without prejudice to the rights of the staff member and shall not constitute a disciplinary measure.

(b) A staff member suspended pursuant to paragraph (a) shall be given a written statement of the reason for the suspension and its probable duration.

(c) If a suspension pursuant to paragraph (a) is without pay and the charge of misconduct is subsequently not sustained, any salary withheld shall be restored.

Rule 110.3 enunciates the following disciplinary measures, depending on the gravity of misconduct:

(i) Written censure by the Secretary-General;

(ii) Loss of one or more steps in grade;

(iii) Deferment, for a specified period, of eligibility for within-grade increment;

(iv) Suspension without pay;

(v) Fine;

(vi) Demotion;

(vii) Separation from service, with or without notice or compensation in lieu thereof, notwithstanding rule 109.3;[3]

(viii) Summary dismissal.

---

3. Rule 109.3 speaks of prior notice to be given before termination of appointment or salary and allowances in lieu of such notice.

However, an oral or written reprimand by a supervisor, recovery of money owed to the United Nations, and suspension of the staff with respect to disciplinary action are not considered disciplinary measures as such. Anyway, before disciplinary measures are imposed, the management must follow the due process as set out in Rule 110.4 (a) through (c), which is as follows:

(a) No disciplinary proceedings may be instituted against a staff member unless he or she has been notified of the allegations against him or her, as well as of the right to seek the assistance in his or her defence of another staff member or retired staff member, and has been given a reasonable opportunity to respond to those allegations.

(b) No staff member shall be subject to disciplinary measures until the matter has been referred to a Joint Disciplinary Committee for advice as to what measures, if any, are appropriate, except that no such advice shall be required:

  (i) If referral to the Joint Disciplinary Committee is waived by mutual agreement of the staff member concerned and the Secretary-General;

  (ii) In respect of summary dismissal imposed by the Secretary-General in cases where the seriousness of the misconduct warrants immediate separation from service.

(c) In cases of summary dismissal imposed without prior submission of the case to a Joint Disciplinary Committee in accordance with subparagraphs (b) (i) and (ii), the staff member or former staff member concerned may, within two months of having received written notification of the measure, request that the measure be reviewed by such a Committee. A request shall not have the effect of suspending the measure. After the advice of the Committee has been received, the Secretary-General shall decide as soon as possible what action to take in respect thereof. An appeal in respect of such a decision may not be submitted to the Joint Appeals Board.

Composition of the Joint Disciplinary Committee (JDC) and its working procedure are spelt out in Staff Rule 110.5 through 110.7. JDC must be composed of management and staff from the relevant main duty station. There is also the provision for Ad Hoc JDCs where JDCs do not exist or cannot be formed.

Appeals

Although points (a) through (c) of the Staff Rule 110.4 dwell on the due process for disciplinary measures, point (d) of the same rule provides for the due process for appeal in respect of a disciplinary measure. It says, "An appeal in respect of a disciplinary measure considered by a Joint Disciplinary Committee pursuant to either paragraph (b) or (c) may be submitted directly to the United Nations Administrative Tribunal."

The Staff Regulations 11.1 and 11.2 deal with appeals in the United Nations. Under the first, SG can establish "administrative machinery with staff participation to advise him or her in case of any appeal by staff members against an administrative decision alleging the non-observance of their terms of appointment, including all pertinent regulations and rules." According to Staff Rule 111.1, SG may establish Joint Appeals Boards for various duty stations to consider and advise him on appeals cases.

Regulation 11.2 provides for the UN Administrative Tribunal that could hear appeal cases and hand its judgment on them. The Tribunal works consistent with its own statute. Staff Rule 111.2 deals with the actual appeal process in detail. It mentions, "The United Nations Administrative Tribunal shall, under conditions prescribed in its statute, hear and pass judgment upon applications from staff members alleging non-observance of their terms of appointment, including all pertinent regulations and rules."

Briefly speaking, the staff member who has faced a disciplinary measure must first request SG in writing to review the administrative decision. If SG responds to the letter, the staff could appeal against the administrative decision and the SG's response together. If SG does not answer within a month for the New York-based staff and two months for the staff based elsewhere, the staff in question may file an appeal within the specified time. Either SG, or the staff, or the Chair of JAB could initiate conciliation, before JAB has been constituted.

Evidently, UN staff members do not have recourse to an external court, as their counterpart civil servants in various countries do.

The UN Staff Regulations and Staff Rules pertaining to disciplinary measures and appeals are presented in Annex A-9.1.

UN staff members have had a serious grudge about the poor state of administration of justice in the world body. Although there is a system in place, it is predominated by administrative measures and mechanisms which by their nature are heavily influenced by management, often stronger between the two. There is no independent body to ensure fairness and unbiased and objective verdict, which could be binding on management. Some efforts have been made to bring improvements in this area, but actual changes have been very difficult to come by. Whatever has happened so far has come about in bits and pieces. Part of the reason for this has been that no strategic endeavour was ever launched to address the shortcomings of this sector in a comprehensive way; and partly, disagreements existed between different areas of the management as well as between the management and staff; both hindered the process of building a reliable administration of justice system in the organisation.

This calls on the United Nations that it must undertake a series of serious measures to reform its system of justice. The kind of outdated system the world body has, cannot be justified in the 21st century. To bring the UN administration of justice to an acceptable level, if not the desirable level, the international community ought to work together in a serious manner. For this purpose, we might be able to draw some useful lessons from the European Commission and member states of the United Nations.

European Commission

In the European Commission, Title VI of the Staff Regulations stipulates, "Any failure by an official or former official to comply with his obligations under these Staff Regulations, whether intentionally or through negligence on his part, shall make him liable to disciplinary action."[4] When the designated appointing authority or the European Anti-Fraud Office (OLAF) becomes aware

4. *http://ec.europa.eu/civil_service/docs/toc100_en.pdf, p.38.*

of the evidence of misconduct, they launch investigation and inform the employee of its result. The appointing authority may, after hearing the employee, choose to warn or reprimand the employee without involving the Disciplinary Board or may involve the Board.

When the Board is involved, the appointing authority submits the report of investigation and communicates to the employee, who has the right to obtain their complete personal file and to be accompanied by a person of his choice in the proceedings. If the employee acknowledges the misconduct before the Disciplinary Board, he could be:

(a) warned in writing,
(b) reprimanded,
(c) prevented from going to higher step for 1-23 months,
(d) relegated to a lower step.

In case the employee does not acknowledge his misconduct, detailed hearings take place from the appointing authority, from the employee and from OLAF if an investigation was conducted. The Board takes a decision by a majority vote. The penalty may be one of those already mentioned or may, depending on the seriousness and repetitiveness of the misconduct, include:

(a) temporary downgrading from 15 days to a year,
(b) downgrading in the same function group,
(c) classification in a lower function group,
(d) removal from post,
(e) reduction in pension.

A single case of misconduct invites only one penalty. In cases of the allegation of serious misconduct, the appointing authority may suspend the employee up to six months with full pay or part pay by withholding some. The withheld pay becomes payable if the employee gets penalty no higher than a written warning, reprimand or deferment to the higher step. If the misconduct is not upheld, the employee may demand that the damage be made good through suitable publicity.[5]

---

5. Ibid, Annex IX.

Member States

We will cursorily look here at only two countries: The United Kingdom and the United States. In the United Kingdom, departments and agencies have to come up with their grievance, disciplinary and dismissal arrangements within the established guidelines set out in the Employment Act 2002 and the Employment (Dispute Resolution) Regulations 2004. There are broad and detailed guidelines for developing operating procedures for grievance and disciplinary matters. The employer must:

> establish fact before taking action; deal with case of minor misconduct or unsatisfactory performance informally; follow formal procedures, including informing the employee of the alleged misconduct or unsatisfactory performance, for more serious cases; invite the employee to a meeting and inform them of the right to be accompanied (by a fellow worker or a union official); when performance is unsatisfactory, explain to the employee the improvement required, the support that will be given and when and how performance will be reviewed; if giving a warning, tell the employee why and how they need to change, the consequences of failing to improve and that they have a right to appeal; if dismissing an employee, tell them why, when their contract will end and that he can appeal; before dismissing or taking disciplinary action other than issuing a warning, always follow the statutory dismissal and disciplinary procedure; when dealing with absences from work, find out the reasons for the absence before deciding on what action to take; if the employee wishes to appeal, invite them to a meeting and inform the employee of their right to be accompanied; where possible, arrange for the appeal to be dealt with by a more senior manager not involved with the earlier decision; and inform the employee about the appeal decision and the reasons for it.[6]

The basics of a good disciplinary procedure have been laid down. Such a procedure should:

> be put in writing; say to whom they apply; be non-discriminatory; allow for matters to be dealt without undue delay; allow for information to be kept confidential; tell employees what disciplinary action might be taken; say what levels of management have the authority to take disciplinary action; require employees to be informed of the complaints

6. *http://www.acas.org.uk/media/pdf/9/5/CP01_1.pdf,* p.4.

> against them and supporting evidence, before a meeting; give employees a chance to have their say before management reaches a decision; provide employees with the right to be accompanied; provide that no employee is dismissed for a first breach of discipline, except in cases of gross misconduct; require management to investigate fully before any disciplinary action is taken; ensure that employees are given an explanation for any sanction; and allow employees to appeal against a decision.[7]

There is also a set of grievance procedures, which are not very different in essence from the disciplinary procedures, except for the fact that preference is given to addressing grievances informally as much as possible.[8] There are some differences in the appeal procedure as well. Further information in this regard—Standard Statutory Dismissal and Disciplinary Procedures in the United Kingdom—is presented in Annex A-9.2 of this chapter.

Many of the fundamental procedures applicable to British civil servants also apply to the US federal civil servants, with some nuances here and there. The US civil servants enjoy, as do civil servants in other countries, several rights on their jobs. They cannot be prosecuted for the inadvertent mistakes they might make; there could be no discrimination between employees on the basis of who they are; and due process of law must always be followed when a departmental or legal action against any employee is instituted. There are detailed investigation procedures with time lines laid out in the US Code.[9]

Evidently the Special Counsel is a key figure in the disciplinary regime of the US federal civil service. The Counsel may determine to take disciplinary action when an employee has committed a prohibited personnel practice; violated any provision of law, rule or regulation; engaged in prohibited political activities; withheld prohibited information; involved in prohibited discrimination and knowingly and willfully refused or failed to comply with an order

7. Ibid: 19.

8. Ibid: 22.

9. *http://www4.law.cornell.edu/uscode/search/display.html?terms=disciplinary%20action&url=/uscode/html/uscode05/usc_sec_05_00001214——000-.html*

of the Merit System Protection Board. The Special Counsel prepares a written complaint together with his determination and facts and presents the complaint to the employee and the Board. After that, the employee is entitled to reasonable time to answer the allegations, to an attorney or representative, to a hearing before the Board or an administrative law judge, and to the transcript of the hearing and decision.

After a careful hearing of the case in question, the Board may decide to remove the employee, reduce their grade, debar them from federal employment for up to 5 years, suspend, reprimand, or impose a penalty not exceeding $1,000. The Merit Protection Board may hear any appeal filed with it or refer it to an administrative law judge, or an employee of the Board experienced in hearing such cases. But the Board hears all those cases involving a removal from the service.[10] The previous decision could be reversed or reaffirmed in the appeal process. A copy of the decision is furnished to each party to the appeal and to the Office of Personnel Management. There is no administrative appeal against the Board's verdict but the employee may file a petition with court for judicial review.[11] If the employee prevails in the process, the Board may require the concerned agency to pay the reasonable attorney fees incurred by the staff in question.

Obviously, the administration of justice in member states is much more objective and advanced than in the United Nations. The United Nations can learn a lot from its own experience, from member states and the European Commission, and adapt their systems to its own.

Status and Observations

The Administrative Law Unit of OHRM handles different sources of disciplinary cases in the Secretariat. Obviously, the Unit logged the following cases in the last few years:

---

10. *http://www4.law.cornell.edu/uscode/5/usc_sec_05_00007701——000-.html*

11. Ibid.

Table 9.1

Year	Review cases		Appeals cases				Disciplinary cases				Total
	Total	Completed	Carried over from previous year	New	Total	Completed	Carried over from previous year	New	Total	Completed	Total
2006	157	79	31	68	99	78	51	72	123	66	379
2007	157	109	21	55	76	67	57	173	230	79	463
2008a	181	84	80	45	125	44	143	277	448	84	754
2008b		240			150				250		

Note: a. Based on the number of cases received as on 24 October 2008.

b. Projected for 31 December 2008 based on the number of cases as on 24 October 2008.

Source: ACABQ report on Administrative of Justice, A/3/545, p.4.

The above figures make it clear that the administration of justice is a major area of concern for the United Nations. Evidently the number of cases is piling up year after year, thanks to increase in the number of staff, in the awareness about staff rights and slow disposal of cases. What is more, there is no credible system of administration of justice, and this has been a major issue for the staff ever since the establishment of the organisation.

Attempts at reforming the UN administration of justice were made as far back as 1976 when the Federation of International Civil Servants' Association (FICSA), following a symposium in January that year, formulated several proposals about the functioning of an administrative tribunal. The Consultative Committee on Administrative Questions (CCAQ) examined the proposals, and in 1979, a joint working group of FISCA and CCAQ considered the proposals but could not decide. Difficulty in harmonisation between the UN administrative tribunal (UNAT) and the ILO administrative tribunal (ILOAT), which the General Assembly wanted, did not allow GA to take any concrete forward action in this area for several years, apart from continue considering the issue for improvement in administration of justice and asking SG to look into the matter. In 1988, however, SG proposed amending the Statute and Rules of UNAT and recommended that ILO do the same.[12]

By resolution 44/185 B of 19 December 1989, the General Assembly noted the significance of an efficient internal administration of justice that prompted SG to present his further report in 1990. At that point, the issue of harmonisation between UNAT and ILOAT was postponed indefinitely. As asked by GA, SG submitted another report in 1994 proposing to change the Joint Appeals Board and the Joints Disciplinary Committee into bodies composed of administrators and chaired by eminent figures recruited from outside the organisation. Resolution 49/222 of 23 December 1994 of GA asked SG to present a report on implementation measures to reform the administration of justice. SG amended his

12. United Nations (2000). *Administration of Justice at the United Nations*. A JIU Report. Geneva. p.1.

previous proposal taking into account the comments of UNAT, but his proposal did not win the support of GA.[13]

In his landmark report on reform of 1997—*A Programme for Reform*—SG Kofi Annan did not address the issue of administrative justice *per se*. However, he did discuss the matter in his report—*An Agenda for Further Change*, presented in 2002—and proposed action 34 which says, "A review of the current system of internal justice will be conducted to improve the efficiency of the system and to allow staff fair and due process."[14] Like his report of 1997, the SG's report—*In Larger Freedom*—submitted to GA in 2005 did not substantively cover the internal administration of justice. In paragraph 25 of his report of 2006—*Investing in the United Nations*—SG admitted, "The internal justice system is slow and cumbersome, and fails to strike the necessary balance between effective managerial control and staff members' right to due process."[15] In paragraph 30 of the same report, SG says, "The redesign panel currently looking at the internal justice system is also critical to the success of these changes. Without a justice system that delivers fair resolution of staff/management disputes in a timely way, the other reforms will be undermined."[16]

The Redesign Panel on the United Nations System of Administration of Justice presented comprehensive recommendations later the same year.[17] The Panel has called for a complete change in the way justice is carried out in the United Nations and for formal and informal systems of justice. Key recommendations include: The existing system should be replaced with a new one which should be professional, indepndent and decentralised; an Office of Administration of Justice, headed by an Assistant Secretary-General should be established; the process of administrative review before action in the formal justice system should be abolished; a new UN

13. Ibid: 2.

14. United Nations (2002). *Strengthening of the United Nations: An Agenda for Further Change*. New York. p.33.

15. United Nations (2006). *Investing in the United Nations*. New York. para 25.

16. Ibid: 30.

17. United Nations (2006). *Report of the Redesign Panel on the United Nations System of Administration of Justice*. New York. July. The Panel was constituted as per GA resolution 59/283.

Dispute Tribunal, composed of professional judges appointed by SG, should replace the existing advisory bodies like the Joint Appeals Boards and the Joint Disciplinary Committees; the UN Administrative Tribunal should be renamed as UN Appeals Tribunal with expanded appeallate jurisdiction, and their judges should be appointed by the General Assembly; managers and staff members should be held accountable for their decisions and actions, and the Dispute Tribunal judges should accept applications to enforce accountability by referring such cases to SG; the heads of missions and offices away from headquarters should have full authority in misconduct and disciplinary cases; a professional Office of Counsel should be established under the proposed Office of the Administration of Justice. A chart of the proposed system of internal justice for the United Nations is presented in Annex A-9.4.

In addition, the Redesign Panel has also made several recommendations with respect to the Ombudsman. It has called for an integrated but decentralised Ombudsman in the UN system; the selection of Ombudsman to be made by a joint committee of representatives of SG, the staff and one of the distinguished outside Ombudsmans; the abolition of the Panels on Discrimination and Other Grievances and transfer of their functions to the Office of the Ombudsman and a Mediation Division to be set up in the Office of the Ombudsman. All the recommendations of the Redesign Panel are produced in Annex A-9.3. Another chart presented in Annex A-9.5 reflects the Redesign Panel's proposal for the Ombudsman.

After Staff-Management consultations, SG submitted in 2007 the first batch of his comments on the Report of the Redesign Panel, in which he asked GA to approve the Panel's recommendations with some adjustments.[18] Subsequently, in its resolution 61/261, the General Assembly—after considering the Redesign Panel's report, the SG's note on the report and ACABQ report on the matter—decided to

> establish a new, independent, transparent, professionalised, adequately resourced and decentralised system of administration of justice. The new system is to be implemented no later than January

---

18. United Nations (2007). *Note of the Secretary-General on the Report of the Redesign Panel on the United Nations system of Administration of Justice.* New York. February.

2009...and requested the Secretary-General to report providing additional information...including on resources required for the implementation of the resolution...[19]

As a response, SG presented his report, in which he sought to address the issue related to different categories of non-staff personnel performing personal services, types of dispute settlement mechanisms, types of grievances raised by non-staff personnel and any other mechanism to provide effective and efficient dispute settlement for non-staff personnel.[20] An Ad Hoc Committee has, after having considered the SG's reports, recommended in April 2008 to the General Assembly that it establish a working group to finalise the draft statute of the UN Dispute Tribunal and the UN Appeals Tribunal.[21] Accordingly an Ad Hoc Committee is considering the draft statutes of these tribunals.

The SG's report—Administration of Justice at the United Nations[22]—of 20 August 2008, responds to GA resolution 62/228 which endorsed the proposal of SG for limited delegation of authority for disciplinary matters and asked SG to report on the issue for further information on full delegation of authority to offices away from headquarters as well as the possible implications for the due process rights of staff members. On this report, GA is yet to take a decision.

This all makes amply clear the poor state of the system of administration of justice in the United Nations, which is still far from satisfactory. Now one sees a glimmer hope that the UN staff will have a reliable and independent recourse to address their grievances and justice needs. However, it will take some time before the General Assembly accepts the Redesign Panel's recommendations, possibly with modifications proposed by SG, and SG implements them fully to replace the existing poor system of administration of justice in the UN house.

---

19. United Nations (2007). *Administration of Justice*. New York. August p.4.
20. United Nations (2008). *Administration of Justice: Further Information Requested by the General Assembly. New York. March*. p.3.
21. United Nations (2008). *Report of the Ad Hoc Committee on the Administration of Justice at the United Nations*. New York. April. p.6.
22. United Nations (2008). *Administration of Justice at the United Nations*, A/63/314 of 20 August.

Finally something has been done in this area. A new internal justice system came into existence on 1 July 2009, which aims to provide a professionalised, independent and expedient way of dealing with work related disputes. There are three entities—a new UN Dispute Tribunal (UNDT) and the UN Appeals Tribunal (UNAT) as well as the Office of Staff Legal Assistance (OSLA). The selection process for the heads of the regional ombudsman branches, and for the Head of Mediation Division are in the final stage, and the system will be fully operational to receive cases from 1 July 2009.

The judges appointed by the General Assembly to the new tribunals are on board. For the first time, the UN has full time judges adjudicating administrative appeals in the Dispute Tribunals located in New York, Geneva, and Nairobi. There are two half time judge to serve on a rotating basis at each of the three UNDT locations.

The Joint Appeals Boards (JAB) and Joint Disciplinary Committees (JDC) were abolished on 30 June 2009.[23]

23. See for details, GA resolution 63/253 of 24 December 2008 published on 17 March 2009. This resolution, which has also approved the Statute of the United Nations Dispute Tribunal and the Statute of the United Nations Appeals Tribunal, has brought significant changes in the administration of justice and rules pertaining to it.

Annex A-9.1

UN Staff Regulations and Rules

Article X

DISCIPLINARY MEASURES

Regulation 10.1

The Secretary-General may establish administrative machinery with staff participation which will be available to advise him or her in disciplinary cases.

Regulation 10.2

The Secretary-General may impose disciplinary measures on staff members whose conduct is unsatisfactory.

The Secretary-General may summarily dismiss a member of the staff for serious misconduct.

Chapter X

DISCIPLINARY MEASURES AND PROCEDURES

Rule 110.1

Misconduct

Failure by a staff member to comply with his or her obligations under the Charter of the United Nations, the Staff Regulations and Staff Rules or other relevant administrative issuances, or to observe the standards of conduct expected of an international civil servant, may amount to unsatisfactory conduct within the meaning of staff regulation 10.2, leading to the institution of disciplinary proceedings and the imposition of disciplinary measures for misconduct.

Rule 110.2

Suspension during Investigation and Disciplinary Proceedings

(a) If a charge of misconduct is made against a staff member and the Secretary-General so decides, the staff member may be suspended from duty during the investigation and pending completion of disciplinary proceedings for a period which should normally not exceed three months. Such suspension shall be with pay unless, in exceptional circumstances, the Secretary-General decides that suspension without pay is appropriate. The suspension shall be without prejudice to the rights of the staff member and shall not constitute a disciplinary measure.

(b) A staff member suspended pursuant to paragraph (a) shall be given a written statement of the reason for the suspension and its probable duration.

(c) If a suspension pursuant to paragraph (a) is without pay and the charge of misconduct is subsequently not sustained, any salary withheld shall be restored.

Rule 110.3

Disciplinary Measures

(a) Disciplinary measures may take one or more of the following forms:

(i) Written censure by the Secretary-General;

(ii) Loss of one or more steps in grade;

(iii) Deferment, for a specified period, of eligibility for within-grade increment;

(iv) Suspension without pay;

(v) Fine;

(vi) Demotion;

(vii) Separation from service, with or without notice or compensation in lieu thereof, notwithstanding rule 109.3;

(viii) Summary dismissal.

(b) The following measures shall not be considered to be disciplinary measures, within the meaning of this rule:

(i) Reprimand, written or oral, by a supervisory official;

(ii) Recovery of moneys owed to the Organisation;

(iii) Suspension pursuant to rule 110.2.

Rule 110.4

Due Process

(a) No disciplinary proceedings may be instituted against a staff member unless he or she has been notified, in writing, of the allegations against him or her, and of the right to seek the assistance of counsel in his or her defence at his or her own expense, and has been given a reasonable opportunity to respond to those allegations.

(b) No staff member shall be subject to disciplinary measures until the matter has been referred to a Joint Disciplinary Committee for advice as to what measures, if any, are appropriate, except that no such advice shall be required:

(i) If referral to the Joint Disciplinary Committee is waived by mutual agreement of the staff member concerned and the Secretary-General;

(ii) In respect of summary dismissal imposed by the Secretary-General in cases where the seriousness of the misconduct warrants immediate separation from service.

(c) In cases of summary dismissal imposed without prior submission of the case to a Joint Disciplinary Committee in accordance with subparagraphs (b) (i) and (ii), the staff member or former staff member concerned may, within two months of having received written notification of the measure, request that the measure be reviewed by such a Committee. A request shall not have the effect of suspending the measure. After the advice of the Committee has been received, the Secretary-General shall decide as soon as possible what action to take in respect thereof. An appeal in respect of such a decision may not be submitted to the Joint Appeals Board.

(d) An appeal in respect of a disciplinary measure considered by a Joint Disciplinary Committee pursuant to either paragraph (b) or (c), or in respect of financial responsibility for gross negligence pursuant to rule 110.5 shall be submitted directly to the United Nations Administrative Tribunal.

Rule 110.5

Joint Disciplinary Committees

(a) A standing Joint Disciplinary Committee is established and shall be available to advise the Secretary-General at his or her request in disciplinary matters at Headquarters; comparable standing committees may be established in the United Nations Office at Geneva, the United Nations Office at Vienna and such other offices as may be designated by the Secretary-General.

(b) The Secretary-General may also establish ad hoc Joint Disciplinary Committees at these or other duty stations for a particular case or series of cases, or may substitute an alternate procedure that conforms to the requirements of due process at duty stations or missions where there is no established staff representative body.

(c) The Joint Disciplinary Committee at Headquarters shall also be available to advise the Secretary-General at his request in matters pertaining to financial responsibility for gross negligence.

Rule 110.6

Composition of Joint Disciplinary Committees

(a) Each standing Joint Disciplinary Committee shall be composed of:

(i) Chairpersons, appointed by the Secretary-General after consultation with the staff representative body or bodies at the duty station at which the Committee is established;

(ii) Members appointed by the Secretary-General;

(iii) Members elected by the staff at the duty station at which the Committee is established.

(b) If necessary, additional members may be selected at any time in the same manner as indicated in paragraph (a).

(c) The chairpersons and members of the Joint Disciplinary Committee shall be appointed or elected for two years, shall be eligible for reappointment or reelection and shall remain in office until their successors are appointed or elected as long as they are staff members assigned to the duty station of the Committee.

(d) A chairperson may be removed from the Joint Disciplinary Committee by the Secretary-General after consultation with the staff representative body or bodies at the duty station at which the Committee is established. The members appointed by the Secretary-General may be removed by him or her. The members elected by the staff may be recalled by a majority vote of the staff at the duty station at which the Committee is established, taken at the initiative of any staff representative body at that duty station.

(e) The Secretary-General shall, in consultation with the staff representative body or bodies at the duty station at which a Joint Disciplinary Committee is established, appoint a Presiding Officer from among the panel of chairpersons.

(f) For the consideration of each case, a panel of the Joint Disciplinary Committee shall be constituted by the Presiding Officer as follows:

(i) A chairperson;

(ii) A member from among those appointed by the Secretary-General;

(iii) A member from among those elected by the staff.

The Presiding Officer, at the request of either party, may disqualify the chairperson or any member from the consideration of a specific case if in the opinion of the Presiding Officer the action is warranted by the relation of that member to the staff member whose case is to be considered or by any possible conflict of interest. The Presiding Officer may also excuse any member at that member's request from the consideration of a specific case.

(g) Ad hoc Joint Disciplinary Committees shall be composed as follows:

(i) At duty stations where there is an established staff representative body or bodies, ad hoc Joint Disciplinary Committees shall be composed, by the Secretary-General or an official designated by him or her, in a manner similar to that of standing Joint Disciplinary Committees, except that staff-appointed members may be substituted for staff-elected members. If no appointments are made within a period set by the Secretary-General, the designated official may make the appointments after consultation with the staff representative body or bodies;

(ii) At duty stations or missions where there is no established staff representative body, the head of office or mission, after reporting the matter to the Secretary-General, shall constitute a panel from among staff present at the duty station to investigate the allegations and to recommend what, if any, disciplinary measure should be imposed. The panel members shall be selected with a view to ensuring that the rights of all parties are respected.

(h) Any case relating to a staff member serving at a duty station where a standing Joint Disciplinary Committee is established shall be referred to that Committee, unless the Secretary-General considers there is a good reason to refer the case to a standing Committee at a different duty station or to an ad hoc Committee at the same or another duty station.

(i) When the advice of the Joint Disciplinary Committee at Headquarters is sought in a matter pertaining to financial responsibility for gross negligence, the level of the members constituting the panel shall be at least the same as the level of the staff member whose financial responsibility may be engaged.

Rule 110.7

Joint Disciplinary Committee Procedure

(a) In considering a case, the Joint Disciplinary Committee shall act with maximum dispatch and shall make every effort to provide its advice to the Secretary-General within four weeks after the case has been submitted to it.

(b) Proceedings before a Joint Disciplinary Committee shall normally be limited to the original written presentation of the case, together with brief statements and rebuttals, which may be made orally or in writing, but without delay. If the Committee considers that it requires the testimony of the staff member concerned or of other witnesses, it may, at its sole discretion, obtain such testimony by written deposition, by personal appearance before the Committee, before one of its members or before another staff member acting as a special master, or by telephone or other means of communication.

(c) Each standing Joint Disciplinary Committee shall adopt its own rules of procedure, which shall be consistent with these Staff Rules and with any applicable administrative instructions, as well as with the requirements of due process. An ad hoc Committee shall apply the rules of procedure of the Headquarters Joint Disciplinary Committee, except to the extent that it decides, consistent with the requirements of due process, to apply other such rules.

(d) A Joint Disciplinary Committee shall permit a staff member to arrange to have his or her case presented before it by counsel, at his or her own expense, at the duty station where the Committee is established.

(e) A representative of the Office of Legal Affairs shall participate in an advisory capacity in the deliberations of the Joint Disciplinary Committee at Headquarters on an ex officio basis when the advice of the Committee has been requested in a matter pertaining to financial responsibility for gross negligence.

Article XI

APPEALS

Regulation 11.1

The Secretary-General shall establish administrative machinery with staff participation to advise him or her in case of any appeal by staff members against an administrative decision alleging the non-observance of their terms of appointment, including all pertinent regulations and rules.

Regulation 11.2

The United Nations Administrative Tribunal shall, under conditions prescribed in its statute, hear and pass judgment upon applications from staff members alleging non-observance of their terms of appointment, including all pertinent regulations and rules.

Chapter XI

JOINT APPEALS BOARDS

Rule 111.1

Establishment

(a) Joint appeals boards shall be established in New York, Geneva, Vienna and Nairobi and at such other duty stations as may be designated by the Secretary-General to consider and advise the Secretary-General regarding appeals filed under the terms of staff regulation 11.1.

(b) Each Joint Appeals Board shall be composed of:

(i) Chairpersons appointed by the Secretary-General after selection by the joint staff-management machinery in respect of the staff representative body or bodies at the duty station at which the Board is established;

(ii) Members appointed by the Secretary-General;

(iii) An equal number of members elected by ballot of the staff under the jurisdiction of the Board.

The number of chairpersons and members of each Board shall be determined by the Secretary-General upon recommendation of the joint staff-management machinery in respect of the staff representative body or bodies at the duty station at which the Board is established.

(c) The chairpersons and members of the Joint Appeals Board shall be appointed or elected for two years, shall be eligible for reappointment or re-election and shall remain in office until their successors are appointed or elected.

(d) A chairperson may be removed from a Joint Appeals Board by the Secretary-General upon recommendation of the joint staff-management machinery in respect of the staff representative body or bodies of the duty station at which the Board is established. The members appointed by the Secretary-General may be removed by him or her. The members elected by the staff may be recalled by a majority vote of the staff under the jurisdiction of the Board concerned, taken at the initiative of any staff representative body at the duty station at which that Board is established.

(e) Each Joint Appeals Board shall establish its own rules of procedure, which shall specify how its presiding officer and, where necessary, any alternate presiding officers shall be selected from among the chairpersons.

(f) Each Joint Appeals Board may, by a majority vote of all its chairpersons and members, recommend to the Secretary-General changes in the present chapter of the Staff Rules.

(g) The secretariat of each Joint Appeals Board shall consist of a secretary and such other staff as may be required for its proper functioning.

[SR 111.1 as amended by ST/SGB/2003/1, effective 1 January 2003]

Rule 111.2

Appeals

(a) A staff member wishing to appeal an administrative decision pursuant to staff regulation 11.1 shall, as a first step, address a letter to the Secretary-General requesting that the administrative decision be reviewed; such letter must be sent within two months from the date the staff member received notification of the decision in writing. The staff member shall submit a copy of the letter to the executive head of his or her department, office, fund or programme.

[effective 1 January 2006]

(i) If the Secretary-General replies to the staff member's letter, he or she may appeal against the answer within one month of the receipt of such reply;

(ii) If the Secretary-General does not reply to the letter within one month in respect of a staff member stationed in New York or within two months in respect of a staff member stationed elsewhere, the staff member may appeal against the original administrative decision within one month of the expiration of the time limit specified in this subparagraph for the Secretary-General's reply.

(b) At any time after a request for review has been submitted, but before a panel of the Joint Appeals Board has been constituted to hear an appeal, conciliation may be sought on the issues involved at the initiative of the Secretary-General, the staff member or the presiding officer of the Joint Appeals Board. The presiding officer shall refer the matter for that purpose to a chairperson or member of the Joint Appeals Board. This procedure is without prejudice to the right of the staff member to pursue an appeal under the provisions of this rule if the issues cannot be resolved through conciliation.

(c) Neither a request for administrative review under paragraph (a) above nor the filing of an appeal under paragraph (d) below shall have the effect of suspending action on the contested decision.

(i) However, the staff member concerned may request a suspension of action on such decision by writing to the

Secretary of the appropriate Joint Appeals Board under paragraph (d) below. The request shall set forth the relevant facts and indicate how implementation would directly and irreparably injure the staff member's rights;

(ii) Upon receipt of such a request, a panel of the Board shall be promptly constituted and shall act expeditiously. If the panel, after considering the views of both parties, determines that the decision has not been implemented and that its implementation would result in irreparable injury to the appellant, it may recommend to the Secretary-General the suspension of action on that decision:

a. Until the time limits specified in subparagraph (a) (i) or (ii) have passed without an appeal having been filed; or

b. If an appeal is filed, until a decision on the appeal is taken;

(iii) The Secretary-General's decision on such a recommendation is not subject to appeal.

(d) An appeal pursuant to paragraph (a) or a request for suspension of action pursuant to paragraph (c) above shall be filed with the Secretary of the appropriate Joint Appeals Board, to be determined as follows:

(i) With respect to staff members serving at a duty station at which a Board has been established or who are administered by organisational units located at such duty station, it shall be the Board;

(ii) With respect to former staff members who last served at a duty station at which a Board has been established or who were administered by organisational units located at such a duty station, it shall be that Board;

(iii) With respect to all other staff members and all other former staff members, it shall be the Board established in New York, provided that the Secretary-General may decide, at the request of the staff member, to refer the appeal to another one of the Boards or to establish an appropriate ad hoc body. Such staff members or former staff members may meet the time limits specified in subparagraph (a) (i) or (ii) by delivering the requisite submissions within such limits to any office of the United Nations for transmission to the appropriate Board.

(e) (i) For the consideration of each appeal, the presiding officer of the appropriate Joint Appeals Board shall constitute a panel of the Board, composed as follows:

a. A panel chairperson from among the chairpersons of the Board;

b. A member selected from among those appointed by the Secretary-General;

c. A member selected from among those elected by the staff;

(ii) In constituting such panels, the maximum possible rotation of chairpersons and members of the Board shall be observed: the modalities of such rotation shall be specified in the rules of procedure of the Board. No person who has assisted the Secretary-General in a conciliation procedure referred to in paragraph (b) shall serve on a panel established to consider an appeal relating to the same case;

(iii) Before a panel undertakes consideration of an appeal, the parties shall be notified of the proposed composition thereof. The presiding officer of the Board may, at the request of either party, disqualify the chairperson or either member if, in the opinion of the presiding officer, such action is warranted to ensure impartiality. He or she may also excuse the chairperson or either member from serving on the panel;

(iv) Subject to the principles set out in subparagraphs (i) to (iii), the presiding officer of the Board shall fill any vacancies arising on the panel.

(f) An appeal shall not be receivable unless the time limits specified in paragraph (a) above have been met or have been waived, in exceptional circumstances, by the panel constituted for the appeal.

(g) At the duty station where the appeal is considered, the designated representative of the Secretary-General shall submit a written reply within two months following the date of receipt of the appeal.

(h) Proceedings before a panel shall normally be limited to the original written presentation of the case, together with brief statements and rebuttals, which may be made orally or in writing, in one of the working languages of the Secretariat.

(i) A staff member may arrange to have his or her appeal presented to the panel on his or her behalf by counsel, at his or her own expense.

[effective 1 May 2003]

(j) Where the competence of the Joint Appeals Board is in doubt, the panel constituted for the appeal shall decide.

(k) In the case of termination or other action on grounds of inefficiency or relative efficiency, the panel shall not consider the substantive question of efficiency but only evidence that the decision was motivated by prejudice or by some other extraneous factor.

(l) The panel shall have authority to call members of the Secretariat who may be able to provide information concerning the issues before it and shall have access to all documents pertinent to the case. Notwithstanding the preceding sentence, should the panel wish to have information or documents relating to the proceedings of the central review bodies in questions involving appointment and promotion, it shall request such information or documents from the Chairperson of the appropriate central review body, who shall decide on the panel's request, taking into account the interests of confidentiality. This decision of the Chairperson of the central review body is not subject to appeal. The Chairperson of the panel shall determine which documents are to be transmitted to all members of the panel and the parties.

[effective 1 May 2002]

(m) In considering an appeal, the panel shall act with the maximum dispatch consistent with a fair review of the issues before it.

(n) Within one month of the date on which the consideration of an appeal has been completed, the panel shall, by majority vote, adopt and submit a report to the Secretary-General. The report shall be considered as constituting a record of the proceedings in the appeal and may include a summary of the matter as well as all recommendations that the panel considers appropriate. Votes on the recommendations shall be recorded, and any member of the panel may have his or her dissenting opinion included in the report.

(o) Notwithstanding the above, if the appeal involves a claim having a cumulative maximum value not in excess of one thousand and five hundred dollars ($1,500) on account of salary, emoluments or any other entitlement under the Staff Regulations and Staff Rules, such claim shall be considered a "small claim" and shall be dealt with accordingly under appropriate rules of procedure which the Joint Appeals Board competent to hear the appeal may have adopted. Such rules may require the designated representative of the Secretary-General to submit comments within thirty days of receipt of the claim from the Joint Appeals Board secretariat.

(p) The final decision on the appeal will normally be taken by the Secretary-General within one month after the panel has forwarded its report, and shall be communicated to the staff member, together with a copy of the panel's report. The Secretary-General's decision and a copy of the panel's report shall also be transmitted to a designated officer of the staff representative body or bodies at the duty station at which the Joint Appeals Board is established, unless the staff member objects.

(q) To enable staff members to exercise their right to make application to the Administrative Tribunal under article 7, paragraphs 2 (b) and (c), of its statute, the Secretary of the Joint Appeals Board concerned shall, at the request of the staff member, communicate to him or her the report of the panel if the Secretary-General has not made a decision on the report within a period of one month after the date on which the report was submitted to him or her.

Annex A-9.2

Standard Statutory Dismissal and Disciplinary Procedure in the United Kingdom[23]

(This is a summary of the statutory procedure which is set out in full in Schedule 2 to the Employment Act 2002.)

This procedure applies to disciplinary action short of dismissal (excluding oral and written warnings and suspension on full pay) based on either conduct or capability. It also applies to dismissals (except for constructive dismissals) including dismissals on the basis of conduct, capability, expiry of a fixed-term contract, redundancy and retirement. However, it does not apply in certain kinds of excepted cases that are described in Annex E.

Step 1

Statement of grounds for action and invitation to meeting

- The employer must set out in writing the employee's alleged conduct or characteristics, or other circumstances, which lead them to contemplate dismissing or taking disciplinary action against the employee.
- The employer must send the statement or a copy of it to the employee and invite the employee to attend a meeting to discuss the matter.

Step 2

The meeting

- The meeting must take place before action is taken, except in the case where the disciplinary action consists of suspension.
- The meeting must not take place unless:
  - i) the employer has informed the employee what the basis was for including in the statement under Step 1 the ground or grounds given in it; and
  - ii) the employee has had a reasonable opportunity to consider their response to that information.
- The employee must take all reasonable steps to attend the meeting.

---

23. ACAS, *Disciplinary and Grievance Procedure, http://www.acas.org.uk/media/pdf/9/5/CP01_1.pdf*, pp. 38-39.

- After the meeting, the employer must inform the employee of their decision and notify them of the right to appeal against the decision if they are not satisfied with it.
- Employees have the right to be accompanied at the meeting (see section 3).

Step 3

Appeal

- If the employee wishes to appeal, they must inform the employer.
- If the employee informs the employer of their wish to appeal, the employer must invite them to attend a further meeting.
- The employee must take all reasonable steps to attend the meeting.
- The appeal meeting need not take place before the dismissal or disciplinary action takes effect.
- Where reasonably practicable, the appeal should be dealt with by a more senior manager than attended the first meeting (unless the most senior manager attended that meeting).
- After the appeal meeting, the employer must inform the employee of their final decision.
- Employees have the right to be accompanied at the appeal meeting. 4 –

Note by authors: There are several appeals bodies in the UK. First line of appeal is the employee's senior; the Commission for Racial Equality and Equal Opportunities Commission take equal opportunities appeals; the Civil Service Appeal Board hears forfeiture of superannuation, dismissal or early retirement, non-payment of staff compensation, and refusal to allow participation in political activities. The Employment Tribunal also hears cases of dismissal.[24] Courts are the next line of appeal.

24. *http://www.cps.gov.uk/Publications/humanresources/pmm/section2/chapter_5.html#17*

Annex A-9.3

Recommendations of the Redesign Panel

152. The Redesign Panel recommends the establishment by the General Assembly of a completely new system of administration of justice in the United Nations. The new internal justice system should be a professional, independent and decentralised one, fully consistent with international human rights standards.

153. The Redesign Panel recommends the early establishment of an Office of Administration of Justice in the United Nations, headed by an executive director with the rank of Assistant Secretary-General.

154. In this context, the Panel recommends the establishment of a two-tiered system of formal justice, comprising a first-instance decentralised tribunal, the United Nations Dispute Tribunal, composed of professional judges with power to make binding decisions and with jurisdiction as set out in annex I. The Tribunal should replace existing advisory bodies, including the Joint Appeals Boards and the Joint Disciplinary Committees, but not including the rebuttal panels and Classification Appeals and Review Committees.

155. The United Nations Administrative Tribunal should be renamed the United Nations Appeals Tribunal and its Statute amended to include a new appellate jurisdiction as set out in Annex A-9.2.

156. The scope and jurisdiction of the informal and formal internal justice system should include all persons employed by the United Nations in a remunerated post or performing personal services under contract with the Organisation.

157. Consultations should be held with the United Nations Joint Staff Pension Fund and other bodies subject to the administrative jurisdiction of the Administrative Tribunal with a view to amending its Statute to expand the definition of staff, to enable it to grant the relief it considers appropriate and otherwise to bring it into harmony with the Statute of the Administrative Tribunal of the International Labour Organisation.

158. The process of administrative review before action in the formal justice system should be abolished.

159. Managers and staff members should be held personally accountable for their decisions and actions. Accordingly, the formal justice system should entertain applications for the enforcement of individual financial accountability, and Dispute Tribunal judges should have power to refer appropriate cases to the Secretary-General for possible action to enforce that accountability.
160. Staff associations should have an independent right to bring a class or representative action on behalf of their members.
161. Full delegation of authority should be granted to special representatives of the Secretary-General heading peacekeeping and political missions and to heads of offices away from Headquarters in misconduct and disciplinary cases.
162. A clear framework of cooperation and coordination between the Office of Internal Oversight Services and the United Nations internal justice system should be established on a priority basis.
163. Standing Boards of Inquiry should be established in all peacekeeping missions of the United Nations, with full-time members in large missions.
164. The Redesign Panel recommends a single integrated but decentralised Office of the Ombudsman for the United Nations Secretariat and the funds and programmes.
165. The Secretary-General should appoint the United Nations Ombudsman; the Ombudsman for funds and programmes will be appointed by the executive heads of those bodies. A selection committee, composed of a staff representative, a management representative and two distinguished outside Ombudsmen, one appointed by the staff and one by management, and chaired by a third distinguished Ombudsman appointed jointly by the Secretary-General and the executive heads of the funds and programmes, should submit a list of not fewer than three names for each position of Ombudsman, taking into consideration the nature and the characteristics of these institutions.
166. The Office of the Ombudsman should be strengthened by combining the functions of formal mediation with proactive monitoring of maladministration.
167. A Mediation Division should be established within the Office of the Ombudsman.

168. The Panels on Discrimination and Other Grievances should be abolished; their functions, as they relate to the informal system, should be transferred to the Office of the Ombudsman and their other functions to the formal system of justice.
169. The Staff Rules and Regulations should be amended to allow the Secretary-General to declare a post vacant where the appointment process has been flawed.
170. A professionalised Office of Counsel should be established and located in the proposed Office of the Administration of Justice.
171. The Department of Peacekeeping Operations should take the necessary steps to identify the peacekeeping missions of adequate size that would benefit most from the services of Ombudsmen and coordinators of the Office of Counsel and ensure the inclusion of such posts in the missions' budget proposals.
172. Proceedings in the formal justice system should be brought against the Organisation or the relevant fund or programme, not the Secretary-General or the executive heads.
173. An Internal Justice Council should be established to compile lists of candidates for appointment as judges in the Organisation's internal justice system, and to monitor that system.
174. Judges of the United Nations Administrative Tribunal should be appointed by the General Assembly from the list of candidates prepared by the Internal Justice Council. In the case of the judges of the United Nations Dispute Tribunal, they should be appointed by the Secretary-General from the list prepared by the Internal Justice Council.
175. The new internal justice system should be provided with post resources as setout in annexes III, IV and V.
176. Subject to the approval of a new system of internal justice by the General Assembly, it should become operational on 1 January 2008.
177. Education and training will be the cornerstone of the successful operation of the new internal justice system. Intensive training should be provided to all persons involved in the internal justice system. Staff members should be provided with a simply written handbook on the new system in all six official languages of the United Nations as a matter of priority.

Note: the paragraph numbers those as they exist in the Panel's Report, and its recommendations start with Paragraph 152.

Annex A-9.4

Redesign Panel: Proposed System of United Nations Internal Justice

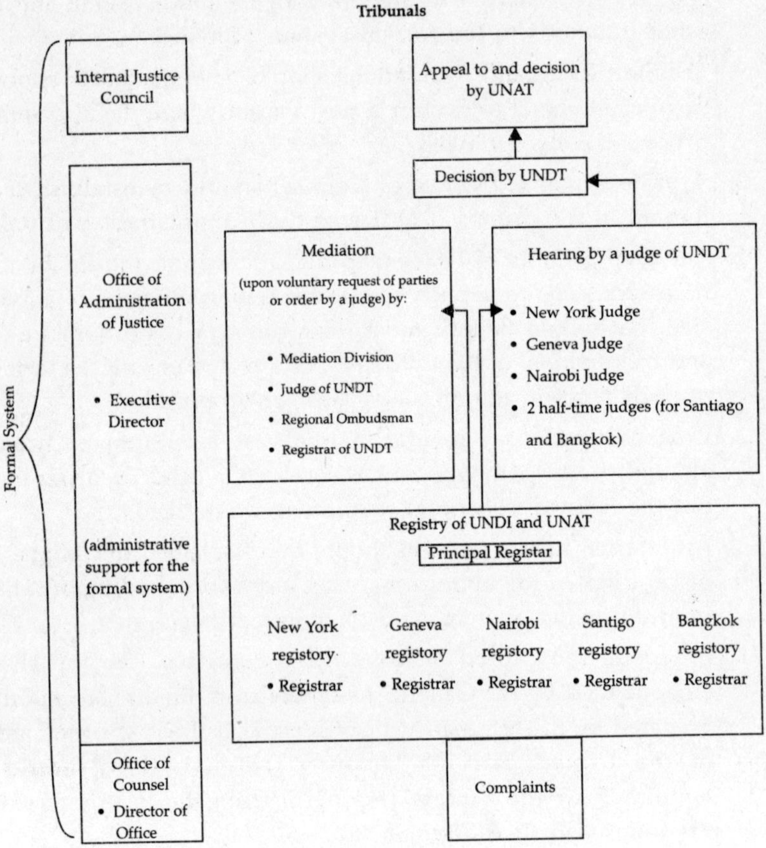

Annex A-9.5

Redesign Panel: Proposed Structure of Office of the Ombudsman

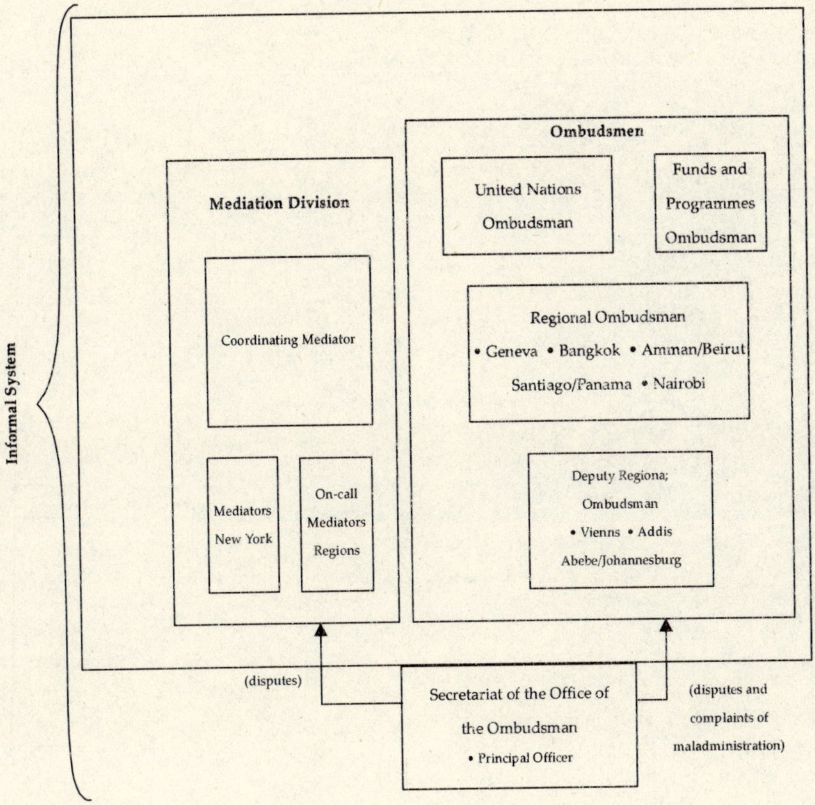

10

Staff Development and Senior Management Programme

Introduction

Growth and change are inherent in all organisations, and they create a plethora of training and management development needs. Existing literature indicates that the concept of "learning organisations" describes the way organisations must cope with their dynamic nature. A learning system is based upon the principle of continuously acquiring new knowledge and widening horizon, or a systematic method designed to increase knowledge within an organisational climate which enables more effective and systematic response to change aimed at new directions and structural readjustment with emphasis on performance. All large and complex organisations aim at training and development, which is primarily concerned with people who are involved with technology and processes, or the precise way an organisation does its business.[1]

To upgrade the capacity of civil service, post-entry and in-service training activities in administration and management have gained wide acceptance in developed and developing countries. Today, most countries have an Institute of Public Administration or at least a focal point for training. A few are in the process of setting up training institutions for senior management development. This is

1. Naquin, Sharon S. (2008). *Approaches to Training and Development*. Dugan Laird: Basic Books.

due partly to the continuing emphasis on training as a strategy for enhancing the level of administrative efficiency and effectiveness, and partly to the high priority attached to human resources development.

Based on the experience of the staff college at Henley, several countries in recent years have established such centres for top management development. In other cases, short-term refresher courses have been instituted. Elsewhere, universities are meeting some of the needs of top management for continuing education.

The United Nations has also embraced a significant staff development and training programme and established a staff college to advance the skill sets of the staff and prepare them for increased responsibilities and challenges. We will cursorily look at the nature and content of UN-related training and staff development programmes in the following sections. Although the P5 and above constitute the team of senior managers in the United Nations, for the purpose of staff development, we will only focus on P5-D2 in this chapter.

Profile of Senior Managers (P5-D2)

The profile of senior UN managers can be viewed from the perspective of the structure, methods and staffing pattern of the International Civil Service. It also depends on the particular source of entry to the senior levels. While a precise definition of senior management is difficult to make, there are basic elements, which could be used as points of reference. In the UN context, the term senior management can properly be used to denote officials from P5 level, D1 and D2 levels in the context of staff development. Generally they hold posts in these levels drawn from the 100 and 200 series of appointments. Numerically, they represent a fairly large group in the service. This group includes persons with differences in background, nationality, age, educational attainments, experience and training. It has largely been customary to draw this group from the source of functional, specialised, technical and professional posts. Some could even be drawn from national competitive examination after formal education and training.

Attracting potentially qualified senior managers is crucial. Recruitment at the entry level is the key factor that links dynamic staff development requirements together. In several countries, the concept of career development, consisting of an orderly progress through a job, or a series of jobs throughout the working life, with increased job complexity, personal responsibility and benefit, has taken firm roots. The United Nations has largely embraced that practice but without the rigour often exercised by those countries. Consequently, the original purpose of career development for providing stability, efficiency and independence in the international civil service is often called into question.

Role of Senior Managers

The functions of senior managers in the world body encompass the formulation of policy, coordination and the exercise of general managerial control over the department/division. Senior managers are also required to supervise the preparation of annual plans, budget estimates, annual report and a series of functions required by legislative organs of the organisation, e.g. General Assembly, ECOSOC and Security Council. The department and division heads are required to justify the budget and posts before the Fifth Committee, ACABQ, and other specialised organs of the Secretariat.

The practice of management covers a variety of activities. Starting with the running of the department, it encompasses advising to higher authorities, preparing such key elements as documents for expert group meetings, drafting resolutions for the legislative organs, managing ad hoc committees, overseeing the preparation and finalisation of technical assistance projects, and also rendering advice to member countries based on specific request.

The United Nations capability to meet the ongoing future tasks by increasing organisational efficiency depends essentially on effective management leadership and on improved administrative structure and processes. In recent times there has been a manifold expansion in staff strength as well as in the complexities of United Nations global operations and mandates, including in the fields of the Millennium Development Goals, peacekeeping and peace-building, security, humanitarian affairs and human rights, climate change and other critical universal issues. These demands have placed enormous responsibility on managerial competencies of members of the international civil service. Senior officials at the USG and ASG levels are expected to provide a range of substantive, political, diplomatic and representational functions in addition to their daily policy and managerial responsibilities. This also puts a major onus on senior and middle staff to help the senior officials do their job by providing leadership and strong management of a multicultural and international workforce at headquarters and those in field locations.

Evidently, the global body has made efforts in recent years to increase the amount of training and management development programmes that staff members receive. There are courses for those who have been freshly recruited at P-2 level, at mid-level at P-4 and P-5 as well as at senior levels. There is no certainty that these efforts and courses will actually be relevant to their work performance. If training is to be effective, the organisation must intervene in their personnel policies to create strong linkages between career development plans and training of personnel, and improve the career prospects of trainers themselves. It is also important to link training and staff development to performance appraisal systems and promote policies to motivate staff members to make better use of training.

Overall, the United Nations now offers a systematic, progressive strategy to managerial and leadership development initiatives as follows:

- The Junior Professional Development Programme, for staff recruited through the national competitive examination (P-2, P-3) and to G to P examinations (P-1, P-2);
- The Supervisory Development Programme, for all staff up to the P-4 level with supervisory responsibility;
- The Management Development Programme, a five-day intensive residential programme that is mandatory for staff at the P-4 and P-5 levels;

The Leadership Development Programme, an intensive residential programme consisting of two 5-day modules over a period of nine to twelve months, which is mandatory for all senior staff at the D-1 and D-2 levels.

Staff Development Programme

In 2009, OHRM of the United Nations has launched a staff development programme. Figure 10.1 illustrates learning and development opportunities for the UN staff.[2]

UN System Staff College

The establishment of a staff college in Turin, Italy, to serve the UN system, was a direct response to the need to strengthen the coherence and effectiveness of the International Civil Service. The College came into operation in January 2002 based on the recommendation of the Independent Evaluation Team, in September 2000.[3]

A number of new techniques have since been introduced to strengthen the management development programmes. They include such programmes as "profile of and effective department" and "profile of an effective manager" which are based on the competency framework of shared values and shared understanding of what constitutes effectiveness at the individual and departmental levels.

In support of the global body's core values, several online and face-to-face learning initiatives on ethics and integrity have been launched. Similarly, programmes on conflict resolution, prevention of harassment and abuse of authority have also been introduced. SG has initiated a retreat of senior managers in collaboration with the UN Staff College in Turin, Italy. It is the intention of SG to hold similar retreats in order to improve coordination among members of the organisation's senior leadership. The Staff College continues to organise on a regular basis development programmes such as Conflict Prevention, Peace and Security, Safe and Secure Approaches in Field Environment, and Development Cooperation

2. United Nations (OHRM) (2009). *2009 Staff Development Programme.* January.

3. United Nations (2009). *UN Staff College Project, Report of the Secretary-General.* September.

Figure 10.1

Learning and Development Oppoptunities for the UN Staff

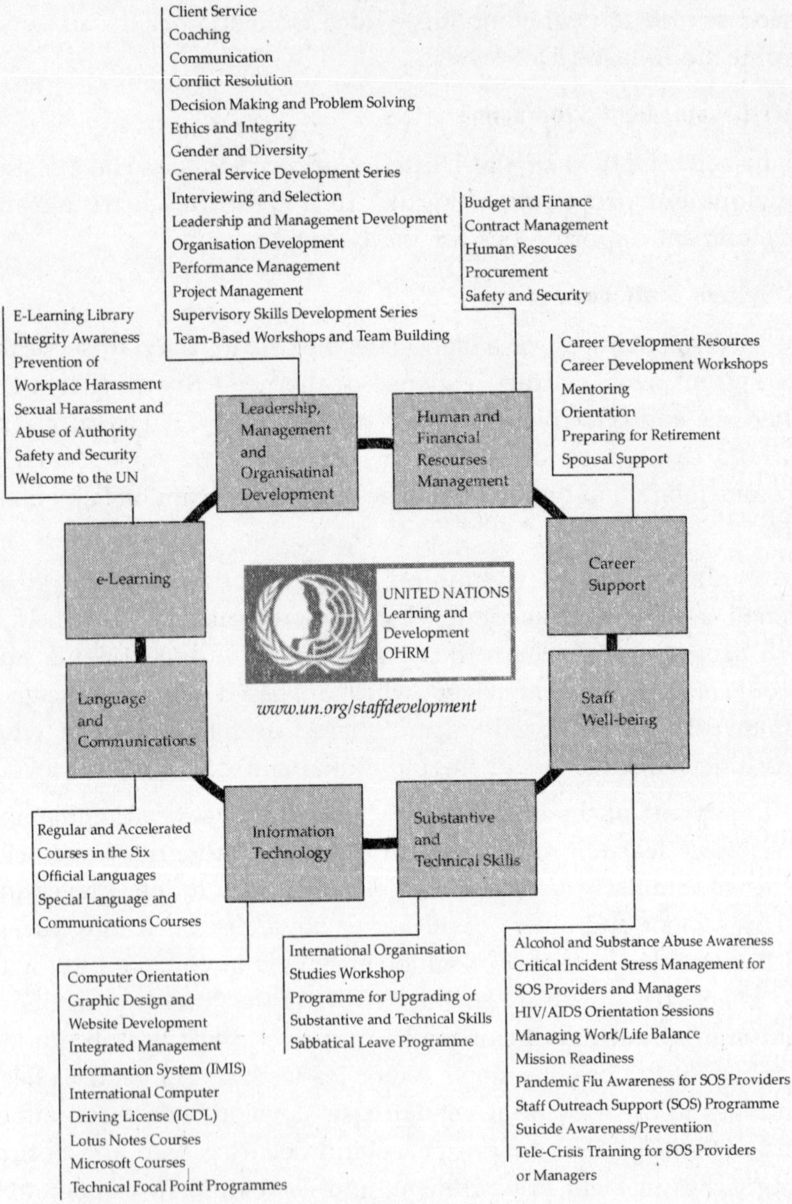

through Learning and Capacity Building, all targeted at UN staff and their development partners, specifically those involved in planning and implementing strategic responses to development problems. The Staff College has also offered programmes to achieve sustainable development within the context of the Millennium Declaration and the MDGs. An important programme of the Staff College is done through its learning and training services with a view to enhancing staff effectiveness as a result of development and learning competencies. This programme is aimed at promoting coherence in staff orientation processes across the UN system, as well as focusing on the specific orientation needs of young professionals at the beginning of their UN careers.[4]

To take advantage of enhancing senior managers' capacity for improved leadership, the Department of Peacekeeping Operations and the Department of Field Support have organised programmes for senior mission leaders, force commanders, police commissioners and heads of mission support.

Initiatives have also been taken to organise mandatory online and face-to-face learning interaction on the subject of ethics and integrity. With the establishment of the Ethics Office, those programmes are being strengthened, and new efforts are being developed to meet emerging needs.

While the establishment of the UN Staff College is a sign of progress, the College has yet to bring to bear innovative, practical and useful approaches and methods on its work. The existing programmes are far from satisfactory. The United Nations needs to think seriously of either closing down the Staff College and outsourcing training activities, or making it a centre of excellence to help build staff capacities and competencies and refresh knowledge and skills necessary for the organisation in a fast-changing world. We propose to reform and revamp the College and develop it into a centre of excellence. There are several experiences out there from which the organisation can learn. Let us have a look at French, British and American experiences.

---

4. United Nations (2007). *Report of the Director of UN Systems Staff College*. ECOSOC. May.

French and British Experience

Two models of institutions are noteworthy. In Strasbourg, France, stands the *Centre des Etudes Europeennes* and the *Ecole Nationale d'Administration (ENA).* Here for six to seven months of every year, the French elite, the 'Enarques' selected after tough competition, decamp from their Parisian heartlands and spend some time in this eminent institution, where the European Parliament has its seat. The institution has no training staff of its own; its trainers come from universities or from Paris.

Sunningdale, in the United Kingdom is the single most important location for training the British civil service. Much of the site of what is now entitled the Civil Service College was established in 1970, inaugurated by Prime Minister of Heath as recommended by the Fulton report. The Fulton committee had debated the long-term British prejudice against 'relevant' university training, but it remained the case that although to become a fast-track official you had to have a 'good degree', there were no advantages in having a degree in Economics or Law rather than Ancient Greek. Hence, training people to become professional meant, above all, getting them versed in the basics of the social sciences.

During the Thatcher period, the Civil Service College increasingly began to focus on management training. At the heart of such training lies the effort to deliver more for less, to treat citizens as customers, to provide value for money, to emulate as far as possible the ground-breaking companies that demonstrated 'excellence' and to waste not a penny of tax payers' money; and all of these characterised the Civil Service College. Training would take the form of focusing upon where officials needed to change their mindsets. Illustrative was a major programme during those years called "the policy programme for managers." This placed emphasis, as relevant training always does, upon the tension points in the system. Among these were the need to apply the techniques of management training to the policy level so that 'policy people' in the British civil service would not feel left behind by the latest developments in policy assessments and evaluation, project management, the use of performance indicators and objectives, benchmarking and the application of quality techniques in their work.

By 1996, the Civil Service College had become entirely self-financing with no budgetary support from the Cabinet Office, raising all its income from charging departments for the training offered to their officials. Subsequently, the College's mission continued to lay emphasis upon customer care and managerial efficiency within its work and its training practice. The arrival of the Labour government in 1997 led to further changes within the civil service and the College. The intellectuals, in the new government's drive to modernise the state machine, go back to the critic of its inefficiency by academics and senior civil servants. Many of these critics did not find fault in the management reforms and the civil service *per se*, but in the policy delivery and constitutional machinery. A new policies division was setup in the Civil Service College and a renewed commitment to research and the involvement of social science expertise in government was added. The College still runs fast-stream courses on Parliament, government and the civil service, effective manager course geared to middle managers who are operating in agencies or departments. The course on Emotional Intelligence is conducted for those senior managers whose success depends on their ability to coordinate the efforts of their staff as part of a team.

The comparison of the Civil Service College and training programme in the United Kingdom with the ENA in France was meant to illustrate certain key factors about their approach to training. The training programmes in the UK, and are brief in duration, conventional in style, contemporary in content, delivered by professional trainers rather than academics, aimed at modest but real improvement in performance. The British emphasis of on-the-job training is distinct from the French style.[5]

American Experience

The American experience is unique. The Office of Personnel Management (OPM) whose job is to identify, recruit, test, train, manage and evaluate the US government employees. OPM's

5. Article by Michael Duggett (2003). "The British Civil Service College in Comparative Perspective," published in Rosenbaum, Alan and Gajdosova, Eudmila (ed), *State Modernization and Decentralization—Implications for Education and Training in Public Administration*, United Nations (with IASIA and NISPAcee pp. 100-108.

workforce has been drastically reduced since the 1993 report of 'Reinventing Government' by David Osborne and Ted Gaebler, which began and fuelled a well-known approach to government as business, citizens as clients and evaluation in the form of National Performance Review. OPM uses a wide variety of methods for recruiting and training of personnel for management positions. Important among them is the presidential management internship (PMI) programme. Talented graduates are recruited annually for this programme from graduate schools, specially those students from public policy/administration institutions. The competition for these positions is fierce, as they carry significant prestige for both the individuals selected and the institutions that train them. OPM also recruits and trains personnel through its Federal Executive Institute and its Management Development Centres. The Office provides unique, customised courses. For example, a course being offered since September 11 attacks is entitled, "Understanding the Enemy". This is a week-long programme of a composite nature.

OPM also has a major responsibility to administer and score the US Civil Service exams at numerous sites across the nation. In marked contrast to France and the United Kingdom, training for federal government service is decentralised and not at all uniform, especially at the highest levels. Preparation may take place in public/private schools and universities, executive training programmes, in-service training, military training academics, public and non-profit agencies and in private companies. For high-level appointments, the role of university-based education in policy and administration is secondary. At lower levels—below political appointees—the schools/colleges of public administration play a much bigger role with departments and agency staff. Another major role of OPM is to improve the performance of all federal departments/agencies. Review of OPM's training programmes and workshops indicate that they focus on "performance management" techniques that include devising mission statements, articulating values and understanding their roles. They also include goal setting and evaluation techniques, and collect and use the statistics needed to measure progress which are reflected in "performance reports" to demonstrate the agency's accountability to the public and facilitate OPM planning.

The work of OPM is limited to federal government jobs. A number of state personnel offices have modelled themselves after the federal system. Recruitment efforts at the state level are more decentralised than at the federal level, and the process is still more decentralised at the county, township and municipal levels. The 250 or so schools and institutes of public administration play a major role in staffing and organising training programmes. The US example can best be characterised as one of great diversity, both in terms of human resources management and education and training activities.[6]

General Observations

There is a need for developing specific guidelines to support the enhancement of internal capabilities. The guidelines must cover the objectives and types of training and management development that the organisation will support for training needs of departmental staff members, the design and preparation of training plan based on needs assessment and resource availability, and the financing of training. In addition, the guidelines must take into account the monitoring and evaluation of training with special emphasis on linkages with career development and the roles and responsibilities of various departments in performing their various tasks.

While the United Nations has introduced a number of training and management development programmes, it is important that the organisation should formulate and continually review its training strategy policy and programmes. A formal training policy can be extremely useful aid to identify training needs and set objectives and priorities of training efforts. It will clarify the roles and responsibilities of different departments and facilitate coordination among them.

A training policy for the United Nations should specify the objectives and types of training, relating them to the different

6. Article by Gordon, Margaret T., "Development and Implementation of Human Resources Management Policy: The Case of the USA," Ibid, pp. 71-75.

categories of personnel. There is a clear need to broaden the objectives and scope of training, so that the needs of all categories of officials are met adequately.

This makes the task of accessing training needs both urgent and complex. A policy statement should emphasise the importance of this task and offer broad guidelines on the subject to the agencies, which are made responsible for this function. A variety of methods (surveys, discussion with departments, job analysis, management skills review, critical incident method, and so forth) are available from which operating departments may choose.

The world body must take into account its changing strategies and functions, new systems and practices introduced in the corporate world, the public service world and the general performance problems of various categories of personnel. The emerging needs may range from general management training for higher-level personnel to functional training and basic skills development for other categories. Mechanisms, such as advisory committees and workshops, may be specified in the policy document to facilitate consultations between the personnel and departments.

Training policy should also spell out the institutional arrangements for meeting the training needs as determined from time to time. While no policy can specify the designs for training programmes, it is important to offer guidelines on the roles of different institutions/university centres, which could play in meeting different types of needs. Training policy should also offer guidelines on the evaluation of training. Institutions must be asked to evaluate training programmes on their own; in addition, the OHRM should be charged with the responsibility of monitoring and evaluating the performance of all training programmes. Since evaluation is a complex matter, the policy statement may provide for a periodic review of performance of the United Nations' own training initiatives through taskforces made up of representatives of user groups and independent experts.

A review of the activities of the Staff College for the period July 2005-June 2007 indicates that there were 75 events for resident coordinator system programme lasting 2-3 days on strategic planning in different regions; partnership/private sector/civil society activities lasting for 2-3 days in several locations; and a number of peace and security programmes such as security learning curriculum, training of trainers, etc., workshops on preventive measures, activities in conflict prevention, senior management network leadership development programme. In addition, the College developed inter-agency learning tools and conducted young professionals orientation programme, and other subsidiary activities. It is not possible to develop a coherent strategy of the College from the cluster of programmes conducted so far. The duration of the programmes seem to be extremely limited to assess the impact on the performance of participants after they receive the training. A rigorous evaluation is called for in association with an established staff college and institute of international studies before repeating such programmes in the future.

The experience of ENA in Paris, Civil Service College in the UK, and the Federal Executive Institute in Virginia and its management development centres deserve to be weighed in to determine the efficacy of the programmes of the UN Staff College. The recurring budget of the College and a staff of 30 instructors seem too high. A viable alternative would be to experiment the idea of outsourcing the training programmes to well known institutions in developed and developing countries. This could be extremely cost effective and beneficial to staff development.

Here are some of the specific observations in this respect.

- There should be clear linkages between training programmes and career paths, and that a more integrated, strategic results-based approach to training, encompassing both headquarters and the field is required, starting with the implementation of a selected number of multiple priority issues, including in particular the development of an inventory of skills.
- There is an urgent necessity to develop a comprehensive training strategy, as referred to earlier in this section, applicable to staff serving both at headquarters and in the

field together with workforce planning techniques and organisational needs.

- At the implementation stage, OHRM should ensure that training programmes are planned and managed in a transparent manner and that staff are adequately informed of the availability of the programmes.
- The impact assessment of such programmes should be carefully evaluated and the efficiency and effectiveness with which such programmes are conducted should be reviewed and acted upon.
- An inventory of management development programmes of excellence available in developed and developing countries should be cataloged by OHRM for use by the United Nations for headquarters and field staff. It would also be useful to prepare an inventory of resource staff with proved competencies in learning methods to be used in appropriate programmes at Headquarters and in the field. Similarly, a condensed form of reading materials based on existing experience should be developed by OHRM specifically focused on: (a) top administrators, (b) senior officers, (c) middle level officers, (d) new recruits through national competitive exams, and (e) general service staff.

11

Conditions of Service

Introduction

The subject of staff regulations and the machinery for their enforcement is most critical in an international civil service. If the head of international administration is judicious in recruitment and selection of his staff, and is skillful in controlling them through his qualities of leadership and administrative capacity, then the actual rules and regulations under which the staff works in the organisation should prove a matter of minor importance. In an environment not torn by dissention, an efficient director would, in all probability, scarcely have an occasion to look at the staff rules.[1]

However, regulations governing salary scales, promotion, leave, pension benefits and other similar entitlements are essential to give the international staff a sense of security. In spite of the best will and greatest managerial skill, occasions will arise in which normal rules of conduct will have to be enforced and appropriate sanctions imposed. Regulations must establish clearly the duties and the obligations of officials; specify and innumerate their rights; act as a check on misbehaviour, and establish a system for their enforcement, and for the settlement of disputes. Chapter 9 of this book on the Administration of Justice provides an annex dealing with UN Staff Regulations pertaining to disciplinary measures and

1. Loveday, A. (1956). *Reflections on International Administration*. Oxford: Clarendon Press. p.108.

appeals procedure (A-9.1), Annex A-9.3 deals with recommendations of the redesigned panel, Annex A-9.4 provides the proposed system of the UN internal justice tribunal, and A-9.5 suggests a new structure for the Office of the Ombudsman.

The United Nations has established a set of Staff Regulations and Rules, which are periodically reviewed and amended by the resolutions of the General Assembly. All contracts with personnel are made with reference to terms and conditions specified therein. Similar sets of such rules exists for the UN specialised agencies and for other inter-governmental organisations. Such regulations articulate the privileges and immunities, the rights and obligations, and other staff-related provisions made in the relevant international conventions of the United Nations or its specialised agencies. They apply to international civil servants around the world regardless of whatever geographical location such bodies have offices or field personnel. International civil servants may be considered as those whose status is governed by such rules, recognised by the international community. In many respects these rules also serve as a code of conduct for international civil servants, although the ethical considerations, characteristic of such codes, are not emphasised.[2]

The Professional and Higher Categories

Levels of Salaries

The level of salaries for professional staff members is determined on the basis of the Noblemaire Principle, which states that the international civil service should be able to recruit staff from its member states, including the highest paid. Therefore, the salaries of professional staff are set with reference to the highest paying national civil service. The International Civil Service Commission (ICSC) makes a periodic review to identify the national civil service of the member state which has the highest pay levels and which by its size and structure lends itself to a significant comparison.

2. Union of International Associations (1988). *United Nations Staff Rules and Regulations, International Association of Statute Series*, Vol. I.

The federal civil service of the United States of America has to date been taken as the highest paid national civil service.

Salary Scales

The salary scales for the professional and higher categories encompass the five Professional grades (P-1 to P-5), Director levels (D-1 and D-2) as well as the levels of Assistant Secretary-General and Under Secretary-General, in some organisations an Assistant Director-General and Deputy Director-General in others. The scales are expressed as gross and net based salaries and applied uniformly, worldwide by all organisations in the United Nations common system. The net-based salary is obtained by deducting staff assessment from the gross base salary. Latest salary scales are annexed to this book.

Staff Assessment

Staff assessment is a form of internal tax administered by the United Nations. Staff assessment rates are derived from income tax rates applicable at the seven headquarter cities of the organisations' in the common system (Geneva, London, Montreal, New York, Paris, Rome and Vienna).

Income Taxes

Most member states have granted United Nations staff exemption from national taxation on their United Nations emoluments. However, a few member states do tax these emoluments of their nationals. In such cases the organisations reimburse the income tax to the staff member.

The General Service and Related Categories

Levels of Salaries

The staff in these categories is paid on a local basis. The level of salaries is established in accordance with Flemming Principle, which provides that the conditions of service for locally recruited staff should reflect the best prevailing conditions found locally for similar work. Consequently, the local salaries are established on the basis of salary surveys, which facilitate the identification of the best prevailing conditions. The local salary surveys are conducted in accordance with the comprehensive methodology approved by ICSC. At headquarters duty stations, ICSC is responsible for conducting salary surveys and for recommending salary scales for final approval by the organisations concerned, mainly the United Nations. At headquarters duty stations, salary surveys are conducted by the United Nations and certain agencies of the United Nations common system.

Salary Scales

There is normally only one local salary scale per country. There are, however, a few cases where more than one salary scale is in effect in the same country, when UN offices are established in more than one duty stations in the country. Local salary scales are expressed in local currency as gross, gross pension, total net, net pension and non-pensionable component per grade and step. They are based on a seven grade level structure, except for some duty stations. Longevity steps may be included in the salary scales while local conditions so justify. At other locations, provision is made for one long-service step in addition to the regular steps for each grade. To qualify, the staff must have been at the top of their grade for five years and have a minimum of 20 years service.

Field Service Category

Salary Structure

The staff in this category, employed in peacekeeping missions and other field operations, are internationally recruited and entitled to a range of international benefits. The salary structure is similar to that of Professional staff, with a single salary scale applicable world-wide. Salary rates for the seven grades in this category are likewise established by comparison with similar jobs in the United States Federal Civil Service.

Post Adjustment

The post adjustment is one of the two main elements (base salary and post adjustment) comprising the salary of staff in the Professional and higher categories.

The cost of living varies significantly between duty stations. The post adjustment is designed to compensate the differences in living costs, thereby providing the staff with the same purchasing power at all duty stations.

Staff members in the Professional and higher categories and in the field service category are entitled to post adjustment assigned to a duty station for one year or more.[3]

Basic Rights and Obligations of Staff

Core Values

Staff members shall uphold and respect the principles set out in the Charter including faith in fundamental human rights, in the dignity and worth of a human person, and in the equal rights of men and women. Staff members shall exhibit respect for all cultures; they shall not discriminate against an individual or group of individuals.

Staff members are required to uphold the highest standards of efficiency, competence and integrity.

General Rights and Obligations

Staff members are subject to the authority of the Secretary-General and to assignments by him/her to any of the activities or offices of the United Nations.

In the performance of their duties, staff members shall neither seek nor accept instructions from any government or any other source external to the organisation. Staff members shall not use their office or knowledge gained from their official functions for private gain, financial or otherwise.

Honors, Gifts or Remuneration

No staff member is allowed to accept any honour, decoration, favour, gift or remuneration from any government.[4]

---

3. *http://www.un.org/Depts/OHRM/salaries_allowances/salary.htm*
4. Staff Regulations of the United Nations, ST/SGB/2003/8, pp. 1-5.

Entitlements

Education Grant

Education grant is available to a staff member, residing and serving outside his home country, whose dependent child is in full time attendance at a school, university, or similar educational institution. The grant is payable in respect of the child up to the end of the fourth year of post graduate secondary studies or the award of the first recognised degree. The amount of the grant per scholastic year for each child is 75 per cent of the admissible educational expenses actually incurred. Travel costs of the child may be paid for an onward and return journey once in each scholastic year between the educational institution and the duty station. The admissible expense reimbursable include the following: tuition (including mother tongue); boarding; transportation; registration and admission fee; books required by the curriculum; computer usage and lab fees; and examination fees.

Children's and Secondary Dependents Allowance

Children's allowance is given to the staff member at the eight headquarters duty stations, weighted by the number of staff at those locations. The secondary dependents allowance is set up at 35 per cent of the children's allowance.

Hazard Pay

Internationally recruited staff are entitled to hazard pay as a special allowance. This allownance is awarded to those who are required to work under hazardous conditions such as war or active hostilities prevailing and where the evacuation of families and non-essential staff has taken place.[5]

Rental Subsidy

Staff members are entitled to claim rental subsidy, which is fixed on the basis of cost of living and rental scheme in the duty station.

5. *Report of the International Civil Service Commission* for 2008, pp. 27-29.

Annual and Special Leave

Staff members are allowed annual leave and special leave authorised by the Secretary-General in special cases. Eligible staff members are granted home leave once in every two years. In the case of designated duty stations having very difficult conditions of life and work, staff members are granted home leave once in every 12 months. A staff member whose home country is either the country of his/her official duty station, or the country of his/her normal residence while in United Nations Service are not eligible for home leave.

Social Security

Provisions are available for the participation of staff members in the United Nations Joint Staff Pension Fund in accordance with the regulations of that fund. The established age of retirement is 60 years, and 62 for those who were recruited after 1995.

Medical Insurance

Staff members are entitled to obtain medical insurance, the cost of which are paid by the staff member and the United Nations based on established regulations.

Travel and Removal Expenses

The United Nations in appropriate cases pays the travel expenses of staff members, their spouses, and dependent children.

Provisions also exist to pay removal costs for staff members.

Separation from Service

The Secretary-General may terminate the appointment of a staff member: (a) if the conduct of the staff member does not meet the highest standards of integrity required by Article 101, para 3 of the Charter; (b) if facts come to light after the appointment of the staff member and relevance to the suitability come to light not known at the time of appointment.

The termination is required to be considered by a special advisory board appointed by the Secretary-General.

Staff members may resign from the Secretariat upon giving the Secretary-General the notice required under the terms of their appointment.[6]

Illustrative Profile of a Staff Member at P-5 Level
Salary, Allowances and Benefits in US Dollars

1. Salary:

   Annual salary (net) $83,089

   Annual post adjustment $58,867

   Annual child allowance (2) $1,936

   Annual deduction for staff assessment $30,000

   Cost of living adjustment: 2-3 per cent annually.

2. Education Grant Annual: 75 per cent of actual cost—maximum $39,096

   High school

   College

   Language allowance (Mother tongue)

3. Rental Subsidy Monthly:

   New York: $3,495 (cost of rental should be higher than $6,500)

4. Home Leave:

   Cost of ticket for a family of two to be determined at time of travel based on the cost of airfare. Home leave entitlement once in two years.

5. Medical Insurance for Family: (Monthly premium) Insurance premium to be paid by staff member—$598 and UN matching payment—$864.

6. Annual Leave: 2½ days a month.

7. Travel and Removal Expenses: New Delhi to New York $18,000 to $25,000 removal cost.

8. Annual Child Disability Benefit: $30,000

6. Staff Regulations of the United Nations, Ibid.

12

Human Resource Planning

Introduction

Human resources planning, through the process of developing and identifying the need for the workforce, is a critical function of personnel management in any large public or private sector organisation. Increasingly, human resources are being treated as strategic and aligned to organisational goals and missions. This has, in fact, marked the transformation of personnel administration, in which you routinely administer the workforce, into human resources management, in which you build and apply your workforce to achieve organisational objectives.

Planning entails anticipating tomorrow to prevent disruption, to prepare for new requirements and to embrace new products, processes and technologies. As Peter Drucker says,

> Management has no choice but to anticipate the future, to attempt to mold it, and to balance short-range and long-range goals...Long-range planning should prevent managers for uncritically extending present trends into the future, from assuming that today's products, services, markets, and technologies will be the products, services, markets and technologies of tomorrow, and above all, from dedicating their resources and energies to the defense of yesterday.[1]

Strategic planning has gained ground in modern organisations. It "allows agencies to map out where they are, where they want

---

1. Drucker, Peter (2008). F., *Management* (Revised Edition). New York: Harper-Collins. pp.122-123.

to go, and how they plan to get there."[2] Human resources planning, in particular, pertain to identifying the current and future required skills sets, determining how the workforce can obtain these skills and setting action plan milestones.[3] In modern organisations, increasingly also in traditional organisations of governments, human resources planning have become integral to strategic planning. So much so that, in the United States, the Government Performance and Results Act, 1993, has corralled government agencies to espouse this linkage between strategic plan and human resources plan.[4] According to OPM, a typical agency strategic planning process, and the place of human resources in it, needs to be conceived with clarity of objectives and processes.[5]

In other words, projection of medium and long-term human resource requirements involves determining the number and types of employees needed by specialisation level. First, departments need to audit the skills of incumbent employees and determine their capabilities and weaknesses. Positions also require to be audited to obtain correct information. Second, along with such data, job analysis is required to obtain information on existing posts. The basic requirement of a job must be defined and converted to job specifications that specify the minimum knowledge, skills, abilities and other characteristics necessary for effective performance. Experience indicates that in complex public organisations the skills and competency requirements of positions do change, so any changes that occur need to be monitored and reflected in the job specifications. It is not enough to monitor changes in positions. Third, a strategic element of human resource planning is aimed to utilise data inventories to integrate the planning and utilisation of functions of human resource management.[6]

---

2. Office of Personnel Management (1999). *Strategic Human Resources Management, Aligning with the Mission*. Washington DC. September p.17.
3. Ibid: 5.
4. US Congress, *Government Performance and Results Act, 1993*
5. Office of Personnel Management, *Strategic Human Resources Management, Aligning with the Mission, op. cit.*, p.6.
6. Pynes, Joan E. (2003). *Public Personnel Administration, Strategic Human Resource Management*. Prentice-Hall. pp. 94-95.

Typical Agency Planning Process

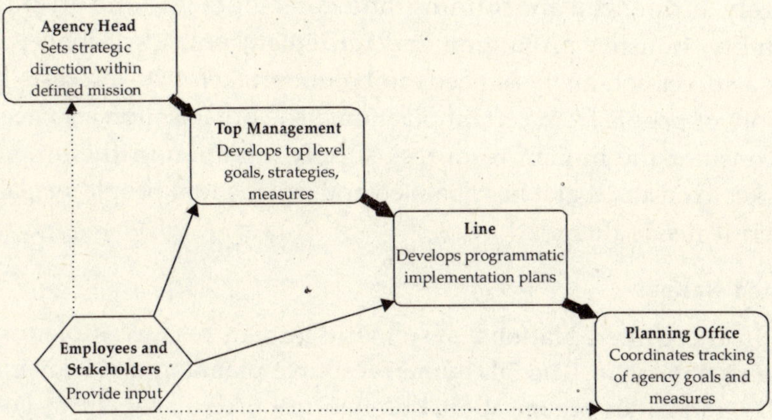

HRM Integration in Agency Strategic Plans

Such planning involves long-term forecasting of the growing need for trained personnel in the international civil service and all its departments and division and preparing plans for their appropriate induction, training and development into the future service. Ideally in all modern civil services, such plans could conceivably cover decades and need to be closely coordinated with the international community in relation to their manpower programmes both inside and outside of their public services. The subject of long term planning for trained human resources is not confined to large organisations, although these tend to be most widely publicised examples. Contemporary experience indicates that, in developing countries, critically important programmes of economic and social development stay in abeyance because of the scarcity of educated, skilled and trained personnel in specialised fields to execute them.

In this context, the methodology of forecasting and/or workforce planning complement each other because such tools identify expectations while plans establish concrete goals and objectives. Methodologically, forecasting human resource requirements has become increasingly important because of retirement, attrition, training of staff and other similar factors. It has been found necessary that when forecasting the availability of human resources, divisions and departments need to consider both the internal and external supply of candidates. The internal supply of candidates is largely influenced by training and development, and through mobility, transfer, promotion and retirement policies. Along with this a succession analysis needs to be undertaken that forecasts the supply of people from certain positions. The organisation also needs to consider the human resources supply situation in the broader market to ensure that it has qualified and experienced people available when it needs them.

United Nations

In the United Nations, systematic human resources planning is of recent origin. The 5th human resource planning cycle covering 2007-08 includes organisational human resource management goals derived from the relevant mandates of the General Assembly. The action plans contain measurable targets in the following key areas: vacancy management, geographical distribution, gender balance, mobility, performance appraisal, staff development and staff-management relations. But this is far from full-blown human resources planning, let alone strategic.

The experience of the United States Federal Government, the United Kingdom, and some developing countries points to the need of succession planning as a tool to identify potential personnel changes, to identify and select backup candidates, and to keep track of attrition. The external supply of candidates is also influenced by a variety of factors, including developments in technology, the actions of competing employers, geographic location and personnel policies. While some countries have strived to go for strategic human resources planning, others are still grappling with workforce planning.

Full-fledged workforce planning in the United Nations is still in the process of emerging due to growing staffing difficulties. Over a period of time, the world body has suffered from a shortage of trained manpower to fill in positions involving diverse skills, background and competencies. This has impacted on the quality of performance particularly in areas requiring contemporary methods and practices. We have been informed that 50 per cent of the UN staff at P5 and above is expected to retire in about five year's time. This prospect prompted the Secretary-General to request heads of all departments in 2008 to engage in strategic workforce planning with the aim of identifying core skills for succession planning, identification and analysis of gaps in the workforce, supply and demand analysis, planning for succession and addressing the high rate of upcoming retirements in a more systematic and cross-organisational manner.[7]

Accordingly, a framework for workforce planning in the Secretariat was developed, and 26 heads of departments were asked to estimate competencies and skills, which would be lost, and also to anticipate how workforce needs in the future could be met. The strategic workforce has now been identified as a key priority for departments, and work, aimed at associating all established posts with the appropriate occupational groups as a basis for subsequent mapping of posts and skills for the planning exercise, has been completed. OHRM and the Department of Field Support are expected to review the results of the pilot programme and introduce action plans for all peacekeeping operations. OHRM has introduced an online "dashboard" system that provides monthly updates of departmental progress in the implementation of action plan targets.

The concept of workforce planning in the world body includes such elements as departmental workforce supply analysis and future workforce requirements. The analysis includes projected staff movement due to the mandatory age of retirement and staff turnover on the supply side, and projected workforce requirements in line with departmental strategic framework on the demand side. The recent acquisition of a new e-staffing talent management tool will support the implementation of strategic workforce planning Secretariat-wide. The tool will also be used for the introduction of a skills inventory.[8]

Recent documentation indicates that OHRM has improved its monitoring of the main demographic indicators of Secretariat staff and continues to report on them annually to the General Assembly. The format and scope of reporting have been expanded considerably in recent years to include all staff employed by the United Nations, including field operations. Recently, departmental planning and

---

7. United Nations (2008). *Recruitment and Staffing in the United Nations: Strategy Going Forward*. A/63/285. August 14, p.3-4.

8. Courtesy of United Nations.

performance in regard to legislative mandates in human resource management are underpinned by the human resource action plan system, which has evolved into an institutionalised system with enhanced elements of accountability.

It is reported that the monitoring system has been improved by the introduction of the senior managers' compacts with the Secretary-General aligning administrative and managerial goals of heads of departments and offices, including major goals in the area of human resources management, with their programmatic objectives. All 26 heads of departments and major offices prepared comprehensive compacts for 2008 after individual discussions between them and the Secretary-General. The Management Performance Board has carried out an interim analysis of their implementation in June 2008. In order to foster transparency and accountability, the United Nations has published the compacts on the Internet. The compacts include four objectives in the area of human resource management: a) to minimise the vacancy level, b) to achieve a 50-50 gender balance in the professional and higher levels, c) to improve the geographical distribution of staff, d) to achieve 100 per cent compliance with the performance appraisal system. The compacts are critical elements of the accountability framework.

Feedback from Departmental Evaluations

1. A recent evaluation of OHRM's initiative in human resource management planning indicates that significant challenges remain, and desired results are not yet fully achieved.
2. The planning and policy development are not fully effective because continuous reform efforts have overburdened OHRM and diminished its ability to plan, prioritise and provide guidance.
3. Human resources management planning, including succession planning, is limited: vacancy rates particularly in the field remain very high. Staff survey rated OHRM capacity planning as "very poor". OHRM acknowledged a lack of annual staffing plans essentially because resources allocated are extremely limited.

4. Current information technology tools do not facilitate a robust planning process. All expressed dissatisfaction with these tools. The IMIS contains significant amounts of incorrect staff data, which requires OHRM staff and others to spend time verifying and correcting records before even basic numbers can be used for planning purpose. Offices away from headquarters cannot fully access and update data.[9]

Way Forward

The United Nations does not need to reinvent the wheel. Many governments and private enterprises have already been doing workforce planning and strategic human resources planning, and the United Nations can learn from them, adapt them and improve them to suit its requirements.

The Office of Personnel Management (OPM), in the Federal Government has practiced workforce planning as a systematic process for identifying and addressing between the workforce of today and the human capital needs of tomorrow. It has developed a five-step workforce-planning model as a useful starting point for understanding the elements of such a methodology. The model is reproduced as a graphic representation of this tool.[10]

OPM's Workforce Planning Model

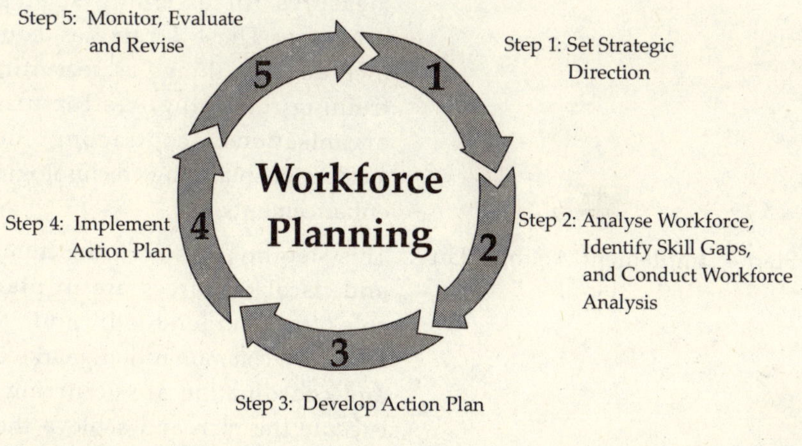

9. Courtesy of United Nations.

10. *http://www.opm.gov/workforceplanning/wfpmodel.htm*

Step 1: Set Strategic Direction	This step involves linking the workforce planning process with the agency's strategic plan, annual performance/business plan and work activities required to carry out the goals and objectives of the strategic plan (long-term) and performance plan (short term).
Step 2: Analyse Workforce, Identify Skill Gaps and Conduct Workforce Analysis	This step involves: • Determining what the current workforce resources are and how they will evolve over time through turnover, etc. • Developing specifications for the kinds, numbers and location of workers and managers needed to accomplish the agency's strategic requirements. • Determining what gaps exist between the current and projected workforce needs.
Step 3: Develop Action Plan	This step involves the identification of strategies to close gaps, plans to implement the strategies and measures for assessing strategic progress. These strategies could include such things as recruiting, training/retraining, restructuring organisations, contracting out, succession planning, technological enhancements, etc.
Step 4: Implement Action Plan	This step involves ensuring human and fiscal resources are in place; roles are understood; and the necessary communication, marketing and coordination are occurring to execute the plan and achieve the strategic objectives.

Step 5: Monitor, Evaluate and Revise.	This step involves monitoring progress against milestones, assessing for continuous improvement purposes and adjusting the plan to make course corrections and to address new workforce issues.

The experience of General Electric indicates their consistent adherence to human resource planning for the purpose of developing rigorous recruitment of policies for new entrants in different divisions as well as to take a whole new look at their talent pools each year and to assess rigorously the achievements of existing staff for promotion, transfer, and/or to offer buyout plans. The success of such a strategy is dependent on people planning process in its entirety.[11]

Human resources planning of the United Nations for the future and the persistent year by year implementation of such plans must be pursued as vigorously as the planning of the use of natural resources and the development of new methods of agriculture and industry within the country context. But the years of study, training and experience, the patient and persistent development of many different skills sets and basic orientation needed to understand, to administer and to coordinate these various skills are factors whose importance is often underestimated in large organisations.

To implement a human resource plan, it is important for OHRM to expand the scope of activities beyond the traditional HRM tasks and functions and enter partnership with divisions and departments. For example, if necessary competencies and skills do not exist in the present employees, they will need to be trained in the new skills or external recruitment may have to be used to bring those competencies to the world body. OHRM has to identify where employees of those backgrounds and skills are likely to be found and appropriate recruitment strategies need to be developed for implementation.

The civil service cannot solve these problems alone. A dynamic organisational programme for the development of United Nations human resources will require the concerted effort of all elements

11. Welch, Jack (2005). *Winning*. New York: Harper-Collins. p.

of the system. But in view of the large areas of activity in which the world body now participates, the international civil service can play a critical role through leadership and other initiatives. In this strategic task the organisation needs to ally itself closely with institutions of excellence, government departments, with corporate management, the leaders of the educational system and professional men in different fields of activity.

OHRM should have a self-contained unit responsible for studying the long term human resources needs of the world body, a unit that should not be preoccupied with day to day operating responsibilities. It should develop methods and techniques for tabulating manning tables for each department, division and section, and projecting their growth and development in harmony with long and medium-term mandates approved by the General Assembly along with census and financial forecasts. It is essential that future personnel needs of the United Nations project for a period of 5 to 10 years, classified by various skills, professions and specialisations. These forecasts must take into account attrition through natural causes, such as retirement and transfer from one to the other department. As experience and data are accumulated, these projections should be revised and updated, at least once a year.

We would like to conclude this chapter with Peter Ducker's comment: "Strategic planning prepares today's business for the future. It asks, What *should* our business be? It asks, What do we have to do today to deserve the future? Strategic planning requires risk-taking decisions. It requires an organised process of abandoning yesterday. It requires that the work to be done to produce the desired future be clearly defined and clearly assigned. The aim of strategic planning is *action now*."[12] The United Nations ought to bear this seriously in mind and get its act together in its human resources planning immediately. In this context, it should be noted that GA resolution 63/250 has underlined the need for strategic workforce planning. We also see the imperative to pursue this matter with diligence and make efforts to improve workforce planning in the United Nations.

---

12. Drucker, Peter F., *Management, op. cit.*, p. 128.

13

Revitalising UN Human Resources Management

Introduction

The United Nations needs consistent reform and revitalisation for it to remain relevant and effective for all times. Continuous efforts have been made to revamp the United Nations ever since the organisation was set up, but they were intensified from the 1990s onwards. And every reform has had implications for human resources management.

Understandably, reform is not new to the organisation; it is as old as the entity itself. Successive secretaries-general have tried their hands at changing the United Nations for the better in response to the demand of time. As Luck says, "The never-ending quest for reform, for improving the function of the United Nations, has been an integral part of the life of the world body since its earliest days."[1] He has aptly summarised reform efforts in the United Nations:

> Through the years, scores of independent commissions, government studies, and individuals scholars have put forward literally hundreds of proposals aimed at making the world body work better, decide more fairly, modify its mandate, or operate more efficiently. Not to be left behind by the reform bandwagon, successive Secretaries-General and units of the Secretariat have engaged in frequent, if

1. Luck, Edward C. (2003). "Reforming the United Nations: Lessons from a History in Progress", *International Relations Studies and the United Nations Occasional Papers*. No.1, ACUNS, p.1.

episodic, bouts of self-examination and self-criticism, offering their own reform agendas.[2]

Yet much expected transformation has eluded the United Nations so far. There have been only three amendments to the Charter of the United Nations in 64 years: To enlarge the Security Council once and to expand the Economic and Social Council twice. Apparently, the polarised global community during the Cold War period, which effectively began with the end of World War II, was not very conducive to reform in the organisation. Still several changes took place during that period, notably the expansion of the Security Council and the Economic and Social Council. Intermittent efforts have been made all along, but they were intensified after Cold War came to an end. At that juncture, the then Secretary-General Boutros-Ghali formulated An Agenda for Peace and An Agenda for Development. Several bouts of reform came in succession after that, but none of them could make a headway, thanks to the North-South divide that replaced the East-West polarisation of Cold War. Therefore, the world body is yet to witness major streamlining in its structures and significant changes in its methods. In fact, the situation has, some may plausibly argue, further deteriorated in some respects.

Consider this. The United States Senate had, as early as 1947, identified "problems of overlap, duplication of efforts, weak coordination, proliferation of mandates and programs and overly generous compensation of staff with the infant, but rapidly growing, United Nations system."[3] This observation could not have been more apt today. Departments and units have increased, overlap and duplication have aggravated, mandates and programmes have proliferated beyond imagination. However, staff compensation has lost much ground, so much so that the best and brightest from the wealthy countries hardly consider the United Nations as an attractive career option now.

---

2. Ibid.

3. Senate Committee on Expenditures in the Executive Departments (1948). *United States Relations with International Organizations*, 80th Congress, Second session. Senate Report 1757.

The US Task Force on the United Nations, headed by the former Speaker Newt Gingrich, has made an apt observation about the reform of the world body:

> Since the late 1980s, U.S. pressures, including financial restrictions, have helped to bring about several reforms: adherence to an informal rule on passing the budget by consensus, creation of the Office of Internal Oversight Services (OIOS), and adoption of results-based budgeting. But by and large, the United Nations has proved resistant to change. The internal management reforms carried out to date have failed to create an institution that meets basic standards of good management, much less one that reflects the profoundly changed nature of what the United Nations is doing. If the United Nations is to carry out those tasks, its ossified managerial structures need more than tinkering...It is a demanding task to make the United Nations work effectively, efficiently, and transparently. The United Nations faces structural problems of oversight and accountability, management, agenda setting and resource allocation, and human resources management.[4]

Reform Initiatives

As we have mentioned above, all secretaries-general of the United Nations have tried their hands at reform in the organisation. The first Secretary-General Trygve Lie (1946-1952) was successful in getting the rules of procedures of the Security Council to be changed in order for him to be able to intervene in the Council's discussions.[5] Secretary-General Dag Hammarskjold (1953-1961) tried to strengthen the world body's role in the midst of rising tensions between the West and the East, and deployed the first peacekeeping mission in the Suez Canal area in 1956 despite strong opposition from the Soviet Union.[6]

Secretary-General U Thant (1961-1971) "played an important part in ending the civil war in Congo, diffusing the missile crisis in Cuba, negotiating Algeria's independence in 1962, and finding a peaceful settlement in the former Dutch East Indies. ...During (his)

4. United States (2005). Institute of Peace, *American Interests and UN Reform, Report of the Task Force on the United Nations*. Washington DC. p.42.
5. See the Global Policy Forum website: *http://www.globalpolicy.org/reform/initiatives/lieindex.htm*
6. Ibid.

tenure, the UN expanded its work on social and economic development in poor countries, and established new programs and funds, such as the UN Development Program and the UN Environmental Program."[7] In the latter half of his second term, U Thant had more contentious and difficult issues to grapple with, including the Vietnam war and the Arab-Israeli war; he was also subjected to criticism for withdrawing UN forces from the Sinai Peninsula. The enlargements of the Security Council from 11 members to 15, and of the ECOSOC from 18 members to 27, took place in 1965 on U Thant's watch.

His successor Kurt Waldheim (1972-1981) took initiative to bring Turkey and Greece to discuss the question of Cyprus and helped end the Israeli-Arab war in 1973. ECOSOC was expanded from 27 members to 54 in 1973 too. In his second term, Mr. Waldheim won accolades for the balanced handling of the war in Afghanistan, the conflict between Iran and Iraq, and Israel's occupation of southern Lebanon.[8] Secretary-General Perez de Cuellar (1982-1991) played a key role in negotiations between Argentina and the UK during the Falklands war, between Israel and Lebanon, and between Afghanistan and the Soviet Union. When the Gulf War broke out with blessings from the Security Council, Mr. de Cuellar urged member states to comply with humanitarian laws. He also asked them to address collectively the growing global problems of HIV/AIDS, drug trafficking and environmental degradation.[9]

Secretary-General Boutros Boutros-Ghali (1992-1996) came with the first major, coordinated thrust for significant change in the United Nations. He presented to member states two landmark documents—*An Agenda for Peace in 1992*[10] and *An Agenda for Development*[11] *in 1994*. In the first document, he emphasised the need for preventive diplomacy, peacemaking, peacekeeping, post-conflict peace-building, cooperation with regional arrangements and

7. Ibid, *http://www.globalpolicy.org/reform/initiatives/thantindex.htm*

8. Ibid, *http://www.globalpolicy.org/reform/initiatives/waldheimindex.htm*

9. Ibid, *http://www.globalpolicy.org/reform/initiatives/perezindex.htm*

10. United Nations (1992). *An Agenda for Peace*, A/47/277-S/24111. 17 June.

11. United Nations (1994). *An Agenda for Development*, A/48/935. 6 May.

organisations, safety of personnel, and financing of peace initiatives. He called on all UN entities and member states to work together and to undertake balanced roles and responsibilities, to practice democracy within the organisation, to resist the temptation for unilateralism, and to engage civil society in the UN's work, among other things.[12]

In *An Agenda for Development*, Mr. Boutros-Ghali declared, "Development is a fundamental human right. Development is the most secure basis of peace."[13] He identified peace as the foundation of development, the economy as the engine of progress, the environment as a basis for sustainability, justice as a pillar of society, and democracy as good governance. Then he proposed to the world to embrace the culture of development, treat development as a comprehensive and collective effort, and provide additional resources to the United Nations to carry out its added responsibilities to advance those five dimensions of development.[14] His two agendas envisaged enhanced role for the United Nations in global governance and implied considerably increased human and financial resources requirements, but he did not specifically translate them in terms of head count and dollars and cents.

During Mr. Boutros-Ghali's term, many other things happened as well. Summit and high-level meetings took place on the environment and development, on human rights, on population, on social development and on women. The Commission on Global Governance, a blue-ribbon panel, called for the strengthening of the major international institutions, particularly the United Nations, and stressed the imperative for better UN funding and for Security Council reform. The Center on Transnational Corporation was abolished, the status of the UN disarmament work was reduced, all economic and social development activities were consolidated into one department, and an Efficiency Board was set up. In 1993, the General Assembly created the post of High Commissioner for Human Rights, the Security Council allowed guests to participate

12. Ibid, see paras 75-86.

13. Ibid, para. 3.

14. Ibid, para 231-245.

in its informal meetings under the "Arria Formula," and the Volcker-Ogata Commission studied UN finances and concluded that member states should pay their dues on time, in full and without conditions. In 1994, the General Assembly established the Office of Internal Oversight Services as an independent department reporting directly to itself—the apex, deliberative body. The United Nations had to curtail its information programmes under the budget crunch. Amidst the serious financial difficulties for the United Nations due to US unwillingness to contribute its share, Mr. Boutros-Ghali proposed global taxes to finance the world body, but the idea was immediately shut down. His proposal to abolish the Trusteeship Council for a lack of work did not find favour with member states either.

On the heels of Mr. Boutros-Ghali's landmark reports, his successor Kofi Annan (1997-2006), the ultimate insider of the organisation, sought to present himself as a reform-secretary-general by making a series of proposals and taking a number of measures within the Secretariat. He announced a reform package, appointed a new Under Secretary-General for Reform, merged several related units in the Department for Economic and Social Affairs, created the post of Deputy Secretary-General, and established a Senior Management Group, set up the Office for the Coordination of Humanitarian Affairs and downsized the staff strength to reduce cost and improve efficiency. The United Nations greatly reduced the use of gratis personnel from member states, and implemented an Integrated Management and Information System (IMIS) for budget and management information. Mr. Annan also set up the Global Compact to develop partnership with the private sector, the Brahimi Panel to suggest measures that would strengthen peacekeeping operations, and the Cardoso Panel to suggest measures to develop relations between the United Nations and civil society.

In 2002, Kofi Annan presented his report—*Strengthening the United Nations: An Agenda for Further Change*[15]—in which he proposed 36 actions. Many of the actions indicate or pledge to present concrete

---

15. United Nations (2002). *Strengthening the United Nations: An Agenda for Further Change*, A/57/387, 9 September.

proposals for consideration in the future, some do ask for concrete action as well, such as the restructuring of the Department of Public Information and the establishment of a policy planning unit in the Department of Economic and Social Affairs. Actions 25 to 36 pertain specifically to human resources management; some of them seem to be quite forward-looking, while others pandering to narrow interest of the staff. These actions have been produced in Annex A-13.3 to this chapter.

Stung by the division over the Iraq war in 2003, Mr. Annan established a blue-ribbon panel on threats, challenges and change to assess global security challenges and recommend institutional and policy measures to address them. Bowing to the pressure from Washington, he fired several of his senior staff and closed several information centers in western Europe. Towards the end of his tenure, Mr. Annan established a high-level panel to look into the possibility of consolidating several UN agencies.

In particular, Kofi Annan presented two landmark reports on reform that have had direct and huge implications for human resources management. The first—*Investing in the United Nations: for a Stronger Organisation Worldwide*[16]—was almost entirely dedicated to administrative change. In this report, Mr. Annan proposed changes for recruitment, mobility of staff, and career development; for the distribution of authority among the leadership; for managing information technology resources better; for getting things done more economically and efficiently; for linking the budget to results and performance; for giving more power to the Secretary-General on managerial and budgetary issues; and for the setting up of change management and one-time staff buyout. The General Assembly approved some of the proposals, but sent back the major ones to the Secretariat to reconsider and fully flesh out the details before resubmission; and rejected some of them in the face of strong opposition from member states.[17] For the complete list of the recommendations, see Annex A-13.1 to this chapter.

---

16. United Nations (2006). *Investing in the United Nations: for a Stronger Organization Worldwide*, A/60/692 of 7 March.

17. US Department of States, *United States Participation in the United Nations, A Report by the Secretary of State to the Congress for the Year 2006*. Washington DC. p.157.

In March 2005, Kofi Annan presented a comprehensive report on reform—*In Larger Freedom: Towards Development, Security and Human Rights for All*—based on the report of the blue-ribbon panel on the Threats, Challenges and Change. In this report, Mr. Annan stressed three freedoms—Freedom from want, Freedom from fear, and Freedom to live in dignity—and the need to strengthen the United Nations to help realise those freedoms. He asked governments to promote freedom from want by working separately and together to realise the 8 Millennium Development Goals, to incorporate them in their national strategies, to increase development assistance and development-oriented trade, ensure environmental sustainability and better manage deadly diseases, natural disasters, migration, etc.

Under the freedom from fear, Mr. Annan asked the international community to find a new security consensus and work collectively to grapple with wars, risks of wars, terrorism, and weapons of mass destruction and to enhance the effectiveness of mediation, sanction, peacekeeping, peace-building, control of small arms and light weapons and to use other tools. He also suggested that the international community had the right and obligation to use force to prevent genocide or other comparable crimes, something that became highly controversial. Under the freedom to live in dignity, Mr. Annan underlined the imperative for the rule of law, better protection of human rights, and promotion of democracy. The United Nations had to be strengthened to be able to help achieve these objectives.

To strengthen the United Nations, the Secretary-General made several proposals. He asked member states to rationalise the work and streamline the agendas of the General Assembly; presented two models for enlarging the Security Council; and suggested that the Economic and Social Council work as a high-level development forum to follow-up on the agreed developmental goals, and to work with the Security Council on rebuilding of countries emerging from conflict. To replace the highly politicised Human Rights Commission, Mr. Annan proposed the creation of a Human Rights Council.

He made several recommendations to strengthen the Secretariat. He asked the General Assembly to review all mandates more than

5 years old and see if the resources devoted to them could be reassigned; to give him the authority and resources to pursue one-time staff buy-out; to review the budget and human resources rules; and to commission a comprehensive review of the Office of Internal Oversight Services. To promote UN system-wide coherence, the Secretary-General asked member states to ensure that there was greater coordination of their positions in various governing bodies, in their humanitarian response, and in development and environmental issues. After some terrorists blasted the Baghdad office of the United Nations in which several UN officials died, the Secretary-General set up in 2005 the Department of Safety and Security, with worldwide presence, under a new Under Secretary-General, who enjoys rather inscrutably considerable degree of independence from SG.

During Mr. Annan's term, the General Assembly held several conferences that took many significant decisions. It convened the Millennium Summit, the Millennium Summit plus Five, the mid-term follow-up meetings on women and sustainable development, among others. In the mean time, the Assembly also agreed to reduce the United States' share in the regular and peacekeeping budgets, establish the International Criminal Court, and create the Peace-building Commission and the Human Rights Council.

No sooner than had he assumed the duty of Secretary-General in 1997 that Kofi Annan presented his first reform report—*Renewing the United Nations: A Program for Reform.*[18] It has had 29 actions and several recommendations. The actions have to do with the measures he himself was going to undertake, while the recommendations were for the General Assembly to approve. He outlined 7 strategies to strengthen and streamline the United Nations. The highlights of the proposed reforms appear in Annex A-13.4 to this chapter.

For the Millennium Summit to consider, Kofi Annan presented the report—*We the People*—in which he sought to persuade heads of states and government to agree on a common vision for development and security. Consequently, through the Millennium

18. United Nations (1997). *Renewing the United Nations: A Program for Reform*, A/51/950, 14 July.

Declaration, governments reaffirmed their common resolve to work together in such areas of shared interest as peace, security and disarmament, development and poverty eradication, the environment, democracy, human rights and good governance, protection of the vulnerable, meeting the special needs of Africa, and strengthening the United Nations.[19] The oft-repeated Millennium Development Goals emanated from this Declaration. Among the measures mentioned, several were related to management. They included the member states' commitment to make resources available to the organisation on a timely and predictable basis, as well as the call on the Secretariat to make the best use of resources by adopting best management practices and technologies, to promote staff safety, and to increase the system-wide coherence.

The Millennium + 5 Summit Outcome Document has a section on management reform.[20] In essence, the document reemphasises the significance of the United Nations in realising the agreed development goals and peace and security measures. It calls on the Secretary-General to establish the Ethics Office, in the wake of the Oil-for-food scandal in which some UN officials were suspected of having siphoned off large sums of money from the Iraqi oil revenue; to strengthen the internal oversight function; and to set up an independent audit advisory body. Mostly, the document also calls on the Secretary-General to submit a series of proposals. The relevant paragraphs of the outcome document have been produced in Annex A-13.5.

Evidently, many of the measures outlined by Kofi Annan were within his purview as Chief Administrative Officer of the United Nations. That is why in some cases he simply informed member states what he wanted to do; in other cases, he pledged to present proposals to intergovernmental bodies; and yet in others, he sought approval from the General Assembly and other decision-making bodies. While the General Assembly accepted several of Mr. Annan's proposals, including the creation of the Human Rights Council, it

19. GA Resolution A/res/55/2 of 8 September 2000.

20. United Nations (2005). Millennium + 5 Summit Outcome Document, A/59/2005. 15 September.

asked him to provide further details on many of them; it also rejected some of them. For instance, the Assembly rejected his proposal to reconstitute the Trusteeship Council with the mandate of "collective trusteeship for the integrity of the global environment and common areas such as the oceans, atmosphere and outer space."[21] Therefore, the Trusteeship Council remains suspended, pending its fate. The Assembly also largely refused to give him greater authority on administrative and budgetary matters.

Even as all this back and forth with inflections and deflections have been going on elsewhere in the UN house, the International Court of Justice has been slugging through almost on the verge of impotency and irrelevance.

Despite all the initiatives he undertook, Kofi Annan left office as a deeply frustrated man in terms of reform, though he had a lot to take personal satisfaction from in other areas, including a Nobel Prize. In his last report on reform, he candidly admitted, "Previous reform efforts, while generating some significant improvements, have sometimes addressed the symptoms rather than the causes of the Organisation's weaknesses, and have failed to adequately address new needs and requirements."[22] That was precisely the reason why Kofi Annan's reforms generated many big waves but did not result in comparable improvements. Substantively speaking, the lowest point in his long career with the United Nations hit when he witnessed the genocides in Rwanda and in Srebrenica, whereas his nadir as chief administrative officer came when the Staff Union adopted a motion of no-confidence against him and his senior management team in March 2006. Unhappy about his proposal to outsource some work or move staff out of the United States to reduce cost of producing documents, the Staff Union took that drastic decision.[23] This demonstrates that keeping both member states and staff happy turns out to be fraught with serious contradictions and dire consequences.

---

21. United Nations (1997). Report of the Secretary-General, *Renewing the United Nations: A Program of Reform* para 84-85.
22. United Nations, *Investing in the United Nations, op. cit.*, p.1.
23. China Daily's website: *http://www.chinadaily.com.cn/english/doc/2006-03/10/content_530479.htm*, 10 March 2006.

Ban Ki-Moon, the new Secretary-General, too has shown his zeal for reform, but he has not tried to project himself as a reform buff. He has broken the Department of Peacekeeping Operations into two departments, Department of Peace Operations and the Department of Field Support. At the same time, he has also combined the works of several erstwhile Under Secretaries-General by bringing their functions under one USG. Mr. Ban is seeking greater streamlining of recruitment and selection and far more authority to fire those staff who fail to perform. This has put him at the loggerheads with the staff already, something Kofi Annan had to face only much later in his tenure.

Either by design or default, founders of the United Nations had sowed some of the seeds of discontent in the UN Charter itself; or it was the circumstances in which the world body was established that were responsible for it. World War II had created victors and the vanquished, and key among the victors—USA, UK, then Soviet Union, France and China—took upon them the privilege of veto power and permanent membership in the Security Council, the most powerful body, of the United Nations, whose decisions, by the Charter, are binding on all member states. However, the dramatically changed global situation does not leave that as an acceptable arrangement anymore. Therefore, several other countries have been trying to get a seat at the top table. Among them, the Group of Four—Japan, Germany, Brazil and India—has been making concerted effort to this effect. Some existing permanent members and those who have no hope to be ones any time soon are opposed to one or an other aspirant to permanent membership in an enlarged Security Council. Divisions are sharp and clear, and evidently irreconcilable. Small countries would rather want to enlarge the non-permanent category of the Security Council membership and strengthen other bodies where they carry numerical weight: The General Assembly and, to a certain extent, the Economic and Social Council.

To make matters worse, the permanent members have been able to expand constantly the scope of the Security Council, further impinging upon the territory of the other two important bodies, where other countries also have a voice. Such issues as HIV/AIDS and children in armed conflict or nation-building aspects of peacekeeping operations—like quick impact projects—that should have been the preserve of the ECOSOC have now become the staples of the Security Council. This is all happening at a time when the permanent members of the Security Council, notably the United States, have been striving hard to reduce their own financial contribution to the organisation. The Security Council has also been defiant to the General Assembly by not sufficiently heeding the latter's resolutions to make the Council's work more transparent and democratic.

A tug of war continues to exist between the General Assembly, which is the final and apex authority on matters of administration and budget, and the Secretariat that has the obligation to service the intergovernmental bodies and to help implement their resolutions and decisions. One hears in the corridors of the United Nations that the permanent members of the Security Council are intent on making the Secretariat more powerful in this struggle, because they themselves then can wield much of such powers through the Secretary-General who stands very much be at their mercy.

As a result, there is a situation where different stakeholders do not trust each other fully and insist on guarding their turf as stringently as possible. This has dragged the United Nations far too long. The GA Working Group on Security Council Reforms has been discussing the issue of Council enlargement well over a decade now, but consensus seems as far as ever. All this has created an enormous friction and generated immense division in the United Nations, made GA to go in circle, using up scarce resources year after year, and retarded reforms elsewhere too.

Observations

From the history of reforms in the United Nations, many things become clear. This is what the US Task Force on the United Nations had to say about it in 2005:

> The United Nations needs top leadership that knows how to manage a complex organisation and is charged with doing so. ▯ The UN Secretariat needs to have a single, very senior official in charge of daily operations and filling the role of chief operating officer (COO). That official should not be the secretary-general, who has too many other responsibilities. But the secretary-general must understand and provide leadership on good management practices: ▯ The United States should insist on management capability as a fundamental criterion for the selection of the next secretary-general. The United States should seek agreement in the General Assembly for a more effective management structure, one that would make the next deputy secretary-general the organisation's COO. The secretary-general must have the authority to remove top management without cause.[24]

Anyway, we, the authors, have come up with our own conclusions. We find many profound problems inherent in the United Nations—partly in its structure, partly in its processes, partly in the member states' attitude towards the world body, and partly in the attitude of staff. We have discussed them in the relevant chapters themselves. In this chapter, we will discuss the most fundamental problems, at the cost of some repetition from the previous chapters, which need to be addressed with priority to improve the HRM of the United Nations in order to have system-wide positive impacts. First, the organisations has shied away from tackling the root causes of problems and sought mostly to address their symptoms only. Secondly, reform in the United Nations is far from easy, amidst contrasting interests of member states and staff with respect to key issues. Thirdly, the demarcation of authority is so blurred that decisive action often becomes difficult, if not impossible. Fourthly, the Chief Administrative Officer has deliberately been made weak. We wish to offer our suggestions to address these strategic issues.

Tackle the Root Causes

Let us start with the root causes. Particularly with respect to human resources management, which happens to be the core subject of this book, we have zeroed in on four root issues to be addressed to make the United Nations a transparent, efficient,

24. United States Institute of Peace, *American Interests and UN Reform*, *op. cit.*, pp. 51-52.

effective, and relevant organisation that can deliver and give value for the money.

1. *Improved Recruitment and Selection:* The recruitment and selection practice in the United Nations is downright unacceptable. The current system gives the impression that the objective of the world body is to hire, retain and promote mediocre staff. There is a huge talent pool out there, but due to its preference system in hiring, no external candidates come to the attention of recruiters as long as they find barely acceptable insiders. Therefore, what they get is the barely acceptable lot. It decimates the capacity of the whole organisation to perform optimally. At the same time, there is also the necessity to keep the existing staff motivated with transfer and promotion opportunities.

   We, therefore, propose that the United Nations apportion, as many countries have done, a certain percentage of vacancies for internal candidates and fill those posts with a rigorous vetting of candidates from the existing staff. In the remaining posts, both internal and external candidates should be able to compete on the strength of their qualification, experience and potential. This arrangement will be consistent with Article 101 of the United Nations Charter. For this, the Galaxy system will have to be upgraded or replaced so that all external and internal candidates could be carefully considered for the open posts.

2. *Independent Selection Agency:* There must be a dedicated and largely independent recruitment agency, as the European Commission and so many governments around the world have. Only such an agency can bring in the kind of expertise and competence that is essential to select and recruit the best fit for the job, without having to accommodate political pressure from different quarters to hire their nationals or friends and cronies of senior managers. This will allow the Secretary-General to focus on substantive issues, rather than staff recruitment and selection, which now happens to consume much of his valuable time.

3. *Increased Authority and Accountability to Secretary-General:* The Secretary-General must have the authority to fire a staff member who consistently underperforms. Those staff members who perform below a certain set of standards for three years in a row or over a period of five years should be subjected to such firing. This calls for a rigorous, objective and regular system of performance evaluation. The General Electric Company, one of the most successful multinationals, has a system of putting its staff in A, B and C categories in terms of their performance; those falling in Category A get raise or promotion; those in B retain their job; and those in Category C get fired. This system keeps staff on their toes and motivates them to perform optimally. To prevent arbitrary firing in the United Nations, the staff in question must perform poorly three years in a row or three years out of five and the Secretary-General must seek the advice of the proposed independent selection agency, as most countries do from their civil service commissions.
4. *Review of Departmental Independence:* There should be a review of independence of various departments and agencies and the degree of such leverage. The independence of those that need it for better performance should be allowed to have it, whereas those that do not deserve it, should be deprived of such privilege. Unwarranted independence often hampers coordination and undermines optimal performance. For instance, the General Assembly has appropriately bestowed a great degree of independence on the Office of Internal Oversight Services, and it should be continued. However, we find no justification whatsoever as to why the Department of Safety and Security needs independence from the Secretary-General. This is inconsistent with the management practice and control measures applicable to security agencies worldwide. We propose that the Department of Safety and Security be brought directly under the Secretary-General.
5. *Comprehensive Human Resources Management Reform:* What the United Nations needs is comprehensive reform in its HRM sector, not tinkering on the margins, as most secretaries-

general have sought to do, simply because the business as usual would not address the root of the multifaceted problem. The Secretary-General must be authorised to hire and fire heads of UN funds and programmes in consultation with the proposed independent selection agency or another high-level panel of eminent people. This will make the Secretary-General accountable for all administrative matters, improve system-wide coherence at the centre, promote collaboration and coordination in the field, make better use of resources, improve delivery and save significant amount of resources for the organisation. A blue-ribbon panel should be set up to look into all these matters and make informed recommendations to improve HRM.

Shape Environment for Reform

The environment for reform is far from conducive in the United Nations. There are numerous stakeholders with varying, and sometimes even conflicting, interests quite difficult to reconcile. It is nearly impossible for all 192 members of the organisation to be on the same page. Member states usually want to contribute to the finances of the United Nations as little as possible, exercise as much influence as possible and to have as many of their nationals working for the body as possible. The existing staff want their promotion; external candidates want fair competition. Each organ of the world body wants more power to itself. Competition also exists between various departments and individuals to encroach upon each other's turf.

Clearly, SG feels entrapped. If he does not pursue certain reforms pet to the powerful, they punish him by withholding their support and contribution, as the United States did in the mid-1990s and the Soviet Union before that. Vigorous reform might impinge on the staff, who could adopt a motion of no confidence against the chief administrative officer and his team and spoil the working environment. While the overall environment could not be dramatically changed anytime soon, that does not mean many important things cannot be accomplished even within the existing framework, climate, and limitations. The best foot forward would be to set up a blue-ribbon panel to suggest reform measures to update and revamp management. Once that has been done, SG ought to determine which suggestions require new mandate from the General Assembly, which are on the borderline of the given mandate, and which require no new mandate; he should then formulate a plan and execute it accordingly. One should not be surprised to find that many sensible reforms could be implemented within the existing mandates.

1. *Reforms not Requiring New Mandate:* Many reforms that are urgently needed require no additional mandate from the General Assembly. Take for instance, improving the recruitment and selection system, training staff, strictly implementing the performance evaluation system; they can be done within the existing resources if they are redeployed or rearranged. SG can simply allocate some additional resources at his disposal and ask OHRM to look at all applicants before settling on the candidates to recruit and promote and give priority to internal candidates if they and external candidates seem equally good. In the field of training, the architecture is already there. However, no previous SG has bothered to implement it rigorously. SG had authorisation for limited managed staff mobility, but he could not use this authority effectively, and now he has asked GA for its suspension. He can stick to having a more rigorous and realistic performance evaluation and use it as the fundamental basis to give staff members promotion and pay raise, to retain them as they are, and or to dismiss those who fail to perform at a certain level over a period. These are just a few examples of far-reaching positive implications that could be generated within the existing mandates. Several other reform issues also fall in this category.
2. The UN Staff Regulations and Rules do already provide a pretty good framework to strengthen and streamline human resources. No new mandate is necessary to issue administrative instructions to implement those regulations and rules. Interestingly for example, while SG thought he did not have

enough power to fire non-performing staff, one of his senior lieutenants opined that he enjoyed that power already, but he was not exercising it enough. Nonetheless, if there are clearly borderline cases, SG can always seek new mandate from the General Assembly.

3. Whenever there is a major restructuring of the Secretariat is proposed, new mandate from the General Assembly might be necessary, but often be difficult to get. However, such cases would be rare. If the Secretariat is able to demonstrate its commitment and resolve to get things done in a credible fashion, GA would be willing to look favourably at the request for greater authority in management matters. If there was no environment conducive for change, then the Secretariat must strive to create one, rather than complaining about it and doing little to change it.

Remove Rigidity from System

Management in the United Nations must be more flexible and result-oriented. Currently, it is anchored to rigid, anachronistic methods and practices, making the world body sclerotic. A senior manager complained to the authors that, when necessary due to the urgency of the matter, he could not pull together a number of staff to work as a team on a project; every staff has had a rigid job description. The Secretary-General should be able to assign staff on priority projects on a temporary basis and get the job done, without jeopardising their substantive work. The General Assembly must choose between making better delivery and binding SG in a rigid bureaucratic rope. If it wants improved delivery from SG, then it should give him the wherewithal he needs to do the job and hold him to account for his performance. On the other hand, if GA wants to maintain its tight control over SG through micro-managing, then it should not expect enhanced accountability from him. GA cannot have a cake and eat it too.

For the same reason, SG either must be prepared to accept greater accountability for his performance or should not complain about micro-management by the General Assembly, as the former

Secretary-General Kofi Annan used to do frequently. There is a big contradiction on both sides: the General Assembly does not want to give more authority to SG but seeks greater accountability from him; conversely, SG wants more authority without agreeing to bear greater accountability. We, the authors, believe authority and accountability must go hand in hand, not only at the top but also down to the lowest echelons of management.

In other words, GA should grant more authority to SG on management related matters and extract greater accountability as well. To suggest how best it could be done, GA in consultation with SG should appoint a blue-ribbon panel on management improvement and task it with making comprehensive recommendations on all key aspects of management, after carrying out careful study of other international organisations, private corporations and government entities. The time has come for such a panel and for a major leap in management reforms in the United Nations.

Increase Staff Mobility

Rigidity manifests itself in the United Nations, among other things, in a lack of staff mobility, a critical factor to keep an organisation vibrant and clean. A lack of mobility is harmful to both, employers and employees. Employers lose by not being able to move the staff where they are needed most; productivity slumps when employees get ossified due to immobility, become complacent about their indispensability and apathetic towards their job; and corruption raises its head when staff members become too much embedded in a post or place. Employees as well lose their zeal to compete; their productivity erodes over time; and they lack the opportunity to acquire broad range of skills and experiences that are critical to promotion and success in senior posts. Increased staff mobility will be beneficial to the United Nations and its staff as well as its member states.

What is rather difficult to understand is why the world body does not yet have a credible mobility policy that works, while every other organisation has it. Governments have always emphasised staff mobility as a matter of course. Large private organisations also value mobility. The European Commission has made staff mobility mandatory since 2004. If the cost was a constraining factor or the utility was suspect, mobility would not have been a widely accepted and practiced principle worldwide, in all sectors. It is long overdue for the United Nations to introduce a workable mobility policy. To minimise the cost of mobility, the work period after which the staff must move mandatorily could be made 5 years, as the European Commission has done.

Strengthen Performance Evaluation

Rewarding performance is a strategic tool to ensure organisational success. Conversely, dis-incentivising non-performance is the other side of the same coin. Reward motivates people, gives them the zeal to compete and to outdo others. In contrast, the fear that one may lose benefits, promotion or even the job for non-performance keeps employees on their toes and makes them bring out their best to prevent the likely uncertainty or humiliation. Not that the United Nations is not aware of it; obviously it is, that is why it has introduced the system of performance evaluation for quite some time. However, the world body has been unable to muster the courage to tell itself that it must survive on its strength, not on life support, and should pull itself up by the bootstraps. To do that, it must have high performing employees who do not fear rating their performance and standing up to the rest of the world on a competitive prism. Therefore, the United Nations must make performance evaluation of the staff the kingpin of decisions related to reward, raise, promotion, chastening and dismissal, depending on their performance. Only this, together with other critical reforms, would be able to help the United Nations rise to its full potential.

The world body can learn a lot from others. It can learn from OPM about 360-degree evaluation and from the rather aggressive, result-oriented, and highly lauded performance evaluation system introduced under Jack Welch, the former CEO of the General Electric Co., one of the most successful multinational organisations in the world. In the scheme, employees would be put in A, B and C categories based on their performance ratings. Those falling in

Category A would get handsome bonus, raise, or promotion; Category B employees retain their jobs; and Category C get dismissal or demotion. One might dismiss this system out of hand by arguing that the United Nations and the General Electric Co. are apples and oranges, which is partly true. However, we believe that at the level of evaluating work assigned to employees, there is no basic difference between the two. Therefore, the GE system, with appropriate modifications to allow for the difference in their nature of work, could be replicated in the United Nations to make the latter truly a centre of organisational excellence.

Change Recruitment Methods

As staff recruitment methods in the United Nations are deeply and inherently flawed, we need to change them to make them more merit-oriented, objective and just to all competent candidates. We have already described the deficient Galaxy system for vacancy announcement and underlined the imperative to change or improve it. Moving one step forward, we find that the basket system for selection from among internal candidates, system-wide candidates and external candidates is guided by innate bias against the injection of new blood and, hence, against long-term vibrancy of the organisation, and must be changed. Evidently, the United Nations selects P1 to P3 levels through national competitive or other examinations. The rest get picked up in a much less rigorous fashion by looking at a limited number of candidates' CV and conducting interview of short-listed candidates. But there is no transparent system to inspire confidence that all candidates have been fairly considered before making a final selection. We have come across employees who accused the United Nations of selecting candidates even before the vacancy announcements have been closed; and we have met the staff members who have rotten in a position for two decades, despite getting good ratings in performance evaluation. This situation is not acceptable.

The world body must ensure that a rigorous vetting process is in place to ascertain that the selection of staff is made based on the highest standards of efficiency and competence, due regard is given to geographical representation, as the UN Charter stipulates. We strongly recommend that the short-listed candidates for key posts, P5-D2 to start with, go through a written test and interview to determine their competence and to minimise personal bias or preference of recruiters. To strike a balance between promotional opportunities for the existing staff and infusion of new talents into the organisation, the world body must divide the number of vacancies between those to be filled from entirely internal competition and those to be filled through open competition with no inherent bias for or against internal or external candidates, other than their merit, competence, and geographical origin. This will ensure that there is a constant infusion of new talent at various levels, without completely blocking promotional opportunities for the existing staff.

Pursue e-Government

e-Government has been gaining ground worldwide, and there is an increasing move from e-Government to connected governance.[25] e-Government, or providing information and services through electronic medium, is a way to make government and organisations leaner and more cost effective. Now they are increasingly moving toward connected governance which "provides better organized, aligned and often integrated information flows, new transactional capacities as well as new mechanism for feedback, consultation and more participative forms of democracy."[26] In other words, it provides better connectivity and coherence across the system than just one-track approach with which e-government started. Sweden, Norway and Denmark have moved forward in this arena by leaps and bounds, and other developed countries are trying to catch up. The United Nations has followed suit in this realm as well. Consequently, we can get much of information on the entity on the web. For instance, we can access virtually all UN resolutions and apply to vacancies electronically. This is the way to go for the world body to enhance its efficiency and productivity, to reduce

25. United Nations. *e-Government Survey 2008: From e-government to Connected Governance.* p.xv.

26. Ibid: xvii.

paperwork, and to make savings. But the UN approach has been rather tentative, if not timid, at least so far.

Review Compensation

To attract best talents and retain them, the United Nations needs to review its compensation policy. The present UN compensation, particularly salary, is insufficient to motivate high achievers from the wealthy countries to join the world body. In the 1980s, the public sector at the central level in such countries as Canada, Japan, Denmark and the Federal Republic of Germany was at least one-third better paid than the private sector.[27] The United Nations has taken US civil service salaries as comparator from its inception, and the compensation was not bad. So much so some from the political right in the United States were decrying the high salaries and lavish pensions of UN civil servants way back.[28]

Not any more. Now things have changed. UN civil servants working with the Secretariat have lost ground to their counterparts elsewhere. Although the basic salaries are similar across the UN family, UN funds, programmes and specialised agencies, some people claim, are more generous to their employees, atleast in some allowances. On the other hand, America, the United Nations' main comparator, does not have the highest civil service pay in the world anymore. Many Western European countries, including the United Kingdom, pay higher salaries to their civil servants, and the European Commission pays its staff higher salaries and pension than member states do to their civil servants.[29] What is more, in the United States, private sector pay has overtaken public sector

27. Heller, Peter S. and Alan A. Tait (1984). "Government Employment and Pay: Some International Comparisons", *IMF Occasional Paper* 24, International Monetary Fund, Revised March. p.18.

28. Melanie L Merkle in 1984 said, "Though most of the U.N's activities are controversial, there is one thing on which just about everyone agrees—the U.N is a very generous employer. It pays its sprawling bureaucracy more than probably any government in the world pays its civil servants. It sends its bureaucrats into retirement secure with the kind of pension that would be the envy of every government and private sector worker worldwide And it says farewell to its workers with a golden handshake retirement bonus that is unknown outside of the most generous private corporations at least one United Nations success story,..it is the breeding of the world's fattest pensions." See the Heritage Foundation website: *http://www.heritage.org/Research/InternationalOrganizations/bg378.cfm*

29. See Harriss, Joseph (1998). "Eurocrats Take the Gravy Train," an article posted in *Reader's Digest*, International Editions, September, posted in *http://www.geocities.com/harriss75007/eurocrat.htm*

salaries. Denise Sherman wrote in the *Eastern Wake News*, "Private sector jobs pay more than similar jobs in the public sector according to information from human resources studies."[30] She, however, admits that it was hard to make neat job comparisons because of the different nature of duties. Anyway, the message is clear: Bright professionals in the rich countries would not consider the United Nations as an attractive career option.

Even in the developing world, many governments presiding over thriving economies have begun to look at the "demand of emerging global economic scenario,"[31] in which human resource could chase better opportunities beyond sectoral and national boundaries. As a result, India's Sixth Central Pay Commission has recommended more than three hundred times increase in the top salary band, from Rs.30,000 a month to Rs.90,000 a month (about US$1,900 at the current exchange rate), exclusive of several compensatory allowances and perquisites. All told, quite an impressive package in terms of absolute amount for India, and quite alluring in terms of its purchasing power parity with the US dollar. Soon, it might be difficult to attract talented young professionals even from India, a large source of UN staff, and so many other developing countries.

Therefore, the United Nations ought to review its compensation package for its civil servants and bring it to a level that can attract competent professionals not only from developing countries but also from the rich countries. Otherwise, the world body will gradually be deprived of talented professionals and lose its competitive edge and vitality, so much-needed to revitalise it and deliver on its umpteen and challenging mandates.

---

30. For anecdotal evidence, see Sherman, Denise (2008). "Public salaries lag behind private sector," an article published in *Eastern Wake News*. March 5. She says, "Chief operating officers of companies with roughly the number of employees as the towns of Knightdale, Wendell and Zebulon start at $333,484 annually and salaries can go as high as $954,642. Compare that to Knightdale Town Manager Gary McConkey's $109,366, Wendell Town Manager David Bone's $85,000 and Zebulon Town Manager Rick Hardin's $86,681."

31. See the Terms of Reference given to the Sixth Central Pay Commission of India in *Report of the Sixth Central Pay Commission*, March 2008, p.1; you can read the report on: *http://india.gov.in/govt/paycommission.php*

Save Avoidable Cost

Several developments have occurred since the last time when the then Secretary-General Boutros-Ghali had asked for a thorough review of the staff strength and reduced it by about 20 per cent. Key among them includes the significant increase in staff numbers, the liberal use of consultants, contractors and retired staff, and the huge investment in information technology. As we have mentioned already, the United Nations has almost invariably resorted to incrementalism in its HRM. Every time policy-making bodies make a demand on the Secretariat, it comes up with a new request for posts and other resources without adequate review of the existing resources and their possible reassignment. This has tremendously distorted the human resources configuration of the organisation and made it difficult to track in an orderly fashion who is doing what and whether what people are doing is consistent with the priority of the organisation and the Secretary-General. Likewise, generous use of consultants and contractors, often without enough and proper justification, should have reduced the need for permanent and temporary staff. That has not happened either. As well, the United Nations has invested large chunks of its resources in information technology and e-government to reduce paperwork and improve staff efficiency and productivity, but there has been no commensurate decline in staff numbers or staff costs.

In view of the above, we strongly see the need for a thorough review of the staff strength and organisational systems and processes and the possibility of substantial reduction in staff numbers, both in the professional and general service and related categories. While occasionally consultants might be needed for the expertise the Secretariat lacks, the liberal and often unjustified use of consultants, contractors and retired staff ought to be stopped immediately. What is more, although there is no scientific basis to quote a specific figure, it is our observation that at least 20 per cent staff reduction will be possible without adversely affecting the present level of the Secretariat's functions and performance. It can be done by removing unwarranted redundancies, streamlining functions, reworking the business plans, merging similar functions scattered at different units and places, and outsourcing non-strategic functions. GS and related staff strength could be reduced by a little bigger number than the Professional staff, particularly because the use of IT and e-government has substantially reduced clerical work in the universal body.

Need for Robust Training Policy

We attach value to training and staff development for the organisation's better performance and support in principal OHRM initiatives in this area. However, we do not find an integrated training policy linked to functions, performance and career development and believe that such policy must be formulated and implemented. The Staff College in Turin is operating as a run-of-the-mill institution with considerable budgetary support and staff that are hard to justify at their present level of activities. Just for an example, the strategic planning training for UNDP resident coordinators is neither sufficient for the target group nor appropriate for the Staff College to conduct. It is our considered view that the United Nations should either close down the Staff College and outsource its current activities to the developed and developing countries, or develop it into a credible centre of excellence with substantive programmes that could justify its continued existence and even enhanced levels of resources.

Imperative for System-wide Coherence

The world community is impatiently waiting for greater system-wide coherence in the United Nations to make it cost effective, more efficient and more coordinated in delivering its services. Such coherence is essential in the conditions of service across the Secretariat and UN funds and programmes and specialised agencies, in the programmatic aspects, and in sharing of common premises and services. As the High-Level Panel on United Nations System-wide Coherence has said, "Effective governance is at the core of coherence," and proposed series of measures at different levels to enable the United Nations to "deliver as one" on global development challenges, and in particular to make the "One United Nations" at the country level a reality for developing countries..."[32] This report

32. United Nations (2006). *Delivering as One*, the Report of the High-Level Panel on United Nations System-wide Coherence, A/61/583, 20 November p.39.

has suggested that several measures for the UN to deliver in an integrated and coordinated fashion. At the organisational level, the Panel has suggested:

- The United Nations System Chief Executives Board for Coordination should improve its decision-making role on overall reform and effectively drive managerial reform.
- The Development Policy and Operations Group should be the central coordinating mechanism for United Nations work on development at the country level. It will bring policy and operational roles together and will be chaired by a Development Coordinator. The Group would comprise the major development organisations in the United Nations.
- A clear firewall and accountability framework should be established between a repositioned UNDP support to the resident coordinator system and its reduced operations role. This will allow the full ownership of the United Nations system in the resident coordinator system (see chap. II.A).
- A Development Finance and Performance Unit should support the Development Policy and Operations Group in providing information and analysis on United Nations system funding, expenditures and results.[33]

Such coherence will go a long way in reducing overhead costs, bringing system-wide synergy in programmatic aspects, fostering greater harmonisation of conditions of service and ensuring considerably improved delivery.

33. Ibid: 39-40.

Annex A-13.1

Investing in the United Nations: For a Stronger Organisation Worldwide

Recommendations

I. People

1. Recruitment should be proactive, targeted and faster.
2. Staff mobility should integrate headquarters and field staff; it should be a condition of service and a prerequisite for promotion; and the authority of the Secretary-General to move staff laterally should be reaffirmed and expanded.
3. Career development should be fostered through targeted training, mandatory requirements for advancement and diverse career paths.
4. Contracts should be streamlined and conditions of service harmonised.

II. Leadership

5. The role of the Deputy Secretary-General should be redefined by the Secretary-General so as to delegate to him or her formal authority and accountability for the management and overall direction of the functions of the Secretariat.
6. The 25 departments and other entities currently reporting directly to the Secretary-General should be reorganised to significantly reduce the reporting span.
7. A major new leadership development plan is needed, covering recruitment, training and career development, to build middle and senior management capacity.

III. Information and communications technology

8. The post of Chief Information Technology Officer should be created, at the Assistant Secretary-General level, to oversee the creation and implementation of an effective information management strategy.

9-10. An urgent upgrading of Secretariat-wide ICT systems should be undertaken.

IV. Delivering services

11. The General Assembly should modify previous guidance, allowing the Secretariat to consider all options for alternative service delivery, including identifying the potential for relocation and outsourcing.

12. Systematic cost-benefit analyses of the potential for applying these options in select administrative services should be completed in the next 12 months.

13-15. A range of measures will be implemented to improve and tighten procedures for United Nations procurement of goods and services.

V. Budget and finance

16. The cycle for reviewing and adopting the budget should be shortened, and budget appropriation consolidated from the present 35 sections into 13 parts; and the Secretary-General should have expanded authority to redeploy posts as necessary, and to use savings from vacant posts.

17. Peacekeeping accounts should be consolidated and trust fund management streamlined; the level of the Working Capital fund and the ceiling of the commitment authority granted by the General Assembly should be increased; and the financial processes of the Organisation should be re-engineered to allow significant delegation of authority within a framework of accountability.

18. The budget and planning process should be explicitly linked to results and managerial performance, as part of a more rigorous monitoring and evaluation framework.

VI. Governance

19. Secretariat reporting mechanisms should be improved, including through the development of a single, comprehensive annual report, and the 30 existing reports on management should be consolidated into six reports.

20. New principles to guide the interaction between the Secretariat and the General Assembly on management and budgetary issues should be introduced to make it more focused, strategic and results-oriented.

21. The General Assembly is urged to consider ways to reform its interaction with the Secretariat on management and budgetary issues.

VII. The way forward: investing in change

22. Dedicated resources should be appropriated to the change management process; in particular, resources will be needed at an early stage for a change management office and a staff buyout.

23. An appropriate intergovernmental mechanism should be set up to work with the change management office.

Annex A-13.2

In Larger Freedom: Towards Development, Security and Human Rights for All

Recommendations

To make the United Nations a more effective and efficient instrument for forging a united response to shared threats and shared needs, I urge Heads of State and Government to:

(a) Reaffirm the broad vision of the founders of the United Nations, as set out in the Charter of the United Nations, for it to be organised, resourced and equipped to address the full range of challenges confronting the peoples of the world across the broad fields of security, economic and social issues, and human rights, and in that spirit to commit themselves to reforming, restructuring and revitalising its major organs and institutions, where necessary, to enable them to respond effectively to the changed threats, needs and circumstances of the twenty-first century;

General Assembly

(b) Revitalise the General Assembly by:

(i) Instructing their representatives to adopt, at its sixtieth session, a comprehensive package of reforms to revitalise the General Assembly, including by rationalising its work and speeding up the deliberative process, streamlining its agenda, its committee structure and its procedures for plenary debates and requesting reports, and strengthening the role and authority of its President;

(ii) Resolving to give focus to the substantive agenda of the General Assembly by concentrating on addressing the major substantive issues of the day, such as international migration and the long-debated comprehensive convention on terrorism;

(iii) Establishing mechanisms enabling the Assembly to engage fully and systematically with civil society;

Security Council

(c) Reform the Security Council to make it more broadly representative of the international community as a whole and the geopolitical realities of today, and to expand its membership to meet these goals, by:

(i) Supporting the principles for the reform of the Council and considering the two options, models A and B, proposed in the present report, as well as any other viable proposals in terms of size and balance that have emerged on the basis of either model;

(ii) Agreeing to take a decision on this important issue before the summit in September 2005. It would be far preferable for Member States to take this vital decision by consensus. If, however, they are unable to reach consensus, this must not become an excuse for postponing action;

Economic and Social Council

(d) Reform the Economic and Social Council by:

(i) Mandating the Economic and Social Council to hold annual ministerial level assessments of progress towards agreed development goals, particularly the Millennium Development Goals;

(ii) Deciding that it should serve as a high-level development cooperation forum, reviewing trends in international development cooperation, promoting greater coherence among the development activities of different actors and strengthening the links between the normative and operational work of the United Nations;

(iii) Encouraging it to convene timely meetings, as required, to assess threats to development, such as famines, epidemics and major natural disasters, and to promote coordinated responses to them;

(iv) Deciding that the Council should regularise its work in post-conflict management by working with the proposed Peace-building Commission;

Proposed Human Rights Council

(e) Agree to replace the Commission on Human Rights with a smaller standing Human Rights Council, as a principal organ of the United Nations or subsidiary body of the General Assembly, whose members would be elected directly by the General Assembly by a two-thirds majority of members present and voting;

Secretariat

(f) Reform the Secretariat by:

(i) Endorsing the Secretary-General's request that the General Assembly review all mandates older than five years to see if the activities concerned are still genuinely needed or whether resources assigned to them can be reallocated in response to new and emerging challenges;

(ii) Agreeing to provide the Secretary-General with the authority and resources to pursue a one-time staff buyout so as to refresh and realign the staff to meet current needs;

(iii) Deciding that Member States should work with the Secretary-General to undertake a comprehensive review of the budget and human resources rules under which the Organisation operates;

(iv) Endorsing the package of management reforms that the Secretary-General is undertaking to improve accountability, transparency and efficiency within the Secretariat;

(v) Commissioning a comprehensive review of the Office of Internal Oversight Services with a view to strengthening its independence and authority, as well as its expertise and capacity;

System-wide Coherence

(g) Ensure stronger system-wide coherence by resolving to coordinate their representatives on the governing boards of the various development and humanitarian agencies so as to make sure that they pursue a coherent policy in assigning mandates and allocating resources throughout the system;

(h) Commit themselves to protecting humanitarian space and ensuring that humanitarian actors have safe and unimpeded access to vulnerable populations; resolve to act on proposals to accelerate humanitarian response by developing new funding arrangements to ensure that emergency funding is available immediately; and support the Secretary-General's effort to strengthen the inter-agency and country-level responses to the needs of internally displaced persons;

(i) Recognise the need for a more integrated structure for environmental standard-setting, scientific discussion and monitoring, and treaty compliance that is built on existing institutions, such as UNEP, as well as the treaty bodies and specialised agencies, and that assigns environmental activities at the operational level to the development agencies to ensure an integrated approach to sustainable development;

Regional Organisations

(j) Support a stronger relationship between the United Nations and regional organisations, including by, as a first step, developing and implementing a 10-year plan for capacity-building with the African Union, and by ensuring that regional organisations that have a capacity for conflict prevention or peacekeeping consider the option of placing such capacities in the framework of the United Nations Standby Arrangements System;

Annex A-13.3

Strengthening the United Nations: An Agenda for Further Change

Recommendations

Action 1. I will submit to the General Assembly in 2003 a thoroughly revised programme budget that better reflects the priorities agreed to at the Millennium Assembly.

Action 2. The United Nations High Commissioner for Human Rights will develop and implement a plan, in cooperation with the United Nations Development Group and the Executive Committee for Humanitarian Affairs, to strengthen human rights-related United Nations actions at the country level.

Action 3. The United Nations High Commissioner for Human Rights will consult with treaty bodies on new streamlined reporting procedures and submit his recommendations to me by September 2003.

Action 4. The United Nations High Commissioner for Human Rights will undertake a review of the special procedures and report back to me by September 2003 with recommendations on how to enhance their effectiveness and improve the support provided.

Action 5: The United Nations High Commissioner for Human Rights will develop a plan to strengthen management, taking into account the recommendations emerging from the management review conducted by the Office of Internal Oversight Services. I expect the report to be submitted to me by March 2003.

Action 6. The Department of Public Information will be restructured as follows:

(a) A Division of Strategic Communications which will devise and disseminate and evaluate United Nations messages around priority themes;

(b) An Outreach Division in which services to delegations, liaison with civil society and activities for the general public will be grouped together;

(c) A strengthened News and Media Division which will incorporate the Department's web-site operation;

(d) Transfer of the Cartographic Section to the Department of Peacekeeping Operations.

Action 7. The Department of Public Information, with assistance from the Office of Internal Oversight Services, will, over a three-year period, conduct a systematic evaluation of the impact and cost-effectiveness of all of its activities.

Action 8. I propose to rationalise the network of United Nations information centres around regional hubs, starting with the creation of a Western European hub.

Action 9. The management of United Nations libraries will be improved as follows:

(a) The Dag Hammarskjöld Library in New York assumes responsibility for setting policy and coordinating the work of all United Nations libraries;

(b) The Department of Public Information, in conjunction with the Department of Management, will prepare a comprehensive plan for the integration of the United Nations library services at various locations, through the use of information and communications technologies;

(c) The Department of Public Information will formulate and implement a plan to improve electronic access to United Nations collections, facilitate the transfer of paper collections to electronic files and provide training to depository librarians.

Action 10. Improvements to publications will be made as follows:

(a) The Executive Committees will plan and coordinate all publications within their respective thematic areas in order to reduce the number of and improve the coherence, focus and scheduling among the Organisation's many publications. The Department of Public Information will do the same for the titles it publishes;

(b) The Publications Board will be reconstituted as a standard-setting body, with appropriate membership and terms of reference to match that function;

(c) The feasibility and cost of online publications delivery, supplemented by a print-on-demand capability will be reviewed;

(d) The Repertory of Practice of United Nations Organs should no longer be produced by the United Nations.

Action 11. Reporting will be improved by:

(a) Consolidating reports on related subjects;

(b) Writing sharper reports with clearly defined actions;

(c) Observing stipulated page limits.

Action 12. I encourage the General Assembly to establish a mechanism to review the continuing need and the frequency of recurring reporting requirements.

Action 13. The Department of General Assembly and Conference Management will implement changes to allow a more integrated approach to planning and managing meetings and documentation.

Action 14. The United Nations Development Group will develop, by September 2003, an implementation plan to strengthen the effectiveness of the Organisation's presence in developing countries. This plan will include such features as joint programming, pooling of resources, common databases and knowledge networks, dedicated support for the resident coordinator and integrated planning, budgeting and resource mobilisation tools for countries emerging from conflict.

Action 15. A document clarifying roles and responsibilities in the area of technical cooperation will be prepared by September 2003.

Action 16. I will propose in the next biennium budget the creation of an additional position of Assistant Secretary-General to support policy coherence and management in the Department of Economic and Social Affairs.

Action 17. A policy planning unit will be established in the Department of Economic and Social Affairs.

Action 18. The Adviser for Special Assignments in Africa will coordinate and guide the preparation of reports and input for the Africa-related debates of the General Assembly and its subsidiary bodies. For this purpose, the resources allocated to the Office of the Special Coordinator for Africa and the Least Developed Countries will be transferred to his office.

Action 19. I will establish a panel of eminent persons to review the relationship between the United Nations and civil society and offer practical recommendations for improved modalities of interaction.

Action 20. A Partnerships Office will be created to regroup under one common umbrella the Global Compact Office and the United Nations Fund for International Partnerships.

Action 21. An improved planning and budgeting system should include the following features:

(a) A shorter, more strategic medium-term plan covering two years rather than four, and submitted closer to the period to which it relates;

(b) A budget outline that could be combined with the medium-term plan;

(c) A shorter, more strategic budget with supplementary detail provided separately;

(d) Flexibility to reallocate resources between programmes and between allocations for personnel and other allocations by up to 10 per cent within a single budgetary period;

(e) A strengthened system of evaluation and monitoring that will better measure the impact of our work.

Action 22. Consistent with the above approach, I recommend that the intergovernmental review of plans and budgets currently performed by both the Fifth Committee and the Committee for Programme and Coordination be absorbed under the aegis of the Fifth Committee itself.

Action 23. Future peacekeeping budgets will be presented in a new format, reflecting a more strategic approach to the process of resource allocation.

Action 24. The management of trust funds will be improved by:

(a) Consolidating and reducing their number;

(b) Harmonizing as much as possible the rules and requirements relating to trust fund management and reporting;

(c) Revising the system of support cost charges;

(d) Streamlining procedures for accessing trust fund monies.

Action 25. In order to enhance staff mobility across the United Nations system, we will:

(a) Review, by the end of 2003, the contractual arrangements and benefits offered to Secretariat staff in field locations, with a view to ensuring that they are comparable or equivalent to those of the United Nations funds and programmes;

(b) Review agreements between the Secretariat and the United Nations funds, programmes and specialised agencies, in order to reduce current barriers to mobility between common-system organisations;

(c) Create longer-term contractual prospects for deserving staff serving in field missions;

(d) Identify special recruitment and reward mechanisms for duty stations at which there are debilitating vacancy rates;

(e) Review all arrangements between the Secretariat and the United Nations funds, programmes and specialised agencies in order to ensure that spouses of United Nations staff with appropriate qualifications are given favourable consideration when applying for posts in field locations;

(f) Approach Governments to explore possibilities for the renegotiation of host country agreements so as to allow United Nations spouses to work in those countries.

Action 26. I urge Member States to consider lifting the restrictions on the numbers of General Service staff eligible for promotion to the Professional category.

Action 27. An implementation plan will be developed over the next 12 months, which will include:

(a) A comprehensive review of General Service functions, responsibilities and competencies;

(b) Improvements to the system of General Service induction and career planning;

(c) Opportunities and incentives for mobility across functions, offices and service in field and peacekeeping missions.

Action 28. Effective 1 January 2003, all employees of the United Nations Secretariat will be referred to as international civil servants.

Action 29. The following measures will be introduced:

(a) Introducing flexible working arrangements in all Secretariat departments, subject to work requirements, from 1 January 2003;

(b) Broadening the opportunities for part-time employment for Secretariat staff.

Action 30. Measures will be introduced to:

(a) Enable better planning for the replacement of departing staff members;

(b) Develop more targeted recruitment mechanisms;

(c) Enhance the existing departure package to include career placement assistance and facilitating transition arrangements.

Action 31. I will recommend in the next biennium budget a significant increase in the resources allocated to training.

Action 32. In order to continue efforts to improve management:

(a) A thorough review will be conducted of delegated authority in order to increase the capacity and flexibility of managers to manage the resources allocated to them;

(b) The roles and responsibilities of the Department of Management, along with those of the executive offices, will be redefined in order to support the increased delegation of authority;

(c) Training of managers will be strengthened across the Organisation, making particular use of the Staff College.

Action 33. A thorough review should be completed to ensure that the Organisation's policy on HIV/AIDS is fully implemented, and additional measures should be implemented, where needed, by the end of 2002.

Action 34. A review of the current system of internal justice will be conducted to improve the efficiency of the system and to allow staff fair and due process.

Action 35. I encourage:

(a) The International Civil Service Commission to finalise its proposals for a more competitive pay and benefits system;

(b) The initiation of an independent review of the operations and functions of the Commission itself.

Action 36. The Deputy Secretary-General will oversee the implementation of the approved reforms.

Annex A-13.4

Renewing the United Nations: A Programme for Reform
Recommendation Highlights

The measures and proposals set out in the present report encompass the reform programme undertaken by the Secretary-General during his first six months in office. It constitutes an extensive and far-reaching set of changes that wil move the Organisation firmly along the road to major and fundamental reform designed to achieve greater unity of purpose, coherence of effort and flexibility in response. Some measures have already been implemented; others will take more time and many require decisions by member states. Reform is, after all, a continuing process not a single event.

The actions and recommendations focus primarily on the following priority areas:

- Establishment of a new leadership and management structure that will strengthen the capacity of the Secretary-General to provide the leadership and ensure the accountability that the Organisation requires. Through:
  - The establishment of the position of Deputy Secretary-General;
  - The estabilishment of a Senior Management Group;
  - Further development and strengthening of the Executive Committees of the sectoral groups established by the Secretary-General in January 1997 which include all the departments, funds and programmes of the United Nations;
  - Decentralisation of decision-making at the country level and consolidation of the United Nations presence under "one flag";
  - Establishment of a Strategic Planning Unit.
- Assuring financial solvency through the establishment of a Revolving Credit Fund of up to $1 billion, financed from voluntary contributions or other means Member States may wish to suggest, pending a lasting solution of the Organisation's financial situation.
- Integration of twelve Secretariat entities and units into five and proposed consolidation of five intergovernmental bodies into two.

- A changed management culture accompanied by management and efficiency measures, which will eliminate at least 1,000 staff posts, reduce administrative costs by one-third, improve performance and effect additional savings in terms of personnel and costs over time.
- Instituting a thorough overhaul of human resources policies and practices to ensure that all staff have the neccessary skills and enjoy the requisite conditions for effective service.
- Promoting sustained and sustainable development as a central priority of the United Nations through:
  - The grouping of United Nations funds and programmes with development operations into a United Nations Development Group, which will faciliate consolidation and cooperation amongst them without compromising their distinctiveness or identity;
  - Proposing a "development divident" to shift resouces from administration to development activities;
  - The establishment of a new Office of Development Financing with the Deputy Secretary-General taking the lead in initiating innovative means of mobilising new financial resources for development.
  - Proposals for burden-sharing and greater predictability through multi-year negotiated and voluntary pledges for the financing of United Nations development operations;
  - Strengthening the environmental dimension of the United Nations activities, particularly UNEP.
- Strengthening and focusing the normative, policy and knowledge-related functions of the Secretariat and its capacity to serve the United Nations intergovernmental bodies through the establishment of the consolidated Economic and Social Affairs sectoral group.
- Improving the Organisation's ability to deploy peacekeeping and other field operations more rapidly, including by enhancing the rapid reaction capacity of the United Nations.
- Strengthening the United Nations capacity for post-conflict peace-building with the designation of the Department of Political Affairs as a focal point for this purpose.

- Bolstering international efforts to combat crime, drugs and terrorism by consolidating United Nations programmes and activities in Vienna under an Office for Drug Control and Crime Prevention.
- Extending human rights activities by reorganising and restructuring the human rights secretariat and the integration of human rights into all principal United Nations activities and programmes.
- Advancing the disarmament agenda by establishing a Department for Disarmament and Arms Regulation to address reduction of armaments and weapons of mass destruction and regulation of armaments.
- Enhancing response to humanitarian needs by setting up a new Emergency Relief Coordination Office to replace the Department of Humanitarian Affairs and focusing its capacities to deal more effectively with complex emergencies.
- Effecting a major shift in the public information and communications strategy and functions of the United Nations to meet the changing needs of the Organisation.
- Addressing the need for more fundamental change through recommendations by the Secretary-General to member states that they consider.
    - Refocusing the work of the General Assembly on issues of highest priority and reducing the length of the Assembly sessions;
    - The establishment of a ministerial-level commission to examine the need for fundamental change through review of the Charter of the United Nations and the legal instruments from which the specialised agencies of the United Nations derive their constitutions.
    - Designation of the session of the General Assembly to be held in the year 2000 as "a Millennium Assembly" to focus on preparing the United Nations to meet the major challenges and needs of the world community in the twenty-first century, accompanied by a companion "People's Assembly".

Annex A-13.5

Millennium Summit + Five Summit Outcome Document
Parts Related to Secretariat and Management Reform

161. We recognise that in order to effectively comply with the principles and objectives of the Charter, we need an efficient, effective and accountable Secretariat. Its staff shall act in accordance with Article 100 of the Charter, in a culture of organisational accountability, transparency and integrity. Consequently we:

(a) Recognise the ongoing reform measures carried out by the Secretary-General to strengthen accountability and oversight, improve management performance and transparency and reinforce ethical conduct, and invite him to report to the General Assembly on the progress made in their implementation;

(b) Emphasise the importance of establishing effective and efficient mechanisms for responsibility and accountability of the Secretariat;

(c) Urge the Secretary-General to ensure that the highest standards of efficiency, competence, and integrity shall be the paramount consideration in the employment of the staff, with due regard to the principle of equitable geographical distribution, in accordance with Article 101 of the Charter;

(d) Welcome the Secretary-General's efforts to ensure ethical conduct, more extensive financial disclosure for United Nations officials and enhanced protection for those who reveal wrongdoing within the Organisation. We urge the Secretary-General to scrupulously apply the existing standards of conduct and develop a system-wide code of ethics for all United Nations personnel. In this regard, we request the Secretary-General to submit details on an ethics office with independent status, which he intends to create, to the General Assembly at its sixtieth session;

(e) Pledge to provide the United Nations with adequate resources, on a timely basis, to enable the Organisation to implement its mandates and achieve its objectives, having regard to the priorities agreed by the General Assembly and the need to respect budget discipline. We stress that all member states should meet their obligations with regard to the expenses of the Organisation;

(f) Strongly urge the Secretary-General to make the best and most efficient use of resources in accordance with clear rules and procedures agreed by the General Assembly, in the interest of all member states, by adopting the best management practices, including effective use of information and communication technologies, with a view to increasing efficiency and enhancing organisational capacity, concentrating on those tasks that reflect the agreed priorities of the Organisation.

162. We reaffirm the role of the Secretary-General as the chief administrative officer of the Organisation, in accordance with Article 97 of the Charter. We request the Secretary-General to make proposals to the General Assembly for its consideration on the conditions and measures necessary for him to carry out his managerial responsibilities effectively.

163. We commend the Secretary-General's previous and ongoing efforts to enhance the effective management of the United Nations and his commitment to update the Organisation. Bearing in mind our responsibility as member states, we emphasise the need to decide on additional reforms in order to make more efficient use of the financial and human resources available to the Organisation and thus better comply with its principles, objectives and mandates. We call upon the Secretary-General to submit proposals for implementing management reforms to the General Assembly for consideration and decision in the first quarter of 2006, and we resolve:

(a) To ensure that the United Nations budgetary, financial, and human resource policies, regulations and rules respond to the current needs of the Organisation and enable the efficient and effective conduct of its work and request the Secretary-General to provide an assessment and recommendations to the General Assembly. The assessment and recommendations of the Secretary-General should take account of the measures already under way for the reform of human resources management and the budget process;

(b) To strengthen and update the programme of work of the United Nations so as to respond to the contemporary requirements of member states. To this end, the General Assembly and other relevant organs will review all mandates older than five years originating from resolutions of the General Assembly and other organs, which would be complementary to the existing periodic reviews of activities. The Assembly and the other organs should complete and take the necessary decisions arising from this review during 2006. We request the Secretary-General to facilitate this review with analysis and recommendations, including on the opportunities for programmatic shifts, that could be considered for early consideration by the Assembly;

(c) To consider a detailed proposal on the framework for a one-time staff buyout to improve personnel structure and quality, including an indication of costs involved and mechanisms to ensure that it achieves its intended purpose.

164. We recognise the urgent need to substantially improve the United Nations oversight and management processes. We emphasise the importance of ensuring the operational independence of the Office of Internal Oversight Services. Therefore:

(a) The expertise, capacity and resources of the Office of Internal Oversight Services in respect of audit and investigations will be significantly strengthened as a matter of urgency;

(b) We request the Secretary-General to submit an independent external evaluation of the United Nations, including the specialised agencies', auditing and oversight system, including the roles and responsibilities of management, with due regard to the nature of the auditing and oversight bodies in question. This evaluation will take place within the context of the comprehensive review of the governance arrangements. We ask the General Assembly to adopt measures during its sixtieth session at the earliest possible stage, based on the consideration of recommendations of the evaluation and those made by the Secretary-General;

(c) We recognise that additional measures are needed to enhance the independence of the oversight structures. We therefore, request the Secretary-General to submit detailed proposals to the General Assembly at its sixtieth session for its early consideration of the creation of an independent oversight advisory committee, including its mandate, composition, selection process and qualification of experts;

(d) We authorise the Office of Internal Oversight Services to examine the feasibility of expanding its services to provide internal oversight to United Nations agencies that request such services in such a way as to ensure that the provision of internal oversight services to the Secretariat will not be compromised.

165. We insist on the highest standards of behaviour from all United Nations personnel and support the considerable efforts under way with respect to the implementation of the Secretary-General's policy of zero tolerance regarding sexual exploitation and abuse by United Nations personnel, both at Headquarters and in the field. We encourage the Secretary-General to submit proposals to the General Assembly leading to a comprehensive approach to victims' assistance by 31 December 2005.

166. We encourage the Secretary-General and all decision-making bodies to take further steps in mainstreaming a gender perspective in the policies and decisions of the Organisation.

167. We strongly condemn all attacks against the safety and security of personnel engaged in the United Nations activities. We call upon States to consider becoming parties to the Convention on the Safety of United Nations and Associated Personnel and stress the need to conclude negotiations on a protocol expanding the scope of legal protection during the sixtieth session of the General Assembly.

System-wide Coherence

168. We recognise that the United Nations brings together a unique wealth of expertise and resources on global issues. We commend the extensive experience and expertise of the various development-related organisations, agencies, funds and programmes of the United Nations system in their diverse and

complementary fields of activity and their important contributions to the achievement of the Millennium Development Goals and the other development objectives established by various United Nations conferences.

169. We support stronger system-wide coherence by implementing the following measures:

Policy

- Strengthening linkages between the normative work of the United Nations system and its operational activities.
- Coordinating our representation on the governing boards of the various development and humanitarian agencies so as to ensure that they pursue a coherent policy in assigning mandates and allocating resources throughout the system.
- Ensuring that the main horizontal policy themes, such as sustainable development, human rights and gender, are taken into account in decision-making throughout the United Nations.

Operational activities

- Implementing current reforms aimed at a more effective, efficient, coherent, coordinated and better-performing United Nations country presence with a strengthened role for the senior resident official, whether special representative, resident coordinator or humanitarian coordinator, including appropriate authority, resources and accountability, and a common management, programming and monitoring framework
- Inviting the Secretary-General to launch work to further strengthen the management and coordination of United Nations operational activities so that they can make an even more effective contribution to the achievement of the internationally agreed development goals, including the Millennium Development Goals, including proposals for consideration of member states for more tightly managed entities in the field of development, humanitarian assistance and the environment.

14

Guidance for Career with United Nations

Introduction

Often people join the United Nations with a lot of enthusiasm and expectations. Some are attracted by its lofty goal of serving humanity; some by its staggeringly international character; some by its fairly good pay and perquisites; and some by the prestige associated with the organisation. But the United Nations has remained an enigma not only for the outsiders, but also for the ultimate insiders.

This has been the case partly because the United Nations has to handle multifarious issues of enormous complexities around the world, and the intricate cobweb of structures and functions we witness has been incumbent on those complexities. Partly, the United Nations has become a huge quilt of multitude patchworks arising from its incremental response to each problem at a time, whereby it has become nearly inscrutable as to how pieces fall together in its elaborate construct. Sometimes in public organisations whose performance is hard to judge by a set of concrete objective criteria—such as profit or the number of clients served, in the private sector—allow their structures to grow unduly complex, functions to spread unyieldingly wide, writing to become unnecessarily obtuse, responsibilities unwarrantedly dispersed, and accountability deliberately diffuse.

Gobbledygook, obfuscation, rhetorical flourishes, and clichés and jargons are commonly associated with public organisations, and the United Nations is a quintessential example of such manifestations, to make the write-ups acceptable to all member states. However, if you are asked to write anything as part of your recruitment test, do not imitate UN reports; write it in an elegant, simple and clear language which the examiner will appreciate.

For outsiders, it is not always easy to cut through such clutters and understand the human resources management practices of the United Nations. So in this chapter we have sought to give some tips to those outsiders who are contemplating to join the United Nations. It will be helpful for them to know what to expect as they seek employment and as they strive to build a career in the world body. We would like to make it absolutely clear that this chapter is not a detailed guide for UN employment, neither is it enough to make a prudent career choice. What we have tried to do here is to draw attention of prospective candidates to key areas on which they need to focus and find out more before they make the United Nations one of their career options among many.

We have covered broad-spectrum steps, caveats and possibilities associated with UN employment and given helpful tips about them. But they are by no means exhaustive. We encourage readers to find out in more detail on their own before they decide to apply for jobs with the United Nations.

Vacancy Announcements

- Check the United Nations jobsite on the web, such as Galaxy or OHRM website.
- Many diplomatic missions in New York and other duty stations might also include such vacancies to their websites.
- Other UN sites also would have links to UN vacancy announcements.
- Visit the United Nations information centres that keep all vacancy announcements.
- Check international news magazines like *The Economist* for some UN vacancy announcements.

- Check local newspapers for local vacancies.

Applications

- You need to fill the Personal History Form and submit it to the United Nations.
- PHF should be written clearly and crisply and should prominently highlight your qualifications and experiences that are relevant to the job being applied to.
- Do not clutter your PHF to demonstrate qualifications and experiences that are not relevant to the job in question, especially if you are an external candidate.
- You can submit your PHP electronically, by hand, by fax and by mail.
- Bear in mind that, if you are an external candidate, your PHF could never meet the eyes of UN recruiters.

Recommendations

- Try and get recommendations from those who are most likely to strongly support you as a candidate, as well as vouch for your qualifications and character; otherwise do not make him/her your referee.
- When you make your supervisor a referee, make sure s/he would write a good report in support of you.
- Do not make your teacher a referee who has given you poor grades.
- If possible, list someone who knows, and is known, in the UN system.
- Recommendations from influential people and powerful countries could be helpful in promoting your candidature.

Selection

- The United Nations organises national competitive examinations for unrepresented and under-representative countries.

- Competitive examinations are also held for certain General Services posts.
- Check the Office of Human Resources Management website to find out when and where such examinations have been planned and whether you could be eligible to participate.
- All other positions are filled either from the established roster of qualified candidates.
- Or through the scruting of curriculum vitae of applicants and interview of shortlisted candidates.
- You need to check this before you apply.

Priority in Processing Applications

- When posts are to be filled through selection of CVs, first priority is given to those applicants who are seeking transfer within the organisation.
- If no such qualified candidates are found, internal promotion and applicants from the UN system get priority consideration.
- External applications are looked at last.

If You are an External Candidate

- Be realistic in your expectations.
- If you have one of the rare qualifications and experiences the United Nations needs, you stand a good chance of getting selected.
- If you are applying for one of the posts or positions in new field offices such as peacekeeping operations and political missions, your chances of getting selected would considerably increase.
- Networking is the key to getting a UN job.
- If you have a powerful country or person in the United Nations to back you up, you are likely to get selected.

Processing Time

- The United Nations generally takes well over 160 days from vacancy announcement to recruitment and placement of staff.

- Some agencies have a slightly better speed in processing applications.

Only Short-listed Candidates are Contacted

- You will hear from the United Nations only if you are short-listed.
- If you do not hear from them, generally your application has been rejected.

If there is a Written Examination

- Use the correct language, verbs and syntax.
- Go straight to the subject matter.
- Do not make your paragraphs too long; no more that 6/7 lines in a paragraph.
- Every paragraph and the whole write up should have a lead statement, information to back it up and conclusion (writing tips are available in books and websites).
- Give complete and full answers.
- If you remember figures and quotes, use them prudently; do not use them excessively or do not make them up.
- Do not stretch your answers unnecessarily long.
- Do not make your answers too short or too cryptic.
- Manage your time carefully.

If You have Multiple Choice Questions

- Read questions carefully.
- More than one answers might look correct, but there would be only one correct answer.
- If you are not too sure about the correct answer, try to eliminate those first that are likely to be incorrect, and concentrate on those one of which is likely to be correct.
- You lose points for incorrect answers.
- Manage your time carefully.

Interview

- Be smartly and decently dressed.
- Read the literature in your area of expertise, including the most recent one.
- Show confidence and energy.
- Look up straight; do not fidget; do not gesticulate too much.
- Be upright and honest in your answers.
- Give precise answers to questions.
- Try and be very articulate and smooth in your responses.
- Do not ask interviewers when the decision would be made.
- If you do not know the answer, just say so.

Getting a Job is Difficult, if not Impossible

- UN jobs are highly competitive, as qualified people from all its member states can apply to them.
- External candidates get third priority, in other words, no priority at all.
- There is too much politicisation of the UN bureaucracy, and candidates from the reasonably represented countries stand little chance unless they are politically pushed by their countries or senior officials in the Secretariat.
- Although in principle the nearest kin of the existing staff are not considered for appointment as long as equally qualified other candidates are available, in reality family relations with powerful people in the Secretariat are tremendously helpful in getting a UN job.
- Knowing someone in the review boards and committees that vet candidates before their appointment also helps a great deal.

Language Skills

- Acquire proficiency in UN languages, as they are an important factor in hiring decisions of the United Nations.

- The United Nations Secretariat works in two languages: English and French.
- Most intergovernmental bodies work in six languages: English, French, Spanish, Arabic, Russian and Chinese.
- Regional Commission secretariats also work in some regional languages.
- Being multi-lingual could be a huge asset in getting hired by the United Nations.
- So build your language skills.

Some Positives and Negatives about UN Jobs

- The United Nations pays almost as much as the US federal government.
- Its allowances—education, non-resident, per diam, language, special post, mobility and hardship, dependency, etc.—are pretty attractive.
- But the world body does not pay as much as some other countries or many private sector organisations in the west.
- It has no bonus or performance related rewards.
- Promotions are often very slow, unless you get pulled up by a senior manager or pushed by a powerful country
- But you get a rewarding multicultural environment for work and feel the sense that you are contributing to the betterment of humanity.
- You may be asked to serve in war-torn and disaster ravaged places.
- You might be passed over by those who you think are inferior to you in their performance.
- Do not forget, the United Nations is a political organisation, and its bureaucracy could not be apolitical.

Types of Recruitment

- Basically two types: International recruitment and Local recruitment.

- Recruitment mainly on the basis of highest standards of efficiency, competence and integrity.
- Due regard to be paid to recruiting staff on as wide a geographical basis as possible.
- No discrimination against anyone on the basis of race, religion or sex.
- Efforts are being made to strike gender balance in UN employment; so if you are a qualified woman, you stand a better chance of getting the job.

Types of Appointments

- Permanent appointment, now being phased out.
- Temporary appointment
    - Probationary appointment
    - Fixed-term appointment
    - Indefinite or continuing appointment
- Appointment of Under Secretary-General and Assistant Secretary-General generally for a period of 5 years.
- You should check what kind of post or position you have been applying to.

Series of Staff

- The United Nations appoints staff in 100-series (staff members appointed by the Secretary-General except technical assistance project personnel and staff members specifically engaged for conferences and other short-term services). Appointments to this series are thought to be most attractive.
- In 200-series (staff members appointed by the Secretary-General for technical assistance project).
- In 300-series for project related posts.
- Conditions of service may vary under these series.
- Check under what series your appointment falls.

UN is a Great Place for Training

- The United Nations is like a work study programme where you learn a lot and at the same time make a fairly good living.
- It provides trainings of all kinds.
- But trainings are not always linked to your job.

Code of Conduct

- Comply with obligations and code of conduct at all times.
- Respect local laws and honour private legal obligations.
- Not engage in any form of discrimination, harassment, and physical and verbal abuse.
- Not engage in any thing that impedes the staff and their colleagues from fulfilling their obligation.
- As a staff member should not alter, destroy, displace or render useless official documents.
- You should not engage in anything or any act for personal gains.
- You should not accept any gift or honour from anyone outside the United Nations other than with the approval of the Secretary-General, nor give anyone any gifts.
- Not share information, without authorisation, with the media or any outsider.

Leaves

- As a UN staff you get 6-week annual leave with full pay.
- The United Nations pays the cost of travel for home leave (as part of the annual leave) every two years to visit your home country.
- Special leave is given for special study or research, normally without pay.
- Sick leave two days per month.
- Maternity leave up to 16 weeks.

- Paternity leave for 4 weeks and 8 weeks for international staff working in a non-family duty station.
- Medical insurance with staff participation.

Mobility/Transfer

- There is limited staff mobility in the United Nations.
- Attractive places are seldom vacant for a transfer.
- The United Nations does not guarantee continued service in temporary appointments, but a good employee may get preference in similar posts when they become vacant, such as moving from a terminating field mission to another.
- In most permanent appointments, which are now being phased out, you may be stuck up with one location or type of work unless you network and be creative.
- The United Nations bears the travel, accommodation and removal allowance of internationally recruited staff upon appointment, upon transfer and upon separation, including for dependents.
- The UN bears staff repatriation allowances and cost of shipping of accompanied and unaccompanied baggage in all those three situations.

Promotion

- The same principles as applicable to appointment apply to promotion.
- Networking plays perhaps the most important role in getting a promotion in the UN system.
- Some mobility is mandatory for a promotion, so try to get a transfer from one office and location to another.
- Try and acquire multi-tasking skills to move faster up the ladder of the UN bureaucracy.
- Do not be surprised if your performance is not given as much weightage in promotion in the United Nations as it gets in your national civil service; performance is important but is

not necessarily a key element in promotional decisions in the world body; it sounds weird but it is true.

Administration of Justice

- An independent Ombudsman tries to redress your grievances.
- There are joint management-staff relations bodies for consultation and elected staff bodies for collective action.
- There are joint disciplinary boards and committees for determining disciplinary actions against staff and joint appeals boards to appeal against those actions.
- The United Nations Administrative Tribunal is the last legal resort for staff to file their cases against management.
- This old system is being replaced with a new one beginning 1 July 2009, which will be a great improvement over the existing system.

Separation

- You retire at the age of 60 or at the age of 62 if appointed after 1990.
- For political appointees, the retirement age could be higher.
- You could also be dismissed for incompetence and serious misconduct.
- You could voluntarily resign.

Post-Retirement Benefits

- You are entitled to a pension based on your contribution to the pension plan.
- You are also entitled to post-retirement health benefits.

These are few, not exhaustive, tips to help prospective UN job applicants understand in a nutshell what to expect and how to go about seeking a job with the United Nations. Each applicant should try and get as much information as possible before they seek to jump aboard the UN ship. They should read as much as possible about how the United Nations works, talk to people who know about it, and develop connections with them.

United Nations Staff Regulations and Rules are a good place to start. The rules expand on the regulations. These regulations and rules provide you understanding of the conditions of service for the staff. GA resolution 63/250 of February 10, 2009 has made many changes in the human resources management system of the United Nations and occasioned changes in staff rules and regulations. Read them thoroughly and try and be conversant with them. As the General Assembly amends them every now and then, you need to read the latest set of these regulations and rules. They could be found at UN libraries and UN information centres worldwide in hard copies or on UN websites, including:

In English: *http://www.un.org/hr_handbook/English/*

In French: *http://www.un.org/french/grh_manuel/French/*

Networking is very important in all organisations: Public, private and international. But nowhere has it assumed the kind of significance as it has in the United Nations. In public organisations, networking helps a great deal, but there are quite rigid criteria laid out by the legislature for human resources decisions. In the private sector, networking is important, so is one's ability to contribute to the bottom line, or the profit, and to productivity growth. However, in the relatively fluid administrative environment of the United Nations, networking and the ability to win the favour of powerful players in the Secretariat or from key member state holds is the greatest secret to success.

Bibliography

Baker, Dean and David Rosnick (2005). *Will a Bursting Bubble Trouble Bernake.* Washington DC: Center for Economic and Policy Research. November.

Banerjee, Ajit, M. and Murari R. Sharma (2007). *Reinventing the United Nations*. India: Prentice-Hall.

Banerjee Ajit M. and K.A. Chandrasekaran (1997). *Renewing Governance*. India: Tata-McGraw Hill.

Beagle, Jan (2007). Assistant Secretary-General of OHRM's statement to ACABQ.

Bhouraskar, Digambar (2007). "Rationalization of UN Functions and Staffing: Economic and Social Field", in Ajit, M. Banerjee and Murari R. Sharma, *Reinventing the United Nations*. India: Prentice-Hall.

Blundell, Brian and Alex Murdock (1997). *Managing The Public Sector*. Butterworth-Heinemann Oxford.

Bouayad-Agha, Fatih and Hernandez, Homero L. (1996). *Comparison of Methods of Calculating Equitable/ geographical Distribution within the United Nations Common System,* Joint Inspection Unit, United Nations, Geneva.

Boutros-Ghali, Boutros (2007) "Foreword", in Ajit M. Banerjee and Murari R. Sharma, *Reinventing the United Nations*. India: Prentice-Hall.

Bowman, C. and D. Asch (1987). *Strategic Management*. Basingstoke: Macmillan.

Carpenter, Ted (2007). "The Great Powers and the Security Council", in in Ajit M. Banerjee and Murari R. Sharma, *Reinventing the United Nations*. India: Prentice-Hall.

Cherrington, David J. (1995). *The Management of Human Resources*. Englewood Cliffs, NJ: Prentice-Hall.

Drucker, Peter, F. (2008). *Management,* Revised Edition. New York: Harper-Collins.

Duggett, Michael (2003). "The British Civil Service College in Comparative Perspective", in Alan Rosenbaum, and Eudmila Gajdosova (eds.), *State Modernization and Decentralization—Implications for Education and Training in Public Administration.* United Nations with IASIA and NISPAcee.

European Economic Commission (EUC) (n.d.) *Staff Regulations.*

Gordon, Margaret T. (n.d.). *Development and Implementation of Human Resources Management Policy: The Case of the USA.*

Government of India (2008). *Report of the Sixth Central Pay Commission of India.* March 2008, *http://india.gov.in/ govt/paycommission.php*

Guillory, Robert D. (n.d.). *Staff Selection.* McNeese State University; *www.nationalforum.com*

Hammarskjold, Dag (1961). *The International Civil Service: In Law and in Fact.* Aa lecture delivered at Oxford University. Oxford: Clarendon Press.

Hariss, Joseph (1998). "Eurocrats Take the Gravy Train", in *Reader's Digest.* International Editions. September. *http://www.geocities.com/harriss75007/eurocrat.htm*

Heller, Peter S. and Alan A. Tait (1984). "Government Employment and Pay: Some International Comparisons", *IMF Occasional Paper* 24. International Monetary Fund, Revised March.

Kudryavstev, Eduard V. (2000). *Senior-Level Appointments in the United Nations, its Programs and Funds*. Geneva: Joint Inspection Unit, United Nations.

Lauria, Joe, U.S. (2007). "Seeks Even More Power at UN", *The Huffington Post*, January 23 at *http://www.huffingtonpost.com/joe-lauria/us-seeks-even-more-power_b_39413.html*

Lawler, Edward E. (1990). *Strategic Pay: Aligning Organizational Strategies and Pay Systems.* San Francisco: Jossey-Bass, Inc.

Loveday, A. (1956). *Reflections on International Administration.* Oxford: Clarendon Press.

Luck, Edward C. (2003). *Reforming the United Nations: Lessons from a History in Progress,* International Relations Studies and the United Nations, Occasional Papers No.1, ACUNS.

Macy Jr., John W. (1971). *Public Service: The Human Side of Government.* Harper Row.

McAdams, Jerry L. (1996). *The Reward Plan Advantage.* San Francisco: Jossey-Bass Inc. .

Merkle, Melanie L. (1984). The Heritage Foundation. website: *http://www.heritage.org/Research/InternationalOrganizations/bg378.cfm*

Mihm, Stephen (2008). "Dr. Doom," in *The New York Times Magazine,* 15 August.

Murphy, Kevin R. and Jeanette Cleveland (1995). *Understanding Performance Appraisal.* Sage International.

Naquin, Sharon S. (2008). *Approaches to Training and Development.* Duganlaird: Basic Books.

Panel's Report (2004). *A More Secure World: Our Shared Responsibility*. United Nations.

Penguin (1998). *Penguin Dictionary of International Relations.*

Pergamit, Michael R. and Jonathan R. Veum (1995). "What is a Promotion?", *BLS Working Paper* 264. US Department of Labor.

Pynes, Joan E. (2003). *Public Personnel Administration, Strategic Human Resource Management.* Prentice-Hall.

Ruben, George (1988). "Work Stoppage at General Electric Ends—Developments in Industrial Relations", in *Monthly Labor Review.* June.

Schneier, Craig Erick and Richard W. Beatty (1979). "Integrating Behaviorally-Based Methods", *The Personnel Administration* XXIV, July.

Schuler, Randall S. and Susan E. Jackson (2005). "A Quarter-Century Review of Human Resource Management in the U.S.: The Growth in Importance of the International Perspective", in *Management Review* 16(1).

Schuler, Randall S. and Susan E. Jackson (1999). *Strategic Human Resource Management*. Oxford: Blackwell Publishing.

Sharma, Murari R. (2003). "Financing The Future", *UN Chronicle* I.

Sherman, Denise (2008). "Public Salaries Lag Behind Private Sector", *Eastern Wake News*, March 5.

Taylor, Frederick W. (1919). *The Principles of Scientific Management.* New York: Harper and Brothers Publishers.

UK Office for National Statistics (2007). *Civil Service Statistics 2006.* London.

UN Civil Service Commissioners (n.d.). *Civil Service Commissioners' Recruitment Code. http://www.civilservicecommissioners.org/web-resources/resources/b0adccaa9dc.doc*

———. (n.d.). *http://www.civilservicecommissioners.org/What_we_do/*

UN General Assembly (2008). Resolution A/res/63/250 (published in February 2009).

———. (2008). Resolution A/res/63/253 (published in March 2009).

———. (2007). Resolution A/res/62/228 (published in 2008).

———. (2000). *Resolution A/res/55/2.* 8 September.

———. (n.d.). *Rules of Procedures of the UN General Assembly,* Rule 31.

———. (n.d.). *UN General Assembly Rules of Procedures.*

UN International Civil Service Commission (2008). *Report of the UN International Civil Service Commission.*

———. (n.d.). *The Statute of the International Civil Service Commission.* Article 1.

Union of International Associations (1998). *United Nations Staff Rules and Regulations, International Association of Statute Series.* Vol. I.

United Nations (2008). *Administration of Justice at the United Nations.* A/63/314 of 20 August.

———. (2008). *Composition of the Secretariat.* A/63/310, 29 September.

———. (2008). *Consultants and Individual Contractors.* A/63/310/Add.3, August 21.

———. (2008). *Employment of Retirees and Retired Former Staff, and Extension of Staff Beyond the Mandatory Age of Separation.* A/63/310/Add.2. August 20.

———. (2008). *Gratis Personnel Provided by Governments and Other Entities.* A/63/310/Add. 1. August 19.

———. (2008). *Human Resources Management.* Report of the Fifth Committee. A/63/639. December 30.

———. (2008). *In-Depth Evaluation of the Office of Human Resources Management.* An OIOS report. Sept. 22.

———. (2008). *Investing in the United Nations.* Box 1. New York.

———. (2008). *Recruitment and Staffing in the United Nations: Strategy going Forward.* A/63/285. August 14.

———. (2008). *Report of the Ad Hoc Committee on the Administration of Justice at the United Nations.* New York. April.

———. (2008). *Report of the Evaluation of National Competitive Examination,* August 2008.

———. (2008). *Report of the Secretary-General on the Work of the Organization,* 2008.

———. (2008). *Report of the Security Council on the Work of the Organization, 2008.*

———. (2008). *Review of the National Competitive Recruitment Examination as a Recruitment Tool.* Note by the Secretary-General (on JIU Report). A/62/707. February 15.

———. (2008). *Information Circular.* ST/IC/2008/52. September 24.

———. (2007). *Report of the Director of UN Systems Staff College.* ECOSOC. May.

———. (2007). *CEB Personnel Statistics as at 31 December 2007. http://hr.unsystemceb.org/statistics/archives/stats/2007*

———. (2007). *Staff Rules.* ST/SGB/2007/3 of 1 January.

———. (2007). *Note of the Secretary-General on the Report of the Redesign Panel on the United Nations System of Administration of Justice.* New York. February.

———. (2006). *Investing in the United Nations for a Stronger Organization Worldwide: Detailed Report—Accountability.* A/60/909. New York.

———. (2006). *Report of the Redesign Panel on the United Nations System of Administration of Justice.* New York. July.

———. (2006). *Delivering As One.* Report of the High-Level Panel on United Nations System-wide Coherence. A/61/583, 20 November.

———. (2006). *Comprehensive Review of Governance and Oversight within the United Nations, Funds, Programs and Specialized Agencies.* Volume III, A/60/883 Add. 1. New York. June.

———. (2005). *Millennium + 5 Summit Outcome Document.* A/59/2005. 15 September.

———. (2005). *Report on the Manipulation of the Oil-for-food Program.* 27 October.

———. (2005). *2005 World Summit Outcome.* General Assembly Resolution 60/1 of 24 October.

———. (2003). *Monterrey Concensus.* Final Text. Monterrey, Mexico. March.

———. (2003). *Staff Regulations and Staff Rules 100.1 to 112.8.* Revised. ST/SGB/2008/1. New York.

———. (2003). *Staff Regulations, ST/SGB/2003/5* of 7 February and *Staff Rules, ST/SGB/2002/1 with amendments contained up to ST/SGB/2006/1.*

———. (2002). *United Nations Staff Rules.* ST/SGB/2002/1 of 1 January.

———. (2002). *Staff Rules.* ST/SGB/2002/2 of 1 January.

———. (2002). *Staff Selection System.* ST/AI/2002/4 of 23 April.

———. (2002). *Strengthening the United Nations: An Agenda Further Change.* A/57/387, 9 September.

———. (2000). *Administration of Justice at the United Nations.* A JIU Report. Geneva.

———. (2000). *UN Staff College Project, Report of the Secretary-General.* September.

———. (1997). *Renewing the United Nations: A Program for Reform.* A/51/950, 14 July.

———. (1997). *Renewing the United Nations: A Program of Reform.* Report of the Secretary-General.

———. (1995). *Inspection of the Application of United Nations Recruitment, Placement and Promotion Policies.* JIU Report. New York.

———. (1994). *An Agenda for Development.* A/48/935, 6 May.

———. (1992). *An Agenda for Peace.* A/47/277-S/24111, 17 June.

———. (1971). *Report of the Special Committee for the Review of the United Nations Salary System.* General Assembly, 26 Session, 28 September, 1971, Statement of the Secretary-General, opening session, 1 June 1971, *Report of the Special Committee*, Official Records, General Assembly.

———. (1951). *Report of the Committee of Experts.* January.

United Nations (n.d.). *Charter of the United Nations.*

———. (n.d.). *Performance Appraisal System*, ST/AI/2002/3.

———. (n.d.) *Introduction to the Position Classification Standards, 1991. http://www.opm.gov/fedclass/gsintro.pdf*

———. (n.d.). *Report of the Secretary-General on the Work of the Organization, 2008.*

———. (n.d.). *UN Staff Regulations and Rules 2003.*

———. (n.d.). *United Nations Resolutions on Gender Balance. http://www.un.org/womenwatch/osagi/gmresolutionsthrdcomm.htm*

———. (n.d.). *E-Government Survey 2008: From e-government to Connected Governance.*

———. (n.d.) *Charter of the United Nations. http://www.un.org/aboutun/charter/chapter15.shtml*

———. (n.d.) *International Civil Service Commission Compendium.*

United Nations International Civil Service Commission (1987). *Statute and Rules of Procedure.* New York.

United States Institute of Peace (2005). *American Interests and UN Reform.* Report of the Task Force on the United Nations. Washington DC.

US Congress (n.d.). *Government Performance and Results Act, 1993*

US Department of State (2006). *United States Participation in the United Nations.* A Report by the Secretary of State to the Congress. Washington DC.

US General Electric (n.d.). *GE 2006 Citizenship Report.*

———. (n.d.). *Investing and Delivering in Citizenship.* GE Citizenship Report, 2007-08.

US Office of Personnel Management. (1999). *Strategic Human Resources Management, Aligning with the Mission.* Washington DC. September.

———. (1997). *360-Degree Assessment: An Overview.* September.

———. (1995). *Introduction to the Position Classification Standards.* TS-134. Washington DC. July.

———. (1991). *The Classifier's Handbook.* TS-107. Washington DC. August.

US Senate Committee on Expenditures in the Executive Departments (1948). *United States Relations with International Organizations.* 80th Congress, Second session. Senate Report 1757.

Welch, Jack with Suzy Welch (2005). *Winning.* New York: Harper-Collins.

Websites:

http://www.chinadaily.com.cn/english/doc/2006-03/10/content_530479.htm, 10 March 2006.

http://www.globalpolicy.org/reform/initiatives/lieindex.htm

http://careers.civil-service.gov.uk/index.asp?txtNavID=136&635132=

http://careers.civil-service.gov.uk/index.asp?txtNavID=137&635132=

http://careers.civil-service.gov.uk/index.asp?txtNavID=141&635132=

http://careers.state.gov/civil-service/development.html

http://daccessdds.un.org/doc/UNDOC/GEN/N02/639/98/PDF/N0263998.pdf?OpenElement

http://ec.europa.eu/civil_service/docs/bs_sexe_age_en.pdf

http://ec.europa.eu/civil_service/docs/toc100_en.pdf

http://ec.europa.eu/civil_service/job/sne/index_en.htm

http://ec.europa.eu/reform/2002/chapter02_en.htm#2

http://ec.europa.eu/reform/2002/chapter02_en.htm#5_2

http://eur-lex.europa.eu/LexUriServ/site/en/consleg/1962/R/01962R0031-20060701-en.pdf

http://europa.eu/epso/working/career/payments_en.htm

http://icsc.un.org/resources/FAQ/default.htm

http://icsc.un.org/resources/pdfs/general/compend/9-70.pdf

http://icsc.un.org/resources/pdfs/ppd/ccog/ccogi_ii.pdf

http://icsc.un.org/resources/pdfs/ppd/ccog/ccogiv-1.a.pdf#search=|vacancies|

http://icsc.un.org/resources/pdfs/ppd/ccog/ccogv.pdf

http://icsc.un.org/resources/pdfs/ppd/hrmframe/ICSC_hrm_eng.pdf

http://www.acas.org.uk/media/pdf/9/5/CP01_1.pdf

http://www.civilservice.gov.uk/documents/doc/pay_reward/CSPayGuidance2007-08.doc

http://www.cps.gov.uk/Publications/humanresources/pmm/section2/chapter_5.html#17

http://www.ge.com/citizenship/priorities_engagement/operational_excellence_co.jsp

http://www.gecareers.com/GECAREERS/html/us/ourPeople/paths.html

http://www.globalpolicy.org/reform/initiatives/hammarskjoldindex.htm

http://www.globalpolicy.org/reform/initiatives/perezindex.htm

http://www.globalpolicy.org/reform/initiatives/thantindex.htm

http://www.globalpolicy.org/reform/initiatives/waldheimindex.htm

http://www.imf.org/external/pubs/ft/weo/2008/update/03/index.htm#table1

http://www.opm.gov/compconf/postconf00/universl/salmons1.pdf; http://icsc.un.org/resources/pdfs/ppd/benchmark/hrm.pdf#search=|vacancies|

http://www.opm.gov/oca/08tables/indexSES.asp

http://www.opm.gov/ses/about_ses/overview.asp

http://www.opm.gov/ses/recruitment/allocate.asp

http://www.opm.gov/ses/recruitment/slpositions.asp

http://www.opm.gov/ses/recruitment/stpositions.asp

http://www.opm.gov/workforceplanning/wfpmodel.htm

http://www.sas.undp.org/documents/Staff_Rules_100_English.pdf

http://www.statistics.gov.uk/downloads/theme_labour/Civil_service_tables_2007.xls

http://www.swlearning.com/management/hrm_news/perform_0404_001.html

http://www.un.org/aboutun/charter/history/

http://www.un.org/aboutun/unhistory/

http://www.un.org/Depts/OHRM/salaries_allowances/classif.htm

http://www.un.org/Depts/OHRM/salaries_allowances/classification/classifs.htm

http://www.un.org/Depts/OHRM/salaries_allowances/salary.htm

http://www.un.org/french/grh_manuel/French/

http://www.un.org/hr_handbook/English/

http://www.usajobs.gov/infocenter/howjobsgetfilled.asp

http://www-03.ibm.com/employment/us/cd_career_dev.shtml

http://www-03.ibm.com/employment/us/li_values.shtml

http://www-03.ibm.com/ibm/history/documents/pdf/hr.pdf

http://www4.law.cornell.edu/uscode/5/usc_sec_05_00007701--000-.html

http://www4.law.cornell.edu/uscode/search/display.html?terms=disciplinary%20action&url=/uscode/html/uscode05/usc_sec_05_00001214--000-.html

https://jobs.un.org/elearn/production/home.html

https://jobs3.netmedia1.com/cp/search_results.jsp

Glossary

ACABQ	Advisory Committee on Administrative and Budgetary Questions
ASG	Assistant Secretary-General
CCAQ	Consultative Committee on Administrative Questions
CCOG	Common Classification of Occupational Groups
CPC	Committee of Program Coordination
CPM	Capital Master Plan
CSS	Central Support Services
D	Director Level
DDA	Department of Disarmament Affairs
DESA	Department of Economic and Social Affairs
DFS	Department of Field Support
DGACM	Department of General Assembly and Conference Management
DOM	Department of Management
DPA	Department of Political Affairs
DPI	Department of Public Information
DPKO	Department of Peacekeeping Operations
DSG	Deputy Secretary-General

DSS	Department of Safety and Security
ECA	Economic Commission for Africa
ECE	Economic Commission for Europe
ECHA	Executive Committee on Humanitarian Affairs
ECLAC	Economic Commission for Latin America Countries
ECOSOC	Economic and Social Council
EOSG	Executive Office of the Secretary-General
ESCAP	Economic and Social Commission for Asia and the Pacific
ESCWA	Economic and Social Commission for West Africa
FAO	Food and Agriculture Organization
FICSA	Federation of International Civil Servants Association
GA	General Assembly
GS	General Service Category
HRM	Human Resource Management
IASC	Inter-Agency Standing Committee
ICAO	International Civil Aviation Organization
ICJ	International Court of Justice
ICS	International Civil Service
ICSC	International Civil Service Commission
IFAD	International Food and Agriculture Development
ILO	International Labor Organization
ITU	International Telecommunications Union
JAB	Joint Appeals Board
JDC	Joint Disciplinary Committee
JIU	Joint Inspection Unit
OCHA	Office of the Coordination of Humanitarian Affairs

OHCHR	Office of the High Commissioner for Human Rights
OHRM	Office of Human Resource Management
OIOS	Office of Internal Oversight Services
OLA	Office of Legal Affairs
OSAA	Office of Special Representative of the Secretary-General for Children in Armed Conflict
P	Professional Level Category
PIPC	Pandemic Influenza Preparedness Committee
PPBA	Program Planning, Budget and Accounts
SC	Security Council
SCC	Special Committee on Coordination
SG	Secretary-General
TC	Trusteeship Council
UNAT	United Nations Administrative Tribunal
UNCTAD	United Nations Conference for Trade and Development
UNEP	United Nations Environment Programme
UNESCO	United Nations Education, Scientific and Cultural Organization
UNFPA	United Nations Population Fund
UNICEF	United Nations Children's Fund
UN-HABITAT	United Nations Human Settlement Programme
UN-OHRLLC	Office of High Representative for the Least Developed Countries, Landlocked Developed Countries, and Small Island Developing States
UNODC	United Nations Office on Drugs and Crime
UNOG	United Nations Office in Geneva
UNON	United Nations Office in Nairobi
UNOV	United Nations Office in Vienna

UNDP	United Nations Development Programme
UPU	Universal Postal Union
USG	Under Secretary-General
USOPM	United States Office of Personnel Management
WFP	World Food Program
WHO	World Health Organization
WMO	World Meteorological Organization

Index